D0619646

KINNERETH
COOKBOOK

Second Edition

ISBN 0-9696054-0-4

This book is dedicated to the memory of
Adèle Freeman, Yona Pattenick, Mary Shendroff and Dolores Weiner,
dedicated members and dear friends.

Introduction

Kinnereth Chapter of Toronto Hadassah-Wizo is proud to present the Second Edition of the Kinnereth Cookbook, honouring the 75th anniversary of Canadian Hadassah-Wizo, and the 40th anniversary of Kinnereth Chapter. We have been prompted by our success and encouraged by your enthusiasm to update our book. We have tried to meet the needs of contemporary taste and fashion without altering the basic simplicity of the Kinnereth Cookbook. With these improvements, our original intent remains the same - to present an inviting cookbook filled with delicious, interesting, and completely reliable recipes. We believe we have.

Our revised book includes over 200 new recipes, as well as treasured old ones from Hadassah-Wizo members, family and friends. Our thanks to all of you who have shared recipes with us. We are sorry that space limitations did not permit us to use all of them.

The first Kinnereth Cookbook was introduced in 1979, and became an instant best seller. We, the members of Kinnereth are very proud of this achievement. It has been a very successful fundraising project.

The proceeds of this book will once again support Hadassah-Wizo projects by providing funds for health, education, youth rescue programs and social and medical services.

Our sincerest thanks to Eli Barr and his associates, Gaetano Leo, Roy Matich, John Sheng and Elaine Thompson for their patience, perseverance and creative expertise in designing our book, and to Hartley Steinberg for his outstanding teaching skills and the unlimited use of his computer.

Our gratitude to Vera Sanders who has shared her artistic talent with us and whose illustrations have greatly enhanced our book.

Thanks too, to Sandra Shleifman and Donna Wise for their encouragement and to Denise Fogel and Barbara Weinberg for their help in bringing this book to fruition. Our appreciation to Margaret Fraser and Ann Bodley, Home Economists, whose assistance on our first edition enabled us to create a best seller. We thank our committee for their enthusiasm and the many hours they spent gathering and testing recipes.

We hope that you'll be as pleased with this updated version of the Kinnereth Cookbook as we are.

Nancy Posluns
Eleanor Steinberg

Cookbook Committee

Elinore Asher	Bianca Israeli	Pam Schwartz
Halle Cohen	Eleanor Maxwell	Eleanor Steinberg
Paula Cohen	Isa Ots	Pauline Toker
Myrtle Coopersmith	Nancy Posluns	Sonia Wachsberg
Gladys Fogler	Honey Rosenthal	Edie Winberg
Lois Friedman	Sheila Rubinoff	Renee Wolfson
Esther Guth	Vera Sanders	Bernice Zwi

Kinnereth Chapter Membership

Barbara Alexander	Esther Guth	Vera Sanders
Elinore Asher	Roz Halbert	Pam Schwartz
Sandra Clavir	Mimi Hollenberg	Sheilah Silverberg
Halle Cohen	Bianca Israeli	Yvonne Stein
Paula Cohen	Lily Katz	Eleanor Steinberg
Myrtle Coopersmith	Chava Kwinta	Dorothy Stone
Betty Deskin	Sheila Lewis	Clara Tepner
Ruth Ehrlich	Eleanor Maxwell	Pauline Toker
Ruby Fidler	Isa Ots	Edith Torobin
June Filler	Judy Pencer	Gilda Tyber
Golda Fine	Nancy Pencer	Sonia Wachsberg
Vera Finkelstein	Joyce Posluns	Valorie Waitzer
Gladys Fogler	Nancy Posluns	Edie Winberg
Nancy Florence	Esterita Rajsky	Florence Winberg
Lois Friedman	Carol Rapp	Donna Wise
Doreen Glick	Coreen Robinson	Renee Wolfson
Raylene Godel	Honey Rosenthal	Joanne Weigen
Clare Goodman	Joyce Rosenberg	Dorothy Zeifman
Ruth Greenspan	Sheila Rubinoff	Bernice Zwi

Table of Contents

Cover Photo: Chicken and Peaches. Recipe on page 223.

Glossary of Terms

Amandine   made with sliced almonds, which have been blanched and browned in butter.

Au Gratin   made with a lightly browned crust, or topping of grated cheese.

Baste   to spoon liquid over a food as it is roasting to prevent drying, and to add flavour.

Beat   to make a mixture smooth by lifting the mixture over and over with a brisk motion.

Blanch   to drop into boiling water and then refresh under cold water.

Blend   to stir 2 or more ingredients until each has lost its own identity.

Bouquet Garni   3 parsley sprigs and 1 bay leaf tied in cheese cloth.

Braise   to brown floured and seasoned food in a small amount of fat in a frying pan, and then to add a small amount of liquid and simmer, covered.

Bread   to cover food with a coating of egg, and seasoned flour or crumbs.

Clarify   to clarify butter is to melt it slowly and let all the sediment settle on the bottom of the pan. What remains on top is clarified butter.

Cream   to stir and beat combination of foods until soft and fluffy (usually shortening and sugar).

Cut In   to combine fat with dry mixture of flour, etc. by using two knives, scissors fashion, or a special wire pastry blender until fat is reduced.

Deglaze   the process of lifting the tasty residue of meat particles and concentrated juices left in a pan after sautéing, by adding liquid and scraping up the particles with a wooden spoon.

Dredge   to coat food evenly and generously.

Fillet   long thin strips of fish or meat which have had the bone removed, usually a choice cut.

Fold In	to blend without losing volume, by cutting through center of batter with edge of a rubber spatula, and to lift batter from bottom to top - turning the bowl, and repeating motion until batter is smooth.
Glaze	to cover a food with a thin film of syrup, forming a transparent sweet coating.
Julienne	to cut food into small thin match-like sticks.
Knead	to work dough to make it more elastic - generally used with yeast mixtures. Lift one half of dough and fold over towards you to give double thickness. Press together with heel of hand, turn dough one quarter turn, and repeat process.
Meringue	stiffly beaten egg whites into which sugar, syrup, and/or flavourings have been beaten.
Mince	to grind or chop very fine.
Pan-Broil	to cook meat on a hot dry surface.
Pan-Fry	to cook in a frying pan, in a small amount of fat.
Par-Boil	to partially cook by boiling.
Partially Set	to chill food until it is the consistency of unbeaten egg whites.
Parve (Parev)	containing no meat or dairy product as an ingredient.
Poach	to cook gently in enough simmering liquid to cover.
Pot-Roast	to cook less tender cuts of meat, by browning first on all sides with high heat, and then to cook in a covered pan with a small amount of liquid.
Sauté	to cook over direct heat, in a small amount of fat.
Scald	to heat to below boiling point. Liquid will form bubbles along side of pan, but not on surface.
Sear	to brown surface quickly at very high temperature.
Simmer	to cook over gentle heat at temperature just below boiling.
Skim	to remove scum from top of liquid which forms as liquid is boiling.
Stock	the liquid in which poultry, meat, fish or vegetables have been cooked.

To Substitute One Ingredient for Another

For	Substitute
1 cup cake/pastry flour	1 cup all purpose flour minus 2 tablespoons
1 cup whole milk	1/2 cup evaporated milk plus 1/2 cup water.
1 cup skim milk	3 tablespoons skim milk powder plus 1 cup water.
1 cup sour milk or buttermilk	1 tablespoon vinegar or lemon juice plus milk to equal 1 cup.
1 cup heavy cream	3/4 cup milk plus 1/3 cup butter.
1 square unsweetened chocolate	3 tablespoons cocoa plus 1 tablespoon butter or shortening.

Herbs and Spices

"Spices" is a term which includes four distinct categories:

Spices themselves are derived from berries, fruits, barks and roots.

Herbs are garnered from only the leaves of annual and perennial shrubs.

Aromatic Seeds come from the seeds of annual plants such as sesame and caraway.

Seasonings are a blend of many spices, herbs and seeds, such as in Poultry Seasoning.

There is also another category which can be added to the marvelous world of "Spice" - that of the **Vegetable spices**. The delightful flavours come from garlic, paprika, horseradish and mushrooms.

Herb Chart

Name	Description	Use
Basil	Leaves and stems of basil plant	Soups, poultry, meat, vegetables, cheese spreads
Bay Leaves	Leaves of laurel tree	Court Bouillon, fish, potted meat, fricasée, vegetables, sauces
Chervil	From a low growing annual related to the parsley family	Avocado and cheese dips, coleslaw, omelets, soufflés, vegetables
Dillweed	Leaf of dill plant	Cheese dips and spreads, soups, coleslaw, potato salad, fish, vegetables
Marjoram	From the mint family	Cheese dips and spreads soups, mixed green salads, poultry, beef, vegetables, eggs
Oregano	Similar to marjoram but stronger	Soups, poultry, dips, beef, lamb, spaghetti sauces, tomato sauces, vegetables, eggs
Parsley	Low growing plant from the celery family	Garnishes, dips, soups, chicken and beef stocks, stews, sauces, vegetables, eggs
Peppermint	Plant of the mint family	Garnishes for fruit salads, vegetables, frosting, tea
Rosemary	Resembles curved pine needles	Fruit, soups, fish, egg, vegetables, fruit compotes

Herb Chart

Name	Description	Use
Saffron	Yellow powder made from stigma of crocus - like flower	Butter, chicken, salads, fish, cream sauces, cakes, frostings, fruit compote, juice
Sage	Plant of the mint family	Cream soups and chowders, meat roasts, baked or broiled fish, poultry
Tarragon	Anise flavoured leaf	Chicken salads, mixed green and fruit salads, salmon, tuna, eggs, veal, lamb, chicken
Thyme	Leaves and stems of bushy plant related to the mint family	Borscht, pea and vegetable soup, baked and fried fish, herb bouquet for sauces, stuffing, fricasée, turkey, chicken

Aromatic Seed Chart

Name	Description	Use
Anise	Licorice flavoured seed	Breads, rolls, cake and cookies, fish sauces, vegetables, fruit salads, sweet pickles
Caraway	Dried fruit of plant similar to the carrot	Cheese spreads and dips, liver, beef, lamb, meat and vegetable marinades, coleslaw, potato and tomato salads

Name	Description	Use
Cardamom	Tiny seeds from small pods of plant related to ginger family	Used whole in fruit punches, pickles and marinades. Used crushed in coffee cakes, Danish pastries, fruitcakes, meatballs, barbecue and basting sauces
Celery	Fruit of plant related to parsley family	Used whole in breads, butter spreads, canapés, pickles and relish. Used ground in cheese sauces, eggs, sour cream or cooked salad dressing, creamed vegetables and soups
Coriander	Similar to anise in shape and size. From parsley family	Danish pastries, coffee cake, apple pie, omelets, meat loaf, beef stew, stuffing for poultry, sweet pickles, lentil, pea and bean soups
Cumin	Looks like caraway seed. Popular in Chinese, Spanish, Mexican and Middle-Eastern cooking	Rye bread, cookies, fruit pies, chili, chutney, sweet pickles and tomato sauce. Add to potatoes, lentils, beets and carrots
Dill	From the parsley family. Seed is more pungent than the weed	Cream cheese dips, herbed butter, sandwich spreads, in sauces for fish, pickles and vegetables
Fennel	Aromatic, from carrot family	Tomato and spaghetti sauces. Add to dry beans and lentils, sweet pickles, macaroni and potato salad, court bouillon

Name	Description	Use
Mustard	Yellow brown in colour with very pungent taste	Dips, meats, salads, sauces, butters, buttered or creamed vegetables
Poppy	Seeds of poppy plant, nut-like flavour	Breads, coffee cakes, dried fruit, cookies, cheese, eggs, vegetable and fruit salads, vegetables
Sesame	Small honey coloured seed with a sweet nutty flavour	Appetizers, breads, meats, vegetables, cooking oil, cookies, cakes, candy

Spices

Name	Description	Use
Allspice	Flavour and aroma similar to combination of nutmeg, cinnamon and cloves	Whole: in pickling, gravies, pot roasts, stews, fruit punches, syrup for stewed and baked fruits. Ground: for cakes, cookies, fruit, puddings and sauces
Cayenne	Small spicy peppers closely related to paprika	Fish and egg dishes, meats and sauces
Cinnamon	Derived from the bark of the plant	Ground: beverages, dessert, fruits, pickled or spiced relishes. Whole: flavour hot chocolate, tea or coffee, desserts, cooked fruit

Name	Description	Use
Cloves	Bud of the clove tree	Whole: beverages, fruits, home canning, beef and fish marinade. Ground: cakes, cookies meat, egg, fish
Ginger	Root of colourful ginger plant	Puddings, gingerbread, chutney, spiced and pickled fruits, sauces, vegetables. Marinade for lamb and turkey
Mace	Skin covering the nutmeg. Flavour resembles nutmeg	Cheese rarebit, cooked fruits, pickles and preserves. Marinades for fish, veal, chicken. Spice cake. Dash in vegetables
Nutmeg	Kernel of the nutmeg fruit	Whole: grate over eggnog, fruit pies, rice pudding and custard. Ground: as above. Also for meat and chicken pie, stuffing for fish, broiled chicken
Paprika	Mild, ground from fruit of pepper plant	Garnish or seasoning for fish, vegetables, meat
Pepper	Berry of a vine Whole: called peppercorn	Meats, gravies, sauces soups, pickling, cheese fish, eggs
Turmeric	Root of plant belonging to ginger family, somewhat medicinal aroma. Should be used sparingly. Used in curry powder.	Mustard, curries, mustard pickles, lamb, beef, cream soups and chowders

Hints for Herbs

Garlic buds can be separated into cloves and frozen for use all winter.

To Freeze Herbs: Wash and dry thoroughly in salad spinner. Discard stems. Place loosely packed in an air tight container. Use as required. Do not defrost.

Parsley: Chop leaves coarsely before packaging and freezing as above.

To Dry Herbs: Wash well - dry on paper towels. Wrap in brown paper bag or parchment paper and keep in cupboard until ready to use. Crumble as you need them.

To Dry Herbs in the Microwave: Herbs such as parsley can easily be dried. Wash well - shake off excess water. Discard stems and loosely fill one cup (250 mL) with leaves. Spread on double layer of paper towelling. Microwave on high for 2 – 3 minutes. Let sit for 10 – 15 minutes. Crumble and place in covered jar to store.

1/2 teaspoon (3 mL) dry herbs can be substituted for 2 – 3 teaspoons (10 - 15 mL) of fresh herbs.

The trend today is to eat less fat. No more than 30% of caloric intake should be from fat. Switch from saturated fats (butter, dairy fats, meat fats, palm oil and coconut oil) to unsaturated fats. Try to limit saturated fat intake to no more than 10% of total caloric intake. Unsaturated fats can be divided into polyunsaturated fats (safflower, sunflower, corn, soybean and cottonseed oils) and monounsaturated fats (canola, olive and peanut oils).

Suggestions for Low Fat Cooking: Choose lean cuts of meat, veal or white poultry. Remove all visible fat from meat and skin from poultry before cooking.

Avoid frying foods. Cook soups, stews and casseroles a day ahead and refrigerate. Remove the hardened fat before reheating.

Soup thickener - use puréed cooked vegetables e.g. squash, potatoes, carrots, noodles, legumes, rice, or barley.

Substitute plain low-fat yogurt, 1% or 2% milk or buttermilk in place of cream.

Salad Dressings - use 1/2 the oil, add a pinch of sugar, orange or apple juice to cut the sharpness of the vinegar.

Use low-fat ("light") mayonnaise instead of regular.

Flavoured vinegars such as raspberry or rice vinegar may be used alone as a simple dressing.

Choose low-fat cheese.

Store bought muffins and cookies often contain more fat than you realize. Try baking your own!

Vegetables are naturally low in fat. Serve them plain or sprinkle them with herbs or lemon juice.

Use herbs for flavouring instead of salt.

Fresh fruits are low in fat, nourishing and delicious. Take advantage of their accessibility.

Sodium (Sodium Chloride), Salt - High sodium foods include wieners, cold cuts, pickles, relishes and canned soups.

Fat - check for both the total fat and the cholesterol contents. Cholesterol free products e.g. potato chips, can be very high in fat. Remember your total fat intake is important.

Labels: Read labels carefully - understand what they mean:

1. "Low Calorie" or "Calorie Reduced" - 50% less calories than the product it is replacing.

2. "Carbohydrate Reduced" - 50% less carbohydrate than the product it is replacing.

3. "Unsweetened - No Sugar Added" - no sugars have been added, but natural sugars e.g. fruit sugars are present. Natural sugars are found in all fruits, juices, milk and starches. Words ending in "OSE" are a form of sugar (sucrose, fructose, lactose, maltose). The exception is cellulose.

4. "Sugar Free" - The product basically contains no sugar in either natural or added form and may also be reduced in calories.

5. "Light" or "Lite" - may mean light in colour or weight and not necessarily lower in fat or calories.

Appetizers and Dips

Antipasto

JUDY ASCH

3 · 6.5 ounce cans	solid white tuna, drained	596 g
11 ounces	chili sauce	313 mL
1 tablespoon	Worcestershire sauce	15 mL
11 ounces	ketchup	313 mL
1 · 9 ounce jar	sweet gherkins, cut up	256 mL
1 · 6 ounce jar	small white onions and/or cauliflower	170 mL
1 · 12 ounce jar	salad olives, drained	341 mL
2	carrots, chopped	2
2 · 10 ounce cans	mushrooms, stems and pieces, drained	568 mL
	juice of 1 lemon	

Mix all ingredients in a large bowl. Store in jars in refrigerator. Will keep for 4 – 6 weeks. Serve with crackers. Serves 24.

Baked Bologna

MAGGIE KATZENBERG

1 · 5 pound	bologna	2.25 kg
1 cup	ketchup	250 mL
1/4 cup	brown sugar	60 mL
2 tablespoons	lemon juice	30 mL
3 tablespoons	Worcestershire sauce	45 mL
1 tablespoon	prepared mustard	15 mL

Preheat oven to 250°F (120°C). Score top of bologna in a diamond pattern. Place on a piece of foil large enough to make a tent. Mix remaining ingredients together and pour over meat. Close foil over top. Bake for 3 hours, basting occasionally. Open foil for last half hour and baste more often. Serve with rye or black bread and mustard.

Pita Cheese Melt

4 – 5	scallions, chopped	4 – 5
1 1/2 teaspoons	capers (optional)	7 mL
1 cup	mayonnaise	250 mL
2/3 cup	grated cheddar cheese	150 mL
6 · 6 inch	pita breads, split in half	6 · 15 cm

Blend together first four ingredients. Spread each half of pita with mixture. Cut again into eighths. Freeze, uncovered, on a cookie sheet. When frozen, store in plastic bags in freezer. Remove 1/2 hour before using. Broil until bubbly. Makes 48 pieces.

Captain's Caps

JUDY ASCH

16 – 20	large fresh mushrooms	16 – 20
1 · 3.5 ounce can	red salmon or tuna	100 g
6 tablespoons	soft fresh bread crumbs	100 mL
2 teaspoons	dried parsley	10 mL
2 teaspoons	minced onion	10 mL
2 tablespoons	melted butter	30 mL
	seasoned with	
	salt and pepper to taste	
	grated Parmesan cheese	

Heat oven to 425°F (220°C). Remove stems from mushrooms. Chop stems to make 6 tablespoons (100 mL). Mix with salmon, bread crumbs and seasonings. Moisten with melted butter. Fill caps with salmon mixture. Place on a cookie sheet and sprinkle with Parmesan cheese. Bake 8 – 10 minutes. Recipe can be doubled or tripled as desired. Can be made a day or two in advance and kept in refrigerator until ready to bake and serve.

Celery with Red Caviar Stuffing

2 bunches	celery	2
1/2 pound	cream cheese	225 g
1 tablespoon	grated onion	15 mL
1/3 cup	chopped parsley	75 mL
1/3 cup	red caviar	75 mL
	salt and freshly ground black pepper to taste	

Use only the choice inner stalks of celery. Wash well. Mix the softened cream cheese with the onion, parsley, caviar, salt and pepper. Stuff the celery stalks with the mixture and refrigerate until serving time.

Variation: Endive or pea pods may be used instead of celery.

Toasted Cheese Rounds

LOIS FRIEDMAN

1/2 cup	butter or margarine	125 mL
1/2 pound	Brie or cheddar cheese	250 g
1 cup	all purpose flour	250 mL
1/2 teaspoon	Tabasco sauce	2 mL
1/4 teaspoon	seasoned salt	1 mL
1/4 cup	sesame seeds	60 mL

In a mixing bowl combine room temperature butter or margarine and cheese. If using Brie, remove the rind before mixing. Add flour, Tabasco and seasoned salt, and blend using hands to form dough into a ball. If using a food processor, use cold butter or margarine. Combine with flour, Tabasco and seasoned salt. Process until dough forms a ball. Divide dough in half. Shape each half into a log about 1" (2.5 cm) in diameter. Wrap in waxed paper and refrigerate overnight or freeze. Preheat oven to 400°F (200°C). Slice chilled log 1/8" – 1/4" (0.3 – 0.6 cm) thick. Dip top of each slice into sesame seeds. Place rounds 1" (2.5 cm) apart on ungreased baking sheet. Bake 8 – 10 minutes or until edges are golden brown. Serve warm or cold. Store in airtight tin. To reheat, bake 5 – 7 minutes in a preheated 375°F (190°C) oven.

Cheddar Cheese and Chutney

LOIS FRIEDMAN

12 ounces	medium cheddar	350 g
1/3 cup	chutney	100 mL
1 loaf	white bread, sliced	1

Grate cheese. Add chutney and mix well. Cut bread into rounds with cookie cutter. Toast under broiler on one side. Turn and spread untoasted side with cheese mixture. Place in 350°F (180°C) oven for 10 – 15 minutes until lightly browned. Rounds may be frozen before baking. If frozen, baking time must be increased.

Easy Cheese Straws

1 · 14 ounce package	frozen puff pastry	397 mL
1 1/2 cups	grated cheddar cheese	375 mL
	Parmesan cheese	
	cayenne or paprika to taste*	

Preheat oven to 400°C (200°C). Thaw the puff pastry just enough to roll on a lightly floured surface. Roll into a 12" (30 cm) square. Sprinkle cheddar cheese over pastry. Sprinkle a little Parmesan over, then very lightly sprinkle just a little cayenne* over the cheese. Fold dough into thirds, then again into a rectangle about 1/4" (0.6 cm) thick. Cut into strips. Twist and place each strip on a foil covered pan. Let rest for 15 minutes. Bake for 10 – 12 minutes or until golden. Yield: about 30.

* If cayenne is too spicy for your taste you can use paprika instead.

Hummus PHYLLIS FLATT

1 · 19 ounce can	chick peas, drained	540 mL
1/4 cup	tahina	60 mL
	juice of 1 whole lemon	
1 clove	garlic, crushed	1
	dash of cayenne	
	pepper to taste	

Put all ingredients in processor and pulse until mixture reaches desired consistency (approximately 15 seconds). If smoother consistency is desired, add water, 1 tablespoon (15 mL) at a time.

 Knishes LOIS FRIEDMAN

1 · 14 ounce package	frozen puff pastry, thawed	397 g
1	egg	1
1 tablespoon	water	15 mL
	sesame seeds	

Preheat oven to 350°F (180°C). Divide pastry dough in half and roll each piece into a rectangle approximately 11" x 16" (27.5 x 40 cm). Place 1/6 of filling along narrow edge. Roll dough around filling. Cut and pinch seam together. Repeat twice. Each rectangle should make 3 rolls.

For spinach and meat knishes, place rolls on a greased cookie sheet, seam side down. Beat egg with water. Paint tops of rolls and sprinkle with sesame seeds. *Bake 30 minutes. Remove to rack and cool. To serve, cut each roll diagonally into 3/4" (0.8 cm) pieces. Bake until hot.

For potato knishes, roll as above, but cut each roll into 1" (2.5 cm) pieces and place, cut side down, onto greased baking pan. Draw dough to center of each and pinch lightly. Bake approximately 20 minutes or until golden brown on the bottom. May be served at this point or cooled and reheated when needed. Freezes well.

* May be frozen before baking. Thaw before baking.

Knish Fillings

L O I S   F R I E D M A N

Meat: use kreplach filling on page 37.

Spinach:

1 · 10 ounce package	chopped spinach	280 g
1	onion, finely chopped	1
1 tablespoon	butter or margarine	15 mL
1/3 cup	Parmesan cheese	75 mL
1	egg, beaten	1
	salt and pepper	

(For a whole package of puff pastry dough, double this recipe.)

Cook spinach according to directions on package and drain well. Sauté onion in butter or margarine until slightly brown. Combine spinach, onion, cheese and egg and mix well. Season with salt and pepper to taste.

Potato:

4	large potatoes	4
2	medium onions, finely chopped	2
1 tablespoon	margarine	15 mL
2 tablespoons	oil	30 mL
1	egg, beaten	1
	salt and pepper	

Boil potatoes until tender. Drain and mash. Sauté onions in margarine and oil until slightly brown. Add to potatoes along with egg. Season with salt and pepper to taste.

Seven Layer Dip

HELAINE ROBINS

First Layer:

1 can	refried beans (el Paso), mashed	1

Second Layer:

1	large avocado, mashed	1
1 1/2 tablespoons	lemon juice	20 mL
	freshly grated pepper	

Third Layer:

1 · 14 ounce can	pitted black olives, drained and sliced	398 mL

Fourth Layer:

1/2 cup	sour cream	125 mL
1/4 cup	mayonnaise	60 mL
1/2 package	taco seasoning mix	1/2

Fifth Layer:

1 cup	chopped tomatoes	250 mL

Sixth Layer:

1/2 cup	green onions, chopped (scallions)	125 mL

Seventh Layer:

4 ounces	cheddar cheese, grated	125 g

Place layers in a large shallow dish. Serve with taco chips.

Savoury Tart

BERNICE ZWI

1 1/3 cups	crushed soda cracker crumbs	325 mL
4 tablespoons	melted butter or margarine	60 mL
2 · 6.5 ounce cans	tuna	368 g
2 – 3 tablespoons	mayonnaise	30 – 45 mL
2 teaspoons	chutney	10 mL
2 – 3	avocados, peeled and pitted	2 – 3
1 tablespoon	lemon juice	15 mL
	salt and pepper to taste	
	chopped parsley	
1/2 pound	smooth cottage cheese	250 g
	with chives	
2 – 3 tablespoons	cream	30 – 45 mL
2 teaspoons	Worcestershire sauce	10 mL
2	eggs, hard boiled	2
	olives for garnish	

Preheat oven to 350°F (180°C). Mix cracker crumbs with melted butter. Press into bottom of greased 9" (22.5 cm) springform pan. Bake about 20 minutes until very firm. Cool.

Spread the following fillings in layers on the biscuit base and refrigerate overnight:

1. Tuna fish mixed with mayonnaise and chutney to taste.
2. Mashed avocados with lemon juice, salt, pepper and chopped parsley to taste.
3. Cottage cheese mixed with chives, Worcestershire sauce, cream, salt and pepper to taste.
4. Hard boiled eggs, grated and sprinkled on top. Garnish with olives.

Refrigerate overnight. To serve cut into slices. Remember to make all fillings of spreading consistency to simplify the building up of the tart.

Yummy Italian Loaf

ELEANOR STEINBERG

1	Italian loaf of bread	1
1 cup	butter	250 mL
3/4 tablespoon	mustard	12 mL
1 1/2 tablespoons	poppy seeds	25 mL
2 tablespoons	grated onion	30 mL
1 · 8 ounce package	cheese slices, Swiss or cheddar	227 g

Trim top and sides from bread. Slice 16 slices almost to bottom of loaf. (Do not cut all the way through). Make a paste of butter, mustard, poppy seeds and onion. Spread between slices, over top and sides. Cut cheese slices into 4 triangles each, and fit one triangle into each slice, point side up. Wrap well in foil and refrigerate a few hours or overnight. Bake at 325°F (160°C) for 20 – 25 minutes. Serve with a big tossed salad.

Mock Pizza

MAGGIE KATZENBERG

4 ounces	cheddar cheese, grated	115 g
1	egg, beaten	1
3/4 cup	all purpose flour	200 mL
1/2 teaspoon	salt	2 mL
1/8 teaspoon	pepper	1 mL
1 cup	milk	250 mL
1/4 cup	chopped red pepper	60 mL
1/4 cup	chopped green pepper	60 mL
1/4 cup	sliced mushrooms, sautéed lightly in butter	60 mL
1/2 teaspoon	oregano	3 mL

Preheat oven to 425°F (220°C). Grease an 8" (20 cm) square pan. Mix half of the cheese with all other ingredients. Pour into prepared pan. Bake for 30 minutes. Remove from oven. Sprinkle with remaining cheese and bake another 2 minutes. Cool slightly before cutting into squares. Double recipe for an 11" x 15" (27.5 cm x 37.5 cm) jelly roll pan.

To freeze: Place squares on a pan lined with waxed paper. Freeze until solid, then place in plastic bag and seal tightly.

Chicken Liver Paté

ADÈLE FREEMAN

1/4 cup	chicken fat	60 mL
1/4 cup	vegetable shortening	60 mL
2	bay leaves	2
1/4 teaspoon	freshly ground black pepper	1 mL
1/4 teaspoon	thyme	1 mL
1 large	onion, chopped	1
1 1/2 pounds	chicken livers, cut up	700 g
1 teaspoon	salt	5 mL
2 tablespoons	cognac	30 mL

In a large frying pan, melt fat and shortening together over medium heat. Add bay leaves, pepper, thyme and onions and cook, stirring, for five minutes. Add livers and cook, stirring, until lightly browned. Add salt and cook 5 minutes longer, stirring from time to time. Cool mixture. Remove bay leaves. Grind mixture in electric blender on high speed, adding cognac until smooth. Pack into a small greased pan and chill. Remove from pan, wrap in waxed paper, and refrigerate until serving.

Note: A double recipe will fill a pyrex loaf pan, but you won't be able to grind the entire mixture at one time. Two or three separate blendings will be needed.

Chopped Liver

ELEANOR STEINBERG

1 pound	chicken livers	500 g
4	eggs, hard boiled	4
2	onions, finely chopped	2
1 tablespoon	oil or chicken fat	15 mL
	salt and pepper	

Broil chicken livers. Turn often to prevent burning. Cool. Sauté onions in oil. Put liver, eggs and onions into food processor, and blend with on/off turns until smooth. Season to taste with salt and pepper. Refrigerate. Serves 8.

Egg and Caviar Mold

ELEANOR STEINBERG

8	eggs, hard boiled	8
1/2 teaspoon	dry mustard	2 mL
	salt and pepper to taste	
2 tablespoons	mayonnaise	30 mL
1	onion, finely chopped	1
1 · 8 ounce package	cream cheese	225 g
	milk as required	
1 small jar	black caviar	1
	lemon slices for garnish	

Grate eggs. Season with mustard, salt and pepper, and mix in mayonnaise. Press into an 8" (1 L) pie plate or quiche pan. Sprinkle onions on top of egg. Mix cream cheese in mixer, adding up to 2 tablespoons (30 mL) of milk if necessary, until it is of spreading consistency. Spread on top of onion. Refrigerate. Before serving, spread caviar over top of cream cheese and garnish with lemon slices. Serve with cocktail rye or crackers.

Note: If desired, mashed avocado seasoned with lemon juice and pepper may be substituted for cream cheese.

No Crust Quiche

VERA SANDERS

6	eggs	6
1 pint	sour cream	500 mL
1 teaspoon	Worcestershire sauce	5mL
1 pound	Swiss cheese, grated	500 g
2 · 3 ounce cans	french fried onion rings	85 g each
2 · 10 ounce cans	sliced mushrooms, drained	284 g each
	Tabasco sauce to taste	

Preheat oven to 325ºF (160ºC). Beat the eggs with a hand beater, and gradually fold in all other ingredients with a wooden spoon. Pour into greased 9" x 13" (3.5 L) baking dish. Bake about 45 – 50 minutes. Cut into squares to serve. May also be baked in muffin tins, but reduce baking time to 20 – 25 minutes. Freezes well.

Spicy Eggplant

D E B B I E   C A M P B E L L

1 1/2 pounds	eggplant (about 2 medium)	750 g
3 tablespoons	vegetable oil	45 mL
2 teaspoons	oriental sesame oil	10 mL
3 cloves	garlic, minced	3
2 tablespoons	chopped fresh ginger	30 mL
3	scallions, trimmed and minced	3
1/4 teaspoon	dried red pepper flakes	1 mL
3 1/2 tablespoons	soy sauce	50 mL
3 tablespoons	light brown sugar	45 mL
1 tablespoon	rice wine vinegar	15 mL
1 tablespoon	fresh lemon juice	15 mL
2 tablespoons	chopped cilantro (fresh coriander)	30 mL

Preheat oven to 425°F (220°C). Place the whole eggplants on a baking sheet and prick in several places with a fork to allow steam to escape. Coat the eggplants with 1 tablespoon (15 mL) of the vegetable oil. Roast, turning once halfway through cooking, until the pulp is quite soft, 30 to 40 minutes. Let stand until cool enough to handle. Cut off the stems and peel the skin from the eggplants. Place the pulp in a food processor and process until smooth.

Heat the remaining 2 tablespoons (30 mL) vegetable oil with the sesame oil in a medium size skillet over medium heat. Add the garlic, ginger, scallions and red pepper flakes, quickly stirring constantly for 1 minute. Whisk together the soy sauce, brown sugar and vinegar just until sugar has dissolved. Add at once to the skillet and bring to a boil. Stir in the puréed eggplant and simmer for 3 minutes. Remove from heat and stir in the lemon juice and cilantro. Can be served either warm, at room temperature or chilled accompanied by cut-up pita or rice crackers.

Microwave Eggplant

1	light coloured eggplant (should be purple, not brown)	1
1	green pepper, seeded and cut into eighths	1
1	green onion, cut into pieces juice of 1/2 lemon	1
1 tablespoon	oil salt and pepper	15 mL
2	tomatoes, peeled and chopped (optional)	2

Prick eggplant with a fork, and cook in microwave at full power - 100% for 6 minutes, turning once. Cool. Slice in half and remove pulp from eggplant and place in processor with green pepper and green onion. Process with on/off motion until coarsely chopped. Add lemon juice and oil and process with on/off motion until blended, but not puréed. Add salt and pepper to taste, and tomatoes, if desired. Chill until ready to serve.

Eggplant Spread

1	medium eggplant	1
3 tablespoons	minced onion	50 mL
2 tablespoons	oil	30 mL
1 1/2 teaspoons	salt	7 mL
1/4 teaspoon	pepper	1 mL

Preheat oven to 475°F (240°C). Bake eggplant until skin turns dark brown. Cool and peel. Chop eggplant and mix until very smooth. Stir in onion, oil, salt and pepper. Chill. Serve with crackers or bread. Serves 6.

14 / APPETIZERS AND DIPS

Mock Chopped Herring

LOIS FRIEDMAN

2 cans	skinless and boneless sardines	2
1 can	flat anchovies	1
1 large	apple, finely chopped	1
1 medium	onion, finely chopped	1
3	eggs, hard boiled and finely chopped	3
1 tablespoon	vinegar (or to taste)	15 mL
1 tablespoon	lemon juice (or to taste)	15 mL
1 tablespoon	mayonnaise (optional)	15 mL
1/2 teaspoon	sugar (or more to taste)	2 mL

Dry sardines and anchovies on paper towel. Mix all ingredients together. Mixture should be crunchy and not too wet. Season to taste.

Delicious Marinated Herring

DOLORES WEINER

2 · 8 ounce jars	herring tidbits in wine sauce	450 g
1 cup	sour cream	250 mL
2	apples, grated	2
4 tablespoons	granulated sugar	60 mL
1	small Spanish onion, sliced	1

Strain liquid from jars of herring and save half of the liquid. Discard onions and spices. Mix together sour cream, apples, sugar and reserved liquid. In a bowl, layer herring, sliced onion and sour cream mixture. Cover and allow to marinate overnight.

Danish Salad International

LILY KATZ

1 · 16 ounce jar	herring tidbits in wine marinade	550 g
1/2 cup	sultana raisins	125 mL
1 cup	granulated sugar (optional)	250 mL
1/4 cup	oil	60 mL
1 cup	white vinegar	250 mL
1/2 cup	tomato paste diluted with	125 mL
1 cup	tomato juice	250 mL
1/2 cup	sweet wine	125 mL
1 cup	apples, peeled and diced	250 mL
1 teaspoon	mustard	5 mL
1/4 teaspoon	pepper (optional)	1 mL

Rinse and drain herring and onions from jar. Herring pieces may be cut in half or left as is. Add raisins. Mix sugar and oil, and add vinegar, paste and juice and remaining ingredients. Pour over herring and onions and place in a bottle or jars. Refrigerate until ready to use.

Guacamole

ELEANOR STEINBERG

1 clove	garlic	1
	salt	
1	large, ripe avocado, pitted	1
1/4 teaspoon	salt	1 mL
1/4 teaspoon	chili powder	1 mL
1 teaspoon	lemon juice	5 mL
2 teaspoons	minced onions	10 mL
	mayonnaise, to taste	

Sprinkle a bowl with a little salt and rub with garlic clove. Mash the avocado pulp in the bowl and season with 1/4 teaspoon (1 mL) salt, chili powder and lemon juice. Stir in onion. Cover with a thin layer of mayonnaise to keep the mixture from darkening. Before serving, stir well. Serve on crisp lettuce as a salad, or as an appetizer with crackers.

Everybody's Favourite Meatballs

2 pounds	ground meat	1 kg
1	egg, slightly beaten	1
1	large onion, grated	1
	salt to taste	
1 · 10 ounce jar	grape or cranberry jelly	284 mL
1 · 12 ounce jar	chili sauce	341 mL
	juice of 1 lemon	

Combine meat, egg, onion and salt. Mix and shape into small balls. Combine chili sauce, grape or cranberry jelly and lemon juice in a saucepan. Drop meatballs into sauce and simmer uncovered for 1 hour. Refrigerate or freeze. To serve, bring to room temperature, and then heat in a chafing dish. Serve with toothpicks. May also be served in the hollow of a scooped out black bread.

Glazed Hot Dog Bites

2 pounds	cocktail size hot dogs	1 kg
1 cup	ketchup	250 mL
1/2 cup	brown sugar	125 mL

Preheat oven to 350°F (180°C). Place hot dogs in 'oven to table' casserole. Cover with ketchup-sugar mixture. Bake uncovered until glazed, about one hour. Spear with toothpicks and serve.

Sweet'n Sour Hot Dogs

3/4 cup	prepared mustard	175 mL
1 cup	currant jelly	250 mL
2 pounds	frankfurters	1 kg

Mix mustard and jelly. Place in top of double boiler. Slice hot dogs 1" (2.5 cm) thick. Add to sauce and cook for five minutes. Refrigerate or freeze. When ready to serve place in a chafing dish and heat thoroughly. Serve with toothpicks.

Marinated Mushrooms

1 pound	fresh button mushrooms	500 g
1/4 teaspoon	salt	1 mL
	pepper to taste	
1/8 teaspoon	oregano	0.5 mL
1/3 cup	red wine vinegar or	75 mL
	lemon juice	
3/4 cup	olive oil or salad oil	175 mL
	pinch of curry powder	0.5 mL

Remove mushroom stems and store if desired for later use. Wash caps and drain immediately. Dry quickly on paper towels. Mix remaining ingredients in a blender. Pour over mushrooms and marinate, covered, for 2 – 3 hours at room temperature. Serve on lettuce leaves or on melba toast rounds as a canapé .

Mushroom Roll Ups   MAGGIE KATZENBERG

1 loaf	thin sliced white bread	1
1 pound	mushrooms, chopped	500 g
1	large onion, diced	1
2 tablespoons	butter	30 mL
1 1/2 ounces	cream cheese,	45 mL
	room temperature	
	additional butter, melted	

Heat oven to 350°F (180°C). Remove crusts from bread and flatten with a rolling pin. Sauté onion in butter and add mushrooms. Cover and cook mixture for 5 minutes. Remove from heat, add cheese and stir until melted. Spread mixture on bread. Roll. Brush with melted butter. Cut each roll in half and place on a cookie sheet. Bake for 30 minutes. Can be frozen on cookie sheet before baking and stored in plastic bags.

Pita Pizzas

2 packages	pita bread, 6" (15 cm)	2
	(5 breads each), separated	
1 clove	fresh garlic, pressed	1
3 ounces	grated Parmesan cheese	100 mL
1 cup	soft butter or margarine	250 mL
1 tablespoon	oregano	15 mL
	sesame seeds	

Preheat oven to 350°F (180°C). Add the garlic and Parmesan cheese to the soft butter or margarine. Mix well, and spread on each pita half. Sprinkle with oregano and sesame seeds. Shake off excess. Cut each half into quarters. Bake 10 – 15 minutes or until golden brown.

To freeze: Place on a cookie sheet before baking until frozen, then place in plastic bags and seal well. It is not necessary to defrost before baking.

Miniature Pizzas

1 loaf	party rye, sliced thin,	1
	or mini pitas	
1 · 7.5 ounce jar	pizza sauce	213 mL
	mozzarella cheese,	
	sliced or grated	

Spread each slice of party rye or pita with pizza sauce. Top with mozzarella cheese. Refrigerate or freeze. When ready to serve, toast under broiler until cheese is melted and beginning to brown.

To freeze: Lay on cookie sheet to freeze, then store in plastic bags.

Potato Kugel Krispies

EDIE WINBERG

6	medium size potatoes, peeled	6
2	eggs	2
1/2 cup	all purpose flour	125 mL
1/2 teaspoon	baking powder	2 mL
1 1/2 teaspoons	salt	7 mL
	pinch of pepper	0.5 mL
1	large onion, chopped	1
1/4 cup	oil	60 mL

Preheat oven to 350°F (180°C). Sift together flour, baking powder, salt and pepper. Grate potatoes quickly so they will not discolour. Squeeze out excess liquid. Add eggs and mix well. Add sifted dry ingredients. Sauté onion in oil until lightly browned, and then add to batter. Stir well. Pour into greased jelly roll pan. Bake for 30 minutes. Remove and cut into squares. Bake again for another 30 minutes. Serve hot with **apple sauce** to dip.

To freeze: Separate squares. Freeze on a cookie sheet. Then store in plastic bags in freezer.

Foo Young Fritters

1/4 pound	fresh mushrooms, sliced	125 g
1/2 cup	finely chopped onion	125 mL
2 tablespoons	oil	30 mL
6	eggs	6
1 cup	all purpose flour	250 mL
1 teaspoon	baking powder	5 mL
1 tablespoon	soy sauce	15 mL
1 teaspoon	Worcestershire sauce	5 mL
1 · 10 ounce can	bean sprouts, drained and rinsed	284 mL
1 cup	cooked chicken, finely chopped	250 mL
	salt and pepper to taste	
	oil for frying	

Sauté mushrooms and onion in oil until onions are golden, but not brown. Cool. Beat eggs slightly. Add flour, baking powder, soy sauce and Worcestershire sauce, blending until smooth. Add bean sprouts, chicken, salt and pepper and mushroom-onion mixture, blending well. Drop by teaspoonfuls into hot oil, about 1/8" (0.3 cm) deep. Fry over medium-high temperature until golden brown. Turn and fry on other side. Drain on paper towels.

To freeze: Place on a cookie sheet. When frozen, store in bags. To reheat, place on foil lined sheet in a single layer. Heat at 400°F (200°C) until crisp and hot. Serve with **sweet and sour sauce**.

Sweet and Sour Sauce

4 tablespoons	granulated sugar	60 mL
4 tablespoons	white vinegar	60 mL
4 tablespoons	ketchup	60 mL
1 cup	water	250 mL
2 tablespoons	cornstarch	30 mL
2 tablespoons	water	30 mL
1/2 cup	chopped green pepper	125 mL
3 tablespoons	canned crushed pineapple, drained	45 mL

Combine sugar, vinegar, ketchup and 1 cup water in a saucepan and bring to a boil. In a small bowl, gradually stir 2 tablespoons (30 mL) of water into cornstarch until smooth. Add to saucepan and bring to a boil, stirring constantly, until mixture is smooth and thick. Remove from heat and stir in green pepper and pineapple. Serve warm.

Petite Quiches

SANDRA HABERMAN, ST. LAURENT

	pastry for single pie crust	
3/4 cup	milk	175 m
2	eggs, slightly beaten	2
1/4 teaspoon	salt	1 mL
	pinch of pepper	0.5 mL
1 cup	grated Swiss cheese	250 mL
1 tablespoon	all purpose flour	15 mL

Preheat oven to 325°F (160°C). Line muffin pans with pastry. Combine milk, eggs and seasoning. Mix well. Toss cheese with flour and add to egg mixture. Fill shells 2/3 full. Bake 30 minutes. For 8" (2 L) square pan: line bottom and 1" (2.5 cm) up the sides of pan with pastry. Pour filling over. Bake for 40 – 45 minutes. Cut into squares to serve.

Hawaiian Salami

DOROTHY GARFINKEL

1 · 2 – 3 pound	salami	1 – 1 1/2 kg
2 tablespoons	prepared mustard	30 mL
1/4 cup	apricot or peach jam	60 mL

Preheat oven to 375°F (190°C). Remove outside plastic casing from salami. Score top half of salami in criss-cross fashion, about 1/2 inch (1.5 cm) deep. Combine mustard and jam. Spread part of this mixture over salami, to glaze. Line a loaf pan with silver foil and grease with non-stick spray. Place salami in pan, and bake for about one hour, until salami swells. Baste while baking with remaining mixture. If salami gets too brown, cover loosely with foil. Serve on a cutting board with a sharp knife and different mustard dips, (e.g. hot mustard, Dijon, etc.)

Hot Salmon Hors D'Oeuvre

ANN BODLEY

1 · 7.5 ounce can	salmon	213 g
1 · 8 ounce package	cream cheese	225 g
1 teaspoon	curry powder	5 mL
1 tablespoon	lemon juice	15 mL
	dash Worcestershire sauce	
	dash Tabasco sauce	

Preheat oven to 325°F (160°C). Soften cheese. Mix all ingredients together, blending well. Place in oven proof serving bowls (such as an onion soup crock). Bake one hour. Serve hot with crackers.

To freeze: Cover tightly and freeze after mixing. Thaw before cooking.

Spinach and Cheese Squares

HELEN BERMAN

	phyllo pastry sheets	
	melted butter	
4 tablespoons	chopped onion	60 mL
3 tablespoons	oil	45 mL
1 pound	spinach, cooked, drained and chopped	450 g
2 tablespoons	fresh dill, chopped	30 mL
1 cup	feta cheese	250 mL
1 cup	cheddar cheese, grated	250 mL
2 tablespoons	Parmesan cheese	30 mL
4	eggs, beaten	4
	salt and pepper to taste	
	Tabasco sauce	

Preheat oven to 350°F (180°C). Grease a 9" x 13" (3.5 L) baking pan. Line pan with 10 buttered sheets of phyllo pastry. Cook the onions in oil until golden. Add spinach, dill and cheeses. Beat eggs thoroughly. Add salt and pepper and several dashes of Tabasco sauce. Combine with spinach mixture and mix thoroughly. Pour over leaves, and cover with 10 more buttered phyllo leaves. Score and bake for 1 hour. Cut into squares to serve. Serves 16.

Spinach Cheese Squares

PAULINE TOKER

2 tablespoons	butter	30 mL
3	eggs	3
3/4 cup	all purpose flour	175 mL
1 cup	milk	250 mL
1 teaspoon	salt	5 mL
1 teaspoon	baking powder	5 mL
1 pound	mild white cheddar cheese, grated (Monterey Jack or any other)	500 g
2 · 10 ounce packages	frozen chopped spinach	283 g each

Prepare spinach according to package directions. Drain well. Preheat oven to 325°F (160°C). Melt butter in 9" x 13" (3.5 L) baking pan in the oven. Remove from oven. In a large mixing bowl, beat the eggs. Add flour, milk, salt and baking powder. Mix well. Add the cheese and well drained spinach. Pour all ingredients into baking pan and bake for 35 minutes. Remove from oven, cool for 45 minutes in order to set. Cut into bite sized squares.

To freeze: Place squares on cookie sheet and allow to freeze. Transfer squares into plastic bags. To serve, place squares on cookie sheet, bring to room temperature and bake at 325°F (160°C) for 12 minutes. Yield: 25 pieces.

Tuna Paté

BARBARA DONSKY

1 · 8 ounce package	cream cheese	225 g
2 tablespoons	chili sauce	30 mL
2 tablespoons	snipped parsley	30 mL
1 teaspoon	instant minced onion	5 mL
1/2 teaspoon	Tabasco sauce	2 mL
2 tablespoons	chopped sweet pickles	30 mL
2 · 6.5 ounce cans	tuna fish, drained	184 g each

Blend all ingredients and pack into a 4 cup (1 L) mold. Chill for three hours or more. Unmold. Serve with crackers.

Hot Cheese Dip (fondue)

JUDY ASCH

2 cups	light cream	500 mL
2 teaspoons	dry mustard	10 mL
1 tablespoon	Worcestershire sauce	15 mL
1 clove	garlic, cut in half	1
1 1/2 pounds	coarsely shredded medium sharp cheddar cheese	700 g
3 tablespoons	all purpose flour	45 mL
	salt to taste	
	bread	

In earthenware, glass or enamel saucepan, heat cream, mustard, Worcestershire sauce and garlic until hot but not boiling. Mix cheese with flour. Drop cheese by handfuls into the hot cream. Stir over low heat with a wooden spoon until cheese is melted and mixture is smooth. If a mild garlic flavour is desired, remove pieces of garlic at this time. For stronger flavour, leave garlic in dip while it is being served. Season to taste with salt. Serve with 1 loaf of French or Italian bread, cut into cubes, or 6 bagels, cut into 1/2" (1.5 cm) thick rounds. Put cheese dip over a warmer to serve, keeping dip hot. Spear breads on forks and dunk away! Can be made a day in advance and reheated.

Delicious Vegetable Dip

HARRIET DENNIS

1 cup	mayonnaise	250 mL
1 cup	sour cream	250 mL
2 tablespoons	parsley flakes	30 mL
2 tablespoons	onion flakes	30 mL
2 teaspoons	dill weed, dried	10 mL
2 teaspoons	'Beau Monde' seasoning	10 mL
	garlic powder to taste	

Blend all ingredients. Serve in a bowl, with crisp fresh vegetables. 'Beau Monde' is made by Spice Islands.

Horseradish Cream Cheese Dip

6 ounces	cream cheese	170 g
1/4 cup	sour cream	60 mL
3 tablespoons	white horseradish	45 mL
	salt and pepper to taste	
	dash paprika	
2 drops	Tabasco sauce	2
2 tablespoons	chopped parsley	30 mL

Mash the cheese and gradually blend in the sour cream. Add the horseradish and seasonings to taste, and beat until the mixture is light and fluffy. Chill. Sprinkle with parsley. Serve with raw vegetables.

California Green Goddess Dip

DOROTHY GARFINKEL

5 tablespoons	white wine vinegar	75 mL
2 cloves	garlic	2
1 can	flat anchovies	1
5	green onions	5
1	bunch parsley	1
1 cup	mayonnaise	250 mL
1 1/2 cups	sour cream	375 mL
1 tablespoon	capers	15 mL

Blend vinegar, garlic and anchovies in blender. Add and blend onions and parsley. Blend in mayonnaise and sour cream. Stir in capers. Chill before serving.

Guacomole Dip

ADÈLE FREEMAN

2	ripe avocados, peeled and chopped	2
1	tomato, skinned and chopped	1
1 tablespoon	finely chopped onion	15 mL
1 clove	garlic, chopped	1
2 tablespoons	lemon or lime juice	25 mL
1 tablespoon	chopped green chili pepper (optional)	15 mL
1 1/2 teaspoons	salt	7 mL
1/4 teaspoon	black pepper	1 mL
1/8 teaspoon	cayenne	0.5 mL

Mix all ingredients in an electric blender just before serving. Yield: about 3 cups.

Hints for Party Sandwiches

Use thin sliced sandwich bread, white or whole wheat, preferably one day old.

Butter should be at room temperature. The butter will keep sandwiches from becoming soggy.

Fill sandwiches generously with your choice of fillings. Sandwiches are best if refrigerated for a few hours, wrapped well in waxed paper, two to a package, and covered with a damp cloth. Sandwiches should be cut while chilled, arranged on platters, covered lightly with waxed paper and a damp cloth, and allowed to remain at room temperature for about 30 minutes before serving. When using tomatoes, slice them thinly, seed lightly, and spread on paper towelling to remove excess moisture. Cucumbers should also be sliced thinly and placed on paper towelling.

One 24 ounce (675 g) loaf of bread will serve 5 – 6 people. Prepare more when company includes men.

When preparing sandwiches, try to keep edges of bread matching so that sandwiches will be neat when trimmed.

Fillings

Egg: Do not boil too many eggs at one time. Place room temperature eggs in one layer in pot. Cover with cold water, bring to a boil and cover pot. Remove from heat and let stand for 20 minutes. Run eggs immediately under cold water to insure easy peeling. Mix chopped eggs with salt and pepper to taste, and moisten with mayonnaise or salad dressing. Finely chopped celery, green pepper, and/or grated onion may be added for variation.

Tuna: Drain tuna well. Rinse solid oil packed tuna under water and drain well. Mix with a fork. Moisten with mayonnaise or salad dressing. Add salt and pepper and finely chopped celery. If desired, add some finely chopped egg. Flaked or solid tuna, or a combination of both may be used.

Salmon: Drain salmon. Remove skin and bones. Mash with a fork. Moisten with mayonnaise or salad dressing. Add finely chopped celery, salt and pepper to taste. Relish, chopped sweet pickle, and/or grated egg may be added if desired. Use red sockeye or a combination of sockeye and cohoe salmon.

Cream cheese: Have cheese at room temperature. Cream in electric mixer. Add milk or sour cream, 1 tablespoon (15 mL) at a time, until cheese is of spreading consistency. If desired, sieved hard cooked egg may be added to cheese mixture.

Cheese: Yellow processed cheese spread mixed with a little mayonnaise and finely chopped egg makes a tasty filling.

Triple Decker: Use 3 slices of bread. Spread first slice with softened butter. Spread with filling and cover with second slice of bread, buttered on both sides. Spread with second filling, cover with top slice of buttered bread.

Combinations:
• Salmon or tuna and egg
• Salmon or tuna and cream cheese with tomato, or cream cheese with cucumber.
Remove crusts and wrap. Cut after chilling in triangles or 1" (2.5 cm) slices.

Rolled sandwiches: Have bread sliced lengthwise. Remove crusts. Flatten bread slightly with rolling pin. Spread with softened butter and desired filling. Place small stuffed olives or gherkins along short side of bread. Roll as for jelly roll. Wrap and chill. Slice after chilling about 1/2" (1.5 cm) thick.

Combinations:
• Cream cheese with olive
• Salmon or tuna with olive or gherkin
• Processed cheese with gherkin
• Peanut butter with banana

Open faced sandwiches: Use small dinner rolls, cut in half. Spread with softened butter and desired filling. Garnish with slices of gherkin, stuffed olive or pimento. Arrange on platter, cover loosely with waxed paper and a damp cloth. Chill. Remove from refrigerator 1/2 hour before serving.

Party loaf: Have bread sliced lengthwise. Remove crusts. Use 5 slices of bread and spread as for triple decker sandwiches, using desired fillings. Frost with:

8 ounces	**cream cheese**	**227 g**
1/4 cup	**milk or sour cream**	**60 mL**

Soften cream cheese, adding milk or sour cream slowly while beating, until of spreading consistency. Frost top and sides of loaf. Chill. Garnish before serving.

Garnishes: Garnish platters with small gherkins, radish roses, green pepper rings, carrot curls, cherry tomatoes, parsley and/or watercress.

Sandwiches for 100 Guests

Suggested shopping list:

12	loaves thin sliced white bread
4	loaves brown sliced bread
3	loaves bread, cut lengthwise
6	dozen eggs
10	cans salmon
10	cans tuna fish
3 1/2	pounds butter (1.75 kg)
3 1/2	quarts mayonnaise or salad dressing (4 L) or a combination of both
2	pounds cream cheese (1 kg)
1	pound processed yellow cheese (0.5 kg)
6	pounds tomatoes (2.75 kg)
6	cucumbers
3	large bunches celery
1	large jar smooth peanut butter
12	small bananas
1	jar small gherkins
1	jar small stuffed olives

Soups and
Accompaniments

Tips for Soup Makers

If soup is too salty, add a raw potato and continue cooking. Potato will absorb the salt. Meat or chicken and bones should be well rinsed before adding to water for soup. Skim well before adding vegetables.

For a very clear chicken soup, line a colander with a linen tea towel and place over a large pot. Pour soup through the towel to strain into the pot.

Egg shells added to soup while cooking will help remove scum. Remove shells when cooking is completed.

To remove fat, refrigerate after cooking. Fat will rise to the top and can be easily removed when congealed.

Basic beef stock or chicken stock can be frozen in 1/2 cup (125 mL) containers for use in other recipes (soups, stews, gravies, etc.)

Basic Beef Stock

3	large beef soup bones	3
1 1/2 pounds	flanken (beef short ribs)	700 g
3 quarts	water	3 L
3	carrots	3
3	stalks celery with leaves	3
1	large onion	1
1	parsnip	1
1	parsley root	1
	salt and pepper to taste	

Bring bones and water to a boil. Skim until clear. Add remaining ingredients and simmer for 2 hours, or until meat is tender. Remove meat. Strain soup through a colander.

Beef Vegetable Soup

ELEANOR STEINBERG

2 or 3 pounds	beef short ribs (flanken), cut into chunks	1 – 1.5 kg
3 quarts	water	3 L
2	marrow bones	2
2 teaspoons	salt	10 mL
1 teaspoon	pepper	5 mL
2 teaspoons	granulated sugar	10 mL
2	onions, peeled and quartered	2
3	carrots, scraped and cut into chunks	3
2	stalks celery, with leaves, cut into 1" (2.5 cm) slices	2
2 cloves	garlic	2
2 packages	soup mix (minestrone, bean and barley, etc.)	2
	parsley	
1/4 cup	ketchup	60 mL

Brown beef ribs, a few pieces at a time in a large soup pot. (You may add a beef cube to enhance colour). Cover the browned beef with water and add marrow bones. Add the salt, pepper and sugar and bring the soup to a boil. Skim, lower the heat to simmer and add the cut up vegetables, the dried vegetables and the parsley. Add ketchup. Cover, and simmer gently for about 2 hours, or until meat and vegetables are tender. Taste for seasoning. Let cool and spoon off the fat. If you wish, remove the meat and bones and purée the liquid in a blender or processor. Add meat to soup when serving. Delicious and wholesome. Can be frozen. Serves 6 – 8.

Split Pea Soup

DOLORES WEINER

1	marrow bone with some meat on it (have butcher crack the bone)	1
2 cups	cold water	500 mL
2 cups	chicken or beef stock	500 mL
2 cups	split peas (buy the ones that need no soaking)	500 mL
2	whole dried chili peppers	2
1/2 cup	chopped celery and leaves	125 mL
2	carrots	2
	salt to taste	
	bay leaf	
	sliced hot dogs (optional)	

Cover bone with cold water. Bring to boil and skim. Add stock, peas and chili peppers and simmer for 1 hour. Add vegetables and simmer another hour. Remove bone from soup. Cut off meat. Remove and discard chili peppers and bay leaf. Strain soup into a bowl. Put vegetables and meat into a blender. Blend and add to soup. Return soup with puréed vegetables to soup pot, and heat thoroughly before serving. Add sliced hot dogs, if desired.

Bean, Barley and Mushroom Soup

To strained beef stock, add:

1 cup	lima beans	250 mL
1/2 cup	pearl barley	125 mL
6	dried mushrooms or	6
1/2 pound	sliced fresh mushrooms	225 g

Bring to a boil. Reduce heat, cover, and simmer for 1 hour.

Green Split Pea Soup

Use basic beef stock recipe. After skimming, add diced carrots and 2 cups (500 mL) of no-soak split peas. Simmer for 3 hours.

Goulash Soup

ESTELLE ZALDIN

4	medium onions, diced	4
2 – 3 tablespoons	oil	30 – 45 mL
1 1/2 pounds	stewing beef, cubed	750 g
1 teaspoon	lemon juice	5 mL
1 tablespoon	tomato paste	15 mL
	salt and pepper to taste	
3 tablespoons	sweet paprika	45 mL
1 tablespoon	granulated sugar	15 mL
6 cups	water	1.5 L
1	bay leaf	1
2	medium potatoes, cut into chunks	2
2	medium carrots, diced	2

Sauté onions in oil until wilted. Add beef chunks sprinkled with lemon juice, and sauté until meat is brown and starts to stick to the pot. Add the tomato paste while meat is sautéing. Add salt, pepper, paprika and sugar. Stir well. Add water and bay leaf. Cover and simmer slowly for 1 hour. Add vegetables. Remove bay leaf and continue to cook until vegetables are tender.

Jeannie's Matzo Balls

ELEANOR STEINBERG

3	eggs	3
1/2 cup	matzo meal	125 mL
1/2 teaspoon	baking powder	2 mL
1/2 teaspoon	margarine or chicken fat	2 mL

Beat eggs with margarine or fat. Add matzo meal, baking powder and a pinch of **salt**, and mix well. Refrigerate for at least 3 hours. Make balls the size of walnuts, and drop into boiling water. Cover, reduce heat and simmer for 45 minutes. Yield: 12 – 15 matzo balls.

Note: For Passover, omit the baking powder.

Chicken Soup

1 · 5 – 6 pound	soup chicken or chicken parts	2.5 kg
3 1/2 quarts	water (enough to cover)	3.5 L
1	large whole onion	1
1 tablespoon	salt	15 mL
5	carrots	5
3	stalks celery with leaves	3
2	sprigs dill	2
3	sprigs parsley	3

Clean chicken thoroughly. Place chicken in a large soup pot and add water and onion. Bring to a boil, skim, and cook over medium heat for 1/2 hour. Add remaining ingredients. Cover and cook over low heat for about 2 hours, or until chicken is tender. Remove chicken and vegetables and strain soup.

For a richer soup, add to the above after skimming:

1	parsley root	1
2	parsnips	2
1	thin slice of lemon	1
1 tablespoon	granulated sugar	15 mL
	lettuce leaves	
1 tablespoon	tomato paste	15 mL

Continue cooking as above.

Egg Drop Soup

Beat 3 eggs with a pinch of flour and salt. Drip slowly into boiling soup. If covered for a few minutes, it will puff up.

Kreplach

LOIS FRIEDMAN

4	eggs	4
4 cups	all purpose flour	1 L
1 teaspoon	salt	5 mL
1 cup	water	250 mL

Place flour and salt in bowl. Make a well. Add eggs to well and beat with a fork, combining flour with the eggs. When dough gets too stiff, begin adding water and continue to do so until all the flour is moistened and a ball of dough is formed. Divide dough into 4 pieces, and knead each piece, adding flour as needed until it is smooth and elastic. Cover until ready to use. Roll out dough, one piece at a time, and cut into 2" (5 cm) squares (approximately 36 per piece). Place 1 teaspoon (5 mL) filling on each square. Fold diagonally in half and pinch edges together well. When finished, drop into boiling salted water and boil 3 minutes. Remove, rinse with cold water, drain and store in plastic bags.

To serve: Heat in boiling chicken soup, or brown in 1 tablespoon (15 mL) chicken fat in a 350°F (180°C) oven for 30 minutes or more until brown and crisp, turning once. Sprinkle with salt before serving.

Filling:

2 cups	diced leftover meat	500 mL
	(roast beef, brisket, steak, etc.)	
4	onions, diced	4
1/2 pound	ground beef	250 g
1	egg	1

Sauté onions. Add diced meat and brown well. Push to side of pan. Add ground beef and cook, stirring, until red disappears. Mix all together and cool. Put through meat grinder, add egg and season with **salt** and **pepper** to taste.

Improved Beet Borscht

ETHEL KLEIN

2 · 19 ounce cans	whole beets	540 mL each
1 · 32 ounce bottle	borscht	896 mL
2 tablespoons	granulated sugar	30 mL
1 tablespoon	lemon juice	15 mL
5	eggs	5
1/2 cup	water	125 mL
1/2 teaspoon	salt	2 mL

Strain borscht into pot and discard beets from borscht. Strain juice from canned beets into pot and grate beets on fine grater. Add beets to pot. Add lemon juice and sugar and bring to boil. Beat eggs with water and salt. Add hot liquid to eggs slowly, beating constantly. Return to pot and heat 2 minutes. Cool. Add dollops of **sour cream** to each serving. Serves 6.

Mother's Easy Cabbage Borscht

CAROL RAPP

2 pounds	flanken	1 kg
2	marrow bones	2
1 1/2 quarts	water or enough to cover meat	1.75 mL
1 · 28 ounce can	tomatoes	796 mL
1 · 28 ounce can	sauerkraut	796 mL
6 tablespoons	granulated sugar	90 mL
1/4 teaspoon	salt	1 mL

Cover meat and bones with water and bring to a rapid boil. Skim. Reduce heat and simmer for 1/2 hour, skimming occasionally. Add tomatoes and sauerkraut, sugar and salt and simmer for 1 hour. As liquid is reduced, you may add another 2 cups (500 mL) of water. Simmer another hour or until meat is very tender. Adjust sugar to taste. Serve hot.

Cabbage Borscht

ADÈLE FREEMAN

2 pounds	flanken	1 kg
2	marrow bones	2
3 quarts	water	3 L
2	onions	2
2 · 14 ounce cans	stewed tomatoes	398 mL each
2	beets, pared and sliced	2
1	medium cabbage, coarsely shredded	1
2 teaspoons	salt	10 mL
1/2 teaspoon	pepper	2 mL
1	whole clove garlic	1
	juice of 1 lemon	
1/2 cup	brown sugar	125 mL
1 · 6 ounce can	tomato paste	156 mL
	boiled potatoes	

Combine meat, bones and water in deep saucepan or stock pot. Bring to a boil and skim. Add onions, tomatoes and beets. Cover and cook over low heat for 1 hour. Add the cabbage, salt, pepper and garlic. Cover and cook for 1 hour longer. Add lemon juice, sugar and tomato paste. Cook another 20 minutes. Taste and correct seasonings if necessary. Serve with boiled potato in each bowl.

French Onion Soup

JOANNE ROSENBERG

2 tablespoons	granulated sugar	30 mL
1 teaspoon	lemon juice	5 mL
4	large onions, cut into 1/4" (1 cm) slices	4
2 tablespoons	butter	30 mL
4 teaspoons	instant parve beef soup mix dissolved in	20 mL
4 cups	water	1000 mL
	salt and pepper to taste	
1 clove	garlic (optional)	1
1 cup	grated Swiss gruyère cheese	250 mL
1/2 cup	grated Parmesan cheese	125 mL
4	slices French bread	4

Combine sugar and lemon juice in a pot. Stir over medium heat until caramelized. Add onions and brown until golden. Do not overcook. Add butter and stock, and simmer about 15 minutes. Season to taste. Place some grated Swiss cheese at bottom of each onion soup crock. Then ladle soup over. Add a slice of hot toasted French bread to each bowl, then more Swiss cheese, then Parmesan cheese. Bake at 400°F (200°C) about 20 minutes, or until bubbly and brown. Serves 4.

Potato Leek Soup

5	medium potatoes	5
3 cups	water	750 mL
3	medium leeks, well rinsed and diced	3
4 tablespoons	butter or margarine	60 mL
3 tablespoons	chopped parsley	45 mL
1 teaspoon	salt	5 mL
1/2 teaspoon	black pepper	2 mL
2	tomatoes, diced (optional)	2

Boil potatoes in water until soft, about 25 minutes. Mash potatoes and water together. Sauté the leeks in butter or margarine until soft. Add to potato mixture. Add parsley, salt, pepper and tomatoes. Serve warm or cold. A dollop of **sour cream** or **yogurt** may be added to each soup bowl, if desired.

Mushroom Leek Soup

PHYLLIS FLATT

2 bunches	**leeks**	**2**
1/2 cup	**butter**	**125 mL**
1/2 – 1 pound	**mushrooms, chopped**	**250 – 500 g**
1/4 cup	**all purpose flour**	**60 mL**
	salt to taste	
	dash cayenne or	
	black pepper	
1 cup	**parve chicken stock**	**250 mL**
3 cups	**milk**	**750 mL**
1 tablespoon	**dry sherry or lemon juice**	**15 mL**

Slice white part of leeks. Sauté in 1/4 cup (60 mL) of the butter until tender. Remove from heat and set aside. Sauté mushrooms in remaining butter until soft, and liquid has evaporated. Blend in flour and seasonings. Gradually stir in broth and milk. Cook until mixture thickens. Add leeks and sherry or lemon juice. Simmer for 10 minutes. Serves 6.

Greta's Potage Crecy

GRETA GREISMAN

1 · 3 pound bag	carrots	1.25 kg
1 · 2 pound bag	parsnips	900 g
6	stalks celery	6
2	large onions, chopped	2
2 tablespoons	oil	30 mL
4 quarts	water	4 L
2 tablespoons	salt	30 mL
1/4 teaspoon	nutmeg	1 mL
1/4 teaspoon	thyme	1 mL
2 tablespoons	instant chicken soup mix (optional)	30 mL

Peel and trim carrots and parsnips. Remove tough fibers from celery. Sauté onions in oil, in a large soup pot. Add carrots, parsnips and celery to pot, and add water and salt. Simmer 2 – 3 hours, uncovered until vegetables are soft. Ladle mixture into blender or food processor (in batches if necessary), and purée. Adjust salt to taste. Add nutmeg, thyme and instant chicken soup mix for flavour, if desired. Before serving, add chopped **parsley** to each bowl.

Creamy Carrot Soup

LOIS FRIEDMAN

2 cups	peeled, sliced carrots (5 – 6)	500 mL
1 1/2 cups	chicken broth	375 mL
1	medium onion, coarsely chopped	1
2 tablespoons	raw white rice	30 mL
	pinch of grated nutmeg	
	salt and freshly ground pepper to taste	

Place all the soup ingredients in a medium sauce pan. Bring to a boil, cover, reduce heat and simmer for 25 – 30 minutes or until vegetables and rice are tender. Allow to cool slightly and then purée the mixture in a food blender or processor until smooth. Just before serving, adjust the seasoning. Reheat the soup. Garnish with **parsley** and serve hot. Serves 4. This soup can also be served chilled.

Carrot Parsnip Soup

2 tablespoons	margarine	30 mL
1 1/2 cups	chopped onion	375 mL
4 cups	chicken stock	1 L
8	large carrots, cut into chunks	8
4	parsnips, cut into chunks	4
1 cup	orange juice	250 mL
	grated orange rind	

In a large pot, sauté onion in margarine over low heat until onions are wilted, about 10 minutes. Add chicken stock and bring to a boil. Add carrots and parsnips and return to boil. Reduce heat, cover and cook until vegetables are tender. Remove from heat and cool. Place a colander in a large bowl and pour vegetables into it. Place drained vegetables into processor bowl, with 1 cup (250 mL) of strained stock. Process until smooth. Return to pot with remaining stock. Add orange juice and **salt** and **pepper** to taste. If soup is too thick, add additional chicken stock. To serve, ladle into soup bowls and sprinkle with grated orange rind.

Old-Fashioned Vegetable Soup

LOIS FRIEDMAN

2 pounds	flanken, cut into pieces	1 kg
6 cups	water	1.5 L
1 · 28 ounce can	tomatoes, not drained	795 mL
1	large onion, diced	1
3	carrots, diced	3
3	stalks celery, diced	3
2 tablespoons	barley	30 mL
1 tablespoon	salt	15 mL
1/4 teaspoon	pepper	1 mL

Cover meat with water in a large pot. Bring to a boil, and skim. Add remaining ingredients, and return to a boil. Reduce heat and simmer, covered, for 2 – 3 hours, until meat is tender. Adjust seasoning to taste.

Note: Any leftover vegetables, or soft fresh tomatoes may be added.

Fish Chowder

3	medium size potatoes, diced	3
4	celery stalks, diced	4
1 1/2 pounds	haddock fillets	675 g
1 1/2 pounds	salmon fillets	675 g
1	large onion, diced	1
1 · 10 ounce can	potato soup	284 mL
1 · 14 ounce can	2% evaporated milk (for richer chowder, use homogenized evaporated milk)	400 mL
1 3/4 cups	2% milk (for richer chowder, use half homogenized milk, and half light cream) salt and pepper to taste	425 mL

Cook potatoes and celery in salted water until tender. Pour off all but 1" (2.5 cm) of water and mash. This is your base. Boil fish and onion in enough water to cover, until tender. Strain and reserve liquid. Cut fish into bite-size pieces and add to base. Stir in reserved cooking liquid. Add potato soup, evaporated and 2% milk or milk-cream mixture. Simmer. Season to taste. Pour into bowls and top with a sprinkling of **paprika**. May be served with hot French bread and a salad.

Tomato Bisque   JOYCE LAMPERT, SAN FRANCISCO

3 tablespoons	butter	45 mL
1 tablespoon	oil	15 mL
1	medium onion, thinly sliced	1
3/4 teaspoon	minced garlic	4 mL
5	large tomatoes, sliced	5
1/2 teaspoon	salt	2 mL
	pinch pepper	
4 tablespoons	tomato paste	60 mL
1 – 2 cups	light cream or milk	250 – 500 mL
2 – 4 tablespoons	dry sherry	25 – 60 mL
2 tablespoons	butter	30 mL

Melt butter with oil in a deep saucepan. Add onion and garlic and cook until golden. Add tomatoes, salt and pepper. Cook over low heat for about 8 minutes. Stir in tomato paste. Bring to a boil, stirring constantly. Purée soup in blender. Strain seeds. Return soup to saucepan and cool. Add cream and heat soup, but do not boil. Add sherry and butter. Garnish with chopped **chives** and/or **croutons**. Serves 6. May be made up to 5 days ahead. Freezes well.

Tomato Rice Soup

PAULINE TOKER

A delicious soup, using left over beef bones!

3	cooked roast beef bones (rib)	3
6 cups	water	1.5 L
1 · 28 ounce can	whole tomatoes	795 mL
1 · 10 ounce can	tomato sauce	284 mL
1	onion, diced	1
2	stalks celery with leaves	2
3	carrots, peeled	3
1 1/2 teaspoons	salt	7 mL
1/4 teaspoon	black pepper	1 mL
1 teaspoon	mixed spices (oregano, Italian, fresh basil)	5 mL
1 teaspoon	granulated sugar	5 mL
2	bay leaves	2
1/2 cup	raw rice	125 mL

Wash bones, cover with cold water and bring to a boil. Skim top if necessary. Reduce heat and add whole tomatoes, tomato sauce, diced onion, celery, carrots and seasonings. Partially cover and allow to simmer 1 1/2 – 2 hours until some of the liquid has reduced. Season to taste. Add raw rice and simmer until rice is cooked, about 1/2 hour. Serves 6 – 8.

Dairy Vegetable Soup

MYRTLE COOPERSMITH

5 quarts	water	5.75 mL
1 cup	baby lima beans	250 mL
1/2 cup	pearl barley	125 mL
1/4 cup	green split peas	60 mL
1/4 cup	yellow split peas	60 mL
4	carrots, shredded	4
4	stalks celery with leaves, diced	4
1	tomato, diced	1
3 tablespoons	salt	45 mL
1 teaspoon	white pepper	5 mL
1	onion, cut fine	1
1/2 cup	butter	125 mL

Place all ingredients except butter and onion in a large pot and bring to a rolling boil. Skim. Cover and reduce heat, and simmer for about 3 hours, or until lima beans are soft. Stir occasionally to prevent sticking. When soup is almost done, brown onion in butter and add to soup. This soup freezes very well.

Turkey Vegetable Soup

MYRTLE COOPERSMITH

1	cooked turkey carcass	1
4 quarts	water (or to cover)	4.5 L
1 cup	lima beans	250 mL
1/2 cup	pearl barley	125 mL
1	onion	1
5	carrots, shredded	5
4	stalks celery, cut into pieces	4
1 - 2	sprigs of parsley	1 - 2
1	parsnip	1
4 tablespoons	salt	60 mL
1 teaspoon	white pepper	5 mL

Place turkey carcass in a large pot with enough water to cover. Bring to a rolling boil and skim. Add remaining ingredients and simmer about 3 hours or until lima beans are soft. Remove carcass and onion (and parsnip if desired) when finished.

# Minestrone Soup

PAULINE TOKER

A terrific way to use that leftover turkey carcass!

1	turkey carcass, cooked	1
2 quarts	water	2 L
1 · 28 ounce can	whole tomatoes, not drained	795 mL
1	onion, chopped fine	1
3	stalks celery, chopped	3
3	carrots, diced	3
1/2	green pepper, diced	1/2
2	medium potatoes, peeled and diced	2
2 teaspoons	salt	10 mL
1/2 teaspoon	pepper	2 mL
1/4 teaspoon	chili powder	1 mL
1 teaspoon	mixed Italian herbs (oregano, tarragon)	5 mL
2	bay leaves	2
1 teaspoon	granulated sugar	5 mL
1/4 teaspoon	basil	1 mL
1 - 2	sprigs of fresh parsley	1 - 2
1/2 – 3/4 cup	macaroni or spaghetti, uncooked	150 mL

Cover washed turkey carcass with cold water and bring to a boil. Skim. Add remaining ingredients, except macaroni, and simmer for 2 hours. Additional leftover vegetables may also be used, such as green beans, peas, zucchini, etc., if desired. Remove carcass and add macaroni or broken spaghetti pieces. Adjust seasonings. Cook an additional 10 minutes, until spaghetti is tender. If too thick, add 1 or 2 cups (250 – 500 mL) boiling water. Remove bay leaves.

Iced Cucumber Soup

FRANKIE BROWN

1 1/2 pounds	cucumber	700 g
1/2 cup	chopped onion	125 mL
3 tablespoons	butter	45 mL
6 teaspoons	instant parve chicken soup mix dissolved in	30 mL
6 cups	water	1 1/2 L
1 1/2 teaspoons	wine vinegar	7 mL
3/4 teaspoon	dried dillweed or tarragon	3 mL
4 tablespoons	quick cream of wheat salt and pepper to taste	60 mL
1 cup	sour cream or yogurt	250 mL
1 – 2 tablespoons	minced fresh dill, tarragon or parsley	25 mL

Peel cucumbers. Slice off 18 – 24 paper thin slices, and set aside for garnish. Cut remainder of cucumbers in 1/2" (1.5 cm) cubes. Cook onion in butter slowly for several minutes until tender, but not brown. Add cucumber chunks, stock, vinegar and herbs. Bring to a boil, and stir in cream of wheat. Simmer, partially covered, for 20 – 25 minutes. Purée and season with salt and pepper. Add 1/2 cup (125 mL) of the sour cream or yogurt, and stir to blend. Allow to cool, uncovered, and then cover and chill.

To serve: Add a tablespoon (15 mL) of sour cream or yogurt to each serving and garnish with cucumber slices and fresh herbs. Serves 8.

Iced Zucchini Soup

Use zucchini instead of cucumber. Do not peel. Cut all of zucchini into 1/2" (1.5 cm) cubes. Follow recipe as above. Garnish with chopped dill or parsley, and a sprinkle of paprika. Serves 8.

Gazpacho

L O I S   F R I E D M A N

1	green pepper, chopped	1
1	cucumber, chopped	1
1/4	large Spanish onion, chopped	1/4
1 · 28 ounce can	tomatoes	796 mL
1	garlic clove, crushed	1
1 cup	tomato juice	250 mL
1/2 cup	water	125 mL
1/4 cup	wine vinegar	60 mL
2 tablespoons	olive oil	30 mL
	juice of 1/2 lemon	
	salt, oregano, thyme to taste	
	few drops of Tabasco sauce	

Combine ingredients in processor or blender. Process, using on and off motion so as not to make soup too thin. Chill at least 6 hours before serving. Garnish if desired with **croutons**, chopped **green onions** or chopped **green pepper**.

Vichyssoise

1 bunch	leeks, white part only, sliced	1
	sliced onions, as needed	
4 teaspoons	parve chicken soup mix	20 mL
4 cups	boiling water	1 L
3 cups	sliced, peeled potatoes	750 mL
3 teaspoons	salt	15 mL
1/4 teaspoon	white pepper	1 mL
2 cups	milk	500 mL

Combine leeks with enough onions to measure 3 cups (750 mL). Dissolve chicken soup mix in water. Add vegetables and simmer until tender. Put in blender (in several stages) and purée. Do not fill blender too full. Return puréed mixture to pot. Add seasoning and milk, and bring to a boil. Cool and put through blender once more. Chill and serve with chopped **chives**.

Cold Red Pepper Soup

IRENE FINK

3 tablespoons	olive oil	45 mL
3 cups	chopped red pepper	750 mL
2 cups	chopped onion	500 mL
1/2 teaspoon	thyme	2 mL
1 tablespoon	minced garlic	15 mL
1/8 teaspoon	ground red pepper	0.5 mL
2	parve chicken cubes dissolved in	2
2 cups	boiling water	500 mL
1 teaspoon	salt	5 mL
2 cups	buttermilk	500 mL
1/4 cup	shredded basil	60 mL

Heat oil and sauté red pepper and onion for 15 minutes. Add thyme, garlic, ground pepper, and sauté 30 seconds. Add chicken stock. Cover and simmer 1/2 hour. Blend when cool and add salt. Whisk in buttermilk and chill. Serve with basil on top. An ideal summer soup! Serves 6 – 8.

Fruit Gazpacho

PHYLLIS FLATT

2 cups	tomato purée	500 mL
3 cups	freshly squeezed orange juice	750 mL
2 teaspoons	granulated sugar	10 mL
	grated rind of 1 orange	
	grated rind of 1 lime or lemon	
2 cups	diced cantaloupe	500 mL
2 cups	diced honey dew melon	500 mL
1	mango, peeled and diced	1
1 cup	fresh blueberries	250 mL
1 cup	halved green or red seedless grapes	250 mL
	fresh strawberries, halved	
1 – 2	kiwis, peeled and sliced	1 – 2

Peel, seed and chop in blender or food processor, enough tomatoes to make 2 cups (500 mL) purée. Combine purée with orange juice, sugar, rinds, cantaloupe, honey dew and mango. Process half of this mixture in food processor or blender until smooth. Stir purée into remaining half of melon mixture. Chill. When serving, add blueberries, grapes, strawberries and kiwi slices.

Cherry Borscht

TOBY DUNKELMAN

1 quart	fresh cooking cherries	1 L
5 cups	water	1.25 L
	pinch salt	
3/4 cup	granulated sugar	175 mL
1 tablespoon	cornstarch	15 mL

Wash and pit cherries. Add water, salt and sugar. Boil until cherries are well cooked. Dissolve cornstarch in a little water and add to soup, stirring until slightly thickened and clear. Cool and chill in refrigerator before serving. May be served with small, hot boiled potato for each serving.

Blueberry Soup

DORIE SOPHER, CLEVELAND

2 cups	water	500 mL
1/2 cup	granulated sugar	125 mL
1 stick	cinnamon	1
1	lemon, thinly sliced	1
1 pint	blueberries	500 mL
1 cup	sour cream	250 mL

Combine water, sugar, cinnamon, lemon and blueberries in a saucepan. Bring to a boil. Reduce heat and simmer for 15 minutes. Remove lemon and cinnamon. Blend in blender. Chill. Add sour cream. Mix with wire whisk. Chill. Serve with a dollop of sour cream. Serves 6.

Chilled Cucumber and Avocado Soup

1	large ripe avocado, peeled	1
1	English cucumber, unpeeled	1
2	green onions, coarsely chopped	2
1 1/2 cups	parve chicken broth	375 mL
3 tablespoons	lemon juice	45 mL
1 tablespoon	fresh snipped dill	15 mL
1/8 teaspoon	granulated sugar	0.5 mL
1/2 cup	sour cream	125 mL
	salt and pepper	
	sour cream for garnish	

Cut avocado into pieces and purée in food processor or blender. Cut cucumber into chunks and drop through feed tube with motor running. Add green onion and process until smooth. Add broth, lemon juice, dill, sugar and sour cream. Blend well. Season to taste with salt and pepper. Refrigerate until ready to serve. Garnish with sour cream if desired. For an elegant touch, top each serving with a slice of cucumber, a dollop of sour cream and caviar. Serves 6. Doubles easily.

Quick and Easy Asparagus Soup

1 pound	asparagus, cut up	500 g
3 cups	parve chicken broth	750 mL
2	tomatoes, cut into chunks	2
1 teaspoon	sweet basil, finely chopped	5 mL

Combine ingredients in a saucepan. Bring to a boil. Reduce heat and simmer for 30 minutes. Purée in a blender or put through a food mill. Stir in 2 tablespoons (30 mL) **sour cream.** Serve hot or cold, with a dollop of sour cream on top if desired.

Salads, Dressings and Molds

Salad Hints

For perfect leaves, soak head of lettuce in cold water to which salt has been added. Place lettuce on wooden board with the stem end up, and hit the core two or three times. Twist out core with fingers. Hold lettuce under faucet, letting cold water flow into the hole. Lettuce leaves will separate beautifully.

After washing and tearing lettuce for a salad, place in a large bowl which has been lined with a terrycloth towel. Wrap towel over top of lettuce. Put into refrigerator until ready to use. Towel will absorb all excess moisture, and lettuce will be crisp and fresh. If you prefer, salad spinners do an effective job of drying lettuce greens.

Bean sprouts are a popular ingredient in many salads. To keep them crisp and white, soak about 10 minutes in cold water to which some lemon juice has been added.

Vinegars

Vinegars come in many different varieties. Try different ones to enhance your salads.

Cider Vinegar - A mild one made from apples.

Fruit Vinegar - Include raspberry, strawberry and many other fruits.

Herb Vinegar - Is made by infusing herbs in the vinegar and include basil, tarragon, dill.

Wine Vinegar - Made from red or white wine. Some may also have herbs added.

Salad Greens

Salad greens vary greatly. Be adventurous. Try new combinations.

Arugula - Intense in colour. Strong taste. Combine with other greens.

Belgian Endive - Crisp, elongated yellow-white leaves. Very special.

Bib Lettuce - Small, tight leaves. Sweet.

Boston Lettuce - Pale green, loosely packed, soft and floppy leaves. Delicate flavour.

Chicory - Tart and crunchy. Curly leaf endive is a variety with slightly bitter taste. Use with other greens.

Iceberg Lettuce - Little flavour. Crisp, keeps well.

Leaf Lettuce - Curly red or green tipped leaves. Tender and tasty.

Radicchio - Ruby red miniature leaf. Slightly bitter flavour. Colour and flavour mix well with other greens.

Romaine - Firm, elongated leaves. Robust taste. Crunchy. Excellent for Caesar salad.

Spinach - Small, rounded, dark leaves. Blends well in many combinations.

Watercress - Dark green, small leaves. Good taste and colour. Mixes well.

Croutons

Trim crusts from sliced bread and cut into cubes. (Leftover stale bread may be used). Sprinkle with garlic salt. Sauté in 2 tablespoons (30 mL) oil until lightly golden. Drain on paper towels.

<u>Or</u>

Place cubed bread which has been sprinkled with garlic salt on a cookie sheet. Bake at 325°F (160°C) about 20 minutes, or until lightly golden.

Orange - Almond Salad

2	large heads of romaine lettuce	2
2 – 3	fresh oranges, peeled and cut into sections	2 – 3
1	red onion, thinly sliced	1
1/2 cup	toasted slivered almonds	125 mL

Dressing:

1/2 cup	oil	125 mL
2 tablespoons	honey	30 mL
4 tablespoons	malt vinegar	60 mL
1/2 teaspoon	salt	2 mL
	pepper to taste	
2 drops	almond extract	2

Toss greens with dressing. Add oranges and onion. Top with toasted almonds. Serves 8 – 10.

Artichoke and Tomato Salad

ELEANOR STEINBERG

2 · 14 ounce cans	artichoke hearts, drained	398 mL each
2 · 14 ounce cans	black olives, pitted and drained	398 mL each
2 · 10 ounce cans	whole mushrooms, drained or	284 mL each
1 1/2 cups	sliced fresh mushrooms	375 mL
4	medium tomatoes, peeled and cut into wedges	4
	sliced red onion rings	
	salt and pepper to taste	
1 1/2 cups	Italian dressing	375 mL
2 tablespoons	chopped parsley	30 mL
	lettuce leaves	
	parsley sprigs	

Place artichoke hearts, olives, mushrooms, tomato wedges and onion rings in a single layer in a large, shallow glass dish. Sprinkle lightly with salt. Combine salad dressing, pepper and chopped parsley, and pour over vegetables. Cover with plastic wrap and chill several hours, turning the tomato wedges once or twice. Lift vegetables out of marinade with a slotted spoon and put on lettuce leaves on individual salad plates at serving time. Garnish with parsley sprigs. May also be placed in an attractive glass bowl for a buffet table.

Mixed Bean Salad

JUDY ASCH

1 · 14 ounce can	red kidney beans	398 mL
1 · 14 ounce can	cut wax beans	398 mL
1 · 14 ounce can	chick peas	398 mL
1 · 14 ounce can	cut green beans	398 mL

Optional:

1	green pepper, chopped fine	1
1	small onion, chopped fine	1
1 tablespoon	finely chopped pimento	15 mL
1/4 cup	chopped celery	60 mL

Mix vegetables together, and marinate in a tart French dressing. (See suggested dressing below). Refrigerate a day or two before serving. Serves 8.

Suggested Dressing

ESTELLE ZALDIN

1/3 cup	oil	75 mL
1/3 cup	cider vinegar	75 mL
1/3 cup	brown sugar	75 mL
1/2 teaspoon	celery seed	2 mL

Blend well.

Chicken Salad

2 cups	cooked chicken breasts, cubed	500 mL
1 tablespoon	lemon juice	15 mL
1 cup	celery, sliced thin, diagonally	250 mL
1 tablespoon	capers (optional)	15 mL
1/2 cup	pineapple tidbits, drained (optional)	125 mL
	salt and pepper to taste	
1/2 cup	mayonnaise	125 mL
2 tablespoons	toasted slivered almonds	30 mL
	lettuce leaves	

Sprinkle lemon juice over chicken. Add celery, capers, pineapple, salt and pepper and toss lightly. Mix mayonnaise through chicken mixture gently. Sprinkle almonds on top. Heap chicken salad on lettuce leaves. Platter may be garnished with small whole **cherry tomatoes**, cold **asparagus spears**, **radish roses**, **olives**, etc. Serves 6.

Green Bean Chicken Salad

MYRTLE COOPERSMITH

2 cups	cooked cut green beans	500 mL
2 cups	cubed cooked chicken	500 mL
1 · 5 ounce can	water chestnuts, drained and sliced	140 g
2	hard boiled eggs, sliced	2
1/3 cup	sweet pickle relish	75 mL
1/2 cup	mayonnaise	125 mL
1 tablespoon	finely chopped onion	15 mL
2 teaspoons	Dijon mustard	10 mL
1 teaspoon	salt	5 mL
	lettuce leaves	

Combine beans, chicken, water chestnuts, egg and relish. Stir together mayonnaise, onion, mustard and salt. Add to bean mixture. Toss lightly. Chill and serve in bowl lined with lettuce leaves.

Fresh Bean Salad

MYRTLE COOPERSMITH

2 pounds	fresh green beans	1 kg
1/2	Spanish onion, sliced	1/2
2	tomatoes, diced	2

Dressing:

1 teaspoon	salt	5 mL
1/2 teaspoon	oregano	2 mL
1/2 teaspoon	pepper	2 mL
1/4 cup	tarragon vinegar	60 mL
1/2 cup	oil	125 mL
	dash of mustard	
	dash of granulated sugar	

Cook green beans in boiling water for one minute. Drain and cool. Add sliced onion and diced tomatoes. Combine ingredients for dressing, and pour over vegetables. Cover and marinate in refrigerator overnight or longer. Serves 12 to 15.

Chinese Salad

MYRNA TECHNER

1	romaine lettuce, torn into bite-size pieces	1
1/2 pound	mushrooms, quartered	250 g
2	zucchini, quartered and sliced	2
1/2 pound	bean sprouts	250 g
1/2	green pepper, slivered	1/2
1 can	Chinese dry egg noodles	1

Combine ingredients and toss just before serving with any creamy dressing. Crunchy and eye appealing. Serves 6 – 8.

Marinated Artichokes and Mushrooms

LOIS FRIEDMAN

1 pound	mushrooms	500 g
1 · 14 ounce can	artichokes	398 g

Wash and dry mushrooms. Cut in half, if large. Place in container with tight-fitting lid. Drain artichokes, and cut in half. Place in another container. Marinate both, separately, in oil and vinegar dressing for 4 – 6 hours. To serve, drain both and mix together in bowl.

Bulgar Salad (Tabouli)

VERA SANDERS

1 cup	bulgar	250 mL
2 cups	water	500 mL
	pinch of salt	

Combine, bring to boil in pot, reduce heat and cook until water is absorbed - about 10 minutes. Cool.

Add:

2	tomatoes, chopped	2
1/2	English cucumber, chopped	1/2
1/2	onion, diced	1/2
1 – 2 cloves	garlic, crushed	1 – 2
1/4 cup	parsley, minced	60 mL
1 each	red, yellow and green pepper, chopped fine	1 each
	juice of 1/2 lemon	
1/4 cup	olive oil	60 mL

Mix well. Serves 6.

Carrot Salad

SANDRA SAMUELS

2 pounds	fresh carrots, sliced	1 kg
	or	
2 pounds	frozen carrots	1 kg
2	medium onions, cut into thin rings	2
1	medium green pepper, cut into strips	1
1 head	cauliflower, blanched and broken into florets	1
1 pound	fresh mushrooms	450 g

Marinade:

1 · 10 ounce can	tomato soup, undiluted	284 mL
3/4 cup	red wine vinegar	200 mL
1/3 cup	granulated sugar	75 mL
1/2 cup	oil	125 mL
1 teaspoon	Worcestershire sauce	5 mL
1/2 teaspoon	salt	2 mL

Cook carrots until just tender. Drain and mix with other vegetables. Mix ingredients for marinade and blend well. Pour over vegetables. Can be made three days in advance. Serves 12 – 15.

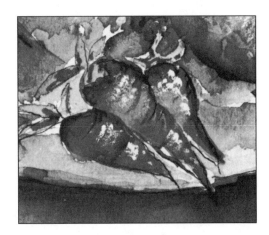

Marinated Cucumbers

LOIS FRIEDMAN

8	cucumbers	8
2 cups	vinegar (scant)	475 mL
	water	
1/2 cup	granulated sugar	125 mL
2 teaspoons	salt	10 mL
1/2 teaspoon	pepper	2 mL

Two days before serving, peel cucumbers, and slice thin. Place vinegar in a 4 cup (1 L) measure and fill with water to equal 4 cups (1 L). Add sugar, salt and pepper - mix and taste. Adjust seasonings. Place cucumbers in jar, pour liquid over, pack down and place heavy object on top. To serve, remove from marinade, and sprinkle with fresh snipped dill.

Cucumbers in Sour Cream

LOIS FRIEDMAN

2	medium cucumbers	2
1	large onion	1
1 1/2 teaspoons	salt	7 mL
3/4 cup	water	175 mL
3/4 cup	vinegar	175 mL
1 teaspoon	granulated sugar	5 mL
1/2 cup	sour cream or yogurt	125 mL
2 teaspoons	fresh dill or	10 mL
1 teaspoon	dried dill weed	5 mL
1 – 2 drops	bottled hot pepper sauce	1 – 2
	dash of freshly ground pepper	

Peel one cucumber. Thinly slice both. Slice onion and separate into rings. Combine cucumbers and onions in a bowl. Sprinkle with salt. Combine water, vinegar and sugar. Pour over cucumbers. Let stand at room temperature one hour. Drain thoroughly. Combine sour cream, dillweed, pepper sauce and pepper. Toss gently with cucumbers and onions. Cover. Chill one hour. Serves 6.

1	medium cabbage, finely shredded	1
10	medium carrots, peeled and finely grated	10
1	green pepper, seeded and finely chopped	1
1	small onion, grated	1

Dressing:

3/4 cup	mayonnaise	175 mL
1/4 cup	white vinegar	60 mL
1/4 cup	granulated sugar (or more to taste)	60 mL
2 teaspoons	salt	10 mL
1/4 teaspoon	black pepper	1 mL

Mix vegetables together. Combine dressing ingredients and blend well. Add to vegetables and mix. Adjust seasoning to taste. Allow to stand in refrigerator 3 to 4 hours before serving. Serves 12 – 15.

Alternative Dressing:

1 cup	white vinegar	250 mL
1/3 cup	salad oil	75 mL
1/2 cup	granulated sugar	125 mL

Mix together.

Creole Salad

LOIS FRIEDMAN

1 bunch	celery, diced and leaves removed	1
1	large green pepper, seeded and diced	1
1	large red onion, sliced into thin rings	1
1 pint	cherry tomatoes, cut in half	500 mL

Dressing:

3/4 cup	oil	200 mL
1/2 cup	vinegar	125 mL
1 teaspoon	salt	5 mL
1/2 teaspoon	pepper	2 mL
	dash of oregano	

Combine dressing ingredients and blend well. Combine vegetables. Pour dressing over and marinate several hours. Serves 8.

Greek Tomato Salad

LOIS FRIEDMAN

3/4 cup	feta cheese	200 mL
1 clove	garlic	1
3	large tomatoes, cut into eighths	3
1	red onion, thinly sliced	1
12	ripe black olives, cut in half	12
3 tablespoons	wine vinegar	45 mL
1/2 cup	olive oil	125 mL
1/2 teaspoon	oregano	2 mL
1/2 teaspoon	thyme	2 mL
1 teaspoon	salt (or to taste)	5 mL
	freshly ground pepper	
	lettuce leaves	

Crumble cheese coarsely. Rub a wooden bowl with garlic. Add tomatoes, onion slices, cheese and olives. Mix vinegar, oil and seasonings. Shake well. Pour over tomatoes and marinate at least 4 hours. Line a serving bowl with lettuce leaves and pour in mixture. Serve chilled.

Gazpacho Salad

4	cucumbers, peeled and finely diced	4
4	tomatoes, seeded and finely diced	4
	salt	
2	green peppers, seeded and finely diced	2
1	onion, finely chopped	1
6	rolled anchovies	6
6	black olives	6

Dressing:

2 cloves	garlic	2
	pinch of salt	
	pinch of ground cumin seed	
1/4 cup	vinegar	60 mL
1/2 cup	oil	125 mL
1 tablespoon	parsley, finely chopped	15 mL
2 tablespoons	shallots, finely chopped	30 mL
	juice of 1 lemon	

In a deep bowl, alternate layers of vegetables. Sprinkle each layer lightly with salt and intersperse with anchovies and olives. Mash garlic with salt and cumin seed. Beat in vinegar and oil. Stir in parsley and shallots. Pour dressing over salad and chill 2 – 3 hours. Sprinkle with lemon juice before serving.

Greek Salad

2 large or 3 small heads	bib, romaine or iceberg lettuce	2 – 3
12	cherry tomatoes or tomato wedges	12
6	thin slices red onion	6
1/2	cucumber, peeled and sliced	1/2
3/4 cup	celery, sliced	175 mL
4	green onions, cut in 1" (2.5 cm) lengths	4
8	radishes, sliced	8
1/2 cup	feta cheese, crumbled	125 mL
8 – 10	Kalamata black olives	8 – 10
1 · 2 ounce can	flat anchovies, drained and halved	57 g

Wash and dry lettuce and break into bite-size pieces in a salad bowl. Add the vegetables, cheese, olives and anchovies. Pour dressing over and toss well. Serves 6.

Dressing:

2 tablespoons	red wine vinegar or lemon juice	30 mL
1 teaspoon	finely minced garlic	5 mL
1/2 teaspoon	freshly ground pepper	2 mL
6 tablespoons	olive oil	90 mL
1 teaspoon	oregano	5 mL
1/4 teaspoon	salt	1 mL

Combine dressing ingredients and blend thoroughly in blender or jar.

Orange and Avocado Salad

J.J. WINBERG

2 heads	Boston lettuce	2
1/2 cup	seedless raisins	125 mL
1	ripe avocado, peeled and sliced	1
1 · 10 ounce can	mandarin oranges, drained	284 mL
2	ripe tomatoes, cut into wedges	2

Dressing:

2 tablespoons	red wine vinegar	30 mL
1/2 teaspoon	salt	2 mL
1/4 teaspoon	pepper	1 mL
2	small shallots, finely minced	2
2 cloves	garlic, crushed	2
1/2 cup	salad oil	125 mL

Croutons:

1/2 loaf	day old French bread	1/2
1/4 pound	garlic butter or margarine	125 mL

Wash and dry lettuce. Tear into pieces and put in bowl. Add raisins, avocado slices, oranges and tomatoes. Combine vinegar, salt, pepper, shallots and garlic. Mix with a wire whisk. Add oil slowly, and continue to whisk. Cut bread into cubes. Melt garlic butter or margarine. Fry pieces of bread in margarine or butter until crisp. Combine salad, dressing and croutons, and toss. Serves 6 – 8.

Oriental Salad

1 · 10 ounce package	spinach (may be mixed with romaine, if desired)	283 g
1 pound	bean sprouts	450 g
3/4 pound	fresh mushrooms, washed, dried and sliced	350 g
1 · 10 ounce can	water chestnuts, drained and sliced	284 mL

Dressing:

1/2 teaspoon	granulated sugar	2 mL
1/2 teaspoon	pepper	2 mL
1/2 cup	oil	125 mL
1/4 cup	soy sauce	60 mL
3 tablespoons	lemon juice	45 mL
1 tablespoon	vinegar	15 mL
1 1/2 tablespoons	grated onion or	20 mL
2 teaspoons	onion flakes	10 mL

Garnish:

	toasted sesame seeds or cashew nuts	

Combine dressing ingredients. Mix well, and let stand in jar for 2 hours. When ready to serve, pour dressing over salad and mix well. Just before serving, add 1 1/2 tablespoons (25 mL) toasted sesame seeds or cashew nuts.

Salad Niçoise

LOIS FRIEDMAN

1 pound	green beans	450 g
1/2 head	lettuce, torn into bite-size pieces	1/2
4 stalks	celery, sliced thin	4
3 · 6.5 ounce cans	tuna, drained	184 g each
6	eggs, hard boiled and quartered	6
1 pint	cherry tomatoes	500 mL
10	stuffed olives	10
10	black pitted olives	10
2	green peppers, seeded and sliced thin	2
1	red onion, sliced thin	1
1/3 cup	chopped parsley	75 mL
1/4 cup	chopped green onion	60 mL
1 teaspoon	dried basil	5 mL
	or	
1 tablespoon	fresh chopped basil	15 mL

Cut green beans into 1" (2.5 cm) pieces. Cook in boiling water for three minutes. Drain and refresh under cold water. Place lettuce in bottom of salad bowl. Add celery. Place tuna chunks on top of lettuce in centre of bowl. Arrange eggs, beans and tomatoes around tuna in mounds. Toss olives, green pepper and onions on top. Sprinkle parsley, green onion and basil on top.

Dressing:

1 – 2 teaspoons	Dijon mustard	5 – 10 mL
2 tablespoons	wine vinegar	30 mL
1 – 2 cloves	garlic, mashed	1 – 2
6 tablespoons	salad oil	90 mL
6 tablespoons	olive oil	90 mL
	pinch of thyme	
	salt and pepper to taste	

Mix all ingredients and chill. Toss salad with dressing just before serving. Serves 8 – 10.

Pear and Pecan Slaw

MARLA FRANKEL, JERUSALEM

2 cups	finely shredded green cabbage	500 mL
1 cup	finely shredded red cabbage	250 mL
2	Bartlett or Bosc pears, halved, cored and diced	2
1/4 cup	diced pecans	60 mL
1/2 cup	seeded grapes	125 mL
1/2 cup	mayonnaise	125 mL
3 teaspoons	grated lemon rind	15 mL
2 tablespoons	lemon juice	30 mL
2 tablespoons	preserved or crystallized ginger, drained and chopped	30 mL
1/4 teaspoon	salt	1 mL

In a large bowl, combine cabbage, pears, pecans and grapes. Combine the remaining ingredients in a second bowl and pour over the cabbage mixture. Toss lightly to mix. Chill well. Serves 6.

Potato Salad

PAULINE TOKER

4	large potatoes, cut in half	4
	or	
24	mini new potatoes	24
1	small bunch green onions, chopped fine	1
5	stalks celery, chopped fine	5
2	hard boiled eggs, diced	2

Cook potatoes in salted water until tender. Peel while hot. Cool and cut into a bowl. Add onions, celery and eggs.

Dressing follows on page 71.

Dressing:

1	egg, beaten	1
1/2 cup	granulated sugar (scant)	115 mL
1 tablespoon	all purpose flour	15 mL
1/2 cup	water	125 mL
1/2 cup	vinegar	125 mL
2 tablespoons	butter	30 mL
1 teaspoon	salt	5 mL
1/4 teaspoon	pepper	1 mL

Combine ingredients in order given, stirring after each addition. Boil until thick. Cool before adding to salad. After mixing salad and dressing, allow to stand at least 8 hours in refrigerator.

Spinach Salad

RUTH SADOWSKI

1 · 10 ounce package	spinach	283 g
	sliced mushrooms	
	croutons	
3	hard boiled eggs, quartered	3
	mandarin orange segments	
	(optional)	

Dressing:

1/3 cup	olive oil	75 mL
2 tablespoons	white vinegar	30 mL
1/2 teaspoon	lemon juice	2 mL
1/4 teaspoon	dry mustard	1 mL
1/2 teaspoon	salt	2 mL
1 clove	garlic, pressed or	1
1/2 teaspoon	garlic salt	2 mL

Wash and dry spinach. Tear into small pieces. Combine dressing ingredients in jar and shake well. Pour dressing over spinach, mushrooms and croutons and toss. Add **salt** and **pepper** to taste. Arrange quartered hard boiled eggs attractively around salad. Serves 6.

Rice Tomato Salad

FAY SANDLER

1 cup	chicken broth or stock	250 mL
1/2 cup	long grain rice	125 mL
1/3 cup	frozen green peas, cooked and drained	75 mL
1 tablespoon	slivered green onions and tops	15 mL
4	large fresh mushrooms, sliced	4
2 tablespoons	diced cucumber	30 mL
1 tablespoon	sliced stuffed olives	15 mL
4 tablespoons	salad oil	50 mL
2 teaspoons	fresh lemon juice	10 mL
	salt and pepper to taste	
1/4 teaspoon	paprika	1 mL

In a small saucepan, bring broth to a boil. Add rice, bring to boiling point and reduce heat to simmer. Cook covered on simmer 15 minutes or until grains are tender. Fluff with a fork. Add peas, and turn into a bowl. Cool. Add onions, mushrooms, cucumber and olives. Blend oil and lemon juice. Mix into rice mixture. Add salt, pepper and paprika to taste. Garnish with **lettuce** and **tomato wedges**.

Waldorf Salad

1/2 cup	mayonnaise	125 mL
1/2 cup	sour cream or yogurt	125 mL
1 tablespoon	honey	30 mL
3 cups	tart apples, peeled, cored and diced	750 mL
2 cups	celery, diced	500 mL
1 cup	coarsely chopped walnuts	250 mL
2 cups	seeded red grapes, halved (optional)	500 mL
	diced fresh pears (optional)	

Mix the mayonnaise, sour cream and honey together. Add the apples and blend well with the dressing to prevent discolouring. Add the celery and walnuts. Mix again and chill. Serve on lettuce leaves. Serves 6 – 8.

Salad Bar Luncheon

A popular luncheon buffet for as many people as you desire!

Salad greens - raw spinach leaves, iceberg, romaine and bib lettuce washed, dried and torn into bite-size pieces.

Carrots - shredded.

English cucumbers - scored with a fork and thinly sliced.

Green peppers - chopped or cut into thin strips.

Mushrooms - washed, dried and sliced.

Eggs - hard boiled, chopped or quartered.

Bean sprouts - washed and drained.

Celery - chopped or thinly sliced.

Tomatoes - cut into wedges.

Radishes - sliced.

Cheese - cottage, feta or shredded brick, cheddar, etc.

Spanish or Bermuda onions - cut in rings.

Green beans - cooked until crisp and barely tender.

Canned artichoke hearts - drained.

Canned chick peas - drained and rinsed.

Tuna fish - drained, rinsed and cut in chunks.

Croutons

Grated Parmesan cheese

Sunflower seeds or pine nuts

Arrange any combination of salad greens in a large bowl. Arrange any or all of the remaining ingredients (your choice) in separate appropriate serving dishes. Set out 3 or 4 different salad dressings in attractive bowls with ladles - Caesar, French, oil and vinegar, lo-cal, Russian, blue cheese. Don't forget the pepper mill! Serve with a variety of breads, muffins and quick breads.

Blue Cheese Salad Dressing

3/4 cup	oil	175 mL
1/4 cup	white vinegar	60 mL
1 teaspoon	salt	5 mL
3 cloves	garlic, pressed	3
	dash of Worcestershire sauce	
1/2 cup	Parmesan cheese	125 mL
3 tablespoons	cottage cheese	45 mL
2 tablespoons	blue cheese	30 mL

Combine all ingredients in blender and blend well. Keep in refrigerator.
If too thick, add a bit more liquid and blend again.

Avocado and Yogurt Dressing

1	very ripe avocado, peeled, pitted and cubed	1
1 cup	plain yogurt	250 mL
1/3 cup	diced onion	75 mL
1/3 cup	diced green pepper	75 mL
1/4 cup	mayonnaise	60 mL
1 teaspoon	snipped fresh dill	5 mL
1/2 teaspoon	lemon juice	2 mL
1/4 teaspoon	granulated sugar	1 mL
1/4 teaspoon	minced garlic	1 mL
	salt and freshly ground pepper to taste	

Combine avocado, yogurt, onion and green pepper in a blender or
food processor. Blend about 20 seconds. Add mayonnaise, dill, lemon
juice, sugar, garlic, salt and pepper. Blend until smooth. Makes about
2 1/2 cups (625 mL). Very nice over greens with a fish dinner.

Caesar Salad Dressing

ADÈLE FREEMAN

3 tablespoons	olive oil	45 mL
1 tablespoon	red wine vinegar	15 mL
1 clove	crushed garlic	1
1 teaspoon	grated Parmesan cheese (optional)	5 mL
1/4 teaspoon	salt	1 mL
1/4 teaspoon	black pepper	1 mL
1/2 teaspoon	dry mustard	2 mL
3	anchovy fillets, mashed	3

Combine all ingredients in blender and blend for a few seconds, or place in jar with tight fitting lid and shake vigorously. Serve over torn romaine lettuce. Toss. Garnish with croutons.

Lo Cal French Dressing

EDIE WINBERG

5 ounces	condensed tomato soup	140 mL
2 1/2 ounces	water	75 mL
1 tablespoon	vinegar	15 mL
1 tablespoon	grated onion	15 mL
2 1/2 tablespoons	finely chopped green pepper	40 mL
1 teaspoon	Worcestershire sauce	5 mL
1/2 teaspoon	dry mustard	2 mL
	pinch of garlic powder	
1/2 teaspoon	liquid sweetener	2 mL

Combine all ingredients and beat well with a wire whisk. Shake well before using.

Garlic Dressing

FAY SANDLER

2 cups	salad oil	500 mL
1 cup	wine vinegar	250 mL
6 ounces	brick cheese, diced	170 g
8 tablespoons	grated Parmesan cheese	125 mL
5 dashes	Worcestershire sauce	5
1 teaspoon	dry mustard	5 mL
1 teaspoon	oregano	5 mL
	salt and pepper	
4 cloves	fresh garlic, peeled	4
	(or more to taste)	

Combine ingredients in a blender and blend at highest speed 2 – 3 minutes. Let sit in refrigerator overnight. The flavour will improve as the dressing sits in the refrigerator.

Italian Dressing

3/4 cup	olive oil	175 mL
1/4 cup	red wine vinegar	60 mL
1 tablespoon	minced onion	15 mL
2 cloves	garlic, crushed	2
1/2 teaspoon	oregano	2 mL
1 teaspoon	dried basil	5 mL
	salt and freshly ground	
	pepper to taste	

Combine all ingredients in a jar and shake well.

Oil and Vinegar Dressing

3/4 cup	oil	175 mL
1/2 cup	vinegar	125 mL
1 teaspoon	salt	5 mL
1/4 teaspoon	pepper	1 mL
	dash of oregano	

Combine all ingredients in a jar and shake well. Very good for marinating vegetables.

Creamy Roquefort Dressing

1 cup	mayonnaise	250 mL
1/2 cup	sour cream	125 mL
1/4 pound	crumbled blue cheese	115 g
1 teaspoon	wine vinegar	5 mL
1 clove	garlic, pressed	1
	salt and pepper to taste	
2 – 4 tablespoons	water, as needed	30 – 60 mL

Combine ingredients in mixing bowl. Stir well to blend. If too thick, add a little water.

Russian Dressing

1 cup	mayonnaise	250 mL
1 tablespoon	minced onion (optional)	15 mL
1 tablespoon	parsley, finely chopped	15 mL
3 tablespoons	chili sauce	45 mL
1/2 teaspoon	Worcestershire sauce	2 mL
	dash of lemon juice	
	salt and freshly ground	
	pepper to taste	

Combine all ingredients. Stir to blend well.

Vinaigrette Dressing

1/2 cup	olive oil	125 mL
1 tablespoon	minced parsley	15 mL
3 tablespoons	red wine vinegar	45 mL
1 teaspoon	salt	5 mL
1 teaspoon	Dijon-style mustard	5 mL
1 clove	garlic, crushed	1
1/8 teaspoon	pepper	0.5 mL
1/4 teaspoon	tarragon (optional)	1 mL

Place all ingredients in a small jar and shake well.

Beet Horseradish Mold

THELMA RACHLIN

1 package	lemon gelatin (4 serving size)	1
1 · 14 ounce can	shoestring beets, drained, reserve liquid	398 mL
2 tablespoons	lemon juice	30 mL
1/2 cup	horseradish	125 mL
1/2 cup	sour cream	125 mL

Place beet liquid in a 2 cup (500 mL) measure, add water if necessary to make 1 1/2 cups (375 mL) of liquid. In a saucepan, dissolve gelatin in beet liquid. Bring to a boil. Add lemon juice and allow to thicken. Stir in horseradish. Add drained beets. Stir gently to mix. Fold in sour cream. Pour mixture into a 4 cup (1 L) mold. Place in refrigerator to set. Good with fish or cold buffet.

Horseradish Mousse

HARRIET DENNIS

1 package	lemon gelatin (4 serving size)	1
1 cup	boiling water	250 mL
2 tablespoons	vinegar dash of salt	30 mL
1 1/2 cups	drained white horseradish dash of Tabasco sauce	375 mL
2 cups	whipping cream, measured then whipped	500 mL

Dissolve gelatin in water. Add vinegar and salt. Congeal slightly in refrigerator for 15 minutes. Add drained white horseradish. Whip until foamy. Add Tabasco sauce. Fold in whipped cream. Pour into 1 1/2 quart (1.5 L) rinsed mold. Chill overnight until firm. Unmold. Serves 12 - 16 as an accompaniment to a fish meal.

Cranberry Pineapple Mold

CONNIE MONSON KUSSNER

3/4 cup	water	175 mL
	juice of 1 lemon	
1 · 14 ounce can	crushed pineapple	398 mL
1 · 14 ounce can	whole berry cranberry sauce	398 mL
2 packages	raspberry gelatin (4 serving size)	2

Mix water and lemon juice with juice of well-drained pineapple in small pot. Bring to a boil, and pour over gelatin. Stir in pineapple and cranberry sauce. Mix thoroughly. Pour into 1 quart (1 L) mold and chill well.

Jellied Gazpacho Mold

LOIS FRIEDMAN

1 1/2 tablespoons	unflavoured gelatin	23 mL
2 1/2 cups	tomato juice	625 mL
2 tablespoons	wine vinegar or tarragon vinegar	30 mL
2 tablespoons	olive oil	30 mL
	a few drops of Tabasco sauce	
	dash of black pepper	
1/2 teaspoon	salt	2 mL
1	medium cucumber, peeled and chopped	1
1/4 cup	onion, minced	60 mL
1/4 cup	green pepper, chopped	60 mL
1/4 cup	celery, chopped	60 mL

Sprinkle gelatin over tomato juice and let stand several minutes. Dissolve over low heat. Let cool. Add next five ingredients. Chop vegetables and place in colander to drain. Add to mixture and pour into mold. Chill to set. Unmold to serve.

Cucumber Mold

1 package	lime gelatin	1
	(4 serving size)	
1 cup	boiling water	250 mL
1 tablespoon	lemon juice	15 mL
1/2 tablespoon	tarragon vinegar	7 mL
1 teaspoon	salt	5 mL
	pinch of pepper	
1/4 teaspoon	dry mustard	1 mL
1/4 cup	mayonnaise	60 mL
2 cups	chopped seedless cucumber	500 mL
2 tablespoons	finely chopped onions	30 mL
1/4 cup	finely chopped green pepper	60 mL
1 cup	cottage cheese, drained and mashed	250 mL

Garnish:

watercress
cherry tomatoes

Dissolve gelatin in boiling water. Add lemon juice, vinegar, salt, pepper and dry mustard. Chill until slightly thickened. Stir in mayonnaise, cucumber, onion, green pepper and cheese. Blend well. Pour into oiled one quart (1 L) mold. Chill. This is better made the day before serving. Unmold on a platter, surround with watercress and cherry tomatoes. Keep refrigerated until serving time. Serves 8 – 10. Tangy, crunchy and delicious!

Raspberry Gelatin Mold

LOIS FRIEDMAN

4 packages	raspberry gelatin (4 serving size)	4
3 cups	boiling water	725 mL
2 · 15 ounce packages	frozen raspberries	850 g
1 · 14 ounce can	crushed pineapple	398 mL
1 pint	sour cream	500 mL

Dissolve gelatin in boiling water. Add partially thawed berries and pineapple including juice. Let stand until gelatin starts to thicken. Pour half into 12 cup (3 L) ring mold. Place mold in refrigerator until quite firm. Spread sour cream over set gelatin, keeping it away from edges of mold. Pour remaining gelatin on top. Refrigerate to set. Unmold to serve.

Raspberry Cranberry Mold

SANDRA HABERMAN, ST.LAURENT

2 packages	raspberry gelatin (4 serving size)	2
2 cups	boiling water	500 mL
2 cups	canned whole berry cranberry sauce	500 mL
1 cup	undrained crushed pineapple	250 mL
1	small apple, diced	1
1/2 cup	Burgundy wine	125 mL
1/3 cup	chopped nuts	75 mL
1/3 cup	chopped celery	75 mL

Dissolve gelatin in boiling water. Stir in cranberry sauce, pineapple, apple and wine. Chill until partially set. Stir in nuts and celery. Pour into 1 1/2 quart (1.5 L) mold and chill. Serves 6 – 8.

Eggs, Cheese
and Side Dishes

Cheese Blintzes

THELMA RACHLIN

3	beaten eggs	3
1/2 teaspoon	salt	2 mL
1 1/2 cups	water	375 mL
1 1/4 cups	all purpose flour	300 mL

Combine eggs, salt and water. Beat flour in gradually. Heat 7" (17.5 cm) frying pan. Grease lightly. Make sure pan is hot. Pour in enough batter to lightly cover bottom of pan, tilting pan to cover evenly. Cook until set. Turn out onto towel. On each blintz place 1 tablespoon (15 mL) filling. Fold over, envelope style, and brown in a little **butter** or **oil**.

Filling: Combine

1 pound	dry cottage cheese	450 g
1	egg, beaten	1
1 tablespoon	melted butter (optional)	15 mL
1 tablespoon	granulated sugar	15 mL
1 teaspoon	cinnamon	5 mL

Serve with blueberry sauce and sour cream. Yield: 20 blintzes.

Hint: Pan may be greased by dipping paper towel or pastry brush in oil or melted butter, then lightly rubbing over pan.

Aunt Sara's Broccoli Soufflé

DOLORES WEINER

1/4 cup	chopped onions	60 mL
6 tablespoons	butter	90 mL
1/2 cup	water	125 mL
2 tablespoons	all purpose flour	30 mL
1/2 cup	water	125 mL
1/2 pound	Velveeta cheese	227 g
2 · 10 ounce packages	frozen chopped broccoli	283 g each
3	eggs	3
1/2 cup	cornflake crumbs	125 mL

Preheat oven to 350°F (180°C). Grease an 8" (2 L) square baking dish. Sauté onions in 4 tablespoons (60 mL) of the butter. Add water gradually to flour, stirring constantly, to make a smooth paste. Add flour paste to onions. Cook over low heat until thick. Blend in cheese, stirring until melted. Add defrosted broccoli. Beat eggs a little and gradually add to broccoli mixture. Pour into prepared baking dish. Mix crumbs and remaining melted butter. Sprinkle over top. Bake for 40 minutes. Freezes well. Serves 5 – 6. Double recipe for 9" x 13" (3.5 L) baking dish.

Mock Cheese Soufflé

NANCY POSLUNS

10 slices	white bread, crusts removed	10
	softened butter	
3/4 pound	grated cheddar cheese	340 g
3/4 pound	grated Swiss cheese	340 g
8	eggs, lightly beaten	8
3 – 4 cups	milk	750 mL – 1 L
1/4 teaspoon	paprika	1 mL
1/4 teaspoon	pepper	1 mL
1 teaspoon	dry mustard	5 mL
1 teaspoon	Worcestershire sauce	5 mL
1/8 teaspoon	cayenne pepper	0.5 mL
1/2 teaspoon	onion powder	2 mL
1 1/2 teaspoons	salt	7 mL

Grease a 9" x 13" (3.5 L) baking dish. Butter bread and cut into cubes. Alternate layers of cubed bread and grated cheese in prepared baking dish. Combine rest of ingredients and pour over bread and cheese. Refrigerate overnight before baking. Preheat oven to 325°F (160°C). Bake 1 1/4 – 1 1/2 hours until puffed up and golden.

To freeze: Bake before freezing. Defrost, then reheat. Serves 8 – 10.

Blintz Soufflé

DOLORES WEINER

18	assorted frozen blintzes, cherry, blueberry, cheese	18
5 tablespoons	butter	75 mL
6	eggs	6
2 1/4 cups	sour cream	550 mL
1 1/2 teaspoons	vanilla	7 mL
1 1/2 tablespoons	orange juice	25 mL
1/3 cup	granulated sugar	75 mL
1/2 teaspoon	salt	2 mL
1/2 teaspoon	cinnamon	2 mL

Preheat oven to 350°F (180°C). Melt butter in 9" x 13" (3.5 L) baking dish. Lay frozen blintzes in pan. Combine rest of ingredients, except cinnamon, in blender or mixer and blend well. Pour over blintzes. Sprinkle with cinnamon. Bake one hour. Serve hot from oven. Serves 9 – 10.

Baked Omelette

LOIS FRIEDMAN

12	eggs, slightly beaten	12
2 1/2 cups	diced salami, cooked and drained	625 mL
1/2 cup	finely chopped onion	125 mL
2	tomatoes, seeded and diced	2
1/2	green pepper, diced	1/2
2 teaspoons	salt	10 mL
1/4 teaspoon	pepper	1 mL
	margarine to grease pan	

Preheat oven to 350°F (180°C). Grease a 9" x 13" (3.5 L) baking dish. Beat eggs, add remaining ingredients and mix thoroughly. Pour into prepared baking dish and bake for 12 – 15 minutes, or until set. Cut into 12 pieces.

Eggplant, Tomato and Cheese Casserole

DOLORES WEINER

2	medium eggplants, peeled and cut into 1/2" (1.5 cm) thick slices	2
	salt	
1/4 cup	olive oil	60 mL
2	onions, finely chopped	2
2 cloves	garlic, finely chopped	2
2	zucchini, sliced (3/4 pound)	2
1 quart	fresh tomatoes, peeled and chopped	1 L
	or	
1 · 28 ounce can	canned tomatoes	796 mL
	salt and pepper to taste	
2	stalks celery, diced	2
1/2 teaspoon	dried basil	2 mL
1/2 cup	grated Parmesan cheese	125 mL
1/4 cup	chopped parsley	50 mL
4 ounces	mozzarella cheese, coarsely grated	115 g

Preheat oven to 375°F (190°C). Sprinkle eggplant slices with salt and let stand 10 minutes. Rinse off and dry well. Cut into cubes. Heat oil in heavy skillet and cook eggplant quickly until lightly browned. Add onions, garlic and zucchini and cook 3 minutes. Add tomatoes, salt and pepper, celery and basil. Bring to a boil, then simmer, covered, stirring occasionally for 15 minutes or until zucchini is just tender. Stir in Parmesan cheese and parsley. Pour into 9" x 13" (3.5 L) baking dish. Sprinkle with mozzarella cheese and bake, uncovered, one hour.

To freeze: Omit mozzarella, cool, chill, wrap well and freeze. To serve, bring to room temperature, sprinkle with mozzarella cheese and bake. Serves 8 – 10.

Eggplant Casserole

SHEILA LOFTUS

2 cups	ricotta cheese	500 mL
1 teaspoon	oregano	5 mL
3	eggs	3
1/2 teaspoon	salt	2 mL
3 tablespoons	chopped parsley	50 mL
1 large or 2 medium	eggplant(s)	1-2
2	eggs	2
1 tablespoon	all purpose flour	15 mL
1 teaspoon	baking powder	5 mL
1/2 cup	milk	125 mL
2 tablespoons	olive oil	30 mL
	mozzarella cheese	

Preheat oven to 375°F (190°C). Combine ricotta cheese, oregano, eggs, salt and parsley. Beat until fluffy. Peel eggplant and slice 3/4" (2 cm) thick. Make a batter out of 2 eggs, flour, baking powder and milk. Lightly flour slices of eggplant. Dip in batter and fry until browned. Place a layer of eggplant in a greased 9" x 13" (3.5 L) casserole, cover with a layer of ricotta cheese mixture, and then with thinly sliced mozzarella. Repeat layers once. Sprinkle top with **Parmesan cheese**. Bake for 1/2 to 3/4 hour. Serves 8 – 10.

Easy Spinach Quiche

JUNE FILLER

1 · 8 ounce can	refrigerated crescent roll dough	227 g
1 · 8 ounce package	natural Swiss cheese slices, cut into thin strips	227 g
1/2 cup	grated Parmesan cheese	125 mL
3 tablespoons	all purpose flour	45 mL
1 1/4 cups	milk	300 mL
4	eggs, slightly beaten	4
1/4 teaspoon	salt	1 mL
1/8 teaspoon	pepper	0.5 mL
1/8 teaspoon	nutmeg	0.5 mL
1 · 10 ounce package	frozen chopped spinach	280 g

Preheat oven to 350°F (180°C). Separate crescent roll dough into large rectangles and place in bottom of greased 9" x 13" (3.5 L) baking dish. Press and seal holes. Cover bottom and 1/2" (1.5 cm) up sides. In mixing bowl, toss cheeses with flour. In another bowl, combine milk, eggs, seasonings, and mix with cheeses. Stir in cooked and very well drained spinach. (Press out as much moisture from spinach as possible). Pour into crescent dough crust and bake 50 minutes on middle rack of oven. Cut into small squares for hors d'oeuvres or larger portions for luncheon. Can freeze and reheat.

Quiche

1	9" (22.5 cm) pastry shell, unbaked	1
4	eggs	4
2 cups	cream or milk	500 mL
3/4 teaspoon	salt	4 mL
1/8 teaspoon	nutmeg	0.5 mL
1/8 teaspoon	granulated sugar	0.5 mL
1/8 teaspoon	cayenne pepper	0.5 mL
1/8 teaspoon	pepper	0.5 mL
1	green onion, thinly sliced sliced fresh mushrooms (optional)	1
1 cup	grated Swiss cheese fresh chopped parsley	250 mL

Preheat oven to 425°F (220°C). Beat eggs. Add cream or milk and seasonings. Add onion and sliced mushrooms if desired. Fold in grated cheese. Pour into pastry shell. Bake 12 – 15 minutes. Lower temperature to 350°F (180°C) and bake an additional 25 minutes. Let stand 10 minutes before serving. Sprinkle with chopped parsley if desired.

Vegetable Quiche

GRETA GREISMAN

1	single pastry for 9" (22.5 cm) pie	1
2 tablespoons	finely chopped green pepper	30 mL
2 tablespoons	minced onion	30 mL
2 tablespoons	butter	30 mL
1/2 cup	sliced cherry tomatoes	125 mL
	all purpose flour	
1/8 teaspoon	thyme	0.5 mL
1 cup	grated Swiss cheese	250 mL
3	eggs	3
1 1/3 cups	light cream	325 mL
1 teaspoon	seasoned salt	5 mL
1/8 teaspoon	cayenne	0.5 mL

Garnish:

3	green pepper rings	3
3	cherry tomatoes, hollowed out	3
	freshly ground pepper	

Preheat oven to 400°F (200°C). Line pan with pastry leaving a high crimped edge. Prick with a fork. Bake for 8 minutes. Remove from oven and allow to cool before filling. Lower temperature to 375°F (190°C).

Sauté chopped green pepper and onion in 1 tablespoon (15 mL) butter until golden. Remove from pan and set aside. Add remaining butter. Dredge tomato slices in flour and sauté quickly. Drain on paper towels. Arrange tomato slices on bottom of pie shell. Sprinkle with thyme. Add green pepper and onions and sprinkle cheese over all. Beat eggs with cream, seasoned salt and cayenne, and pour over. Garnish top. Bake for 40 minutes or until set. Remove and season with black pepper. Let stand 15 minutes before serving.

Tip for cholesterol conscious: You may substitute canned condensed skim milk for cream, and margarine for butter.

Spinach Ricotta Tart

PAULINE TOKER

1	9" (22.5 cm) single baked pie crust	1
2 · 10 ounce packages	frozen chopped spinach	280 g each
1	small onion, minced	1
3 tablespoons	butter or margarine	45 mL
1/2 teaspoon	salt	2 mL
1/4 teaspoon	ground nutmeg	1 mL
1 · 15 ounce package	ricotta cheese	425 mL
1 cup	light cream or half and half	250 mL
1/2 cup	grated Parmesan cheese	125 mL
3	eggs, slightly beaten	3
1/4 pound	grated Swiss cheese	113 g

Preheat oven to 350ºF (180ºC). Cook spinach. Drain in strainer and squeeze out liquid well. Sauté onion in butter. Stir in spinach, salt, nutmeg and a dash of **black pepper**. Combine ricotta cheese, cream, Parmesan cheese and eggs. Stir in spinach mixture. Sprinkle baked pie crust with Swiss cheese. Pour mixture into pastry shell. Bake for 50 minutes until custard is set and top is lightly browned. Serves 6 – 8.

Noodle Pudding #1

LOIS FRIEDMAN

1 · 12 ounce package	medium noodles	340 g
4	eggs	4
1/4 cup	butter or margarine	60 mL
2 teaspoons	granulated sugar	10 mL
1 teaspoon	salt, to taste	5 mL
1/4 teaspoon	white pepper, to taste	2 mL

Preheat oven to 375ºF (190ºC). Boil noodles in lightly salted water until tender. Drain and rinse. Drain again. Melt butter or margarine in 9" x 13" (3.5 L) baking dish. Add butter to noodles. Beat eggs slightly with sugar, salt and pepper. Add to noodles and mix well. Pour into baking dish and bake for 45 minutes. Pudding will be crispy and thin. Serves 8.

Noodle Pudding #2

DIANE FINSTEN

1 · 12 ounce package	broad noodles	340 g
3	eggs	3
1 cup	sour cream	250 mL
1 cup	milk	250 mL
3	onions, diced and browned	3
2 teaspoons	salt	10 mL
1/2 teaspoon	pepper	2 mL
2 tablespoons	margarine	30 mL

Preheat oven to 350°F (180°C). Grease and flour a 9" (2.5 L) baking dish. Boil noodles in salted water until tender. Drain and rinse well with cold water. Drain again. Add beaten eggs, sour cream, milk, onions, salt, pepper and margarine. Pour into prepared baking dish and bake for 1 hour. Serves 6.

Snow Capped Pineapple Cheese Pudding

TILLY SPEARS

1 · 12 ounce package	broad noodles	340 g
8	eggs, separated	8
1 1/2 pounds	cottage cheese	700 g
2 cups	sour cream	500 mL
1 1/2 cups	granulated sugar	375 mL
1/2 teaspoon	salt	2 mL
1/2 cup	butter, melted	125 mL
1 · 19 ounce can	crushed pineapple, not drained	540 mL

Heat oven to 350°F (180°C). Grease a 9" x 13" (3.5 L) baking dish. Cook noodles until tender and rinse under cold water. Drain. Cream cottage cheese and add egg yolks, sour cream, sugar and salt. Add butter to yolk/cheese mixture. Add half the cottage cheese mixture to noodles. Add pineapple. Pour into prepared baking dish. Beat egg whites until stiff. Fold whites into remaining half of cheese mixture. Pour this on as top layer. Bake 1 hour until golden brown. This is a lovely party pudding. Serves 10 – 12.

Buttermilk Noodle Pudding

SHEILA ALEXANDER

8 ounces	medium noodles	225 g
2	eggs	2
2 cups	buttermilk	500 mL
1/3 cup	granulated sugar	75 mL

Topping:

1 cup	cornflake crumbs	250 mL
1/4 cup	brown sugar	60 mL
1/4 cup	melted butter	60 mL

Preheat oven to 350°F (180°C). Boil noodles in salted water. Drain and rinse well in cold water. Mix beaten eggs, buttermilk, sugar and salt to taste. Combine with noodles. Pour into buttered 8" (2 L) baking dish. Combine cornflake crumbs and brown sugar. Sprinkle over top. Drizzle melted butter over top and bake for 1 hour.

No-Egg Luncheon Noodle Pudding

MYRTLE COOPERSMITH

1 pound	broad noodles	450 g
2 cups	sour cream	500 mL
1 pound	cottage cheese	454 g
1 cup	milk	250 mL
2 1/2 teaspoons	salt	12 mL
6 tablespoons	granulated sugar	90 mL
6 tablespoons	melted butter	90 mL
	crushed Cornflakes	
2 tablespoons	additional butter	30 mL

Preheat oven to 350°F (180°C). Cook noodles according to package. Drain and rinse well. Mix with sour cream, cottage cheese, milk, salt, sugar and melted butter. Place in greased 9" x 13" (3.5 L) baking dish. Top with crushed Cornflakes, and dot with 2 tablespoons (30 mL) butter. Bake for 1 1/2 hours.

To freeze: Freeze uncooked, well wrapped, and bring to room temperature before baking. Serves 10 – 12.

Pearl Barley Casserole

HALLE COHEN

1/4 pound	butter or margarine	125 g
1/2 pound	fresh mushrooms, sliced	250 g
2	medium onions, chopped	2
1 3/4 cups	pearl barley	425 mL
2 3/4 cups	chicken broth	675 mL
1 teaspoon	salt	5 mL

Preheat oven to 350ºF (180ºC). Sauté mushrooms in butter or margarine until soft. Remove from pan. Add onions to pan and cook until wilted, about 5 minutes. Add barley and cook until golden. Return mushrooms to mixture. Combine and place mixture in 9" x 13" (3.5 L) baking dish. Add 1 3/4 cups (425 mL) of the chicken broth and bake for 30 minutes, covered. Add remaining chicken broth and bake uncovered for an additional 30 minutes. Serves 10.

Vegetable Luncheon Cheesecake

HONEY ROSENTHAL

3 cups	coarsely grated zucchini	750 mL
1 cup	minced onion	250 mL
2 tablespoons	butter	30 mL
2 cloves	garlic, minced	2
1 cup	grated carrots	250 mL
3 tablespoons	all purpose flour	45 mL
1 teaspoon	dried basil	5 mL
1 teaspoon	dried oregano	5 mL
1/2 cup	fresh parsley, minced	125 mL
2 tablespoons	lemon juice	30 mL
4	eggs	4
3 cups	ricotta cheese, drained	750 mL
1/2 cup	grated Parmesan cheese	125 mL
1 1/2 cups	grated mozzarella cheese	375 mL
1/4 cup	breadcrumbs	60 mL
	freshly ground pepper	
	salt to taste	

In a colander over the sink, salt the grated zucchini. After 15 minutes, squeeze out all the moisture. In a large frying pan sauté the onion in butter until soft. Add garlic, carrots, zucchini, flour, basil and oregano. Cook over medium heat about 8 minutes, stirring occasionally. Remove from heat, stir in parsley and lemon juice. In an electric mixer beat eggs and cheeses. Fold in cooled vegetables, mixing well. Season with salt and pepper. Butter heavily the bottom of a 10" (25 cm) spring form pan. Sprinkle with bread crumbs. Pour vegetable mixture into pan carefully. Bake at 375°F (190°C) for 30 minutes. Reduce heat to 350°F (180°C) and bake another 30 minutes. Turn off oven, open door, and leave cake for 15 minutes. Remove from oven and cool for 10 minutes before serving.

Risotto

7 cups	chicken stock (parve)	1.75 L
3 tablespoons	butter	45 mL
1	onion, finely chopped	1
1 cup	sliced mushrooms	250 mL
2 cups	arborio rice	500 mL
	(short grain Italian)	
1/4 cup	dry white wine	60 mL
1/2 cup	grated Parmesan cheese	125 mL
2 tablespoons	minced parsley	30 mL

Bring chicken stock to a simmer on stove. In a large heavy pot melt butter and sauté onions and mushrooms until onions are transparent, but not brown. Add rice, and cook, stirring constantly, about 2 minutes. Add wine and cook, stirring until almost completely absorbed. Add 2 cups simmering stock slowly, and cook, uncovered, stirring gently occasionally, until almost all the liquid is absorbed. Repeat with another 2 cups of stock. Add stock 1/2 cup (125 mL) at a time, cooking and stirring very gently until liquid is absorbed and rice is moist, creamy and al dente. Remove from heat and stir in grated Parmesan cheese. Season to taste with salt and pepper and sprinkle with chopped fresh parsley. Serve at once. Serves 6.

Rice Pilaf

ADÈLE FREEMAN

1/3 cup	finely chopped onion	75 mL
6 tablespoons	butter or margarine	100 mL
2 1/4 cups	uncooked rice	550 mL
4 1/2 cups	boiling chicken broth	1125 mL
	salt and freshly ground	
	black pepper to taste	

Preheat oven to 375°F (190°C). In a heavy casserole sauté onion in butter until tender and transparent. Do not brown. Add rice and continue to cook over low heat until rice grains turn opaque, stirring occasionally. Do not allow rice to brown. Note: You can do up to this point ahead of time, and proceed with the recipe 25 minutes before serving. Add chicken broth, and season with salt and pepper. Cover tightly and bake 5 minutes. Reduce heat to 350°F (180°C) and bake 15 – 20 minutes longer, or until rice has absorbed all the stock.

Options: Just before serving you can add broiled chicken livers cut into small pieces, and/or 1/2 pound (225 g) of fresh mushrooms which have been sliced and sautéed in 1/4 cup (60 mL) butter or margarine, and/or chopped fresh parsley.

Fried Rice

SHEILA RUBINOFF

3 tablespoons	peanut oil	45 mL
2 slices	fresh ginger	2
1/2 cup	cooked chicken, chopped (optional)	125 mL
1/2 cup	frozen peas, thawed	125 mL
1	stalk celery, chopped	1
4 cups	cold cooked rice	1 L
1/2 cup	scallions, sliced	125 mL
1	egg, lightly scrambled	1
2 tablespoons	soy sauce	30 mL
1/2 cup	snow peas, trimmed and diagonally cut	125 mL

Heat wok or frying pan well. Add oil. Stir fry ginger. Discard. Add chicken, peas and celery, cooking about 30 seconds. Add rice and stir fry about 3 minutes until thoroughly heated, breaking up any lumps while stirring. Add scallions, scrambled egg, snow peas and soy sauce. Stir well, heating another minute. Remove from heat and serve immediately.

Curried Rice with Dried Fruit

ELEANOR STEINBERG

3 tablespoons	butter or margarine	45 mL
1	medium onion, diced	1
1	tomato, seeded and chopped	1
1/4 teaspoon	cumin	1 mL
1/2 – 1 teaspoon	curry powder	2 – 5 mL
1 cup	long grain white rice	250 mL
2 cups	chicken stock or water	500 mL
1 tablespoon	raisins	15 mL
2 tablespoons	chopped dried apricots	30 mL

Melt butter or margarine in saucepan. Sauté onion until transparent. Add tomato and cook for 2 minutes. Add cumin, curry powder, rice and stock. Bring to a boil. Reduce heat to low, and simmer, covered 20 minutes. Add raisins and apricots. Recover, and simmer 10 minutes more, until the liquid is completely absorbed and rice is tender. Serves 6.

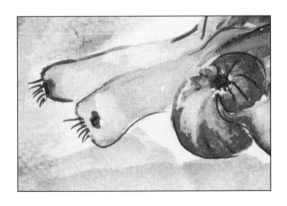

Armenian Rice

SANDY GRANATSTEIN, OTTAWA

1/4 cup	melted butter or margarine	60 mL
1/2 cup	fine uncooked noodles, broken into 1" (2.5 cm) pieces	125 mL
1/4 cup	chopped walnuts	60 mL
1 1/2 cups	uncooked rice	375 mL
3 cups	consommé (parve)*	750 mL
2 tablespoons	currants	30 mL
1/4 teaspoon	allspice	1 mL

Melt butter or margarine. Add noodles and walnuts. Cook over medium heat until lightly browned, stirring. Add rice and cook 2 minutes. Add consommé, currants, allspice, salt and pepper. Stir well. Bring to a boil. Cover, reduce heat to low and cook 20 minutes. Sprinkle with parsley. *If using instant soup mix, dissolve 3 teaspoons (15 mL) in 3 cups (750 mL) of boiling water. Serves 6.

Couscous

VERA SANDERS

1 cup	couscous	250 mL
6	dried apricots, cut up	6
1/2 cup	raisins	125 mL
	dash of salt	
2 cups	boiling water	500 mL

Place couscous in a bowl with apricots, raisins and salt. Pour boiling water over. Cover and let sit for 10 – 15 minutes. Fluff with a fork and serve. Serves 4 as a side dish.

Fruited Cranberries

4 cups	whole fresh cranberries	1 L
2 cups	granulated sugar	500 mL
1 cup	water	250 mL
1	large apple, peeled and thinly sliced	1
1	orange, sectioned	1
	grated rind of 1 orange	
	walnut halves (optional)	

Combine first four ingredients. Cook over medium heat, stirring occasionally, until cranberries pop, about 15 minutes. Fold in orange sections and rind. Remove pan from heat, and cool. Add nuts, if desired, before serving. Can be made a few days in advance. A delicious accompaniment for poultry or meat. Yield: 1 quart (1 L) of sauce.

Curried Fruit Compote

JUNE FILLER

1 large can each	pears, pineapple, peaches and black pitted cherries	1 each
2	sliced bananas (add last half hour)	2
2/3 cup	dark brown sugar	150 mL
2 tablespoons	curry powder	30 mL
1/2 cup	melted butter	125 mL
	juice of 1 lemon	
2	rusks or zwieback, crumbled	2
	shredded coconut (optional)	

Preheat oven to 325°F (160°C). Place fruit in strainer and drain well. Leave fruit whole and place in a greased baking dish or roaster. Mix remaining ingredients and spread over fruit. Bake for 1 1/2 hours, covered. Do not stir cooked fruit. When serving, top with shredded coconut, if desired.

Vegetable and Cheese Puff

2 cups	assorted vegetables	500 mL
	e.g. mushrooms, green onion,	
	tomatoes	
4	eggs, well beaten	4
1 cup	cottage cheese	250 mL
1 cup	yellow cheese, grated	250 mL
1 tablespoon	all purpose flour	15 mL
	salt and pepper	

Chop vegetables coarsely. Mix together with eggs and cheeses. Add flour, salt and pepper to taste. Pour into a greased 9" (22.5 cm) baking dish and dot with **butter**. Refrigerate for 1 1/2 hours. Preheat oven to 325°F (160°C) and bake for 35 - 40 minutes. Serves 4.

This recipe is easily doubled. Allow 1 hour baking time for doubling.

Microwave Red Pepper and Zucchini Frittata

1 tablespoon	olive oil	15 mL
1	small onion, chopped	1
1 clove	garlic, minced	1
1 cup	red pepper, chopped	250 mL
1 cup	zucchini, unpeeled and chopped	250 mL
6	eggs	6
1/2 teaspoon	basil, dried	2 mL
1/4 teaspoon	oregano	1 mL
1/4 teaspoon	salt and pepper, each	1 mL
1/2 cup	Parmesan cheese, grated	125 mL

Combine oil, onion, garlic, red pepper and zucchini. Place in 9" (22.5 cm) microwavable dish. Microwave uncovered on high for 4 - 6 minutes or until softened. Stir half way through cooking. Lightly beat eggs with seasonings. Stir in cheese. Pour egg mixture over vegetables and combine. Microwave uncovered for 2 - 3 minutes. Stir mixture with a fork, moving outer cooked parts towards center. Microwave for 3 - 5 minutes or until set. Let stand for 5 minutes before serving. Serves 4.

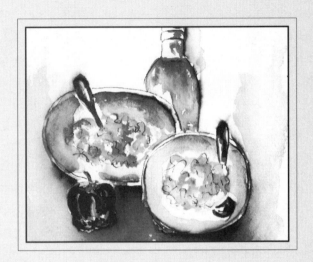

Pasta

How to Cook Pasta

VERA SANDERS

When cooking pasta, it is important to use a large pot and plenty of water. For one pound (454 g) of pasta use at least a seven quart (7 L) pot and four quarts (4 L) cold water with 1 1/2 tablespoons (20 mL) of salt (optional). One tablespoon (15 mL) of oil may be added to keep pasta separated and shiny.

Make sure water is boiling rapidly before adding pasta. Stir pasta well after adding to water to separate. Cook pasta 'al dente' – firm to the bite. Homemade pasta takes very little time to cook, in most cases 2 – 5 minutes. Test for doneness. Packaged pasta takes longer to cook. For times, consult instructions on package.

When cooked to your taste, rinse and toss pasta in a colander under cold running water.

One pound (454 g) of pasta and sauce will serve six people generously.

Heat sauce separately and add to pasta. Serve immediately. To reheat cooked pasta, plunge into boiling water, and return to boil for one minute. Drain and mix with sauce.

Quick and Easy Pasta

SHANEA RAKOWSKI

2 pounds	fresh pasta, cooked al dente	1 kg
4 cups	fresh tomato sauce (commercial or your favourite recipe)	1 L
1/4 pound	Chèvre cheese	125 g
	handful of chopped fresh basil	
1/4 cup	chopped fresh herbs, i.e. dill, chives or parsley	60 mL
2 teaspoons	brown sugar	10 mL
	sliced mushrooms or peas (optional)	
	Parmesan cheese	

Combine ingredients, except pasta, and simmer until lukewarm and well blended. Serve over hot pasta. Sprinkle with Parmesan cheese.

Primavera

1/4 cup	butter	60 mL
2 cloves	garlic, crushed	2
	(or more to taste)	
1	sweet red pepper, cut julienne	1
24	asparagus tips	24
1 cup	broccoli florets, blanched	250 mL
1/2 cup	chopped fresh parsley	125 mL
1	large ripe tomato, diced	1
2/3 cup	cream	150 mL
	salt and freshly ground pepper	
3 tablespoons	grated Parmesan cheese	45 mL
1 teaspoon	dried tarragon	5 mL

Melt butter in heavy skillet. Add garlic, red pepper, asparagus and broccoli. Sauté five minutes. Stir in parsley and tomato. Cook five minutes more. Add cream, salt and pepper to taste, and cook gently until sauce thickens. Stir in Parmesan cheese and tarragon. Serve over hot pasta.

Fettucini Alfredo

1 pound	fresh or dried fettucini	454 g
	boiling water	
	salt	
1 – 1 1/2 cups	soft or melted butter	250 – 375 mL
2 cups	grated Parmesan cheese	500 mL
3/4 cup	heavy cream	175 mL
1/2 teaspoon	nutmeg	2 mL
	freshly ground pepper	

Cook noodles in a large quantity of lightly salted boiling water until tender. Drain well. Rinse and drain again. Place noodles in a hot casserole over low heat. Combine butter, cheese, cream and nutmeg. Add mixture a little at a time to noodles, tossing gently after each addition. Season with freshly grated pepper to taste.

Dairy Lasagna

VERA SANDERS

1 · 12 ounce package	lasagna noodles	340 g
2 cups	tomato sauce (commercial or your favourite recipe)	500 mL
1 cup	grated mozzarella cheese	250 mL
1/2 cup	grated Parmesan cheese	125 mL
2 cups	béchamel sauce	500 mL

Béchamel sauce:

4 tablespoons	butter	60 mL
6 tablespoons	all purpose flour	90 mL
2 cups	milk	500 mL
	salt and pepper to taste	

Melt butter in saucepan. Add flour gradually and cook gently on low heat until bubbly, stirring constantly with a whisk. Do not allow mixture to brown. Remove from heat. Slowly add milk and continue to stir. Return pan to low heat and cook gently, stirring, until thick. Season to taste with salt and pepper. Cook lasagna noodles according to package directions.

Preheat oven to 350°F (180°C). In a 9" x 13" (3.5 L) greased baking dish, place a small amount of tomato sauce, covering bottom of dish. Then layer noodles, tomato sauce, béchamel sauce and cheeses until all ingredients have been used, ending with cheese. Bake 30 minutes.

Variation: 2 cups (500 mL) chopped vegetables such as onions, green or red peppers, mushrooms, and/or zucchini which has been lightly dusted with flour, may be sautéed with one clove of minced garlic in 2 tablespoons (30 mL) of olive oil until wilted. Layer these vegetables alternately with above ingredients, still ending with a layer of cheese.

Zucchini Lasagna

PAULINE MENKES

2	large zucchini	454 g each
1 cup	chopped onion	250 mL
1 teaspoon	minced garlic	5 mL
3 tablespoons	olive oil	45 mL
2 cups	chunky spaghetti sauce	500 mL
1 pound	ricotta cheese	454 g
1/2 pound	grated mozzarella cheese, divided	225 g
2	eggs	2
1 teaspoon	parsley, chopped	5 mL
1 teaspoon	dried basil	5 mL
1/2 teaspoon	salt	2 mL
1/2 teaspoon	pepper	2 mL

Bring large pot of salted water to a boil. Cut zucchini lengthwise into 1/8" (0.3 cm) thick slices. Parboil in three batches for 5 – 6 minutes. Remove from pot and drain well on paper towels.

Sauté onion and garlic in oil over medium heat until soft but not brown, 5 – 6 minutes. Add spaghetti sauce. Bring to a boil and reduce heat. Simmer uncovered 10 minutes. Combine ricotta, half of mozzarella, eggs and parsley, basil, salt and pepper in a large bowl. Blend with wooden spoon. Preheat oven to 375°F (190°C). Butter a 9" x 13" (3.5 L) baking dish. Spoon thin layer of sauce on the bottom. Cover with slices of zucchini cut to fit. Spread 1/2 cup (125 mL) of sauce over zucchini. Top with half of ricotta-mozzarella mixture. Repeat a layer of zucchini, sauce and cheese mixture. Finish with layer of zucchini and remaining sauce. Sprinkle remaining mozzarella cheese on top. Bake 40 – 45 minutes until cheese is melted and golden brown. Let stand 10 minutes before serving. Garnish with basil. Serves 8 – 10.

Fettucini Lasagna

HONEY ROSENTHAL

1 pound	fettucini noodles	500 g
6 ounces	grated Swiss cheese	175 g
6 ounces	grated mozzarella cheese	175 g
1/2 cup	grated Parmesan cheese	125 mL
3 1/2 cups	tomato sauce	875 mL

Boil noodles in salted water al dente. Drain and rinse. Combine cheeses. Reserve 1 cup for topping.

Custard:

2	eggs	2
1 1/2 pounds	ricotta or cottage cheese	680 g
	salt and pepper to taste	

Mix together and set aside.

Preheat oven to 350°(180°C). Combine noodles, cheeses and tomato sauce. Place half in casserole. Spoon custard over noodles. Spread and cover top with remaining noodle mixture. Sprinkle with reserved cheese. Bake 30 – 35 minutes. Serves 6 – 8.

Eggplant Parmesan for Microwave

VERA SANDERS

1	large eggplant	1
2	peppers, red, yellow or green, seeded and thinly sliced	2
2 tablespoons	fresh snipped dill	30 mL
2 tablespoons	fresh chopped parsley	30 mL
1 · 14 ounce jar	meatless spaghetti or tomato sauce or your favourite recipe	375 mL
12 ounces	partly skimmed milk mozzarella cheese, thinly sliced or grated	340 g
3 tablespoons	grated Parmesan cheese	45 mL

Wash and thinly slice unpeeled eggplant. Salt lightly and let rest for 30 minutes to soften and remove bitter taste. Wipe dry with paper towels. Spray a 9" x 13" (3.5 L) baking dish with cooking spray and layer eggplant, peppers and herbs with sauce and cheeses, ending with a top layer of cheese. Cover with plastic wrap. Uncover one corner to vent. Microwave on High (100%) for 30 minutes. Let rest 10 minutes before serving. Serves 6 – 8.

Noodle Bake with Spinach Ricotta Sauce

8 ounces	broad noodles	250 g
Sauce:		
1 · 10 ounce package	frozen chopped spinach, thawed and well drained	284 g
2 cups	ricotta cheese	500 mL
2	eggs, lightly beaten	2
1/4 cup	grated Parmesan cheese	75 mL
2 tablespoons	finely chopped fresh basil	30 mL
2 tablespoons	finely chopped fresh parsley	30 mL
1 teaspoon	finely minced garlic	5 mL
1/4 teaspoon	grated nutmeg	1 mL
	salt and pepper to taste	
2 tablespoons	grated Parmesan cheese	30 mL

Cook pasta in a pot of boiling water until just tender. Drain. Preheat oven to 350°F (180°C). Combine the sauce ingredients in a large bowl and stir until smooth, or use processor and pulse until smooth. Toss the hot pasta with the sauce, coating the noodles well. Pour into a well greased 8" - 9" (22.5 – 25 cm) square baking dish. Top with the Parmesan cheese and bake for 25 – 30 minutes. Bow tie pasta can be substituted for broad noodles. Garnish with additional chopped parsley.

Linguini with Broccoli and Anchovies

YONA PATTENICK

1/3 cup	olive oil	75 mL
1/4 cup	butter	60 mL
2 – 3 teaspoons	minced garlic	10 – 15 mL
1/4 teaspoon	crushed chilies	1 mL
1 can	flat anchovies, not drained	48 g
1/2 pound	linguini	225 g
2 cups	broccoli florets, steamed	500 mL
2 tablespoons	chopped parsley	30 mL

In a small saucepan, sauté garlic and chilies in the oil and butter. Add the anchovies, and cook the mixture until the anchovies disintegrate, about 5 minutes. Remove the sauce from heat, and set aside. Cook the pasta al dente. Drain. Return pasta to pot and add the anchovy sauce. Gently stir in the broccoli florets. Sprinkle with parsley. Add freshly grated **Parmesan cheese**, if desired. Serves 4.

Meat Sauce for Pasta

1	large onion, finely chopped	1
3 tablespoons	olive oil	45 mL
1 pound	lean ground beef, chicken or veal	500 g
1 clove	garlic, finely chopped (or more to taste)	1
1 · 28 ounce can	plum tomatoes	796 mL
1 · 7 1/2 ounce can	tomato sauce	225 mL
	pinch of sugar	
	pinch of crushed red pepper flakes	
1/2 teaspoon	oregano	2 mL
1/2 teaspoon	basil	2 mL
1/2 teaspoon	thyme	2 mL
	salt and pepper to taste	

Sauté onion in olive oil in a large skillet until soft, but not brown. Add ground meat and garlic and sauté, stirring, about five minutes. Add rest of ingredients. Simmer, uncovered, for one hour, stirring frequently.

Simple Tomato Sauce

PAULINE TOKER

1 clove	garlic, finely chopped (or more to taste)	1
1/2	onion, grated	1/2
2 tablespoons	olive oil	30 mL
1 · 28 ounce can	Italian plum tomatoes, including juice or	796 mL
3 cups	fresh tomatoes, peeled, seeded and chopped (preferably plum)	750 mL
1/2 cup	chicken stock	125 mL
2 tablespoons	tomato paste (optional)	30 mL
1	bay leaf	1
	salt and pepper	
1/2 teaspoon	basil, dried	2 mL
1/2 teaspoon	oregano, dried	2 mL

Sauté garlic and grated onion in olive oil. Add tomatoes, chicken stock and herbs to taste. Simmer gently for 30 minutes. For thicker sauce, add tomato paste.

Pesto Sauce

1/4 cup	pine nuts	60 mL
2 cloves	garlic	2
1 cup	fresh basil	250 mL
1/2 cup	fresh parsley	125 mL
1/2 cup	olive oil	125 mL
1/3 cup	grated Parmesan cheese	75 mL
	salt and pepper to taste	

Spread pine nuts in single layer in a heavy unoiled skillet. Place on moderate heat and stir until browned. Combine pine nuts, garlic, basil and parsley in a food processor and chop. Continue processing while adding olive oil in a slow steady stream. Add cheese, salt and pepper and process briefly to combine. Serve over warm pasta.

1 pound	orzo (rice shaped pasta)	454 g
2 cups	chopped onion	500 mL
1/2 pound	mushrooms, sliced	225 g
1/2 cup	butter or margarine	125 mL
	salt and pepper	
	paprika	

Preheat oven to 350ºF (180ºC). Boil orzo in lightly salted water until tender, about 8 minutes. Drain, rinse, and set aside. Sauté onions and mushrooms in butter or margarine until soft, but not brown. Season to taste with salt, pepper and paprika. Add orzo and mix well. Place in covered casserole and bake 45 minutes.

Variation: Canned french fried onion rings may be added. Mix half with orzo. Sprinkle remaining half on top before baking. Bake another 10 minutes uncovered, so the onion rings will brown.

Garden Pasta Salad

2 pounds	plum tomatoes, sliced	1 kg
1/2 cup	olive oil	125 mL
1/4 cup	fresh basil, chopped	60 mL
3 tablespoons	white wine vinegar	45 mL
1/2 teaspoon	salt	3 mL
1 pound	penne or fusilli	454 g
1	small English cucumber, sliced	1
1/2 cup	red onion, chopped	125 mL
1/2 cup	red pepper, chopped	125 mL

Combine tomatoes, oil, basil, vinegar and salt in a large bowl. Boil pasta in a large pot of lightly salted boiling water until al dente. Drain well. Combine pasta with tomato mixture, sliced cucumber, onion and pepper. Blend thoroughly. Serve at room temperature. Serves 6.

Variation: Try using roasted red pepper (see page 126).

Tomato and Red Pepper Pasta

3	sweet red peppers	3
4	red potatoes, peeled, cooked and cut into chunks	4
4	large tomatoes, cut into chunks	4
1/4 cup	pitted black olives, halved	60 mL
1/4 cup	sun dried tomatoes, sliced	60 mL
1/4 cup	chopped fresh basil	60 mL
1/4 cup	chopped fresh parsley	60 mL
1 pound	penne noodles, cooked and drained	500 g
1	small head lettuce, shredded	1

Dressing:

1/2 cup	olive oil	125 mL
2 tablespoons	red wine vinegar	30 mL
1 clove	garlic, minced	1
1 teaspoon	anchovy paste	5 mL
1/2 teaspoon	salt	2 mL
1/4 teaspoon	hot red pepper flakes	1 mL
1/4 teaspoon	pepper	1 mL

Halve red peppers. Remove seeds and membranes. Place skin side up on baking sheet. Broil until blisters form and skin is black. Let cool, peel, and julienne. Whisk dressing ingredients together. Combine all ingredients except lettuce, and toss with dressing. Adjust seasonings to taste. Serve on a bed of lettuce.

Pasta Niçoise

See Salad Niçoise on page 69. Omit lettuce, and replace with 4 cups (1 L) of cooked pasta such as fusilli, penne, shells, etc. Toss well. Pasta may require extra dressing. Serves 6.

Pasta Salad with Lime Ginger Mayonnaise

MYRTLE COOPERSMITH

1/2 pound	pasta shells	250 g
2 tablespoons	vegetable oil	30 mL
4	carrots, thinly sliced diagonally	4
1/2 pound	snow peas, trimmed and cut diagonally	250 g
1	avocado	1
1 pint	cherry tomatoes	500 mL

Dressing:

1	egg, at room temperature	1
1 teaspoon	dry mustard powder	5 mL
	pinch of salt	
3 – 4 tablespoons	fresh lemon juice	45 – 60 mL
	pinch of cayenne pepper	
1/4 teaspoon	freshly ground pepper	1 mL
1/2 cup	olive oil	125 mL
3/4 cup	vegetable oil	175 mL
1/2 teaspoon	curry (optional)	2 mL
1 clove	garlic, minced	1
1 tablespoon	finely chopped ginger root	15 mL
3 tablespoons	fresh lime juice	45 mL
	grated zest of 1 lime	

Garnish:

lemon slices
chopped green onions

Boil pasta in a large pot of lightly salted boiling water until tender. Drain and rinse with cold water. Shake dry and toss with vegetable oil. Set aside.

Cook carrots until barely tender, 2 – 3 minutes. Refresh under cold water and pat dry. Cook snow peas in boiling water for 1 minute. Refresh and pat dry. Combine pasta with carrots, snow peas and tomatoes. Set aside.

In a food processor with steel blade, or blender, combine egg, salt, mustard, lemon juice, cayenne, pepper and 1/4 cup (60 mL) olive oil with quick on/off turns. With machine running, very slowly drip in remaining olive oil, and then vegetable oil. Add remaining ingredients.

Gently combine dressing with salad. Dice avocado into salad and toss. Refrigerate until ready to serve. May be made a day ahead. Serve on a lettuce lined platter and garnish with lemon slices and chopped onions.

Variation: 2 cans of salmon or tuna may be added if desired.

Pasta Salad

MYRTLE COOPERSMITH

1/2 pound	pasta	250 g
2 tablespoons	olive oil	30 mL
1 · 6.5 ounce can	tuna	184 g
1	fennel bulb	1
1/2 cup	pimento stuffed olives	125 mL
1	tomato, seeded and chopped	1
1/4 cup	diced, sun dried tomatoes	60 mL
1 tablespoon	capers	15 mL
3 tablespoons	chopped fresh parsley	45 mL
3 tablespoons	chopped fresh basil	45 mL

Cook pasta al dente. Drain and rinse. Toss with olive oil. Remove spears from fennel bulb. Wash spears, trim, and cut into 1" (2.5 cm) lengths. Combine with tuna, olives, tomato, sun dried tomatoes, capers, parsley and basil. Toss with pasta.

Dressing:

1/2 cup	olive oil	125 mL
3 tablespoons	red wine vinegar	45 mL
2 cloves	garlic, minced	2
1/2 teaspoon	anchovy paste	2 mL
1/4 teaspoon	oregano	1 mL
	salt and pepper to taste	

Blend well. Pour over pasta mixture and gently toss.

Summer Pasta Salad

MYRTLE COOPERSMITH

1/2 cup	olive oil	125 mL
1/2 teaspoon	hot red pepper flakes	2 mL
5	tomatoes, diced	5
1/3 cup	fresh chopped basil or	75 mL
1 teaspoon	dried basil	5 mL
1/4 cup	fresh chopped chives or	60 mL
3	green onions, sliced	3
1 pound	penne pasta, cooked	454 g

Place olive oil in a large bowl. Stir in all other ingredients except pasta. Combine well, add **salt** and **pepper** to taste and let sit at least 30 minutes. Add hot pasta to sauce, toss to mix well. Serves 6 - 8.

Pasta Primavera Salad

MARILYN BROWN

1 pound	linguini	454 g
8 ounces	Italian dressing	225 mL
1 bunch	broccoli, cut into florets, blanched	1
1 bunch	cauliflower, cut into florets, blanched	1
3 – 4	scallions, green part only, cut diagonally	3 – 4
2 cups	snow peas, trimmed and cut diagonally	500 mL
1 pint	cherry tomatoes	500 mL
2	red peppers, diced	2
2	green peppers, diced	2
6 – 8	mushrooms, sliced	6 – 8
1 · 14 ounce can	chick peas, drained and rinsed	398 mL

Cook linguini al dente. Drain. Do not rinse. Marinate in Italian salad dressing overnight. On day of serving, add rest of ingredients. Add more Italian dressing if necessary, and salt and pepper to taste. Serve at room temperature. Serves 10 – 12.

Vegetables

Hints for Vegetables

When purchasing vegetables, buy the freshest ones you can. Avoid vegetables that are damp or wilted, or green vegetables that are turning yellow.

Store most vegetables in plastic bags in the refrigerator. Potatoes, onions, winter squash (e.g. acorn, butternut), eggplant and rutabaga are best stored out of the refrigerator but in a cool place. Vegetables may be cooked by boiling, using as little water as possible, and just long enough to be crisp-tender.

Potatoes and other root vegetables require more water and longer cooking time. Vegetables to be mashed should be cooked until soft and tender.

Methods of Cooking Vegetables

Steaming: Use a small folding steamer placed in a saucepan with about 1/2 inch (1 1/4 cm) boiling water. Cover pan and cook until vegetables are tender. Remove steamer from saucepan. Drain and add seasonings as desired.

Butter steaming: Melt a small amount of butter or margarine in a frying pan. Add vegetables in a single layer with 2-4 tablespoons water (30-60 mL). Cover pan tightly and cook quickly over high heat, until vegetables are crisp-tender. Stir often, and add a little more water if necessary to prevent sticking.

Stir frying: Cut vegetables into small pieces - either julienne or slices or squares. Add to hot oil in frying pan or wok and stir over high heat until just tender.

Baking: Whole vegetables such as potatoes or winter squash can be pricked with a fork and baked for 45 minutes to an hour until tender. Vegetables in casseroles can be baked according to individual recipes.

Microwave: Different vegetables require different cooking times. Follow instructions in microwave manual.

Asparagus with Fresh Tomato Sauce

ADÈLE FREEMAN

3 pounds	asparagus	1.5 kg
1/4 cup	mayonnaise	60 mL
1 1/4 teaspoons	lemon juice	6 mL
1/4 teaspoon	salt	1 mL
	dash of white pepper	
1/3 cup	diced, peeled fresh tomatoes	75 mL

Cook asparagus in a small amount of water until just tender. Meanwhile combine next 4 ingredients in top of a double boiler. Stir over hot but not boiling water, until heated through. Stir in tomato and serve over hot, freshly cooked asparagus. Serves 6.

Broccoli Vinaigrette

ADÈLE FREEMAN

1 bunch	fresh broccoli	700 g
	(about 1 1/2 pounds)	
1 tablespoon	finely chopped onion	15 mL
1 tablespoon	prepared mustard	15 mL
	(imported preferably)	
	freshly ground pepper	
1 tablespoon	red wine vinegar	15 mL
6 tablespoons	oil	90 mL

Wash broccoli well and drain. Trim off large coarse leaves and tough lower parts of stalk. Cook in small amount of boiling salted water until just tender. Meanwhile, combine remaining ingredients in a small saucepan and heat over very low heat, stirring with a whisk, until sauce is lukewarm. Do not boil, and do not heat too far in advance. Arrange warm broccoli on a platter and spoon sauce over. Serve warm.

Note: One pound (500 g) of fresh green beans may be used instead of broccoli.

Harvard Beets

A D È L E   F R E E M A N

2 1/2 cups	cooked or canned small beets	625 mL
1/4 cup	granulated sugar	60 mL
2 teaspoons	cornstarch (for Passover, use potato starch)	10 mL
1/4 cup	vinegar	60 mL
1 tablespoon	butter or margarine	15 mL

Drain beets, saving 1/4 cup (60 mL) liquid. Combine sugar and cornstarch and stir in vinegar and reserved beet liquid. Cook, stirring over low heat until mixture is thickened and smooth. Add the beets and butter and heat through. Serves 4 – 6.

Cauliflower Pudding

C H A R L O T T E   K A M I N S K Y

1 head	cauliflower, cooked, drained and mashed well	1
1	large onion, chopped	1
2 stalks	celery, chopped	2
1 · 10 ounce can	drained mushrooms	280 g
2 tablespoons	oil	30 mL
2	eggs, separated	2
1 cup plus 1 tablespoon	bread crumbs or matzo meal	265 mL
	salt and pepper to taste	

Preheat oven to 325ºF (160ºC). Grease an 8" (2 L) square ovenproof baking dish. Sauté onion, celery and mushrooms in oil. Beat 2 egg whites until frothy. Add slightly beaten yolks to whites, then add to cauliflower. Add bread crumbs or matzo meal. Add sautéed mixture, salt and pepper. Place mixture into prepared pan. Bake for 30 minutes or until done. Cut into squares.

Sweet and Sour Red Cabbage

BERNICE ZWI

1	medium size red cabbage	1
1	medium size onion	1
10	cloves (more or less to taste)	10
2 tablespoons	oil or chicken fat	30 mL
3 – 4 tablespoons	malt vinegar	45 – 60 mL
4 – 5 tablespoons	granulated sugar	60 – 75 mL
3	medium size sour apples	3
	salt and pepper to taste	
1 tablespoon	raisins	15 mL
1 tablespoon	all purpose flour (optional)	15 mL

Remove outer leaves of red cabbage and discard. Shred cabbage. Peel onion and insert cloves. Heat oil or chicken fat in a large pan and add shredded cabbage. Cook for about 5 minutes. Add vinegar, whole onion, sugar and peeled, cored and sliced apples. Season to taste. Simmer for 1 1/2 – 2 hours, being careful not to burn the cabbage. Remove onion. If desired, flour made into a paste with a little water may be stirred into mixture. Taste and adjust seasonings. Add raisins. This dish becomes even tastier when heated a second time. Serves 6 – 8.

Brandied Carrots

MYRTLE COOPERSMITH

24	small, peeled carrots	24
2 tablespoons	Triple Sec	30 mL
1/4 cup	brandy	60 mL
1/4 cup	honey	60 mL
	juice of 1 lemon	

Preheat oven to 350°F (180°C). Cook carrots in salted water until just tender, about 15 minutes. Drain and place in a buttered casserole. Combine remaining ingredients. Pour over carrots. Bake for 15 minutes. Garnish with chopped parsley. Serves 4.

Glazed Carrots with Walnuts

MYRTLE COOPERSMITH

2 pounds	carrots, peeled and cut into strips	1 kg
1/2 cup	water	125 mL
2 tablespoons	butter or margarine	30 mL
1 teaspoon	salt	5 mL
1/4 teaspoon	cinnamon	1 mL
2 tablespoons	honey	30 mL
2 teaspoons	lemon juice	10 mL
1/2 cup	chopped toasted walnuts	125 mL

Place carrots, water, butter or margarine and salt in large frying pan. Cover tightly and cook gently until crisp-tender. If necessary, add just a little water as it cooks to keep from sticking. Gently stir in cinnamon, honey and lemon juice. Simmer a few minutes, add nuts and simmer a minute or two longer. Serves 6 – 8.

Carrot Pudding #1

1 cup	vegetable shortening	250 mL
1/2 cup	brown sugar	125 mL
1	egg	1
1 1/4 cups	all purpose flour	300 mL
1 teaspoon	salt	5 mL
1 teaspoon	baking powder	5 mL
1/2 teaspoon	baking soda	2 mL
1 1/4 cups	grated carrots	300 mL
	rind and juice of 1/2 lemon	

Preheat oven to 375°F (190°C). Grease a 9" (22 cm) ring mold. Cream shortening and brown sugar. Add egg and continue creaming. Sift flour, salt, baking powder and baking soda. Add dry ingredients to creamed mixture. Fold in carrots, which have been mixed with rind and juice of 1/2 lemon. Bake in greased ring mold for 30 – 45 minutes. To freeze, put batter in greased ring mold and wrap well. Defrost before baking.

Carrot Pudding #2

LOIS BUCKSTEIN

5	medium carrots, finely grated	5
1/2 cup	brown sugar	125 mL
1	egg	1
2 tablespoons	orange juice or water	30 mL
1 tablespoon	lemon rind	15 mL
1 tablespoon	lemon juice	15 mL
1/2 cup	oil	125 mL
1 1/4 cups	all purpose flour	300 mL
1 teaspoon	baking powder	5 mL
3/4 teaspoon	baking soda	4 mL
1/2 teaspoon	salt	2 mL

Preheat oven to 350°F (180°C). Grate carrots into a bowl. Add sugar, egg and all wet ingredients. Combine flour, baking powder, baking soda and salt. Add carrot mixture to flour mixture, blending well. Pour into small greased mold. Bake 45 minutes. Recipe doubles easily, and is delicious served with meat. Can be frozen after baking. Defrost before reheating. Double recipe to serve 10 – 12.

Carrot Soufflé

EDIE WINBERG

3 pounds	carrots	1.5 kg
1/2 cup	margarine, melted	125 mL
1 1/2 cups	graham cracker crumbs	375 mL
	pinch of ginger	
3	eggs, separated	3
1/4 – 1/3 cup	brown sugar	60 – 75 mL

Preheat oven to 375°F (190°C). Cook carrots until tender. Purée. Combine margarine, 1 cup (250 mL) of the crumbs and the ginger. Beat in egg yolks. Add to the carrots and cool. Beat egg whites until stiff and fold into the carrot mixture. Pour into greased 6 cup (1.5 L) soufflé dish or casserole. Combine sugar and remaining crumbs. Spoon over soufflé. Bake for 45 minutes. Serves 12.

Sweet and Sour Carrots

VERA SANDERS

1 pound	carrots, peeled and diagonally sliced	500 g
1	green pepper, seeded and cut into 1" (2 1/2 cm) cubes	1
1 · 8 ounce can	pineapple chunks in their own juice	250 g
1/3 cup	granulated sugar	75 mL
1 tablespoon	cornstarch	15 mL
1/2 teaspoon	salt	2 mL
2 tablespoons	vinegar	30 mL
2 teaspoons	soy sauce	10 mL

In a saucepan, cook carrots in a small amount of lightly salted water, about 10 minutes. Add green pepper and cook three minutes more. Drain. Drain pineapple, reserving juice. Add water to juice to make 1/3 cup (75 mL) of liquid. In saucepan, combine sugar, cornstarch and salt. Stir in pineapple liquid, vinegar and soy sauce. Cook and stir until clear and bubbly. Stir in vegetables and pineapple. Heat thoroughly. Serves 6.

Carrot or Zucchini Latkes

6	medium carrots, grated	6
	or	
3	medium zucchini, grated and squeezed very dry	3
1	onion, chopped fine	1
3	eggs, lightly beaten	3
	salt and pepper to taste	
1/2 cup	all purpose flour	125 mL
1/2 teaspoon	baking powder	2 mL
	oil for frying	

Combine all ingredients except oil. Heat oil in a large skillet. Drop mixture from a large spoon into hot oil. Flatten and brown on both sides on medium heat. Drain on paper towelling. Yield: about 16 pancakes. Freezes well. To reheat, place on lined cookie sheet and place in 400°F (200°C) oven until crisp and heated through.

Eggplant and Zucchini Casserole

LIBBY HOFFMAN

2	Spanish onions, diced	2
2	green peppers, cut into chunks	2
	oil for frying	
2	medium eggplants, peeled and cut into cubes	2
8	small zucchini, cut into cubes	8
1 · 28 ounce can	plum tomatoes	796 mL
	salt and pepper	
1/4 cup	brown sugar (or more to taste)	60 mL

Fry onions and green peppers in a generous amount of oil until transparent, but not brown. Add eggplant and zucchini, and cook until transparent. Add tomatoes, and salt and pepper to taste. Add brown sugar. Cook until vegetables are tender and liquid has disappeared, about 40 minutes. Place in oiled 9" x 13" (3.5 L) casserole.

Topping:

1 cup	bread crumbs	250 mL
1/2 cup	margarine, melted	125 mL
2 cloves	garlic, crushed	2
	ground almonds and/or Parmesan cheese (optional)	

Preheat oven to 350°F (180°C). Combine topping ingredients and place over vegetables. Bake until bubbly, about 30 minutes.

Grandmother's Corn Fritters

E D I E   W I N B E R G

1	egg	1
1/2 cup	milk	125 mL
2 cups	canned corn, cream style	500 mL
1 1/2 cups	all purpose flour	375 mL
2 teaspoons	baking powder	10 mL
1/2 teaspoon	salt	2 mL
	dash of pepper	
2 teaspoons	oil	10 mL
1 tablespoon	parsley, chopped	15 mL

Beat egg. Add remaining ingredients and beat well. Drop by spoonfuls into hot oil until golden in colour. Drain on paper towelling. Can be frozen, uncovered, on a cookie sheet and then stored in plastic bags in freezer. Reheat on cookie sheet at 375°F (190°C) while still frozen.

Variation: For an appetizer, make into 32 bite-size fritters.

Grilled Eggplant

2 tablespoons	salt	30 mL
2 cloves	garlic, crushed	2
1/2 teaspoon	oregano leaves, finely minced	2 mL
2 cups	cold water	500 mL
1 large or 2 small	eggplant(s)	1 – 2

Place salt, crushed garlic and oregano in a 9" x 13" (3.5 L) shallow dish. Add about 1 cup (250 mL) water and stir until salt is dissolved. Cut eggplant into slices 3/4" (2 cm) thick. Peel, if you wish. Arrange slices in a single layer in prepared dish and add enough cold water to cover. Weight them down with a plate and refrigerate overnight.

To Barbecue: Rinse eggplant slices under cold water. Dry well. Coat both sides with vegetable oil. Grill about 5" (12.5 cm) from hot coals. Turn frequently, brushing with oil before turning. Takes 5 minutes on each side. Serves 4.

Meatless Moussaka

ROZ HALBERT

1	medium eggplant	1
1/2 cup	zucchini, thinly sliced	125 mL
	salt	
	vegetable oil	
1	small clove garlic, crushed	1
1	onion, chopped	1
	all purpose flour	
1	large tomato, sliced	1
1/2 pound	mozzarella cheese, grated	225 g
	chopped fresh parsley	
2 teaspoons	parve chicken or beef powder	10 mL
	dissolved in	
3 ounces	water	75 mL
2 tablespoons	tomato paste	30 mL

Preheat oven to 375°F (190°C). Peel and slice eggplant and zucchini. Place on towel and sprinkle with salt. Let stand for 30 minutes. Pat dry. Fry or broil the eggplant to brown both sides. Drain on paper towelling. Fry garlic and onions for a few minutes.

In a large casserole, place in layers: half of the eggplant sprinkled with a little flour; tomato and zucchini; garlic-onion mixture; half the mozzarella; other half of the eggplant; other half of the mozzarella; chopped parsley. Mix tomato paste and consommé and pour over casserole. Bake for 35 minutes.

Topping:

1	egg, beaten	1
1 1/2 tablespoons	whole wheat flour	20 mL
5 ounces	plain yogurt	150 mL
	or sour cream	

Spread onto baked casserole and bake 10 – 15 minutes longer.

Note: Flavour is improved if made the day before. Cover with foil, unbaked, and without topping. Next day, bake as above. Good served with brown rice and salad.

Tri-Coloured Roasted Peppers

PAULINE TOKER

Any combination of peppers - red, yellow, green.

Preheat oven to 450°F (230°C). Brush whole peppers with a little olive oil. Bake on a foil lined pan, turning frequently, until charred, about 40 minutes. Remove from oven. Place in a plastic bag and allow to steam. Peel peppers when they are just warm, starting at stem end. Discard stem, skin, seeds and ribs. Cut peppers into strips.

To serve, arrange on a serving dish and drizzle with oil and wine vinegar. Season lightly with salt and pepper, and sprinkle with capers if desired.

Italian Potato Soufflé

BARBARA DONSKY

3 tablespoons	Parmesan cheese	45 mL
9	boiled mashed potatoes	9
3	eggs, beaten	3
1/2 pound	mozzarella cheese	225 g

Preheat oven to 375°F (190°C). Combine Parmesan cheese, potatoes and eggs. Alternate layers of potato mixture and sliced mozzarella cheese in a greased casserole. Top with **buttered bread crumbs** and **parsley**. Bake for 45 minutes. May be frozen prior to baking.

Oven Fried Potatoes

HARRIET DENNIS

4 – 5	medium potatoes, peeled if desired	4 – 5
	ice water	
1/4 cup	oil	60 mL
1/4 cup	butter or margarine	60 mL
	grated cheese (optional)	
	salt and pepper	

Preheat oven to 400ºF (200ºC). Slice potatoes thinly into discs. Soak in ice water for at least 1 hour. Drain and pat dry. Line a large cookie sheet (with sides) with foil and grease with oil or non-stick spray. Arrange potatoes overlapping in rows. Melt oil and butter or margarine together. Sprinkle over potatoes. Sprinkle with grated cheese (optional). Bake for 45 minutes. Sprinkle with salt and pepper before serving. To reduce fat, just drizzle a small amount of oil and/or butter over potatoes before baking.

Potato Skins
VERA SANDERS

4 – 5	baking potatoes	4 – 5
2 teaspoons	vegetable oil	10 mL
1 clove	garlic, crushed	1

Preheat oven to 450ºF (230ºC). Scrub potatoes well. Peel skin in wide strips, lengthwise, removing a thin layer of flesh. Combine oil and crushed garlic. Coat potato skins well with oil/garlic mixture. Arrange strips, skin side up on foil lined baking sheet. Bake about 20 minutes or until crisp. Salt if desired. Serve immediately or reheat at 450ºF (230ºC) for 3 – 5 minutes. Do not freeze.

Potatoes Au Gratin
MRS. J. SCHIPPER

2 tablespoons	butter	30 mL
4 1/2 cups	diced cooked potatoes	1.125 L
4 tablespoons	grated cheese	60 mL
1/2 cup	dry bread crumbs	125 mL
1	egg	1
1/4 teaspoon	paprika	1 mL
	salt and pepper to taste	

Preheat oven to 400ºF (200ºC). Melt shortening in a shallow baking dish. Toss cheese, crumbs, egg and seasonings with potatoes. Bake 10 – 20 minutes. Serves 4.

Potato Latkes

NANCY POSLUNS

4	medium potatoes	4
2 tablespoons	grated onion	30 mL
2	eggs, well beaten	2
2 tablespoons	matzo meal	30 mL
1 teaspoon	baking powder	5 mL
	salt and fresh pepper to taste	

Grate potatoes into ice water. Drain well, and squeeze out excess moisture. Combine potatoes, onion, eggs, matzo meal, baking powder, salt and pepper. Drop by spoonfuls onto very hot, well greased frying pan. Cook over medium heat, until golden, about 5 minutes on each side. Serve with **apple sauce** and/or **sour cream**. Serves 4.

Potato Pudding

LOIS FRIEDMAN

4	medium potatoes, peeled	4
1	medium onion	1
3	eggs	3
1 tablespoon	all purpose flour	15 mL
	oil	

Preheat oven to 425°F (220°C). Put oil in 9" x 13" (3.5 L) baking pan, to cover bottom (about 4 tablespoons – 60 mL). Let oil heat in pan in oven while mixing rest of ingredients. Grate potatoes and onion. Drain excess liquid. Add beaten eggs. Blend in flour and **salt** and **pepper** to taste. Make sure oil is very hot. Pour batter into pan. Oil will sizzle up around potato mixture. Bake for 1/2 hour. Reduce heat to 400°F (200°C) and bake an additional 1/2 hour. Cut into squares while hot. Warm in moderate oven 350°F (180°C) for 15 minutes before serving. This makes a flat, crispy pudding.

Ratatouille

1/4 cup	oil	60 mL
2	large garlic cloves, crushed	2
2	large onions, sliced	2
3 tablespoons	all purpose flour	45 mL
2	medium zucchini, sliced	2
1	medium eggplant, cubed	1
1	green pepper, seeded and cut into chunks	1
1	red pepper, seeded and cut into chunks	1
1	bay leaf	1
4	large ripe tomatoes, cut up or	4
1 · 28 ounce can	tomatoes	796 mL
1 teaspoon	salt	5 mL
1/4 teaspoon	pepper	2 mL
	capers (optional)	
	chopped parsley	

Heat oil in a large frying pan or Dutch oven. Add garlic and onions and sauté until soft and transparent. Sprinkle flour over all vegetables except tomatoes, and add to frying pan. Cover and cook on low heat 45 – 60 minutes, stirring occasionally. Add tomatoes and simmer, uncovered, until mixture is thick. Season with salt and pepper to taste. Add capers, if desired for last 15 minutes of cooking. Remove bay leaf. Garnish with parsley. Serve hot or cold. Serves 6 – 8.

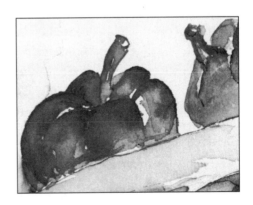

Sweet Potato Pie
SANDRA HABERMAN, ST. LAURENT

Filling:

4 – 6	medium sweet potatoes, boiled, peeled and mashed	4 – 6
1 cup	crushed pineapple	250 mL
1/8 teaspoon	nutmeg	0.5 mL
1/2 teaspoon	salt	2 mL
2 – 4 tablespoons	brown sugar	30 – 60 mL
1/4 cup	margarine	60 mL

Mix all ingredients and spoon into a greased pie plate or casserole.

Topping:

1/3 cup	brown sugar	75 mL
1/4 cup	margarine	60 mL
2 cups	crushed cornflakes	500 mL

Preheat oven to 350°F (180°C). Mix all ingredients and spread over filling. Bake for 40 minutes. May be made ahead and refrigerated until baking time.

Candied Sweet Potatoes
JUDY ASCH

2/3 cup	brown sugar, packed	150 mL
1/4 cup	orange juice	60 mL
1/3 cup	butter or margarine	75 mL
1/4 teaspoon	salt	1 mL
1 tablespoon	grated orange rind (optional)	15 mL
2 · 19 ounce cans	sweet potatoes or	540 mL each
5 – 6	medium size fresh sweet potatoes	5 - 6

If using fresh sweet potatoes, peel, cut into thick slices, cover with water and boil until tender. Preheat oven to 375°F (190°C). Combine all ingredients except potatoes in a small saucepan. Bring to a boil, stirring until sugar is dissolved. Remove from heat. Arrange potatoes in a shallow baking pan. Pour sauce over. Bake 20 minutes until bubbling. Can be made a few days ahead. Serves 6.

Vegetable Stir Fry

VERA SANDERS

Any vegetables may be used in this dish. Some to keep in mind are celery, shredded cabbage, peppers, mushrooms, snow peas, broccoli, cauliflower and carrots. Consider the following as a colourful combination.

2 tablespoons	vegetable oil	30 mL
2 cups	broccoli florets, blanched	500 mL
2 cups	cauliflower florets, blanched	500 mL
3	medium carrots, peeled, cut into julienne and blanched	3
1/2 cup	chicken stock	125 mL
2	red peppers, halved, seeded and sliced	2
2	yellow peppers, halved, seeded and sliced	2
1 cup	snow peas, trimmed	250 mL
3	green onions, sliced	3
2 tablespoons	fresh ginger root, grated	30 mL
1 clove	garlic, minced	1
2 tablespoons	soy sauce	30 mL
1/4 cup	cornstarch dissolved in	60 mL
1/2 cup	cold water	125 mL
1/4 cup	sesame seeds for garnish	60 mL

Before beginning to stir fry, wash, cut and blanch all vegetables where indicated. In a wok or large frying pan, heat oil. Add broccoli, cauliflower and carrots. Stir fry on medium heat for about 3 minutes. Add chicken stock, cover and steam for 2 – 3 minutes. Uncover. Add peppers, snow peas and onions. Stir fry for 1 minute. Add ginger root, garlic and soy sauce and cook 1 minute longer, stirring. Add cornstarch, stir and cook until thickened. Sprinkle with sesame seeds. Serve immediately.

Note: For a different taste and texture add 1 cup (250 mL) cooked thin noodles such as vermicelli and mix with vegetables.

Spinach Fritters

2 tablespoons	butter or margarine	30 mL
1/4 cup	minced onions	60 mL
1 clove	garlic, minced	1
4	eggs	4
1 teaspoon	salt	5 mL
	pinch of pepper	
	pinch of thyme	
1/4 cup	grated Parmesan cheese	60 mL
1 cup	chopped cooked spinach	250 mL
1/2 cup	dry bread crumbs	125 mL
4 tablespoons	vegetable oil	60 mL

Melt butter in a large skillet. Sauté the onion and garlic until soft and yellow. Discard the garlic. Beat together the eggs, salt, pepper and thyme. Mix in cheese, spinach, bread crumbs, onion and a scant tablespoon of oil. Taste for seasoning. Wipe skillet clean of any onions. Heat the remaining oil in the skillet. Drop the mixture into it by heaping tablespoons. Cook over low heat until browned on both sides.

Souffléd Acorn Squash

ELEANOR STEINBERG

3 · 3/4 – 1 pound	small acorn squash	500 g each
3 tablespoons	melted unsalted margarine	45 mL
2 1/2 tablespoons	brown sugar	40 mL
1/2 teaspoon	cinnamon	2 mL
1	egg, separated	1
	salt and pepper	

Preheat oven to 400°F (200°C). Halve the squash with a knife. Cut a thin slice from the bottom of each half, so it will stand. Scoop out seeds and fibre and discard. Place squash, cut side down, in a baking pan. Add 1/2" (1.25 cm) water. Cover pan with foil, and bake 30 – 45 minutes or until flesh is tender. Pour off water and turn squash over. Cool. Scoop cooked flesh carefully into a bowl, leaving approximately 1/8" (.65 cm) layer all around cavity. Do not pierce the shells. Purée pulp with margarine, brown sugar, cinnamon and egg yolk. Transfer to a bowl.

In a clean bowl, beat egg white until stiff. Fold into purée. Season with salt and pepper. Divide purée evenly among squash shells and bake on a lightly greased cookie sheet for 25 minutes or until tops are lightly golden. Serves 6 – 8.

Squash-Apple Casserole

GOLDIE DAVIS, SAINT JOHN

2 pounds	squash (acorn or butternut)	1 kg
1/4 cup	margarine	60 mL
1 tablespoon	brown sugar	15 mL
1/2 teaspoon	salt	2 mL
1/2 teaspoon	pepper	2 mL
1/4 cup	granulated sugar	60 mL
2 tablespoons	margarine	30 mL
7 – 8	tart apples, peeled and sliced	7 – 8
1 tablespoon	sugar	15 mL
2 cups	cornflakes, crushed	500 mL
1/2 cup	pecans, chopped	125 mL
2 tablespoons	margarine, melted	30 mL
1/4 cup	brown sugar	60 mL

Cut squash in half. Discard seeds. Bake squash in oven at 350°F (180 °C) cut side down on a greased pan until tender - about 1 hour.

Or

Microwave: Prick squash with fork on all sides. Place in microwave on high power for 8 – 10 minutes, or until tender. Remove, cut in half. Discard seeds.

Scoop out pulp. Add next 5 ingredients to pulp, mix well and set aside. Heat 2 tablespoons (30 mL) margarine in a frying pan. Add sliced apples. Sprinkle with 1 tablespoon (15 mL) sugar and simmer until barely tender. Spread apples on bottom of greased casserole. Add squash mixture. Combine crushed cornflakes, pecans, melted margarine and brown sugar. Sprinkle over squash. Bake at 350°F (180°C) for 20 minutes.

Zucchini Niçoise

ADÈLE FREEMAN

2 tablespoons	oil	30 mL
1	medium onion sliced	1
1/2 pound	fresh mushrooms, sliced	225 g
1 cup	chopped tomatoes, canned or fresh	250 mL
	freshly ground pepper to taste	
1/2 teaspoon	salt	2 mL
1/2	bay leaf	1/2
3	medium zucchini cut into 1" (2.5 cm) pieces	3

Heat oil. Add onions and mushrooms and sauté until onions are transparent. Add tomatoes and spices and simmer 5 minutes. Add the zucchini to the sauce, cover and simmer until tender, about 10 minutes.

Note: Tomato sauce can be made in the evening. Add zucchini 10 minutes before serving. Serves 4 – 6.

Stuffed Zucchini

ADÈLE FREEMAN

6	medium zucchini	6
1	medium onion, finely chopped	1
1 clove	garlic, finely minced	1
2 tablespoons	butter or margarine	30 mL
1/2 cup	bread crumbs	125 mL
1/4 cup	parsley, finely minced	60 mL

Heat oven to 350ºF (180ºC). Place the zucchini in a saucepan. Cover with water and boil for five minutes. Remove zucchini immediately and plunge into cold water to stop cooking. Split in half lengthwise. Invert on paper towelling to drain. Sauté onion and garlic in butter or margarine until tender but not brown. Scoop out part of the pulp of the zucchini, leaving enough of a shell to hold stuffing. Mash pulp lightly. Add sautéed onion and garlic, bread crumbs, parsley, a pinch of oregano and **salt** and **pepper** to taste. Mix well. Fill zucchini with stuffing. Drizzle additional **melted butter** or **margarine** over top. Bake in greased open baking dish 30 minutes or until tender.

Sauces

What You Should Know About Making Hollandaise Sauce

1. Hollandaise sauce is made of warmed egg yolks flavoured with lemon juice, into which butter is gradually incorporated to make a thick, yellow, creamy sauce.

2. Egg yolks must be heated slowly and gradually so that they will thicken into a smooth cream. You may beat them over hot water or over low heat, as long as the process is slow and gentle.

3. A small quantity of butter should be added at a time. When too much is added at one time, the sauce will not thicken.

4. A teaspoon of cornstarch beaten into the egg yolks at the beginning, will help to hold a sauce that is to be kept warm for a long period of time.

5. If the sauce does not thicken, rinse out a bowl with hot water. Put in a teaspoon of lemon juice and a tablespoon of the sauce. Beat with a wire whisk until the sauce creams and thickens. Then beat in the rest of the sauce, a little at a time, beating until each addition has thickened in the sauce before adding the next.

6. If sauce starts to separate, a tablespoon of cold water or butter beaten into it will often bring it back.

7. If leftover sauce is to be used again, beat 2 tablespoons (30 mL) of it in a saucepan over very low heat or hot water. Gradually beat in the rest of the sauce by spoonfuls.

8. Keep sauce warm in a pan of lukewarm water.

Hollandaise Sauce

3	egg yolks	3
1 tablespoon	cold water	15 mL
1/2 cup	soft butter, unsalted	125 mL
1/4 teaspoon	salt	1 mL
1 teaspoon	lemon juice	5 mL

Combine the egg yolks and water in the top of a double boiler and beat with a wire whisk over simmering water. Add a few spoonfuls of butter to the mixture and beat continuously until the butter has melted and the sauce starts to thicken. Never let the water in the double boiler come to a boil. Continue adding the butter bit by bit, stirring constantly. Blend in the salt and the lemon juice.

Quick Blender Hollandaise Sauce

3	egg yolks	3
2 tablespoons	lemon juice	30 mL
1/4 teaspoon	salt	1 mL
1/4 teaspoon	pepper	1 mL
1/2 cup	unsalted butter	125 mL

Place the egg yolks, lemon juice and seasonings in the blender jar. Cut the butter into pieces and heat to foaming hot in a small saucepan. Blend the egg yolk mixture at top speed for two seconds. Still blending at top speed, start pouring the hot butter in a thin stream of droplets. Try and cover the blender with a towel just leaving a corner through which to dribble in the butter. By the time most of the butter has gone in, the sauce will be a thick cream.

Hollandaise with Beaten Egg Whites

3	stiffly beaten egg whites	3
1 1/2 cups	hollandaise sauce	375 mL

Just before serving, fold the egg whites into the hollandaise. Delicious with fish, soufflés and/or egg dishes.

Microwave Béchamel Sauce   VERA SANDERS

1 tablespoon	butter	15 mL
2 tablespoons	all purpose flour	30 mL
1/2 teaspoon	salt	2 mL
1 cup	milk	250 mL

In a 1 quart (1 L) glass casserole place butter, flour and salt. Microwave at High (100%) 2 minutes, stirring after 1 minute. Gradually stir in milk. Microwave at High (100%) 3 1/2 – 4 1/2 minutes, stirring every minute until thick.

For thicker sauce, use 3 tablespoons (45 mL) flour instead of 2 tablespoons (30 mL).

For cheese sauce variation add 2 cups (500 mL) shredded sharp cheese to white sauce. Stir to melt cheese after microwaving.

Béarnaise Sauce

1 teaspoon	chopped shallots	5 mL
1 teaspoon	dried tarragon	5 mL
1/2 teaspoon	ground black pepper	2 mL
1/2 teaspoon	salt	2 mL
1/4 cup	tarragon vinegar	60 mL
5	egg yolks	5
3/4 cup	melted butter	175 mL

Simmer the shallots, tarragon, pepper and salt in the vinegar over low heat until the vinegar has been reduced by two-thirds. Cool to lukewarm. Add the egg yolks and beat briskly with a wire whisk. Place over low heat and gradually add the butter. Whisk until the sauce thickens. (Do not try to re-heat or it will curdle.) See note on hollandaise sauce, page 136.

White Sauce (Béchamel)

	Thin	Medium	Thick
Butter or marg.	1 tbsp.(15 mL)	2 tbsp.(30 mL)	3 tbsp.(45 mL)
Flour	1 tbsp.(15 mL)	2 tbsp.(30 mL)	3 tbsp.(45 mL)
Salt	1/4 tsp.(1 mL)	1/4 tsp.(1 mL)	1/4 tsp.(1 mL)
Pepper	dash	1/8 tsp.(.5 mL)	1/8 tsp.(.5mL)
Milk	1 cup (250 mL)	1 cup (250 mL)	1 cup (250 mL)

In a small saucepan, melt the margarine or butter. Stir in the flour, salt and pepper. Add the milk all at once. Cook and stir over medium heat until thickened and bubbly. Cook and stir one minute more. Makes 3/4 cup (175 mL).

Cucumber Sauce   MILDRED GORDON, BUFFALO

1	cucumber	1
1 cup	sour cream	250 mL
1/4 teaspoon	salt	1 mL
	dash of white pepper	
1 1/2 tablespoons	vinegar or lemon juice	25 mL
1 teaspoon	finely cut chives	5 mL

Chop or grate cucumber coarsely. Drain well. Mix rest of ingredients and fold in the drained cucumber. A lovely fish accompaniment.

Dill Sauce

ELEANOR STEINBERG

1/2 cup	fresh dill	125 mL
2 tablespoons	chopped onion	30 mL
1 large clove	garlic	1
1/2 teaspoon	salt	2 mL
1/4 teaspoon	black pepper	1 mL
1 cup	sour cream	250 mL
1/2 cup	mayonnaise	125 mL
2 tablespoons	olive oil	30 mL

Place all ingredients except oil in food processor. Blend until well mixed. Gradually add oil while machine is running. Blend until smooth.

Herb Sauce for Fish

6 tablespoons	sour cream	100 mL
6 tablespoons	mayonnaise	100 mL
1 teaspoon	tarragon	5 mL
1 teaspoon	chopped parsley	5 mL
1 teaspoon	Dijon mustard	5 mL
1/2 teaspoon	lemon juice	2 mL
1 tablespoon	minced chives	15 mL
	freshly ground pepper	
	coarsely ground salt, to taste	

Combine all ingredients in food processor and mix until well blended.

Mustard Cream Sauce

1	large egg yolk	1
2 tablespoons	lemon juice	30 mL
2 tablespoons	Dijon style mustard	30 mL
1/2 teaspoon	salt	2 mL
1/4 cup	olive oil	60 mL
1/2 cup	heavy cream	125 mL

In a food processor fitted with the steel blade, or in a blender, blend the egg yolk, lemon juice, mustard and salt. With the motor running add the olive oil in a stream and the cream. Blend the mixture until it is smooth. Transfer the sauce to a bowl and chill, covered, for one hour. Makes about 3/4 cup (175 mL).

Phyllis' Green Sauce

ADÈLE FREEMAN

1 cup	chopped frozen spinach, cooked according to package directions and well drained	250 mL
1/2 cup	chopped fresh parsley	125 mL
1 teaspoon	salt	5 mL
1 teaspoon	freshly ground pepper	5 mL
1/2 cup	finely chopped chives or green onions	125 mL
2 cups	mayonnaise, thinned with a little cream	500 mL

Combine and mix well. Adjust seasoning to taste. Serve well-chilled. A good accompaniment for hot or cold poached salmon, baked trout, etc.

Mushroom Velouté Sauce

DOROTHY STONE

2 tablespoons	margarine	30 mL
2 tablespoons	all purpose flour	30 mL
1 cup	parve chicken flavoured stock	250 mL
1/4 pound	fresh mushrooms, sliced	115 g
2 tablespoons	butter	30 mL
1 teaspoon	lemon juice	5 mL

Melt margarine. Add flour and cook, stirring, until beige in colour. Blend in chicken stock. Bring to a boil, and simmer for a few moments. Sauté the sliced mushrooms in butter and lemon juice. Combine mushrooms and sauce. Serve hot with baked fish, etc.

Apricot Glaze or Sauce

1 · 10 ounce jar	apricot jam	280 mL
1/4 cup	granulated sugar	60 mL
1/4 cup	water	60 mL
1 tablespoon	rum, cognac or Kirsch	15 mL

Blend first three ingredients on low heat until smooth. Using small sieve, strain glaze. Cool. Stir in liqueur. Pour over fruit pie, fruit flan, or cheese cake topped with fresh berries.

Mixed Berry Sauce

1 · 10 ounce package	frozen raspberries	300 g
2 tablespoons	orange or raspberry liqueur	30 mL
2 cups	fresh strawberries, hulled and cut into quarters	500 mL
1 cup	fresh raspberries	250 mL
1 cup	fresh blueberries	250 mL

Defrost berries and strain. Reserve juices. Purée berries through a food mill to remove seeds (or in a food processor and then strain). Add enough reserved juices to make a medium thick sauce. Add liqueur. Gently stir in strawberries, raspberries and blueberries. Serves 8.

Hint for Quick Sauce: Melted raspberry ice or sherbet makes a very nice sauce.

Blueberry Sauce

THELMA RACHLIN

3/4 cup	granulated sugar	175 mL
1 tablespoon	cornstarch	15 mL
1 cup	water	250 mL
1/3 cup	crushed fresh blueberries	75 mL
3/4 cup	fresh whole blueberries	175 mL
1 tablespoon	lemon juice	15 mL

Combine sugar and cornstarch in saucepan. Gradually stir in water. Stir slowly, cooking, until smooth and clear. Add crushed berries and cook one minute. Add rest of berries and lemon juice.

For canned berries: Drain can. To 1 cup (250 mL) of juice add 1/4 cup (60 mL) sugar. Bring to a slow boil. Mix 2 teaspoons (10 mL) cornstarch with a little water to make a paste. Add to juice and cook for 3 minutes, stirring. Stir in blueberries. Serve with blintzes.

Elegant Fruit Sauce

2 · 15 ounce packages	frozen strawberries, thawed and drained rind of 1 lemon and 1 orange	425 g each
1/4 cup	orange liqueur	60 mL
1/4 cup	Kirsch	60 mL
1/4 cup	Cognac	60 mL
3 tablespoons	red currant jelly	45 mL

Combine all ingredients in food processor and blend. Serve over fresh or canned fruit and top with whipped cream or ice cream.

Raspberry Coulis

2 · 10 ounce packages	frozen raspberries, thawed	560 g
2 tablespoons	granulated sugar	30 mL
2 teaspoons	cornstarch	10 mL
	dissolved in	
2 tablespoons	cold water	30 mL
2 tablespoons	framboise liqueur	30 mL

Simmer raspberries with sugar in a small saucepan about 2 minutes, stirring occasionally. Add cornstarch mixture and stir until clear. Strain sauce through fine sieve, pressing with the back of a wooden spoon to extract as much juice as possible. Cool. Mix in framboise.

Grand Marnier Sauce

2	egg yolks	2
1/4 cup	granulated sugar	60 mL
1 1/2 tablespoons	Grand Marnier	25 mL
1/2 cup	heavy cream	125 mL

Use a 1 quart (1 L) mixing bowl that will rest snugly on top of a slightly larger saucepan. Add about 2" (5 cm) of water to saucepan and bring to a boil.

Place yolks and sugar into the mixing bowl not on heat, and start beating with portable mixer. Scrape all around the inside bottom of bowl to cover entire surface to insure mixture is well blended.

Set mixing bowl inside saucepan (over but not in the water). Continue beating constantly until the yolks are thick and pale, 5 – 7 minutes. Remove bowl from saucepan and stir in Grand Marnier. Put bowl in freezer to chill. Do not freeze. Whip cream until stiff and fold into chilled sauce. Serve over fresh berries or sliced fruit. Also excellent over apple pie. Makes 4 servings. Can be doubled.

Butterscotch Sundae Sauce

1/2 cup	light cream	125 mL
1/2 cup	water	125 mL
1 cup	corn syrup	250 mL
2 tablespoons	butter or margarine	30 mL
1 cup	granulated sugar	250 mL
1/4 teaspoon	salt	1 mL

Combine all ingredients in saucepan. Cook over medium heat, stirring constantly until mixture boils. Cook to 230°F (115°C) stirring occasionally. (Soft ball stage). Remove from heat. Serve hot. May be stored in refrigerator, and reheated by placing over hot, not boiling water until thinned to pouring consistency.

Coffee Sauce for Ice Cream

ESTELLE ZALDIN

1 cup	granulated sugar	250 mL
1/2 cup	water	125 mL
1 tablespoon	corn syrup or honey	15 mL
	few drops lemon juice	
2 tablespoons	instant coffee,	30 mL
	dissolved in a little water	

Combine ingredients in a saucepan. Boil, stirring occasionally, until thick, about 10 minutes.

Super Chocolate Sauce

SALLY KERR, CALGARY

4 ounces	semi-sweet chocolate, broken into pieces	4 squares
1 cup	brown sugar	250 mL
2/3 cup	light cream	150 mL
2 tablespoons	grated orange rind	30 mL
4 tablespoons	rum	60 mL

Combine chocolate, sugar, cream and orange rind in a saucepan. Stir over low heat. To serve, scoop vanilla ice cream into bowls. Put chocolate mixture in chafing dish. Heat. Add rum and ignite. Spoon over ice cream.

Thick Fudge Sauce

4 ounces	unsweetened chocolate	4 squares
2 cups	icing sugar	500 mL
1 · 6 ounce can	evaporated milk	170 g
3 tablespoons	butter	45 mL
1/2 teaspoon	vanilla	2 mL

Melt chocolate. Gradually add sugar. Add milk and cook until smooth, stirring constantly. Add butter. Cook until butter is melted, stirring occasionally. Add vanilla. Serve warm, or store in covered jar in refrigerator. Reheat in double boiler before using. If too thick, add a little evaporated milk, cream or hot water.

Fish

Fish

When buying fish, always purchase the best available. A good fish merchant will advise you on the freshest of the day. Fish must be very fresh or flash frozen.

Fish does not require long cooking. When cooked quickly at high temperature, fish will retain its flavour and stay moist. Fish is cooked when it has an opaque, whitish look at its thickest part, and separates easily into flakes when touched with a fork.

To avoid strong fish odours while cooking, place a small piece of fresh peeled ginger root in the corner of the pan.

Basic Methods for Cooking Fish

1) Dry Heat – Bake, Broil, Charcoal Grill

Baking is good for whole fish, steak and fillets. Bake in 425°F (215°C) oven allowing 10 minutes per inch (2.5 cm) of thickness.

Broiling is good for steaks or fillets which should be about 3/4"(2 cm) thick. Brush the pan with melted butter or oil, arrange fish on pan and broil 3 1/2 – 4 inches (8.75 – 10 cm) away from heat. Allow approximately 10 minutes cooking time.

Charcoal Grilling is recommended for whole fish, fillets or steaks. Cook on a greased preheated grill. Oil and flour the fish well before grilling. Brush fish with oil while cooking 10 minutes on each side.

2) Moist Heat: - Poach, Steam, Poach in Foil or Lettuce

Poaching in water or milk is suitable for whole fish or fillets 3/4" to 1" (2 – 3 cm) thick. Bring liquid to a boil, add the fish tied in cheesecloth. When liquid returns to a second boil, reduce heat to simmer. Cover and cook for 10 minutes per inch of thickness. Remove from liquid as soon as fish is cooked.

Steaming is the same as poaching except fish is over liquid, not in it. If you do not have a steamer, partially fill a deep saucepan with water, place fish, wrapped in cheesecloth in a sieve or colander and place over the boiling water. Do not let fish touch water. Cover and steam for 10 minutes per inch of thickness.

Poaching in Foil: (Whole fish). Clean and season fish to taste. Add lemon and onion slices in cavity and around fish. Add 1/2 cup (125 mL) of white wine. Wrap tightly in foil. Place in baking pan. Bake at 400°F (200°C) ten minutes per inch of thickness.

Larger fish: 6 – 8 pounds (3 – 4 kg) should be cooked an extra 20 minutes. When done, remove from oven, cool, and unwrap. Peel off skin. Garnish and serve.

Wrap in lettuce (any kind) and poach the same way. Skin is easily discarded with lettuce.

3) Pan Frying: Popular method for steaks, fillets and small whole fish. Season with salt and pepper, dip in milk or beaten egg, coat with flour or bread crumbs. Fry fish in hot oil until golden on one side, turn and brown other side.

4) Microwave: Easiest and fastest way to prepare fish. Be sure to follow recipe instructions carefully to avoid overcooking. Fish should be opaque and flake easily when done. It should be moist and succulent to taste.

Freezing Fish: Fish should be very fresh and very well wrapped. Fish is at its best when used within two months. Maximum freezing time is three to four months. Defrost as quickly as possible in a basin of cold water while fish is still in its freezer wrap or a seal-tight plastic bag. Depending on the size of the fish, it should take from forty minutes to four hours. Gradual overnight defrosting in the refrigerator causes loss of texture and taste. Thawed fish should **never** be refrozen.

Sauces for Fish

1. Hollandaise
2. Mousseline - 1/2 Hollandaise, 1/2 whipping cream
3. Lemon Butter - melted butter with lemon juice to taste
4. Mustard and Mayonnaise - 1 teaspoon (5 mL) mustard to 2 teaspoons (10 mL) mayonnaise - coat fish steaks or fillets before baking or broiling.

Familiar Types of Fish

Bass: Good all-around fish. Good in almost any recipe from broiling to saucing.

Bluefish: Adapts well in most recipes. A relative of mackerel. Very good when grilled.

Carp-Buffalo: Both fish are very similar. Good for baking. Used solely in Middle European style gefilte fish.

Cod: Called Scrod in New England. Very delicate. Has a spotted skin and pure white meat. Excellent when broiled.

Flounder: May be substituted for sole. Very good when broiled or pan fried.

Grouper: Good when fried or broiled.

Haddock: Like cod, but not as delicate. One of the least costly and most plentiful fish. Can be prepared in almost any way.

Halibut: A large firm fish. Fairly bland. Good with sauces.

Herring: Very good for pickling and smoking. When fresh, it is difficult to work with and very bony. Tends to fall apart when cleaned and cooked. Smaller mackerel can be used instead.

Mackerel: Fresh mackerel has almost unlimited uses. Can be baked, broiled, or fried. The richness can be cut by a little marinating.

Orange Roughy: Flat fish similar to sole. Can be pan-fried, broiled or baked.

Perch: Versatile fish. Good fried, broiled, or under sauces.

Pickerel or Pike: Very bony. However, once boned it is delicious simply prepared or with sauces.

Plaice: Used extensively in England for Fish and Chips. Very tasty when fried.

Pompano: A Gulf fish. Delicate with excellent flavour. Delicious when broiled with brown butter or amandine style.

Red Snapper: A Gulf fish. May be used in most recipes. Its firm texture makes it a good choice for fish stews and sauces.

Salmon: Fresh salmon is superb when simply prepared. Poached or broiled, it is excellent. Can be smoked, cured as in Gravlax, or canned and used in salads and salmon patties.

Smelts: Very small fish. Delicious when crisply pan fried.

Sole: A versatile flat fish. Dover sole is the best and most expensive.

Trout: All variations are delicious when fresh. Best when prepared simply. A pan fried whole trout is delicious.

Tuna: Fresh tuna is very different from the canned variety. Fresh may be grilled. Canned tuna is used mainly for casseroles, sandwiches and salads.

Turbot: A mild tasting fish in the sole-flounder family.

Walleye Pike: Delicious, difficult to bone. Can be broiled, baked, or pickled. Wonderful when freshly caught and eaten at a shore cook-out.

Whitefish: One of the great versatile fish along with salmon, trout, bass, sole, and pompano. Can be panfried, baked, or broiled.

Pickled Fish

CLARA FREEDMAN

3 pounds	fish (salmon, pike or pickerel), in slices	1.5 kg
2 1/2 cups	water	625 mL
1 1/2 cups	vinegar	375 mL
1 scant cup	granulated sugar	200 mL
1 1/2 teaspoons	salt	7 mL
1 1/2 teaspoons	mixed pickling spices	7 mL

Place all ingredients (except pickling spices) in a large pot and bring to a boil. Simmer for 1/2 hour, adding pickling spices for the last 5 minutes. Cool. Lift out fish very carefully and place in a casserole. Strain the liquid into a bowl and add strained liquid to fish to cover.

Add:

	sliced onions	
	sliced carrots	
1/2	lemon, sliced	1/2
	juice of 1/2 lemon	

Cover and let sit in refrigerator for 2 – 3 days before serving.

Fish Casserole #1

ELINORE ASHER

2	potatoes, boiled and sliced	2
1	medium onion, chopped	1
	salt and pepper to taste	
1/3 cup	white wine	75 mL
1 pound	fish fillets (flounder, sole or turbot)	450 g
1/2 cup	sour cream	125 mL

Place potatoes and onion in bottom of greased casserole. Sprinkle with salt and pepper. Pour in white wine. Place fish fillets on top. Spread fish with sour cream. Bake uncovered 1/2 hour at 350°F (180°C). Serves 3 – 4.

Fish Casserole #2

ELINORE ASHER

1 1/2 pounds	fish fillets (turbot or halibut)	675 g
	salt and pepper	
1 tablespoon	lemon juice	15 mL
1/2 cup	chopped green pepper	125 mL
1	medium onion, chopped	1
1 cup	buttered bread crumbs	250 mL
3 tablespoons	water	45 mL
1/4 cup	sherry	60 mL

Sprinkle fish with salt and pepper and lemon juice. Combine green pepper and onion and spread over fish. Pack bread crumbs on top of fish. Add water and sherry. Bake uncovered at 375°F (190°C) for 25 minutes.

Baked Carp

ROSE KAY

4	slices of carp	4
	coarse salt	
2 cloves	garlic, pressed	2
1/2 teaspoon	salt	2 mL
1/4 teaspoon	pepper	1 mL
1/4 teaspoon	paprika	1 mL
2 tablespoons	oil	30 mL

Wash carp and lightly salt with coarse salt. Let stand 1/2 hour, then wash and pat dry. Combine garlic, salt, pepper, paprika and oil. Soak carp in this mixture for 1 hour, basting often. Lift carp from oil mixture, and place in lightly greased shallow ovenproof baking dish. Bake, uncovered, at 350°F (180°C) for 45 minutes to 1 hour depending on how dry or moist you like the fish. Remove from pan and drain on paper towelling.

Stuffed Baked Whitefish

| 4 pounds | whitefish | 2 kg |
| 1/2 cup | melted butter | 125 mL |

Have merchant butterfly fish (remove bone). Soak fish in very cold water for 1/2 hour. Remove and pat dry with paper towel. Put three or four slashes on each side of skin to keep from cracking. Fill cavity of fish with stuffing, and secure firmly with toothpicks. Place fish in a well greased ovenproof baking dish and pour melted butter over fish. Season with **salt** and **pepper**. Bake uncovered for 1 1/2 hours at 350°F (180°C). Remove toothpicks and serve on platter garnished with **parsley** and **lemon wedges**.

Stuffing:

1 cup	chopped celery	250 mL
1 cup	chopped onions	250 mL
3 cups	bread crumbs	750 mL
1/2 cup	butter	125 mL
1 teaspoon	salt	5 mL
1/2 teaspoon	pepper	2 mL
1 teaspoon	chopped parsley	5 mL

Sauté celery and onions in butter, add remaining ingredients and blend well. Sauté until onions are golden in colour.

Fillet of Whitefish

FAYE BIGMAN

3 pounds	whitefish, filleted (2 fillets)	1.5 kg
2	egg whites	2
1/2 cup	mayonnaise	125 mL
2 teaspoons	prepared mustard	10 mL

Preheat oven to 450°F (230°C). Beat egg whites until firm. Fold in mayonnaise and mustard. Grease cookie sheet and place fish fillets skin side down. Spread egg white mixture over fish. Bake for 15 minutes. Reduce heat to 375°F (190°C) and bake for an additional 15 – 20 minutes.

Note: 1 cup (250 mL) seedless grapes added to egg white mixture is a nice addition. Serves 4.

Whole Baked Whitefish in Foil

3 pounds	whitefish	1.5 kg
	salt and pepper	
6	slices of lemon	6
6	slices of orange	6
	butter	
4	carrots, sliced	4
1	tomato, sliced	1

Have your merchant butterfly the fish. Soak fish in cold water for 1/2 hour. Remove and dry well with paper towels. Place on a piece of buttered foil large enough to make a generous fold. Rub fish generously with butter inside and out. Sprinkle with salt and pepper, and place 3 slices of lemon and orange inside cavity of fish. Place 3 slices of lemon and orange on top. Add carrots and tomato slices. Fold foil to make an envelope. Place on a cookie sheet and bake for about 1 hour at 350°F (180°C).

Baked Fillet of Sole
RUTH GOLDBERG

1 pound	fillet of sole (about 4 slices)	450 g
1 quart	water	1 L
2 tablespoons	vinegar	30 mL
	crushed cornflake crumbs	
3 tablespoons	butter or margarine	45 mL
1/4 teaspoon	fresh lemon juice	1 mL
1/8 teaspoon	garlic powder	0.5 mL
1 teaspoon	chopped parsley	5 mL

Combine water and vinegar. Wash fish and allow to soak in this mixture for about 45 minutes. Preheat oven to 350°F (180°C). Remove fish from water and pat dry with paper towelling. Sprinkle well with crushed cornflake crumbs. Place in well-greased oven proof baking dish. Melt butter or margarine and mix with lemon juice, garlic powder and parsley. Spoon over fish. Bake for 20 to 30 minutes.

Easy Lo-Cal Sole

1 pound	sole fillets	500 g
10 ounce package	frozen asparagus, cooked and drained, or	284 g
7 – 8	fresh asparagus, cooked lightly and drained	7 – 8
1/2 teaspoon	salt	2 mL
1/8 teaspoon	dried thyme	0.5 mL
1/8 teaspoon	pepper	0.5 mL
1 teaspoon	salad dressing mix (dry) for buttermilk dressing	5 mL
1/2 cup	plain yogurt	125 mL

Arrange fillets evenly in baking dish. Layer asparagus over fillets. Combine all seasonings and dressing mix with yogurt and spoon mixture evenly over asparagus.

For oven: Bake uncovered at 375°F (190°C) for 15 – 20 minutes or until fish flakes easily with a fork.

For microwave: Use pyrex or microwavable baking dish. Cover loosely with heavy duty plastic wrap. Cook 4 – 6 minutes or until fish flakes easily with a fork. (Fish will continue to cook for 5 minutes after removal from microwave).

Baked Fillets of Sole in White Wine

6 – 8	sole fillets	6 – 8
1 cup	dry white wine	250 mL
	lemon wedges	
	chopped parsley	

Preheat oven to 350°F (180°C). Place fillets in a greased ovenproof baking dish. If the fillets are large, cut in half. Pour wine over fish and bake until just done (flakes when touched with a fork). Serve covered with the liquid from the dish. Garnish with lemon wedges and chopped parsley.

Baked Fillets of Turbot or Sole

LIL PEARL

1 1/2 pounds	turbot or sole	675 g
2	tomatoes, peeled and sliced	2
	salt and (lemon) pepper	
2 tablespoons	butter	30 mL
2	onions, thinly sliced	2
1 clove	garlic, finely chopped	1
4 ounces	Edam cheese	120 g
1/2 cup	dry white wine	125 mL

Preheat oven to 375°F (190°C). Arrange fish and tomato slices on a lightly greased baking dish. Sprinkle with salt and pepper. Sauté onions in butter. Add garlic and cook until soft. Spread over fish. Cut cheese into small cubes about 1" (2.5 cm) square, and arrange on top of onions. Pour wine on top. Bake for 30 minutes until cheese is bubbly and golden.

Vina's Fish Luncheon

VINA SECTER

1 pound	fillet of sole	500 g
2 tablespoons	oil	30 mL
1	onion, chopped	1
1/2	green pepper, seeded and chopped	1/2
3	zucchini, chopped, unpeeled	3
2	carrots, peeled, diced	2
1 · 14 ounce can	tomato juice	398 mL
1/2 teaspoon	oregano	2 mL
	salt and pepper to taste	

In a skillet, brown vegetables in oil. Remove vegetables from pan. In same pan, brown fish, 10 minutes on each side. Remove fish to baking dish that can be placed on burner. Cover fish with vegetables. Add tomato juice, oregano, and salt and pepper. Cover with foil. Simmer on top of stove for 20 minutes. Sprinkle with **fresh chopped dill** to taste, and cook another 2 – 3 minutes. Remove from heat. Garnish with partially cooked **broccoli** and **cauliflower** florets.

Sole with Herbs and Vegetables

ROZ HALBERT

2 tablespoons	butter	30 mL
1 cup	thin noodles	250 mL
	or	
1/2 cup	raw rice	125 mL
1/4 cup	thinly sliced green onions	60 mL
1/4 cup	butter	60 mL
12	small white onions, cut in halves or quarters	12
1/2 pound	fresh mushrooms	225 g
2 cloves	garlic, crushed	2
6	medium carrots, diagonally sliced	6
2	celery stalks, sliced	2
1	green pepper, seeded and sliced	1
1 tablespoon	all purpose flour	15 mL
1 teaspoon	basil	5 mL
1/2 teaspoon	oregano	2 mL
1 1/2 teaspoons	salt	7 mL
1/4 teaspoon	pepper	1 mL
	juice of 1 lemon, plus water or tomato juice to make 1 1/2 cups / 375 mL	
1 1/2 pounds	sole or haddock fillets, fresh or frozen	675 g
	salt and pepper to taste	
	sliced mozzarella - enough to cover fish	
3 tablespoons	butter	45 mL
2 tablespoons	parsley	30 mL
	any other fresh vegetable - broccoli, cauliflower, beans.	

Preheat oven to 400°F (200°C). Butter a 9" x 12" x 3" (3.5 L) baking pan. In a skillet, heat 2 tablespoons (30 mL) butter. Add uncooked noodles and a little water. Cook gently until browned. If using rice, follow package directions. Spread half of noodles or rice down each side of baking dish. Heat 1/4 cup (60 mL) butter in a large pan. Add onions and cook until golden. Add crushed garlic, carrots, celery and other vegetables. Cook gently, and stir for five minutes (add green pepper last). Add flour, basil, oregano, salt and pepper, and mix well.

Add water/lemon juice mixture to pan, stir, bringing to boil. Cover and simmer 10 minutes.

Sprinkle fish well with salt and pepper. Cut into serving pieces, and cut cheese the same size as the fish. Lay fish on noodles. Lay cheese on fish. Melt 3 tablespoons butter (45 mL). Stir in **1 tablespoon (15 mL) lemon juice**. Drizzle over fish and cheese. Pour vegetables and sauce into middle of pan. Sprinkle parsley over all. Cover pan with foil. Bake 15 minutes. Uncover and bake 10 more minutes, until fish is flaky. Serve with salad for a lovely buffet supper. Serves 6 – 8.

Note: For easier preparation, substitute frozen pasta and vegetable prepackaged mix instead of fresh vegetables and noodles. Lightly preboil and drain before adding.

Orange Roughy or Sole in Yogurt Sauce

ADÈLE FREEMAN

Preheat oven to 350°F (180°C). Place desired quantity of fish in an open casserole. Sprinkle with salt, pepper and your favourite herbs and cover with a layer of sliced fresh mushrooms. Make a mixture of equal parts of yogurt and Parmesan cheese and spread over fish. Bake for 30 minutes.

Sole in Lemon Butter

ADÈLE FREEMAN

2 pounds	fillet of sole	1 kg
1/2 cup	butter or margarine	125 mL
3 tablespoons	lemon juice	45 mL
	salt and pepper to taste	

Preheat oven to 350°F (180°C). In baking pan, melt butter with lemon juice. Place sole in butter, top side down, then turn over. Bake 20 minutes. Sprinkle chopped **parsley** over top of fish before serving.

Baked Fillet of Fish, Amandine

MYRTLE COOPERSMITH

8 slices	fillet (sole, haddock, etc.)	8
1/2 cup	lemon juice	125 mL
4 tablespoons	butter or margarine	60 mL
3/4 cup	bread crumbs	175 mL
1 teaspoon	paprika	5 mL
	salt and pepper to taste	
3 ounces	blanched, slivered almonds	85 g
1 tablespoon	butter	15 mL

Pour lemon juice over fish. Add enough ice cold water to cover, and soak for 1/2 hour. Remove fish and pat dry with paper towels. Melt butter or margarine in a 9" x 13" (3.5 L) baking dish. Dip fish in bread crumbs and sprinkle with paprika, salt and pepper. Place fish in baking dish and bake at 350°F (180°C) for 20 minutes. Remove fish to platter and keep in a warm oven. Brown almonds in 1 tablespoon (15 mL) of butter, and pour over fish. Serve immediately. Serves 4 – 6.

Baked Fish Au Gratin

4	servings fish fillets or steaks	4
	salt and freshly ground black pepper to taste	
1 cup	tomato sauce	250 mL
1/2 cup	grated Parmesan cheese	125 mL
2 tablespoons	melted butter	30 mL

Preheat oven to 425°F (210°C). Place fish in buttered, shallow baking dish and season with salt and pepper. Spread tomato sauce over fish and sprinkle with cheese. Drizzle with melted butter. Bake uncovered 15 – 20 minutes.

Baked Fish Rollups

MYRTLE COOPERSMITH

6	fillets of sole	6
1 cup	white wine	250 mL
1 cup	sliced onions	250 mL
1 cup	sour cream or yogurt	250 mL
1 cup	mayonnaise	250 mL

Marinate sole in wine for two hours. Drain fish, and roll up, holding fish in place with a toothpick. Spread onions in a greased, ovenproof pan. Place rolled fish on top. Combine mayonnaise and sour cream and pour over fish. Bake for 30 minutes, uncovered, at 350°F (180 °C).

Fish Piquant

LILY KATZ

Prepare gefilte fish mixture on page 162, using sautéed onions, instead of raw. Form into flat fish cakes, and fry in deep oil.

Sauce:

1 · 14 ounce can	apricots	398 mL
1 cup	vinegar	250 mL
2 teaspoons	curry powder	10 mL
2	cloves	2
2	large onions	2
1/4 teaspoon	salt	1 mL
4	ginger snaps	4
1 cup	sultana raisins	250 mL
2 tablespoons	tomato sauce (optional)	30 mL

In a saucepan, combine apricot syrup, vinegar, curry, cloves, one sliced onion and salt. Boil for 1/2 hour. Slice second onion thinly. Soak ginger snaps in a little boiling water just to cover. Add thinly sliced onion, soaked ginger snaps, raisins and tomato sauce to apricot sauce. Boil together for only 1 minute. The onion should still be crisp. Pour over fish and garnish with apricot halves. Slivered almonds may be sprinkled on top if desired. Serve cold.

To freeze: Fish with sauce can be placed in a casserole, and wrapped well to freeze. Defrost in refrigerator to serve.

Gefilte Fish

2 pounds	chopped fish (whitefish and pickerel only - more of latter)	1 kg
2	medium onions, grated	2
2	eggs	2
1 1/2 teaspoons	salt	7 mL
1 teaspoon	granulated sugar	5 mL
1 tablespoon	matzo meal	15 mL
1/4 teaspoon	white pepper	1 mL
1 cup	water (approximately - less may be required)	250 mL

Stock:

2	onions, sliced	2
	bones and heads of fish	
2	carrots	2
	salt and pepper to taste	

Place sliced onions, heads and bones in a pot with water to cover. Bring to a boil and simmer while the fish is being made. Add carrots just before adding fish. Season to taste.

In large mixer bowl, combine chopped fish and grated onion and mix at low speed for several minutes. Add eggs, salt, sugar, matzo meal and white pepper with the mixer going. Add water slowly until mixture has a gluey consistency and comes away from the sides of the bowl. Continue to mix slowly for 15 – 20 minutes.

Keep hands wet while making fish balls. Use 1/4 cup or 50 mL measure to scoop fish. Make a ball, tossing fish lightly into air while forming. Drop gently into boiling stock. (Keep stock at a boil while adding the fish balls). When all the balls are in the pot and have turned white, cover the pot, leaving the lid slightly ajar, and reduce heat so that juice boils up around the fish gently. Cook for 1 1/2 hours, adding more water when necessary and tasting and adjusting seasoning.

Remove pot from heat. Close lid tightly and let sit for 5 minutes. Carefully remove fish balls to a bowl and strain juice over fish. Cover bowl with waxed paper and then a plate smaller than the top of the bowl. Refrigerate when cool.

To Freeze: Freeze fish and juice separately. **Two days** before serving, remove from freezer and thaw. Bring fish to a boil in juice and simmer several minutes. (This should be done day before serving). Chill overnight, placing fish in bowl and straining juice over as before.

Baked Gefilte Fish

RUTH GREENSPAN

2	medium carrots, peeled	2
1	large Spanish onion	1
1/4 cup	oil	60 mL
2 pounds	ground fish (whitefish, pickerel, salmon combined)	1 kg
3	eggs	3
3/4 cup	water	175 mL
2 1/2 teaspoons	salt	12 mL
1/4 teaspoon	liquid sweetener or	1 mL
1 tablespoon	granulated sugar	15 mL
3/4 teaspoon	pepper	3 mL
3 tablespoons	matzo meal	45 mL
	lime juice	
	paprika (optional)	

Preheat oven to 350°F (180°C). Grate carrots. Dice onions fine. Sauté carrots and onions in oil until soft. Allow to cool. Place remaining ingredients except lime juice and paprika in bowl of electric mixer. Add onions and carrots and mix together on low speed for 3 – 4 minutes. Spray a 9" x 5" x 3" (1.5 L) loaf pan with vegetable spray. Line pan with foil and spray again. Place mixed ingredients in loaf pan. Spread a little lime juice on top and sprinkle with paprika. Bake for approximately 1 1/4 hours. Remove from oven and cool 15 minutes. Turn out of pan onto cooling rack. When cool, remove foil. Refrigerate up to 4 days. Slice before serving.

Whole Baked Fish

ROZ HALBERT

1	whole fish, cleaned (trout, red snapper, whitefish, grouper, etc.)	1
	paprika	
1 clove	garlic, crushed	1
	salt	
	lemon pepper	
	butter or margarine	
	parsley	
	dill	
	onions	

Season fish very generously the day before serving with a paste of paprika, fresh garlic-crushed, salt, (lemon) pepper, etc. inside and out. Dot with butter or margarine. Place sprigs of fresh parsley and dill, and a few chopped onions inside, on top and on under side of fish. Wrap air tight in heavy foil, place in plastic bag, and refrigerate overnight or for 24 hours. Next day, open foil and bake, uncovered at 350°F (180°C) until fish flakes, about one hour. Cool. Fish may be eaten at this time, or wrapped in heavy foil and plastic bag and refrigerated until next day when flavours have blended beautifully. Serve at room temperature. Great to take to a cottage or to have on hand for a weekend!

Easy Broiled Salmon Steaks

SHIRLEY LAZARUS

salmon steaks,
cut 3/4" (2 cm) each
milk
salt and pepper
lemon juice
butter or margarine

Soak steaks in milk to cover for 1/2 hour. Remove steaks. Sprinkle with salt, pepper and lemon juice. Top with dabs of butter or margarine. Broil one side only, for 15 minutes.

Salmon Patties

1 · 15 ounce can	salmon	430 g
1/2 teaspoon	salt (optional)	2 mL
1/4 cup	bread crumbs or matzo meal	60 mL
2	eggs	2
1/2 teaspoon	baking powder	2 mL
1/2 teaspoon	onion powder	2 mL
	butter or margarine	

Remove skin and bones from salmon. Mash salmon well. Mix with remaining ingredients. Form into patties and fry in butter or margarine until well browned.

Salmon Loaf

RUTH GREENSPAN

1 · 15 ounce can	salmon	430 g
3	eggs	3
1	Spanish onion, grated	1
1/4 teaspoon	pepper	1 mL
3/4 cup	sour cream or low-fat yogurt	175 mL
3/4 cup	bread crumbs parsley for garnish	175 mL

Preheat oven to 350°F (180°C). Combine salmon, eggs, onion, pepper and sour cream and blend well. (May be blended in food processor with quick on/off turns). Fold in bread crumbs, mixing well. Turn into 1 quart (1 L) greased loaf pan. Bake 45 minutes – 1 hour until done. Turn out onto platter. Garnish with parsley.

Variations:

1. 1/2 cup (125 mL) chopped celery or canned, drained mushrooms may be added to mixture.

2. Canned fried onion rings or Chinese noodles may be placed on top before baking.

3. This recipe also works well with canned tuna.

Salmon Wellington

TOBY DUNKELMAN

2 ·15 ounce cans	salmon	860 g
3 – 4	beaten eggs	3 – 4
1 1/2 cups	soft bread crumbs	375 mL
1/4 teaspoon	grated lemon rind	1 mL
1/2 cup	mayonnaise	125 mL
1/2 cup	milk	125 mL
1/2 teaspoon	lemon juice	2 mL
1/4 teaspoon	pepper	1 mL
2 – 3 teaspoons	grated onion	10 – 15 mL

Preheat oven to 325°F (160°C). Mix all of the above ingredients. Line a cookie sheet with foil and grease lightly. Form the salmon mixture into a loaf and place on cookie sheet. Bake about 1 hour until set and lightly brown.

Puff Pastry: Prepare your favourite puff pastry recipe, or frozen pastry as package directs. If frozen pastry is used, you will need 2 packages. Roll out pastry. Arrange salmon in center. Seal edges with **beaten egg**. Prick top with a fork, brush with **beaten egg**, and bake at 450°F (230°C) for 30 - 40 minutes until brown.

Microwave Salmon Steaks

VERA SANDERS

4	salmon steaks, 1/2 inch (1.2 cm) thick	4
2 tablespoons	melted butter or margarine (optional)	30 mL
2 teaspoons	lemon juice	10 mL
1/2 teaspoon	fresh chopped dill	2 mL

Line microwave baking dish 12" x 2" x 8" (3.5 L) with paper towel. (It absorbs juices for best appearance). Brush steaks with melted butter mixed with lemon juice, and place in one layer in baking dish. Sprinkle with dill. Cover with waxed paper. Microwave on High (100%) for 5 – 6 minutes, or until fish begins to flake easily. Keep covered. Fish will continue to cook after removal from microwave. Turn fish onto serving plate. If desired serve with yogurt-cucumber sauce.

Yogurt Cucumber Sauce

1/2 cup	plain yogurt	125 mL
1/4 cup	grated, peeled cucumber	60 mL
1/4 teaspoon	dried dill	2 mL
	salt and pepper to taste	

Combine ingredients and mix well.

Sweet and Sour Salmon ETHEL KLEIN

Sauce:

4 cups	water	1 L
2	onions, chopped fine	2
1 cup	raisins	250 mL
3/4 cup	brown sugar	175 mL
1 teaspoon	ginger	5 mL
1 teaspoon	salt	5 mL
	pepper to taste	
	juice of 2 lemons	
1/2	lemon, sliced thin	1/2
6	ginger snaps	6
1/2 cup	water	125 mL

Boil onions in 4 cups (1 L) water for 1/2 hour. Add raisins and boil another 1/2 hour. Add brown sugar, ginger, salt and pepper and lemon juice and lemon slices. Dissolve ginger snaps in water to cover and add to mixture. Boil until clear and thick. Adjust sugar and lemon to taste.

To prepare fish:

4	slices of salmon steak, 1 1/2 inches (4 cm) thick	4
2	onions	2
	celery tops	

Slice onions and place in large frying pan with celery tops. Add water to cover and salt to taste. Bring to boil and put fish in pan. Poach for 15 minutes. Cool fish in juice. When cool remove skin and bones. Carefully break each steak into four serving pieces, place in a dish and pour sauce over. Chill and serve.

Salmon Florentine

YONA PATTENICK

6	salmon fillets	1 kg
1/4 cup	parve chicken flavoured stock	60 mL
1/4 cup	water	60 mL
1/4 cup	dry white wine	60 mL
	salt and pepper	
1 1/2 tablespoons	butter or margarine, cut into bits	15 mL
3 packages	frozen spinach, thawed	3
1 tablespoon	bread crumbs	15 mL
1 tablespoon	Parmesan cheese	15 mL
1 tablespoon	melted butter or margarine	15 mL

Preheat oven to 375°F (190°C). Place fillets in single layer in a shallow baking dish. Combine stock, water, wine and salt and pepper. Pour over fish. Dot with butter or margarine. Bake, covered with foil, for 8 – 10 minutes. Squeeze as much liquid as possible from spinach. Spread spinach over a baking dish large enough to hold fillets in one layer. Prepare Mornay sauce and set aside. Place warm fish over spinach. Add 1/3 cup (75 mL) of liquid from fish to Mornay sauce (the consistency should be like hot pudding). Pour sauce over fish. Sprinkle bread crumbs and Parmesan cheese over top. Drizzle butter or margarine over.* Increase oven temperature to 400°F (200°C) and bake for 10 minutes. Then broil 6 inches (15 cm) from heat until sauce is glazed on top.

* This may be prepared and refrigerated overnight, and then baked for 20 – 25 minutes in a preheated 400°F (200°C) oven.

Mornay Sauce

2 tablespoons	butter or margarine	30 mL
2 tablespoons	all purpose flour	30 mL
1 cup	milk	250 mL
	salt to taste	
	dash of thyme	
1/3 cup	grated Emmenthal cheese	75 mL
2	egg yolks	2
2 tablespoons	cream	30 mL
2 tablespoons	butter or margarine	30 mL

In a small saucepan, melt butter or margarine. Add the flour, stirring, to make a paste. Cook on medium high heat, stirring until bubbly, about 1 minute. Slowly stir in the milk and continue to cook until sauce is thick, about 4 minutes. Turn heat to medium low. Stir in the salt, thyme and Emmenthal cheese. Remove pan from heat. Combine egg yolks and cream and slowly pour into cheese mixture, stirring constantly. Return pan to heat. Simmer, stirring for 2 minutes. (Do not boil). Remove from heat. Stir in butter or margarine.

Broiled Salmon Trout
ELEANOR STEINBERG

4 – 6	fillets of salmon trout	4 – 6
1 – 2 tablespoons	butter or margarine	15 – 30 mL
1/4 teaspoon	garlic powder, to taste	1 mL
1/4 teaspoon	lemon pepper	1 mL
1/4 cup	bread crumbs	60 mL
2 tablespoons	melted butter or margarine	30 mL
	oil as necessary	
	lemon wedges for garnish	

Brush fillets with melted butter or margarine. Season with garlic and lemon pepper. Line a cookie sheet with foil. Brush foil with oil to prevent fish from sticking. Lay fillets skin side down on foil. Sprinkle top side of fish with bread crumbs. Sprinkle melted butter or margarine over top. Broil on rack about 5" (12.5 cm) from heat for 10 – 12 minutes or until done. Do not turn. Garnish with lemon wedges.

Salmon Teriyaki

EDIE WINBERG

1	whole salmon	1
	or	
15	fillets	15
	about 6 – 7 pounds (3 kg)	
Sauce:		
6 cloves	garlic, crushed	6
1/2 cup	honey	125 mL
1/2 cup	brown sugar	125 mL
1 cup	soy sauce	250 mL
1/4 cup	sherry	60 mL
2 teaspoons	powdered ginger	10 mL

For whole fish: Combine ingredients for sauce and mix well. Place fish in a bowl. Pour marinade over and let marinate overnight.* Preheat oven to 350ºF (180ºC). Remove fish from marinade and place in greased baking dish. Cover with foil and bake 45 minutes. Uncover and baste. Bake an additional 15 minutes, basting occasionally. Serve on a platter. Serve excess sauce on the side.

For fillets: Follow above recipe to *. Place fish fillets on a greased broiler pan and broil approximately 10 minutes per inch of thickness, or until fish is no longer translucent and flakes easily. Baste occasionally with sauce while cooking.

Coulibiac

ANNE ALLEN

Crust:		
4 cups	sifted all purpose flour	1 L
2 teaspoons	salt	10 mL
1 cup plus	butter	280 mL
2 tablespoons		
6	egg yolks	6
4 tablespoons	olive oil	60 mL
1/2 cup	ice water	125 mL

Cut butter into flour and salt. Add yolks, oil and water, stirring with a fork until blended. Form into a ball and refrigerate for a few hours or overnight. Or use your favourite prepared puff pastry. (Frozen is available).

Crumb Mixture:

1 cup	bread crumbs	250 mL
2 teaspoons	dry mustard	10 mL
1 teaspoon	salt	5 mL
1 teaspoon	pepper	5 mL
1/2 cup	melted butter	125 mL
1/2 cup	grated Parmesan cheese	125 mL

Mix all ingredients together.

Filling:

1 pound	unsalted sliced smoked salmon (Nova Scotia salmon)	500 g
1 cup	sour cream	250 mL
3	hard cooked eggs, chopped	3
2	onions, chopped	2
1/4 cup	snipped fresh dill	60 mL
1/4 cup	melted butter	60 mL
1 clove	garlic, minced	1

Preheat oven to 375°F (190°C). Roll out 2/3 of the pastry. Place on greased jelly roll pan. Layer with the following down the middle, leaving 1" (2.5 cm) margin all around the filling: Bread crumb mixture, sliced salmon, sour cream, eggs, onion, dill and melted butter mixed with garlic. Roll out remaining pastry and place on top of mounded filling. Brush edges with **1 egg white** mixed with **1 teaspoon (5 mL) water**. Turn bottom edges over upper and press down with fork, or flute edges. Decorate top with waste trim of edges if desired. Make 2 slits in top or prick with a fork. Brush entire surface with remainder of egg wash. Bake 1 hour at 375°F (190°C). Serve with **hot melted butter** and **lemon juice** on the side. Serves 8 – 10.

Tuna Casserole for 30

E D I E   W I N B E R G

8 · 6 1/2 ounce cans	tuna fish	184 g each
4 · 10 ounce cans	cream of mushroom soup	284 mL each
4 · 12 ounce packages	frozen peas, not cooked	340 g each
2 · 10 ounce cans	sliced mushrooms, drained	568 mL
2 1/4 cups	minute rice, not cooked	550 mL
5 cups	milk	1250 mL
2	onions, diced	2
1	bunch celery, diced	1
1	green pepper, seeded and chopped	1
1 teaspoon	curry powder	5 mL
	juice of 2 lemons	
2 pounds	grated cheddar cheese	1 kg
	cornflake crumbs	
2/3 cup	melted butter	150 mL

Preheat oven to 325°F (160°C). Grease an 8 quart (8 L) casserole with butter. Cut tuna into chunks and pour boiling water over. Drain well. Add all ingredients except cornflake crumbs and melted butter and mix well. Pour into casserole. Sprinkle with cornflake crumbs, and pour melted butter over top. Bake 1 hour. Freezes well. Defrost before baking.

Tuna Cashew

E D I E   W I N B E R G

1 · 8 ounce can	chow mein dry noodles	227 g
1 · 10 ounce can	cream of mushroom soup	284 mL
1 · 6.5 ounce can	tuna fish, drained	184 g
1/4 pound	unsalted cashew nuts	113 g
1 cup	diced celery	250 mL
1/4 cup	minced onion	60 mL
1/2 cup	milk	125 mL
1 · 10 ounce can	sliced mushrooms, drained	284 mL

Preheat oven to 325°F (160°C). Mix all ingredients, setting aside half of the noodles. Pour into 1 quart (1 L) casserole. Sprinkle remaining noodles on top. Bake for 45 minutes. Serves 4.

Broiled Fish Steaks with Walnuts

ELEANOR MAXWELL

1 1/4 – 1 1/2 pounds	fish steaks 1" (2.5 cm thick) (halibut, salmon, salmon trout, etc.)	575 – 700 g
1/4 cup	dry white wine juice of 1/2 lemon	60 mL
1 tablespoon	butter or margarine salt and pepper	15 mL
Sauce:		
3 tablespoons	chopped walnuts	45 mL
1/2 cup	chopped parsley leaves loosely packed	125 mL
1 tablespoon	dried basil	15 mL
2 tablespoons	liquid parve chicken flavoured broth	30 mL
2 tablespoons	grated Parmesan cheese	30 mL
1 tablespoon	olive oil	15 mL
1 tablespoon	vinegar	15 mL
1 teaspoon	granulated sugar	5 mL
1	garlic clove, minced	1
1/2 teaspoon	fresh ground pepper	2 mL

Blend sauce ingredients in food processor. Add more broth if thinner sauce is desired. Arrange fish steaks in a shallow pan. Pour wine and lemon juice over fish. Dot with butter or margarine. Season with salt and pepper to taste. Broil for 5 minutes. Turn over. Spoon sauce over fish. Broil another 5 minutes or until it is done. Fish is done when it flakes easily and is opaque, about 10 minutes per inch (2.5 cm) of thickness.

Tuna or Salmon Quiche

EDIE GOSSIN

Pastry Shell:

1 cup	all purpose flour	250 mL
1/4 teaspoon	salt	1 mL
1/2 cup	margarine	125 mL
1 tablespoon	vinegar	15 mL

Combine flour, salt and margarine. Work in with fingers. Add vinegar, and work in until mixture holds together. Pat into 9" (1.5 L) pan.

Filling:

1/2 cup	mayonnaise	125 mL
2	eggs, beaten	2
1/2 cup	milk	125 mL
1 · 6.5 ounce can	flaked tuna or red salmon	184 g
1/2 pound	Swiss cheese, diced	227 g
1/3 cup	chopped green onion	75 mL

Preheat oven to 350°F (180°C). Combine mayonnaise, eggs and milk. Mix until well blended. Stir in tuna or salmon, cheese and onion. Pour into pastry shell. Bake for 40 – 45 minutes.

Salmon Blintzes

FRAN KIRSHENBAUM

1	recipe blintzes (page 84)	1
1 · 7.75 ounce can	salmon	220 g
1 tablespoon	lemon juice	15 mL
1 · 10 ounce can	cream of mushroom soup	280 mL
	Parmesan cheese	

Preheat oven to 350°F (180°C). Prepare blintzes, using a pan approximately 9" (22.5 cm). Fry blintz on both sides. Combine salmon, lemon juice and 1 tablespoon (15 mL) of the soup. Divide mixture evenly between blintzes and fold up envelope style. Place blintzes in a lightly greased baking dish. Pour remaining soup over and sprinkle with Parmesan cheese. Bake 15 – 20 minutes until heated through.

Meat

Hints for Cooking Meat

1) If you are running late for dinner and are cooking a roast at a higher temperature than usual, wrap the meat in lettuce leaves. They keep the moisture and heat in, and the meat doesn't dry out.

2) Use a pan that is the correct size for the meat you are roasting. A small piece of meat in a large pan will dry out quickly.

Stuffed Peppers

ZOZO LAFTSIDIS

2	medium onions, chopped	2
4 tablespoons	oil	60 mL
2 pounds	lean minced beef	1 kg
1/4 cup	parsley, chopped	60 mL
1 clove	garlic, pressed	1
1 · 14 ounce can	tomatoes, not drained	398 mL
	salt and pepper to taste	
3/4 cup	raw rice	175 mL
12	long medium size sweet peppers, red or green	12
1 cup	water	250 mL
1 teaspoon	salt	5 mL
	bread crumbs	
1/4 cup	pine nuts (optional)	60 mL

Brown chopped onions lightly in 2 tablespoons (30 mL) of the oil. Brown meat, scrambling with a fork until red is gone. Add parsley, garlic and tomatoes with juice. Mash tomatoes lightly with a fork. Add salt and pepper to taste. Simmer 1/2 hour. Rinse rice under cold water. Add to meat and simmer until the liquid is absorbed - about 15 minutes. Heat oven to 350°F (180°C). Clean, core and seed peppers. Salt insides lightly. Keep tops of peppers. Stuff peppers with filling, and place tops back on. Lay peppers in one layer in baking dish. Add water and salt to pan in which you have browned meat. Stir well, then add to baking pan with peppers. Sprinkle peppers with remaining 2 tablespoons (30 mL) oil. Sprinkle bread crumbs on top. Bake one hour. If desired, pine nuts may be added to mixture before stuffing peppers. Serves 6.

Beef Bourguignon

J U D Y   A S C H

3 tablespoons	salad oil	45 mL
3 pounds	stewing beef (chuck)	1.5 kg
1 cup	chopped onion	250 mL
1 cup	chopped green pepper	250 mL
1 cup	sliced celery	250 mL
1 clove	garlic, finely chopped	1
1 · 8 ounce can	tomato sauce	227 mL
1 1/2 tablespoons	salt	20 mL
1/8 teaspoon	thyme	0.5 mL
2 tablespoons	chopped parsley	30 mL
1 cup	red wine	250 mL
1 tablespoon	beef soup mix	15 mL
1/4 teaspoon	pepper	1 mL
1	bay leaf	1
2 cups	water	500 mL

In a Dutch oven, heat oil. Cut beef into cubes, and brown well in oil on all sides. Remove and set aside. Add onion, green pepper, celery and garlic to pot. Sauté until tender - about 8 minutes. Return beef to pot. Add remaining ingredients. Bring to boil. Reduce heat and simmer, covered, 1 1/4 hours.

Add vegetables:

2	potatoes, cut into pieces	2
4	carrots, cut into halves	4
6	white pearl onions	6

Cook 1 hour longer or until tender. Skim off fat.

Mix:

2 tablespoons	all purpose flour	30 mL
2 tablespoons	water	30 mL

Make a smooth paste. Stir into beef stew. Cook a few minutes until stew is thickened. Cut a **tomato** into 6 wedges. Arrange skin side up on top of stew. Simmer covered 10 minutes. Nice if served from large tureen. Can make and freeze well ahead of time. Serves 6 – 8.

Beef Wellington

1 · 5 pound	fillet of beef	2.5 kg
	salt and pepper	
3 cloves	garlic, crushed	3

Season meat with salt, pepper and garlic and refrigerate overnight.

Pastry:

2 cups	all purpose flour	500 mL
1 cup	soft wheat flour	250 mL
1 1/2 teaspoons	salt	7 mL
1 cup	shortening	250 mL
	at room temperature	
2	eggs	2
2 tablespoons	lemon juice	30 mL
	or	

your favourite frozen puff pastry dough

Coating:

1 pound	paté or chopped liver	500 g
1 cup	chopped mushrooms	250 mL
	sautéed with	
1/2 cup	chopped onions	125 mL
	in	
1 tablespoon	oil	15 mL
	salt and pepper	

Sauce:

1/2 cup	sliced mushrooms	125 mL
2 tablespoons	chopped onions	30 mL
2 tablespoons	all purpose flour	30 mL
3/4 cup	broth	175 mL
1/2 cup	dry red wine	125 mL
	salt	

Early next day, preheat oven to 450°F (230°C). Place fillet on a rack and roast for 50 minutes. Meanwhile, make pastry as follows or use frozen puff pastry dough as directed. Blend together well with a pastry blender, and then with fingertips, the flours, salt and shortening. Mix the eggs and lemon juice together, and then sprinkle over pastry. Mix well and form into a ball. Allow to rest until ready to use.

After roast has cooled completely, mix together: the paté, sautéed mushrooms and onions, salt and pepper, and spread mixture evenly over the entire cold roast.

Roll out pastry (reserve some for decoration). Place roast in center of pastry and bring up sides and ends to seal. Brush with a **beaten egg** after decorating. Set aside on a greased cookie sheet until approximately 1 hour before serving time.

To make wine sauce: Sauté mushrooms in pan drippings, remove and set aside. Add chopped onions to pan and cook until golden. Mix in flour, then gradually add broth and wine. Add salt and mushrooms.

Approximately 1 hour before serving, bake roast at 400°F (200°C) for 20 minutes or until golden brown. Cover lightly with foil and bake an additional 15 minutes. Remove from oven and allow to stand for 15 minutes before serving. Reheat the wine sauce just before serving. The beauty of this recipe is that all the work is done early in the day.

Baked Stuffed Steak

1 1/2 – 2 pounds	shoulder steak,	1 kg
	cut thin and pounded	
1	onion, chopped fine	1
1 tablespoon	oil	15 mL
1 tablespoon	all purpose flour	15 mL
2 tablespoons	Worcestershire sauce	30 mL
2 tablespoons	stock or gravy	30 mL
1 cup	cooked rice	250 mL
1 tablespoon	parsley	15 mL
	salt to taste	
	mushrooms (optional)	

Preheat oven to 325°F (160°C). Brown the onion in the oil. Stir in the flour, Worcestershire sauce and stock, and cook until thick. Stir in rice, parsley and salt. Spread stuffing on the steak, roll, tie or fasten with skewers and bake, covered, for 1 1/2 hours. Mushrooms may be added at bottom of pan. Add a little water if necessary, for gravy. Slice crosswise and serve hot. Serves 4 – 6.

Beef Oven Stew

ADÈLE FREEMAN

2 – 3 pounds	stewing beef	1 – 1.5 kg
1/3 cup	all purpose flour	75 mL
1 teaspoon	salt	5 mL
1/4 teaspoon	pepper	1 mL
3 tablespoons	shortening	45 mL
1	large cooking onion, sliced	1
1 · 10 ounce can	tomato soup	284 mL
1 1/4 cups	water	300 mL
1/2 cup	sliced celery	125 mL
2 tablespoons	finely chopped fresh parsley	30 mL
	or	
2 teaspoons	dried parsley	10 mL
4	medium potatoes	4
6	medium carrots	6
1 cup	drained canned peas	250 mL

Preheat oven to 350°F (180°C). Wipe beef with a damp cloth, and cut into 1" (2.5 cm) cubes. Combine flour, salt and pepper, and dredge meat. In a large skillet, brown meat on all sides in heated shortening. Transfer meat to a large casserole with a close fitting cover. Add onion to skillet, and cook gently until tender. Add tomato soup and water and heat thoroughly. Add the celery and parsley. Pour sauce over meat in casserole. Cover and bake about 1 1/2 hours. Peel potatoes and cut into quarters. Peel carrots and cut into quarters lengthwise. Add potatoes and carrots to meat mixture. Sprinkle lightly with salt and pepper and add a little water if necessary. Combine well. Cover closely and continue to bake until vegetables are tender - about 1 1/2 hours longer. Add the peas and heat for 10 minutes. Serve with crusty rolls. 4 – 5 servings.

Standing Rib Roast with Mustard Crust

MYRTLE COOPERSMITH

Buy best quality first cut ribs, well trimmed. To simplify carving, have your butcher remove the backbone (chine), and tie it back to the ribs. This is called "French Cut".

1 · 9 – 10 pound	rib roast (1st 4 ribs)	4 1/2 kg
2	garlic cloves, crushed	2
2 tablespoons	Dijon mustard	30 mL
1/2 teaspoon	ground black pepper	2 mL
1/2 teaspoon	paprika	2 mL
1 tablespoon	Worcestershire or soy sauce	15 mL

Preheat oven to 325°F (160°C). Combine garlic, mustard, pepper, paprika and Worcestershire or soy sauce, and smear all over roast. Place meat in roasting pan and bake, uncovered, until meat registers desired doneness on a meat thermometer placed into the large end of the meat, not touching bone, or resting in fat.

	Approximate Cooking Time (min. per pound)	Internal Temperature (°F)	Internal Temperature (°C)
Rare	18 - 20	130°F - 140°F	55°C - 60°C
Medium	24 - 26	150°F - 160°F	65.5°C - 70°C
Well Done	30 - 32	170°F - 185°F	76.5°C - 85°C

Cabbage Rolls

ETHEL KLEIN

Remove core from cabbage by placing cabbage in a large pot of boiling water and separating leaves with two forks or place cabbage in freezer just long enough to freeze. When defrosted, the leaves can be separated easily.

Meat:

2 pounds	**ground beef**	**1 kg**
2	**slices of bread**	**2**
1 tablespoon	**raw rice**	**15 mL**
	salt and pepper to taste	

Soak bread in cold water and squeeze most of it out. Mix with meat and seasoning. Add rice and mix well.

Sauce:

1 · 28 ounce can	**tomatoes**	**795 mL**
1 cup	**brown sugar**	**250 mL**
	juice of 1 lemon	
	salt to taste	

Combine sauce ingredients in saucepan and bring to a boil. Place a generous tablespoon of meat mixture onto each cabbage leaf. Roll up, tucking ends in securely. Chop heart of cabbage and place in bottom of a large pot. Arrange cabbage rolls on top. Add 1 cup (250 mL) of boiling water and cook for 30 minutes uncovered. Add sauce and cook another 1 1/2 hours. Can be refrigerated or frozen at this point. To serve, place in single layer in shallow baking pan and bake in 350°F (180°C) oven for 1 hour. Serves 8 as a side dish.

Chili Con Carne

Beans: Soak 2 1/2 cups (625 mL) of raw red kidney beans in cold water, covered, overnight. Next morning, drain, cover with fresh salted water, and boil until tender (approximately 35 – 45 minutes).

6 tablespoons	oil	90 mL
4 cups	finely chopped onions	1 L
4 cloves	garlic, finely minced	4
3 pounds	ground beef	1.5 kg
6 tablespoons	chili powder	90 mL
4 cups	fresh or canned tomatoes (preferably plum)	1 L
4 cups	beef broth	1 L
	pinch oregano	
	cayenne pepper to taste	
	salt to taste	
4 cups	cooked red kidney beans	1 L

Heat oil in large saucepan and cook onions and garlic until onions are wilted. Add meat and cook, breaking it up until it loses its red colour. Add chili powder. Add tomatoes and half of broth. Reserve remaining broth to add as chili cooks. Add seasoning and cook, stirring occasionally, 1 – 2 hours, adding broth as necessary. Add beans. Serves 8 – 10.

Note: If desired, two 19 ounce (540 mL) cans of red kidney beans may be used instead of raw beans. Rinse beans before adding to chili.

Brisket

Brisket is one of the most popular cuts of beef, and there are many variations of recipes. Note that in any of the following recipes, the brisket may be prepared ahead of time, cooled for easy slicing, and sliced across the grain. Reheat the meat in the gravy before serving.

Glazed Corned Beef

L O I S   F R I E D M A N

Purchase a prepared **pre-cooked pickled brisket** which may be available from your butcher or delicatessen, and is ready for glazing or purchase a **raw pickled corned beef**, 5 – 6 pounds (2.5 – 3 kg). Cook as follows: Wash well to get all the spices off. Place in a large pot and cover with water. Add **large onion**, **celery tops** and boil for 3 – 4 hours until tender. When tender, remove from liquid and cool.

Glaze #1

1/2 cup	brown sugar	125 mL
1/2 teaspoon	dry mustard	2 mL
	juice and rind of	
	1 orange and 1 lemon	

Glaze #2

1 cup	orange marmalade	250 mL
4 tablespoons	Dijon mustard	60 mL
4 tablespoons	brown sugar	60 mL

Place cooled corned beef in baking pan. Combine your choice of glaze ingredients, spread over corned beef and bake at 350°F (180°C) for 30 minutes, basting often. When cooled, slice across the grain. Serve at room temperature.

Brisket with Mustard Sauce

ADÈLE FREEMAN

1 · 5 pound	brisket	2.5 kg
4 tablespoons	all purpose flour	60 mL
24 ounces	cola	670 mL
1/2 cup	prepared mustard	125 mL
1/2 cup	ketchup	125 mL
2 teaspoons	soy sauce	10 mL
1/2 teaspoon	finely chopped garlic	2 mL
1 teaspoon	Italian seasoning	5 mL

Preheat oven to 325°F (160°C). Place roast in a baking pan and season with **salt** and **pepper**. Mix together the remaining ingredients to form a smooth sauce. Pour sauce over roast and bake, covered, on middle shelf of oven for 40 minutes per pound. Remove cover and bake an additional 30 minutes or until tender when pierced with a fork. The roast should be basted every half hour. Great for leftovers. Refrigerate leftover meat and sauce separately and combine to reheat.

Brisket #1

MYRTLE COOPERSMITH

1 · 5 pound	brisket	2.25 kg
2	large cooking onions, sliced	2
1/2 cup	brown sugar	125 mL
1/2 cup	ketchup	125 mL
2 teaspoons	dry mustard	10 mL
4 – 5	carrots	4 – 5
4 – 5	celery stalks	4 – 5
1/2 cup	dried apricots	125 mL

Line roasting pan with one sliced onion. Grate **pepper** over onion slices. Place brisket on top, fat side up. Place second sliced onion on top of brisket. Combine brown sugar, ketchup and dry mustard, and pour over top. Sprinkle with additional grated pepper to taste. Place carrots, celery and apricots around sides and cover pan tightly with foil. This can sit overnight refrigerated, or be cooked immediately. Bake in preheated 350°F (180°C) oven 4 hours, basting frequently (every 30 – 45 minutes). Cover tightly in between bastings. **Par boiled potatoes** may be added the last half hour, if desired.

Brisket #2

L O I S F R I E D M A N

1 · 5 – 6 pound	brisket	2.5 – 3 kg
	salt, pepper, seasoned salt	
	and garlic salt to taste	
2	onions, chopped	2
2 tablespoons	oil	30 mL
1/2 · 10 ounce can	tomato soup	150 mL

Heat oven to 375°F (190°C). Season brisket well. Place in shallow pan and roast, uncovered, one hour. In the meantime, sauté onion in oil. Add tomato soup. Remove brisket from oven. Pour off most of the fat that has melted off. Pour tomato soup-onion mixture on top of meat. Cover pan tightly with foil. Lower oven temperature to 325°F (160°C). Return pan to oven and cook an additional 2 – 3 hours depending on size of brisket. Baste often. When meat is done, remove from pan, taste gravy, and if it is too strong, add water. Strain into a bowl.

It is a good idea to make brisket the day before it is to be served. It is easier to slice and to remove fat from gravy. To serve, slice brisket and stand slices up close together in baking dish. Remove fat from gravy and pour gravy on top of meat. Cover and heat in 350°F (180°C) oven just until hot.

Barbecue Sauce for Chili Burgers

A D È L E F R E E M A N

1 · 14 ounce can	kidney beans	398 mL
1/2 cup	canned or chopped	125 mL
	fresh tomatoes	
1 tablespoon	vinegar	15 mL
2 teaspoons	brown sugar	10 mL
1 – 2 teaspoons	chili powder	5 – 10 mL
1/2 teaspoon	dry mustard	2 mL

In a saucepan combine all ingredients. Heat until boiling, stirring occasionally. Spoon over cooked barbecued burgers. Also good for hot dogs. Makes enough for 8 burgers.

Basic Burgers or Meatballs

2 pounds	lean minced meat (veal, beef or a combination of both)	1 kg
1	egg, beaten	1
2 tablespoons	ketchup	30 mL
2 tablespoons	water	30 mL
2 tablespoons	matzo meal or bread crumbs	30 mL
1 teaspoon	Worcestershire sauce	5 mL
	salt and pepper	
	garlic powder	
	onion salt	
	paprika	

Mix very well. Wet hands and form into patties. Fry, broil or barbecue as desired. Yield 8 patties.

Country Hash

CONNIE MONSON KUSSNER

3 tablespoons	oil	45 mL
1/2 cup	chopped onion	125 mL
1 1/2 cups	chopped seeded green pepper	375 mL
1 pound	ground beef	500 g
1/2 cup	rice, uncooked	125 mL
2 cups	cooked or canned tomatoes, not drained	500 mL
1 teaspoon	chili powder	5 mL
1 teaspoon	salt	5 mL
1/4 teaspoon	pepper	1 mL

Heat oil in skillet. Add onion, green pepper and ground beef. Brown well. Add remaining ingredients. Cover tightly. Cook over high heat until steaming freely, then turn heat down and simmer for about 30 minutes. Serves 4.

Easy Meat Loaf

LOIS FRIEDMAN

3 pounds	lean minced beef or a combination of beef and veal and/or chicken	1.5 kg
1 cup	bread crumbs	250 mL
2	eggs, slightly beaten	2
1	medium onion, grated	1
1 1/2 teaspoons	salt	7 mL
1/2 teaspoon	pepper	2 mL
1 · 10 ounce can	tomato juice (or less)	284 mL

Preheat oven to 375°F (190°C). Combine bread crumbs, eggs, onion, salt and pepper. Add meat, and mix lightly. Gradually add enough tomato juice to hold mixture together. Mix lightly, but thoroughly. Shape into a loaf, and place in a shallow rectangular baking dish. Bake for 1 1/2 hours or until well browned. Serves 6.

Sweet and Sour Meatballs #1

ELINORE ASHER

Per pound (500 g) of lean ground meat:

1/2 cup	ketchup	125 mL
1/2 cup	water	125 mL
1	onion, diced	1
1 or 2	bay leaves	1 or 2
1 tablespoon	granulated sugar	15 mL
2 tablespoons	lemon juice	30 mL
	paprika, salt, pinch of ginger	

Season meat to taste. Combine remaining ingredients in a saucepan, and bring to a boil. Shape meat into 1" – 2" (2.5 – 5 cm) balls and drop into sauce. Reduce heat and simmer for one hour.

Sweet and Sour Meatballs #2

PAULINE TOKER

3 pounds	ground meat (chuck, veal and/or chicken)	1.5 g
4 slices	white bread, crusts removed	4
	salt and pepper	
2	medium sized onions	2
1 tablespoon	oil	15 mL
1 tablespoon	brown sugar	15 mL
1 · 28 ounce can	whole tomatoes	795 mL
1 · 14 ounce can	tomato sauce	397 mL
	juice of 1/2 lemon	

Sauce: Dice onions. Add salt and pepper and gently sauté in oil until golden. Add brown sugar stirring until dissolved. Add tomatoes and tomato sauce. Let sauce boil gently, stirring occasionally.

Meat: Soak 4 slices of bread in cold water just to cover. Crumble with hands. Add the soaked bread, salt and pepper to meat, continuing to work with hands until meat is a smooth consistency with no sign of bread in it. Form into balls and drop in boiling sauce. Reduce heat to simmer. Cover pot and cook for 1 1/2 hours. Season at end with lemon juice and more brown sugar to taste. This dish may be made ahead and reheated in casserole in oven. Serve over rice. Freezes well. Defrost before reheating. Serves 6.

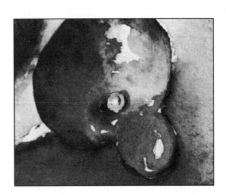

Meat Loaf

EDIE WINBERG

1 1/2 pounds	lean ground beef or combination of beef and veal and/or chicken	750 g
1	egg, beaten	1
1 cup	fresh bread crumbs	250 mL
1	medium onion, chopped	1
1 1/4 teaspoons	salt	6 mL
1/4 teaspoon	pepper	1 mL
1 · 7 ounce can	tomato sauce	200 mL
2 tablespoons	vinegar	30 mL
2 tablespoons	prepared mustard	30 mL
2 tablespoons	brown sugar	30 mL
1 cup	water	250 mL

Preheat oven to 350°F (180°C). Combine meat, egg, bread crumbs, onion, salt, pepper and 1/2 can of tomato sauce. Mix lightly and form into a loaf. Place in a shallow rectangular baking pan and place in oven. Combine the other half can of tomato sauce with vinegar, mustard, brown sugar and water. Baste meat loaf with sauce frequently while the meat loaf cooks. Baking will take about 1 1/2 hours. Serve any sauce that is left on the side. Serves 4 – 6.

Miami Ribs

DOLORES WEINER

3 pounds	Miami ribs (thinly sliced flanken or veal ribs) garlic powder, salt and pepper	1.5 kg
1 · 12 ounce bottle	prepared garlic sauce for spareribs	341 mL
1/2 cup	soy sauce	125 mL
1 tablespoon	molasses	15 mL
1 tablespoon	lemon juice	15 mL
2 tablespoons	honey	30 mL
1 – 2 tablespoons	corn starch, mixed with a little water	15 – 30 mL
1 tablespoon	brown sugar	15 mL

Preheat oven to 350°F (180°C). Season ribs with garlic powder, salt and pepper and bake, covered, for 30 minutes. Pour off fat. Combine remaining ingredients and heat until well blended. Pour over ribs and bake for 30 minutes more. Check with fork for doneness. Serve on **rice**.

Shepherd's Pie

LOIS FRIEDMAN

6 – 8	medium sized potatoes	6 – 8
1	whole egg	1
1	egg white	1
1 tablespoon	all purpose flour	15 mL
1 teaspoon	baking powder	5 mL
3 tablespoons	oil	45 mL
1 cup	chopped onion	250 mL
4 cups	leftover cooked meat, (e.g. brisket)	1 L
1 pound	minced beef or veal	500 g
1/2 cup	gravy, beef broth or consommé	125 mL
1 · 14 ounce can	creamed style corn paprika	398 mL

Boil potatoes until tender. Mash well. While hot, add beaten eggs, flour, baking powder and 1 tablespoon (15 mL) of the oil. Cream well. Sauté onion in remaining 2 tablespoons (30 mL) of oil until golden and transparent. Add cooked meat, cut into cubes. Brown well. Push aside. Add raw minced meat and brown well, scrambling with a fork as it browns. Drain off fat. Let mixture cool slightly and then process in food processor using on-off motion, or put through food grinder. Do not overprocess. Combine meat with gravy, beef broth or consommé. Place mixture on bottom of 2 1/2 quart (2 L) baking dish. Add corn. Spread mashed potatoes on top. Sprinkle with paprika. Bake at 350°F (180°C) for 1 hour. Serves 4 – 6.

Pickled Tongue in Raisin Sauce

PAULINE TOKER

1	pickled tongue	1
1/2 cup	light brown sugar	125 mL
1 teaspoon	dry mustard	5 mL
2 tablespoons	corn starch	30 mL
2 tablespoons	vinegar	30 mL
2 tablespoons	lemon juice	30 mL
1 cup	water	250 mL
1 cup	tomato sauce	250 mL
1/2 cup	raisins	125 mL
2 tablespoons	margarine	30 mL

Cook tongue in boiling water until tender, approximately 2 1/2 – 3 hours. Cool, peel, and slice thin. Mix brown sugar, dry mustard and cornstarch. Slowly stir in vinegar. Add lemon juice, water, tomato sauce, raisins and margarine. Stir over low heat until thickened. Pour over tongue and serve hot.

Tongue in Sweet and Sour Tomato Sauce

ESTELLE ZALDIN

1	pickled tongue	1
1 · 10 ounce can	tomato soup	283 mL
1/3 cup	cider vinegar	75 mL
1/3 cup	brown sugar	75 mL

Cook tongue in boiling water until tender, about 2 1/2 – 3 hours. Cool, peel, and slice. Preheat oven to 325°F (160°C). Combine soup, vinegar and brown sugar in baking dish and heat. Add sliced tongue and bake one hour. Best served reheated the next day.

Pot Roast

ELINORE ASHER

3 – 4 pounds	shoulder steak, sliced	1.5 – 2 kg
2	onions, diced	2
2	green peppers, sliced	2
3	stalks celery, sliced	3
1 · 10 ounce can	sliced mushrooms (reserve liquid for sauce)	284 mL

Place meat on bottom of 9" x 13" (3.5 L) pan. Place vegetables on top. Make the following sauce:

1/2 cup	ketchup	125 mL
1 tablespoon	brown sugar	15 mL
1/4 cup	boiling water	60 mL
	mushroom liquid	

Blend all ingredients together and pour over meat and vegetables. Press vegetables so flavour will penetrate meat. Refrigerate over-night, covered. Cook in 350°F (180°C) oven for 2 1/2 hours, covered. **Potatoes** and **carrots** may be added before cooking.

Spaghetti Sauce

ESTELLE ZALDIN

1 clove	garlic, finely chopped	1
1	small onion, chopped	1
2 tablespoons	olive oil	30 mL
1 teaspoon	sweet basil	5 mL
1 teaspoon	oregano	5 mL
1/2 teaspoon	fennel seed	2 mL
1/2 teaspoon	chili powder	2 mL
1 tablespoon	tomato paste	15 mL
1 · 14 ounce can	stewed tomatoes	398 mL
1 · 14 ounce can	tomato sauce	398 mL

Brown garlic and onion in olive oil. Add rest of ingredients. Bring to a boil. Stir, reduce heat and simmer to blend for 10 minutes. Sauce can be used for pizza, veal scallopini, lasagna, etc.

Meat Sauce Bolognese

2	medium onions, chopped	2
1	large green pepper, seeded and chopped	1
2 tablespoons	olive oil	30 mL
1 pound	minced beef, chicken or veal	500 g
1 · 28 ounce can	tomatoes	795 mL
1 · 5 1/2 ounce can	tomato paste	156 mL
2 tablespoons	parve beef soup mix	30 mL
1 teaspoon	Worcestershire sauce	5 mL
1 teaspoon	mixed herbs, oregano, basil, etc.	5 mL
1 teaspoon	paprika	5 mL
1 teaspoon	chopped parsley	5 mL
8	bay leaves	8
1 teaspoon	garlic powder or	5 mL
1 clove	garlic, freshly minced	1
1/2 teaspoon	chili powder	2 mL
2 tablespoons	ketchup	30 mL
1/2 teaspoon	granulated sugar, (or more to taste)	2 mL

Brown onions and pepper in olive oil. Add meat, stir and cook until lightly browned. Drain fat from meat, add tomatoes and tomato paste. Gradually add remaining ingredients and simmer one to two hours, stirring occasionally. Good for lasagna or spaghetti. Freezes well. Can be tripled.

Tzimmes

ADÈLE FREEMAN

1 · 3 pound	brisket	1.5 kg
2 pounds	carrots, sliced	1 kg
2	sweet potatoes, sliced	2
1	onion, quartered	1
1 teaspoon	salt	5 mL
1/4 teaspoon	pepper	1 mL
1/2 cup	honey	125 mL
1/2 cup	water	125 mL
1 · 14 ounce can	pineapple bits	398 mL

Preheat oven to 350°F (180°C). Season meat lightly and quickly sear on all sides. Transfer meat to a roaster, arrange vegetables around meat and add salt, pepper and honey. Add water, cover and bake for 2 1/2 – 3 hours. Discard onion. Slice brisket carefully and arrange meat and vegetables in an open casserole. Add drained pineapple. Bake uncovered 30 minutes longer or until browned.

Sweet Potato and Prune Tzimmes

THELMA RACHLIN

2 pounds	lean flanken	1 kg
1/2 cup	water	125 mL
1	onion, sliced	1
	salt and pepper	
5	carrots, cut into chunks	5
4	sweet potatoes, peeled and cut into chunks	4
1 cup	prunes (soaked overnight)	250 mL
1 tablespoon	brown sugar	15 mL
1 tablespoon	honey	15 mL
	juice of 1/2 lemon	
3 – 4	white potatoes	3 – 4
1	small onion	1
2 tablespoons	all purpose flour	30 mL
1	egg, slightly beaten	1
1 tablespoon	chicken fat or oil	15 mL

Cook meat in covered pot with water, onion, salt and pepper on top of stove for 1 1/2 hours. Add carrots, quartered sweet potatoes and prunes. Cook until tender. Remove from stove, and cover with a mixture of brown sugar, honey and lemon juice. Preheat oven to 350°F (180°C). Grate white potatoes and onion. Add flour, egg and chicken fat or oil. Pour over whole mixture and bake uncovered 1 hour.

Sweet and Sour Veal

PEARL GREENBAUM

1 1/2 pounds	veal shoulder, 1/2" (1.25 cm) thick, cut into strips	675 g
2	eggs, lightly beaten	2
1/2 teaspoon	salt	2 mL
	fine dry bread crumbs	
2 tablespoons	vegetable shortening	25 mL
1	green pepper, seeded, and cut into strips	1
1/2 cup	water	125 mL
4	slices canned pineapple, drained (reserve syrup)	4
5 tablespoons	pineapple syrup	75 mL
2 teaspoons	juice from sweet mixed pickles	10 mL
1 cup	ketchup	250 mL
1/4 cup	granulated sugar	60 mL
2	large tomatoes, cut into eighths	2

Combine eggs and salt. Dip veal strips first in egg mixture and then in crumbs until well covered. Sauté until browned. Place in covered baking dish and bake for 35 minutes at 350°F (180°C). Boil green pepper strips in water for 3 minutes. Drain. Combine pineapple which you have cut into pieces, peppers, pineapple syrup, pickle juice, ketchup and sugar in a saucepan, and heat well but do not boil. Place cooked meat in serving dish and pour hot sauce over. Garnish with wedges of tomato and serve with hot cooked **rice**. Serves 6.

Veal Stew

NANCY POSLUNS

2 pounds	stewing veal, cut into cubes	1 kg
4 tablespoons	oil	50 mL
12	small white pearl onions	12
1 clove	garlic, crushed	1
1 cup	red or white wine	250 mL
1 · 28 ounce can	tomatoes	795 mL
	salt and pepper to taste	

Brown veal cubes in oil in deep saucepan. Remove meat and set aside. Sauté onions and garlic in same pan. Add wine, tomatoes, salt and pepper. Stir until blended. Return meat to pan. Cover and simmer over low heat 2 hours or until tender. If desired, quartered **potatoes** and **carrots** may be added the last half hour of cooking. Serves 4.

Veal and Beef Stew

PHYLLIS PEPPER

1 1/2 pounds	stewing veal, cut into cubes	700 g
1 1/2 pounds	stewing beef, cut into cubes	700 g
6	carrots, peeled and chopped	6
3	parsnips, chopped	3
2	leeks, chopped	2
1	Spanish onion, chopped	1
1	bay leaf	1
1	bouquet garni	1
	(2 sprigs parsley, marjoram,	
	celery leaf, tied together)	
	salt and freshly ground	
	pepper to taste	
1/2 cup	dry sherry or red wine	125 mL
1 cup	beef broth	250 mL
1 cup	water	250 mL
1 tablespoon	Worcestershire sauce	15 mL
1 tablespoon	oil	15 mL
	(or enough to just cover	
	the bottom of the pan)	

Preheat oven to 300°F (150°C). In a heavy casserole or Dutch oven, heat oil, and brown meat on all sides. Remove meat. Add vegetables to pan, and sauté for 3 minutes. Add the meat and all the other ingredients to the vegetables. Bake, covered, for 3 hours. Discard bouquet garni and bay leaf before serving. Serves 4 – 6.

Escalope of Veal with Herbs

ADÈLE FREEMAN

3 pounds	thinly sliced veal, cut into small pieces	1.5 kg
2 tablespoons	margarine	30 mL
2 tablespoons	vegetable or peanut oil	30 mL
2	medium onions, thinly sliced	2
2	medium green peppers, sliced	2
2 cloves	garlic, minced	2
1/2 pound	mushrooms, thinly sliced	225 g
3/4 cup	finely chopped celery	175 mL
2 · 10 ounce cans	tomato or tomato rice soup	566 mL
1/2 cup	water	125 mL
2 tablespoons	lemon juice	30 mL
	salt and freshly ground pepper to taste	
1/2 teaspoon	dried rosemary	2 mL
2	sprigs parsley	2
1	bay leaf	1
12	small white onions	12
2 teaspoons	finely chopped parsley	10 mL

Heat margarine and oil in heavy skillet and cook meat, a few pieces at a time, until browned. Remove meat and set aside. In same skillet, sauté onions until transparent. Add the green pepper, garlic, mushrooms and celery and cook until tender. Return meat to skillet. Combine soup, water and lemon juice and add to skillet, stirring to blend. Add salt and pepper, rosemary, parsley sprigs, bay leaf and onions. Cover and cook over low heat for 45 minutes or until onions and meat are tender. Stir occasionally. Sprinkle with chopped parsley and serve with **rice** or **noodles**. Serves 4 – 5.

Breaded Veal Chops or Cutlets

6	veal chops or cutlets	6
3	eggs	3
2 cups	seasoned bread crumbs	500 mL
3 tablespoons	oil	45 mL

Preheat oven to 350°F (180°C). Beat eggs. Dip veal in eggs and then in bread crumbs. Brown in oil on both sides. Transfer to baking dish, and bake covered for 1 hour.

Veal or Chicken with Lemon and Vermouth

J.J. WINBERG

2	chickens, cut up	2
	or	
6	veal chops or cutlets	6
3 tablespoons	oil	45 mL
	juice of 2 lemons	
1 teaspoon	salt	5 mL
1/4 teaspoon	fresh ground pepper	1 mL
2 tablespoons	chopped parsley	30 mL
2 tablespoons	chopped chives	30 mL
1 teaspoon	marjoram	5 mL
1 tablespoon	paprika	15 mL
1 cup	chicken stock	250 mL
1/4 cup	white vermouth	60 mL
2 tablespoons	cornstarch	30 mL
	dissolved in	
3 tablespoons	water	45 mL

Preheat oven to 350°F (180°C). Brown meat in oil. Transfer meat to baking dish, and add lemon juice, salt and pepper. Cover dish with foil and bake for 45 minutes. Remove from oven, and sprinkle meat with parsley, chives, marjoram, and paprika. Broil 5 minutes until brown. Keep meat warm. Pour off juices into a small frying pan. Heat and add broth, vermouth, cornstarch-water mixture. Simmer until thick. Pour over meat. Serve with **rice** or **noodles**. Serves 6.

Stuffed Veal Roast

1 · 4 pound	veal shoulder or brisket	2 kg
2 teaspoons	salt	10 mL
1/2 teaspoon	pepper	2 mL
1 teaspoon	paprika	5 mL
2 tablespoons	oil	30 mL
3	onions, sliced	3
1 cup	water or red wine	250 mL
	potatoes	

Ask butcher to make a pocket in your veal roast.

Preheat oven to 325°F (160°C). Stuff roast* and fasten securely with skewers. Make a paste of seasonings and oil and rub over meat. Place onions, roast and liquid in roasting pan. Cover tightly with foil. Bake for 2 3/4 hours. Uncover, add potatoes and roast uncovered 3/4 hour longer, basting meat and potatoes occasionally. Serves 6 – 8.

* See stuffing recipe on page 225.

Veal Shanks à la Milanese (Osso Bucco)

MARJORIE KATES

	flour for dredging	
6 · 6 1/2 ounce	veal shanks	185 g each
1/2 cup	olive oil	125 mL
1	carrot, chopped	1
1	celery stalk, chopped	1
1	onion, chopped	1
1 clove	garlic, pressed	1
1 cup	white wine	250 mL
1 tablespoon	tomato paste	15 mL
2 cups	water, beef or chicken stock	500 mL

Preheat oven to 325°F (160°C). Roll the veal in flour. Sauté veal in foaming oil. Add the carrot, celery, onion and garlic, sautéing until slightly coloured. Add the dry white wine, tomato paste, **salt** and **pepper** and stock. Place in covered casserole, and bake approximately 2 1/2 hours.

Veal Marengo

4 tablespoons	vegetable oil	60 mL
20	small white pearl onions	20
1/2 pound	fresh mushrooms cut in halves	225 g
2 pounds	shoulder of veal, cut into 1" (2.5 cm) cubes	1 kg
	salt and pepper	
2 tablespoons	all purpose flour	30 mL
2 tablespoons	tomato paste	30 mL
1 clove	garlic, minced or chopped fine	1
1 cup	dry white wine	250 mL
1 cup	chicken stock	250 mL
1	bouquet garni (2 sprigs parsley, 1 bay leaf, 1 celery leaf tied together)	
1 teaspoon	thyme	5 mL
1 pint	cherry tomatoes	500 mL
1 tablespoon	fresh parsley, finely chopped	15 mL

Heat oil in heavy casserole or saucepan. Add onions and mushrooms. Sauté until brown. Remove from pan and set aside. Add cubes of veal into oil in pan, a few at a time, browning well on all sides. Transfer browned veal to a plate. After all the veal has been browned, return to pan, season with salt and pepper, then sprinkle flour on top. Combine well. Add tomato paste, garlic, wine, chicken broth, garni and thyme. Stir, bring to a boil, reduce heat and simmer for an hour.*

Return mushrooms and onions to casserole. Cook over low heat for another 30 minutes or until heated through. Add cherry tomatoes and simmer five more minutes. Remove and discard bouquet garni, sprinkle parsley over top and serve.

* Dish can be prepared to this point early in the day.

Veal Shoulder Roast

1 · 3 pound	veal shoulder roast	1.5 kg
	salt and pepper	
	Dijon mustard	
	water	

Sauce:

1/4 cup	margarine	60 mL
2	small onions, finely chopped	2
2 cloves	garlic, finely chopped	2
4 tablespoons	chopped parsley	60 mL
4 tablespoons	seasoned bread crumbs	60 mL
	freshly ground black	
	pepper to taste	
1 tablespoon	Worcestershire sauce	

Preheat oven to 325°F (160°C). Sprinkle meat with salt and pepper and roast uncovered about 25 minutes. Remove meat, and brush surface with paste made of mustard and water. Return to oven, and roast an additional 1 – 1 1/2 hours until tender. Transfer meat to a platter and keep warm. Heat the margarine in a saucepan. Add onions and garlic and sauté until golden, about 1 minute. Stir in parsley, bread crumbs, ground pepper, and Worcestershire sauce. Simmer and pour over sliced meat. Serve at once.

Veal Shoulder Florentine   ELEANOR STEINBERG

1 · 3 1/2 – 4 pound	boned shoulder of veal,	1.5 – 2 kg
	with pocket	
1/3 cup	margarine	75 mL
1/2 cup	chopped onion	125 mL
1 · 10 ounce package	frozen chopped	280 g
	spinach, thawed and drained	
1 cup	cooked rice	250 mL
1 teaspoon	salt	5 mL
1/4 teaspoon	pepper	1 mL
1 teaspoon	dried thyme leaves	5 mL
1	egg, slightly beaten	1

Preheat oven to 325°F (160°C). Wipe veal well with damp paper towel. Melt margarine in medium skillet. Add onion and sauté until golden. Remove from heat. Add spinach, rice, salt, pepper, thyme and egg, stirring until well combined. Spoon stuffing into pocket. Close with skewers or string. Place on rack in shallow baking pan, and bake uncovered for 2 1/2 to 3 hours, or until tender. Remove the skewers or string. Serves 6.

Universal Marinade

JACK KWINTER

1 clove	fresh garlic, pressed or chopped	1
1/2 teaspoon	fresh ground pepper	2 mL
1/2 teaspoon	ground chili pepper	2 mL
1/2 teaspoon	ground coriander	2 mL
1 teaspoon	sugar	5 mL
	juice of 1/2 lemon	
	or	
1/2 cup	vinegar or wine	125 mL
1/4 cup	oil	60 mL

Combine ingredients. Yields enough for approximately 10 steaks or equivalent.

Special flavours for:

Chicken - add 1/2 teaspoon (2 mL) oregano.

Lamb - add 1/2 teaspoon (2 mL) ground mint.

Beef - add 1 teaspoon (5 mL) teriyaki or Worcestershire sauce. Marinate for about an hour before cooking.

Fish - should not be marinated more than 5 minutes as the flavour penetrates the fish very quickly. The longer you leave it in the marinade, the stronger it becomes.

To Start Barbecue:

Gas, Propane or Electric: Always have lid open to light – then close cover and preheat on medium heat for 10 minutes before cooking.

Charcoal or Briquettes: One 5 pound (2.25 kg) bag will last about 1 1/2 hours. One half of a bag will last about 3/4 hour. Stack coal or briquettes into a pyramid. Ignite with liquid starter fluid or electric starter according to directions. Let the coal burn until all the black is gone. (Coals are still stacked and solid, but covered with a white ash.) Spread coals out evenly and you're ready to barbecue.

To Cook:

Beef, Chicken or Lamb: Barbecue 5 minutes with lid open to sear, turning after 3 minutes. For a heavy crust, leave lid open. To retain moisture cook with lid closed. The thicker the meat, the longer the lid should be open. The longer the lid is open, the thicker the crust will be.

Fish: If desired, a basket or aluminum foil can be used directly on grill. Place flesh side down (towards heat) to start, and turn onto skin side to finish. If using foil, it can be opened after turning to let smokey flavour penetrate. Fish cooks very quickly. Internal temperature should not go over 140°F (60°C).

Hamburgers: leave lid open a little longer than for steak in order to char them more.

Hotdogs: (which are fully pre-cooked) should be ready in 3 to 5 minutes, depending on the thickness.

If your barbecue has adjustments, use the middle rack. There should be a 3"– 4" (7.5 – 10 cm) space between the bed of coals and the rack.

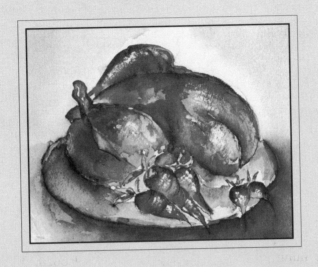

Poultry

Roasting Chart for Poultry

Eviscerated Weight	Oven Temperature	Approximate* Cooking Time
Chicken and Duck:		
Stuffed Bird		
3 – 4 pounds (1.5 – 2 kg)	350°F (180°C)	2 – 3 hours
4 – 5 pounds (2 – 2.3 kg)	350°F (180°C)	2 1/2 – 3 1/2 hours
5 – 6 pounds (2.5 – 2.75 kg)	350°F (180°C)	3 – 3 1/2 hours
Turkey:		
6 – 8 pounds (2.75 – 3.5 kg)	325°F (160°C)	3 – 3 1/2 hours
10 – 15 pounds (4.5 – 7 kg)	325°F (160°C)	4 – 5 hours
16 –18 pounds (7.2 – 8.2 kg)	325°F (160°C)	5 1/4 – 6 hours

* To estimate cooking time for unstuffed bird, deduct 5 minutes per pound (0.5 kg).

Roast until your meat thermometer registers 185°F (85°C) when inserted between the thigh and body of the bird. Be careful that the tip is not in contact with the bone. When thermometer is inserted into breast, temperature should be at 170°F (77°C). Meat should be fork tender, and juices no longer pink when pierced with a fork. On removal from oven cover loosely with foil and let stand 10 – 15 minutes before carving.

To clean, scald inside and outside of bird with boiling water. Scrape skin, wash thoroughly with cold water.

Stuff bird just before roasting.

Roast Chicken

YONA PATTENICK

1 · 6 pound	capon	2.5 kg
2	large onions, coarsely chopped	2
1 teaspoon	celery salt	5 mL
1 teaspoon	onion powder	5 mL
1 teaspoon	garlic salt	5 mL
1 – 2 teaspoons	paprika	5 – 10 mL
1/4 cup	water	60 mL

Place onions in bottom of roasting pan with cover (one not much larger than the chicken). Season the cleaned, dried chicken all over with the spices. Place chicken over the onions. Pour water into bottom of roaster around chicken and cover. Roast at 350°F (180°C) for 2 hours, basting occasionally and adding a small amount of water to pan, if necessary. After the 2 hours uncover and cook 10 – 15 minutes more to brown.

Baked Chicken

LOIS FRIEDMAN

2	chickens, cut into eighths	2
3/4 cup	oil	175 mL
1 large clove	garlic	1
1 cup	bread crumbs, seasoned	250 mL
3 tablespoons	sesame seeds	45 mL

Season bread crumbs with salt, pepper and paprika to taste. Add sesame seeds and set aside. Crush garlic into oil and heat until garlic starts to sizzle. Remove from heat. Line pan with foil. Dip chicken in oil and then in crumbs. Place on pan skin side up. Bake in 375°F (190°C) oven for 1 hour.

Almond Chicken with Ginger and Snow Peas

2	whole chicken breasts, skinned, boned, and sliced into thin strips	2
2 tablespoons	oil	30 mL
1 cup	celery, diagonally sliced	250 mL
1 clove	garlic, minced	1
2 tablespoons	instant chicken broth powder dissolved in	30 mL
1 1/2 cups	boiling water	375 mL
1 tablespoon	soy sauce	15 mL
1 tablespoon	finely chopped ginger	15 mL
1/2 pound	snow peas	225 g
2 tablespoons	cornstarch	30 mL
1/4 cup	toasted slivered almonds	60 mL
3 cups	hot cooked rice	750 mL

Heat oil in a large skillet. Add chicken and sauté for 5 minutes, stirring. Stir in celery and garlic and sauté until chicken is tender, about 3 – 4 minutes. Add broth, soy sauce and ginger. Bring to light boil. Add snow peas and simmer 5 minutes. Make a paste with cornstarch and a little cold water. Pour into chicken mixture and stir until it thickens. Place in serving dish and top with toasted almonds. Serve with rice. Serves 6.

Baked Chicken Italian

ADÈLE FREEMAN

3 1/2 pound	chicken, cut into eighths	1.5 kg
8 ounces	Italian salad dressing, regular or diet	227 mL
1 cup	bread crumbs	250 mL
2 cloves	garlic, finely chopped	2
1/3 cup	parsley, chopped	75 mL

Preheat oven to 350°F (180°C). Line a baking sheet completely with foil. Marinate chicken for at least one hour in salad dressing. Combine bread crumbs with garlic and parsley. Dip chicken pieces in crumbs to coat all over. Place chicken on foil lined pan. Bake for 1 1/2 hours, or until tender. Serves 4.

Baked Chicken in Honey Curry Sauce

ADÈLE FREEMAN

2	squabs quartered	2
	or	
1	broiler cut into eighths	1
1/3 cup	margarine	75 mL
1/2 cup	honey	125 mL
1/4 cup	prepared mustard	60 mL
4 teaspoons	curry powder (or to taste)	20 mL

Melt margarine in large roasting pan. Stir in honey, mustard, curry powder, and mix well. Remove from heat. Add chicken pieces, skin side down. Bake uncovered at 375°F (190°C) for 25 minutes, basting often with sauce. Turn chicken, baste and bake 15 minutes longer or until golden. Serve hot with sauce, or cold. Cool chicken on rack. Serves 4. When doubling recipe, adjust curry.

Barbecued Chicken Wings

LOIS FRIEDMAN

4 pounds	chicken wings	2 kg
1	onion, chopped	1
2 tablespoons	oil	30 mL
1 cup	ketchup	250 mL
2 tablespoons	vinegar	30 mL
2 tablespoons	brown sugar	30 mL
1/4 cup	lemon juice	60 mL
3 tablespoons	Worcestershire sauce	45 mL
1/2 tablespoon	prepared mustard	10 mL
1 cup	water	250 mL
1/2 cup	chopped celery	125 mL
1/2 teaspoon	salt	2 mL
1/8 teaspoon	cayenne	0.5 mL

Brown chicken wings in hot fat or under hot broiler. Sauté onion in oil. Add remaining ingredients and simmer for 30 minutes. Pour over chicken and bake in 325°F (160°C) oven for 1 hour. Serves 6. Can also be done with cut up chickens.

Barbecued Chicken Breasts

Marinate boneless, skinless chicken breasts in the following marinade for one hour.

1/3 cup	white wine or lemon juice	75 mL
1/3 cup	vinegar	75 mL
1/3 cup	olive oil	75 mL
2	shallots or green onions, chopped	2
2 teaspoons	fresh basil, chopped fine	10 mL
1/2 teaspoon	freshly grated pepper	2 mL

Remove chicken from marinade. Cook over hot coals 7 minutes per side.

Chicken on Rice
LOIS FRIEDMAN

2	chickens cut into quarters	2
	seasoned flour	
2 tablespoons	oil	30 mL
1 cup	raw rice, washed	250 mL
1/2 cup	chopped onion	125 mL
1/2 cup	chopped green pepper	125 mL
1/2 cup	sliced mushrooms	125 mL
3 cups	chicken broth	750 mL

Preheat oven to 400°F (200°C). Season flour with salt, pepper and garlic powder. Cut chicken in pieces, dust with seasoned flour and brown in oil. Set aside. Sauté onions, green pepper and mushrooms for five minutes. Mix with raw rice and place in baking dish large enough to hold chicken in a single layer. Pour chicken broth over and bake for 20 minutes. Arrange chicken pieces on top and bake an additional 45 – 50 minutes. Serves 6.

Broiled Chicken

LOIS FRIEDMAN

2	chickens cut into quarters	2
1	medium onion, chopped	1
2 tablespoons	margarine	30 mL
2 tablespoons	oil	30 mL
	seasoned salt to taste	

Place onion, margarine and oil in pan large enough to hold chicken in a single layer. Place under broiler until onions become glazed and start to sizzle. Remove from oven. Roll chicken around in pan to coat with oil and place it skin side down. Season with seasoned salt and broil on first side for 20 minutes, basting several times. Turn, sprinkle with more seasoned salt and broil 20 minutes more, again basting frequently. Watch carefully to make sure the skin does not burn.

Grilled Chicken Burgers

1 1/2 – 2 pounds	lean ground chicken	750 g – 1 kg
3 tablespoons	grainy style Dijon mustard	45 mL
3 tablespoons	minced green onions, white parts only	45 mL
1 tablespoon	sodium-reduced soy sauce	15 mL
2 teaspoons	Worcestershire sauce	10 mL
	salt and pepper to taste	

Combine chicken with mustard, scallions, and seasonings, mixing with your hands until well blended. Chill until mixture is easy to handle, about 10 – 15 minutes. Form into 4 – 6 patties. Preheat barbecue. Grill patties for 5 – 10 minutes, turning once, until cooked through but not overdone. To Broil: Preheat broiler. Broil 4" (10 cm) from heat for 5 – 10 minutes, turning once, until cooked through, but not overdone. For firmer patties add 2 – 3 tablespoons (30 – 45 mL) **whole grain bread crumbs** to mixture.

Note: Ground veal or ground turkey can be used if desired.

Chicken Breasts with Wild Rice

LOIS FRIEDMAN

6	whole chicken breasts, skinned and boned	6
2 tablespoons	margarine	30 mL
3/4 cup	wild rice	175 mL
1	onion, chopped	1
1	stalk celery, chopped	1
	margarine	
	salt and pepper	
	paprika	

Cook rice according to directions on package. Sauté onion and celery in margarine until golden. Add to cooked rice and season with salt and pepper to taste. Sprinkle chicken breasts inside and out with salt and pepper. Stuff with wild rice and sew together. Rub chicken with softened margarine, season with salt, pepper and paprika and bake in 400°F (200°C) oven for 1 hour, basting frequently with pan juices. Remove from oven.

Sauce:

1	medium onion, chopped	1
2 teaspoons	thyme	10 mL
1	bay leaf	1
1 cup	port wine	250 mL
2	chicken boullion cubes	2
1/3 cup	boiling water	75 mL
1 tablespoon	cornstarch	15 mL
2 teaspoons	granulated sugar	10 mL

Take 2 tablespoons (30 mL) of the pan drippings and place in frying pan. Add chopped onion and sauté for 5 minutes. Add remaining ingredients except cornstarch. Dissolve cornstarch in small amount of water and add. Boil until thick and clear, about 5 minutes. Place a teaspoon (5 mL) of sauce over each chicken breast and return roasting pan to oven for chickens to heat and glaze. Remove chicken to serving platter. Strain remaining sauce into a gravy boat and serve on the side.

Company Chicken Breasts

JUNE FILLER

8 single	boneless and skinless breasts cut into bite size pieces	8
6 tablespoons	margarine seasoned flour for coating	90 mL

Sauce:

3/4 cup	dry cooking sherry	175 mL
3 tablespoons	soy sauce	45 mL
3 tablespoons	lemon juice	45 mL
1/2 teaspoon	powdered ginger	2 mL
1 cup	water	250 mL
3/4 pound	sliced mushrooms, sautéed	325 g

Place the above sauce ingredients, except mushrooms, in a sauce pan. Bring to a boil and set aside.

Preheat oven to 325°F (160°C). Coat chicken in flour with seasonings of your choice. Sauté in margarine until brown. Place chicken in a casserole, and top with sauce which has been boiled. Add mushrooms. Pour over chicken. Bake about 1 hour and 20 minutes. Serve with your favorite rice pilaf.

Note: If serving with rice pilaf, substitute half the amount of water required with orange juice for a delicious flavour. Serves 8.

Sticky Chicken

JENNY KLOTZ & HONEY ROTENBERG

1	broiler, cut into eighths	1
2 tablespoons	brown sugar	30 mL
2 tablespoons	soy sauce	30 mL
2 tablespoons	liquid honey	30 mL

Preheat oven to 375°F (190°C). Sprinkle chicken with **garlic powder**, **ground ginger** and **salt**. Sprinkle brown sugar over each chicken piece. Drizzle soy sauce over. Bake for 45 minutes. Drizzle honey over each piece and cook an additional 15 minutes, or until browned. Chicken wings may be substituted for cut up chicken. Serves 4.

Chicken Cacciatore

JUDY ASCH

2	small broilers, cut into pieces	2
	salt, pepper, paprika	
	all purpose flour	
2 tablespoons	oil	30 mL
1 · 28 ounce can	stewed tomatoes, not drained	795 mL
1	green pepper, chopped fine	1
2 tablespoons	pimento, chopped fine	30 mL
1 clove	garlic, minced	1
1/2 teaspoon	marjoram	2 mL
1/4 teaspoon	thyme	1 mL
1/2 cup	white wine	125 mL
2 – 3 bunches	green onions or shallots, chopped	2 – 3
1/2 pound	fresh mushrooms, sliced	225 g

Season chicken with salt, pepper and paprika to taste. Coat well with flour. Brown well in oil in frying pan. Put chicken in large pot with tomatoes, green pepper, pimento and seasonings. Add wine. Simmer slowly about 1 hour. Twenty minutes before serving, add onions or shallots and mushrooms which have been sautéed. Can be made day before and reheated. Serves 6 – 8.

Chicken with Currant Jelly

SHEILA LOFTUS

6	whole chicken breasts,	6
	cut into halves	
1 · 12 ounce jar	currant jelly	340 mL
1/2 cup	water	125 mL
	salt and pepper	
1 tablespoon	cornstarch	15 mL
2 teaspoons	allspice	10 mL
1 tablespoon	Worcestershire sauce	15 mL
2 tablespoons	lemon juice	30 mL

Preheat oven to 450°F (230°C). Place chicken breasts in open roaster. Slowly stir some of the water into the cornstarch to make a paste. Combine remaining ingredients in a saucepan and bring to a boil. Add cornstarch mixture and cook, stirring until clear. Pour over chicken. Bake for 15 minutes. Lower oven temperature to 375°F (190°C) and continue to bake for 45 – 60 minutes, basting frequently.

Chicken Chow Mein

ADÈLE FREEMAN

2 tablespoons	cornstarch	30 mL
1/4 cup	water	60 mL
3 tablespoons	oil	45 mL
1	medium onion, diced	1
1	green pepper, cut into strips	1
1/2 pound	fresh mushrooms, sliced	225 g
3	stalks celery, sliced diagonally	3
3 tablespoons	soy sauce	45 mL
2 teaspoons	granulated sugar	10 mL
1 cup	chicken broth	250 mL
2 cups	bean sprouts, washed and drained	500 mL
1 · 4 ounce can	water chestnuts, sliced	113 mL
2 cups	diced cooked chicken	500 mL

Dissolve cornstarch in water and let stand. Heat oil and sauté onion, green pepper, mushrooms and celery for 2 minutes. Add soy sauce and sugar. Mix well. Add broth and bring to a boil. Add bean sprouts, water chestnuts and chicken. Add cornstarch mixture, cover and simmer for 10 minutes. Serve over **dry noodles** or **boiled white rice**. Serves 4.

Creole Chicken Gumbo

HALLE COHEN

Stock:

3 1/2 – 4 pounds	chicken pieces	1.5 – 2 kg
3 quarts	water	3 L
2	stalks celery with leaves	2
1	carrot, cut into thirds	1
1	medium onion, quartered	1
1 teaspoon	salt	5 mL
1	bay leaf	1

In a stock pot place chicken, water, celery, carrot, onion, bay leaf and salt. Bring to a boil and cook over medium heat for 30 minutes, skimming foam and fat. Remove chicken from broth and bone. Set meat aside and return bones to broth. Simmer 1 – 1 1/2 hours.

Gumbo:

2 – 3 tablespoons	oil	30 – 45 mL
1 – 1 1/4 pounds	okra, washed and cut into 1/4" (0.6 cm) pieces	500 – 750 g
1 cup	chopped onion	250 mL
3/4 cup	chopped celery	175 mL
1/2 cup	chopped green pepper	125 mL
2 cloves	garlic, pressed	2
1 · 19 ounce can	whole tomatoes with juice	540 mL
1 · 10 ounce can	tomato soup	284 mL
1 small package	frozen white corn	1
1 – 2 teaspoons	Worcestershire sauce	5 – 10 mL
	black pepper	
	cayenne pepper	
	Tabasco sauce	
3 – 4 cups	steamed rice	750 mL – 1 L

In a large 4 quart (4 L) pot, heat oil. Add okra, onions, celery and green pepper. Cook over medium heat, stirring until okra is no longer stringy. Add garlic, tomatoes with juice, tomato soup and corn. Cook slowly, until tomatoes are almost puréed. Add chicken and strained stock into gumbo. Simmer 1 – 1 1/2 hours, stirring as often as necessary to prevent sticking. Taste after cooking and season to taste with Worcestershire sauce, salt, pepper, cayenne and Tabasco sauce. Serve over steamed rice. Freezes well. Serves 6 – 8.

Chicken Crepes

This dish can be used as an appetizer, or as a buffet dish.

Crepes:

2	eggs	2
1/2 cup	all purpose flour	125 mL
1/2 teaspoon	granulated sugar	2 mL
1 cup	liquid (may be tomato juice, chicken soup, consommé, etc.)	250 mL
1 tablespoon	chopped parsley (optional)	15 mL

Beat eggs slightly. Add flour and sugar and beat until well mixed. Add liquid gradually, beating after each addition. Let stand at least one hour at room temperature. Grease a small pan (teflon is best). Heat until bubbling, and pour about 1 1/2 tablespoons (25 mL) of batter into the pan, swirling it around so that the batter covers the pan. Cook on one side about a minute until brown. Turn crepe over and cook on other side about half a minute. Yield: 16 – 20 five inch (12.5 cm) crepes.

Filling:

2 1/2 cups	cooked chicken or turkey	625 mL
2 tablespoons	oil	30 mL
1 large	onion, chopped	1
	fresh mushrooms, celery, green pepper, washed and chopped	
4 small cans	parve mushroom gravy	4
	chopped parsley to garnish (optional)	

Preheat oven to 375°F (190°C). Cut the chicken or turkey into bite size pieces. Heat oil in a large skillet, and sauté onion until clear. Add vegetables and cook about 5 minutes. Add chicken and stir to combine all flavours and juices. Add enough mushroom gravy to bind ingredients together, and heat over low heat. Put a spoonful or two of filling down center of each crepe. Roll and turn seam side down, and place in a lightly greased baking dish. Pour the remaining mushroom gravy over the filled crepes. Bake for 15 minutes. Sprinkle with chopped parsley if desired.

Chicken Delight

ELEANOR STEINBERG

2	broilers, cut into eighths	2
	or	
4	whole breasts, cut in half	4
1/2 cup	seasoned flour	125 mL
3 – 4 tablespoons	oil	45 – 60 mL
1 clove	garlic, pressed	1
2	medium Spanish onions, sliced	2
1/4 cup	chopped parsley	60 mL
1/2 pound	mushrooms, sliced	225 g
2	green peppers, coarsely chopped	2
1 · 19 ounce can	tomatoes	540 mL
1/2 teaspoon	salt	2 mL
1/4 teaspoon	curry powder	1 mL
1/4 teaspoon	thyme	1 mL
1/2 cup	dried currants	125 mL
1/4 cup	white wine	50 mL

Preheat oven to 350ºF (180ºC). Shake chicken in flour in a paper bag. Brown in oil and remove to a large pan for baking. In same frying pan, add garlic, onions, parsley, mushrooms and green pepper. Sauté until limp, 5 – 8 minutes. Add tomatoes with juice, spices and currants. Add wine. Blend and cook 5 minutes. Pour over chicken and bake uncovered for one hour.

Delicious Chicken

MOLLY TITLE

2	chickens cut into eighths	2
	pepper and garlic powder	
1 envelope	onion soup mix	1
1 · 8 ounce jar	apricot jam	225 mL
1 · 8 ounce bottle	thick Russian dressing	225 mL

Season chicken with pepper and garlic and place in a baking pan. Combine soup mix, jam and dressing together to make a sauce. Pour sauce over chicken and marinate overnight. Bake uncovered, basting from time to time for 1 – 1 1/2 hours at 350ºF (180ºC). For a zesty variation, add 1 teaspoon (5 mL) freshly chopped **ginger**.

Potato Crusted Chicken

EDIE GOSSIN

1	large potato, peeled	1
3 - 4 tablespoons	Dijon mustard	45 - 60 mL
1 - 2 cloves	garlic, crushed	1 - 2
2	whole chicken breasts, skinned and halved	2
1 - 2 teaspoons	olive oil	5 - 10 mL
	freshly grated black pepper	
	parsley and rosemary	

Preheat oven to 425°F (210°C). Grate potatoes by hand or in processor. Transfer to a bowl of ice water and let stand 10 minutes. Combine mustard and garlic and mix well. Rinse chicken and pat dry. Brush mustard mixture on meaty side of chicken. Drain potato and dry well. A salad spinner does an excellent job of spinning the potatoes dry. Toss with olive oil. Top each piece of chicken with 1/4 of the potato mixture, spreading evenly to form a skin. Sprinkle with pepper and herbs. Bake 40 minutes. Place under broiler for about 5 minutes to brown. Watch carefully. Serves 4.

Easy Chicken and Pineapple

LORETTA ROSNICK

This is not as sweet as it sounds!

3	chickens, cut into eighths	3
	salt, pepper, garlic salt to taste	
2 cups	corn syrup	500 mL
1 cup	ketchup	250 mL
1 · 14 ounce can	pineapple chunks, partially drained	398 mL
2 teaspoons	lemon juice	10 mL

Preheat oven to 350°F (180°C). Season chicken lightly with salt, pepper and garlic salt. Place in a shallow baking dish. Combine corn syrup, ketchup, pineapple and lemon juice. Pour over chicken pieces. Bake 1 1/2 hours, uncovered, basting occasionally. Sauce is a light sweet and sour sauce, and any leftover sauce can be used with meatballs.

Chicken Jubilee

ROZ HALBERT

4	broilers, cut into eighths	4
	salt, pepper, garlic salt,	
	paprika to taste	
1/4 pound	parve margarine	125 mL

Night before or early in the day: Season chicken well. Cover and refrigerate. Place chicken in deep broiler pan, skin side up. Pour melted parve margarine over chicken and broil until browned. Flavour improves as it stands.

Sauce:

1 cup	water	250 mL
3/4 cup	raisins	175 mL
3/4 cup	brown sugar	175 mL
1 1/2 teaspoons	garlic salt	7 mL
1/2 teaspoon	pepper	2 mL
1 · 12 ounce bottle	chili sauce	340 mL
1 tablespoon	Worcestershire sauce	15 mL

Preheat oven to 325°F (160°C). Combine ingredients. Pour over chicken. Cover with heavy foil. Bake 45 minutes.** Twenty minutes before serving,

Combine:

1 · 14 ounce can	pitted cherries, drained,	398 mL
	dark (if available) or red	
3/4 cup	dry sherry	175 mL

Remove foil from chicken. Pour cherry-sherry mixture over chicken. Bake at 325°F (160°C) for 15 – 20 minutes, basting once or twice. Serves 8.

** At this point chicken may be refrigerated or frozen. Defrost and heat slightly before proceeding with cherry-sherry mixture.

Chicken with Rice
Spanish Style

ADÈLE FREEMAN

Your whole meal in one pot!

2	broilers, cut into eighths	2
	salt, pepper, paprika to taste	
2 cups	raw rice	500 mL
1/2 pound	mushrooms, sliced	225 g
	or	
1 · 14 ounce can	mushrooms, well drained	398 mL
1	large onion, chopped	1
1 large clove	garlic, finely chopped	1
2 tablespoons	olive oil	30 mL
1	green pepper, chopped	1
2 cups	water	500 mL
1 · 28 ounce can	tomatoes	795 mL
2 teaspoons	chicken soup mix	10 mL
1/4 teaspoon	saffron	1 mL
1	bay leaf	1
1/2 teaspoon	oregano	2 mL
2 cups	raw rice	500 mL
1 · 14 ounce can	artichoke hearts, well drained	398 mL
1 small jar	pimento, well drained and cut into strips	1

Preheat oven to 350°F (180°C). Place rice in bottom of a large baking dish which has a lid. Season chicken pieces with salt, pepper and paprika, and arrange on top of rice. Cover with sliced mushrooms. Sauté onion and garlic in oil until tender, but not browned. Add green pepper and continue to sauté a few minutes. Add the water, the tomatoes, soup mix and seasonings. Bring to a boil, and pour over chicken. Cover closely. Bake for 45 – 50 minutes. Add the artichoke hearts and pimento and bake, covered, 10 minutes more. To reduce baking time: brown seasoned chicken pieces in olive oil before placing on rice. Bake for half the time. Serves 6 – 8.

Chicken Pie

BERNICE ZWI

3 cups	cooked chicken	750 mL
	(leftovers of any type will do)	
4 tablespoons	oil	60 mL
1	onion, finely chopped	1
2 pounds	mushrooms, finely chopped	1 kg
2 tablespoons	green pepper, chopped	30 mL
2 tablespoons	all purpose flour	30 mL
2 cups	chicken stock	500 mL
1 tablespoon	lemon juice	15 mL
1 teaspoon	Worcestershire sauce	5 mL
	salt and pepper	
	puff pastry	
	egg yolk	

Preheat oven to 375°F (190°C). Heat oil. Add onion, mushrooms and green pepper, and sauté until limp. Add flour, and stir until smooth. Gradually add chicken stock, lemon juice, Worcestershire sauce, and seasoning to taste. Add cut up chicken, taste again, and allow to cool. Thinly roll out puff pastry. Spread pastry into greased 9" (22.5 cm) pie plate, to cover bottom and sides. Fill with chicken mixture. Add pastry to top of pie plate and seal. Brush with beaten egg yolk. Bake for 1 hour. Serves 6.

Orange Baked Chicken

ADÈLE FREEMAN

2	broilers, cut into eighths	2
1	egg, beaten	1
1 cup	corn flake crumbs	250 mL
1/4 teaspoon	paprika	1 mL
1/4 teaspoon	pepper	1 mL
4 tablespoons	orange juice	60 mL
1 teaspoon	curry powder	5 mL
1/4 cup	granulated sugar	60 mL
1/2 teaspoon	salt	2 mL

Preheat oven to 400°F (200°C). Dip chicken pieces first in beaten egg, then in crumbs. Place in a large foil-lined pan in a single layer, skin side down. (If desired, this can be done early in the day. Refrigerate until cooking time, then proceed with recipe). Bake uncovered for 30 minutes. Turn chicken pieces over. Combine remaining ingredients and pour over chicken. Continue baking for 30 minutes, or until tender, basting several times. Serves 4. When multiplying recipe, adjust sugar and seasonings according to taste.

Chicken and Peaches — SHIRLEY LAZARUS

4	broilers, cut into quarters	4
	oil, salt, pepper and paprika	
2	onions, cut into eighths	
2	green peppers, seeded and	2
	cut into slivers	
2 tablespoons	cornstarch	30 mL
2 cups	peach juice	500 mL
2 tablespoons	soy sauce	30 mL
4 tablespoons	vinegar	60 mL
1 teaspoon	granulated sugar	5 mL
2 teaspoons	instant chicken soup powder	10 mL
2 · 19 ounce cans	sliced peaches	1080 mL
	or	
4 - 6	fresh peaches, sliced	4 - 6

Preheat oven to 350°F (180°C). Brush chicken pieces lightly with oil and season with salt, pepper and paprika. Bake 1 hour, covered. Add onions and green peppers and bake another 15 minutes.

Sauce: Add cornstarch to peach juice and blend well. Add soy sauce, vinegar, sugar and soup powder, and cook, stirring until thick and clear. Add sliced peaches to sauce and pour over chicken. Bake another 15 minutes uncovered. If you like it extra brown, place under the broiler for a few moments.

Note: If using fresh peaches, use bottled peach juice.

Coq Au Vin

1 · 5 pound	roasting chicken, cut into eighths	2.4 kg
	flour for dredging	
1/2 cup	oil	125 mL
10	small whole white onions, peeled	10
1 clove	garlic, finely chopped	1
1/4 teaspoon	thyme	1 mL
1 sprig	parsley	1
1	bay leaf	1
12	whole mushrooms	12
	salt and freshly ground pepper to taste	
1/4 cup	warmed cognac	60 mL
1 cup	dry red wine	250 mL

Preheat oven to 325°F (160°C). Dredge chicken with flour. In a skillet, heat oil, add chicken and brown on all sides. Transfer chicken to casserole. Add onions, garlic, thyme, parsley, bay leaf, mushrooms, salt and pepper. Pour in cognac and ignite. When flame dies, add wine. Cover and bake until tender, about 2 1/2 hours. Serves 4 – 6.

Chicken Teriyaki

RENEE WOLFSON

2	broilers, quartered	2
1 · 8 ounce jar	orange marmalade	225 mL

Marinade:

1/2 cup	soy sauce	125 mL
1/4 cup	oil	60 mL
2 tablespoons	granulated sugar	30 mL
2 tablespoons	white wine vinegar	30 mL
1 clove	garlic, minced	1
1 tablespoon	chopped fresh ginger	15 mL

Combine ingredients for marinade. Marinate chicken pieces for 4 hours or longer, turning frequently. Place in large shallow pan and bake at 325°F (160°C) for 1 1/2 hours. Baste every 15 minutes with marinade. Spread orange marmalade over chicken after chicken has been in oven for 1/2 hour. Bake uncovered.

Stuffing For Veal or Chicken SANDY GOTTFRIED

2	large baking potatoes	2
1	large cooking onion	1
1/3 cup	fine kasha (uncooked)	75 mL
4 tablespoons	chicken fat (rendered)	60 mL
	or	
4 tablespoons	oil	60 mL
	salt and pepper to taste	

Grate potatoes and onion finely. Add kasha and fat or oil. Season to taste. Sufficient for a 6 bone veal brisket or an 8 – 9 pound (4 kg) capon.

Wild Rice Stuffing

1 cup	wild rice	250 mL
1/2 cup	celery, diced	125 mL
1/2 cup	canned water chestnuts, drained and sliced	125 mL
1/2 cup	mushrooms, sliced	125 mL
4 tablespoons	oil	60 mL
1 tablespoon	soy sauce	15 mL
	salt and pepper to taste	

Prepare rice according to directions on package. Add remaining ingredients and combine well. This makes 4 cups (1000 mL) of stuffing.

Rendered Chicken Fat

To render chicken fat, cut the chunks of fat that you remove from the tail end of chickens into little pieces. Include pieces of the skin. Make a bed of cut up onion in a frying pan. Add pieces of fat and skin and a drop of water to keep the pan from burning. Cover and cook over low heat until skins are brown and crisp. Strain fat into heatproof glass jar. Cool and refrigerate.

Roast Turkey

Preheat oven to 325°F (160°C). Place bird breast side down on heavy duty foil, large enough to make a tent. Brush bird with **oil, juice of 1/2 lemon**, crushed **fresh ginger**, crushed **fresh garlic** and season well with **salt, pepper, paprika** and **dry mustard**. Close foil. Roast, basting often. Add **1 · 12 ounce (355 mL) can of frozen orange juice** when half cooked. Uncover for last half hour. Turn bird over and allow breast to brown. See chart on page 206 for time.

Honey Lemon (or Orange) Glaze for Turkey

2/3 cup	liquid honey	175 mL
1/4 cup	lemon or orange juice	60 mL
1/2 cup	water	125 mL
1 1/2 tablespoons	cornstarch	20 mL

Combine honey and lemon juice in a saucepan and bring to a boil. Add water to cornstarch to make a smooth paste. Gradually add to honey, stirring constantly. Cook until glaze thickens and becomes clear. Spoon over roasted turkey to glaze surface.

Turkey Meat Loaves

1	onion, chopped	1
1 clove	garlic, minced	1
2 tablespoons	olive oil	30 mL
2	tomatoes, peeled, seeded and chopped	2
1/2 teaspoon	dried oregano, crumbled	2 mL
1/2 teaspoon	dried basil, crumbled	2 mL
1/4 cup	dry red wine	60 mL
1	large green pepper, seeded and chopped	1
1	zucchini, scrubbed, trimmed and chopped	1
1 cup	fresh parsley leaves	250 mL
6	fresh basil leaves, chopped	6
2 pounds	ground turkey	900 g
1 1/2 cups	fresh bread crumbs	375 mL
1 teaspoon	white pepper	5 mL
1	large whole egg, beaten lightly	1
2	large egg whites, beaten lightly	2
	salt to taste	

Preheat oven to 350°F (180°C). In a saucepan, cook half the onion and the garlic in the oil over moderately low heat, stirring until the onion is softened. Add the tomatoes, oregano, dried basil and the wine. Simmer uncovered, stirring occasionally, for 15 minutes. In a food processor, finely chop the remaining onion with the green pepper and zucchini. Transfer to a large bowl and combine the chopped vegetables with the tomato sauce, the parsley, basil, turkey, bread crumbs, white pepper, egg, egg whites and salt to taste. Divide the mixture between 2 loaf pans, each 8 1/2" x 4 1/2" x 2 1/2" (1.5 L), and bake for 1 hour and 15 minutes. Serves 10 – 12.

Turkey Cantonese

2 cups or more	diced, cooked turkey	500 mL
1 cup	celery, sliced diagonally	250 mL
1 cup	carrots, peeled, thinly sliced	250 mL
1	medium onion, chopped	1
1/4 cup	slivered almonds	60 mL
1/4 cup	margarine	60 mL
3/4 cup	canned pineapple chunks	175 mL
1/4 teaspoon	salt	2 mL
1 tablespoon	cornstarch	15 mL
1/4 teaspoon	ginger	1 mL
1/8 teaspoon	nutmeg	0.5 mL
1 tablespoon	soy sauce	15 mL
1 teaspoon	lemon juice	5 mL
1 · 10 ounce can	water chestnuts, thinly sliced	284 mL
	hot cooked rice	
	chow mein noodles	

Cook celery, carrots, onion and almonds in margarine until nuts are lightly browned. Drain pineapple and add enough water to the syrup to make 1 1/4 cups (300 mL). Add salt, cornstarch, ginger, nutmeg, soy sauce and lemon juice to pineapple juice and blend. Stir into celery-nut mixture and cook, stirring constantly until thickened. Add pineapple, turkey and chestnuts. Heat. Serve over rice. Sprinkle noodles over top. Serves 4.

Lemon Turkey Schnitzel

HONEY ROSENTHAL

1 pound	boneless, skinless turkey breasts	500 g
	juice of 1 lemon	
1/4 cup	all purpose flour	60 mL
1/2 teaspoon	thyme	2 mL
1/2 teaspoon	celery salt	2 mL
1	egg	1
1 teaspoon	water	5 mL
1/2 cup	fine bread crumbs	125 mL

Preheat oven to 400°F (200°C). Cut turkey into 1/2" (1.25 cm) slices. Flatten, and sprinkle with lemon juice. Combine flour, thyme, and celery salt. Mix beaten egg with water. Dip turkey schnitzels into flour mixture, then into egg mixture, then into bread crumbs. Place in a lightly greased baking dish. Bake for 10 – 15 minutes. If using microwave oven, bake uncovered on high for 4 – 6 minutes or until turkey is done. Serves 4.

Roast Duckling à l'Orange   ESTHER SCHWARTZ

2 · 4 – 5 pound	whole ducklings	2 – 2.5 kg each
	salt and pepper	
2	onions sliced	2
2	oranges with rind, sliced	2
	potatoes, peeled and	
	parboiled for 10 minutes	
	watercress or parsley	

Preheat oven to 375°F (190°C). Wash ducklings well. Drain and dry with paper towels. Season cavities and outsides of birds with salt and pepper. Stuff loosely with recipe below. Truss each duckling. Prick the skin at wings, back and breast to allow excess fat to escape. Place ducklings side by side, breast side up, on rack in shallow roasting pan. Arrange sliced onions and sliced oranges over ducklings. Roast uncovered, for 1 hour. Prick skin to allow more fat to drip off. Turn over, to brown on other side. Add potatoes and roast for 1 hour longer, turning to brown evenly on all sides. Baste with orange sauce (see page 223) the last 10 – 15 minutes of roasting time. Garnish with watercress or parsley, and orange slices dipped in orange sauce.

Orange Stuffing

3 cups	dry bread crumbs	750 mL
1 cup	diced apple, peeled	250 mL
1/4 cup	oil or melted margarine	60 mL
4 tablespoons	granulated sugar	60 mL
2/3 cup	orange juice	150 mL
1/2 cup	raisins	125 mL
	salt and pepper	

Mix ingredients together, seasoning to taste. Use enough liquid to moisten. You may need a bit more or less. Stuff ducklings loosely.

Orange Sauce

4 tablespoons	margarine	60 mL
4 tablespoons	frozen orange juice concentrate, thawed	60 mL
4 tablespoons	honey	60 mL
1/2 teaspoon	allspice	2 mL
2 tablespoons	lemon juice	30 mL
1 teaspoon	ground ginger	5 mL
2	oranges, sliced, for garnishing	2

Mix all ingredients together in a saucepan, except orange slices. Heat just to boiling. Dip orange slices in sauce to use as garnish. Baste ducklings with remaining sauce for the last 10 – 15 minutes of roasting time. Serves 8.

Cornish Hens

4	Cornish hens, well cleaned	4
1	medium onion, diced	1
1 cup	celery, diced	250 mL
1/2 cup	green pepper, diced	125 mL
1/4 pound	mushrooms, sliced	125 g
2 tablespoons	oil	30 mL
1/4 pound	ground beef	125 g
3 cups	cooked rice	750 mL
	salt and pepper	
	garlic salt, onion powder,	
	paprika	
1 tablespoon	water	15 mL
1/2 cup	orange juice	125 mL
2 tablespoons	honey	30 mL

Preheat oven to 350°F (180°C). Sauté onion, celery, green pepper and mushrooms in oil until limp. Scramble in meat until browned. Add rice. Season to taste with garlic salt. Stuff birds. Flap skin over and truss. Smear chickens with paste made of salt, pepper, garlic salt, onion powder, paprika and a little water. Arrange chickens in roasting pan. Pour in orange juice and dribble honey over. Bake uncovered 1 1/2 hours. Turn and baste while cooking. Remove thread and cut in half to serve. Serves 6 – 8.

Orange Glaze for Duck or Chicken

1 cup	orange marmalade	250 mL
1/4 cup	Triple Sec	60 mL

Combine, and heat thoroughly. Brush on the duck or chicken occasionally as it is cooking.

Bread Crumb Stuffing

This is enough to stuff a 10 pound (4.5 kg) turkey.

2	onions, chopped	2
2	stalks celery with leaves, chopped	2
1/2 cup	chicken fat or oil	125 mL
5 cups	stale challa or other white bread soaked in water	1250 mL
1	egg, beaten	1
1 – 2 teaspoons	poultry seasoning or sage	5 – 10 mL
1/2 teaspoon	salt	2 mL
1/2 teaspoon	pepper	2 mL
2 tablespoons	chopped parsley	30 mL

Sauté the onion and celery in oil until tender. Squeeze the water out of the bread and add beaten egg, seasonings and parsley. Toss together with onion mixture.

Mushroom Stuffing: Cook 1/2 pound (250 g) sliced mushrooms with the onion and celery. If a fruit flavor is desired add one grated apple to bread and proceed.

Quick Breads
and Muffins

Apple Bread

2 cups	all purpose flour	500 mL
2 1/2 teaspoons	baking powder	12 mL
1/4 teaspoon	baking soda	1 mL
3/4 cup	granulated sugar	175 mL
1/2 teaspoon	salt	2 mL
1/2 teaspoon	cinnamon	2 mL
2	eggs	2
3/4 cup	milk	175 mL
1/3 cup	margarine, melted	75 mL
1/2 cup	seedless raisins	125 mL
1 1/2 cups	peeled and grated apples	375 mL

Preheat oven to 350°F (180°C). Sift flour once before measuring. Sift with baking powder, soda, sugar, salt and cinnamon. Beat eggs until light and mix in milk and melted margarine. Add to dry mixture, stirring just enough to moisten. Fold in raisins and apples. Turn into well greased 9" x 5" x 3" (2 L) loaf pan, and let stand at room temperature for about 10 minutes. Bake for 60 to 70 minutes, until loaf tests done. Slice and butter when cold.

Corn Bread

HELEN BERMAN

1 cup less 2 tablespoons	all purpose flour	225 mL
1/2 teaspoon	salt	2 mL
1 cup	yellow cornmeal	250 mL
1/4 cup	granulated sugar	50 mL
4 teaspoons	baking powder	20 mL
1 cup	milk	250 mL
1	egg	1
1/4 cup	oil	60 mL

Preheat oven to 400°F (200°C). Grease an 8" (2 L) square baking pan. Mix dry ingredients. Mix liquids. Make a well in dry ingredients and quickly pour in the wet ingredients. Mix until blended. Pour into prepared pan. Bake 30 minutes. Freezes well. Wrap securely.

Banana Loaf

SANDY GRANATSTEIN, OTTAWA

1/2 cup	butter, melted	125 mL
1 cup	granulated sugar	250 mL
1	egg	1
2 cups	all purpose flour	500 mL
1 teaspoon	baking soda	5 mL
	pinch of salt	
1 cup	bananas, mashed	250 mL
1/2 cup	chopped nuts	125 mL

Preheat oven to 350°F (180°C). Grease a 9" x 5" x 3" (2 L) loaf pan. Combine butter and sugar in bowl. Add egg and mix well. Sift flour, baking soda and salt into the butter mixture. Fold in bananas and nuts, just until blended. Pour into prepared pan. Bake one hour or until loaf tests done. Cool on rack. Keep wrapped in foil in refrigerator.

Banana Nut Bread

NANCY POSLUNS

1/2 cup	margarine or butter	125 mL
1 cup	granulated sugar	250 mL
2	eggs	2
1 teaspoon	vanilla	5 mL
1 1/2 cups	mashed ripe bananas	375 mL
1 1/4 cups	all purpose flour	300 mL
1 1/2 teaspoons	baking soda	7 mL
1 teaspoon	baking powder	5 mL
1/2 teaspoon	salt	2 mL
1 cup	sour cream or yogurt	250 mL
1 cup	oatmeal	250 mL
1/2 cup	chopped walnuts or pecans	125 mL

Preheat oven to 350°F (180°C). Grease a 9 cup (2.5 L) bundt or two small loaf pans. Cream margarine and sugar well. Add eggs, one at a time, and continue beating. Add vanilla and mashed bananas. Gradually add sifted dry ingredients, alternately with sour cream and/or yogurt. Stir in oatmeal and nuts. Do not overmix. Pour into prepared pans. Bake for 50 minutes or until loaf tests done.

Parve Banana Bread

MYRTLE COOPERSMITH

2 cups	mashed ripe bananas (about 4)	500 mL
2 cups	granulated sugar	500 mL
4	eggs	4
1/2 cup	vegetable oil	125 mL
2 1/2 cups	all purpose flour	625 mL
2 teaspoons	baking soda	10 mL
1/2 teaspoon	salt	2 mL
1/2 cup	chopped nuts, chocolate chips or raisins (optional)	125 mL

Preheat oven to 350°F (180°C). Lightly grease and flour a 9" x 5" x 3" (2 L) loaf pan. In a large mixing bowl, using electric mixer, beat bananas, sugar, eggs and oil until well combined. In a separate bowl, mix flour, baking soda and salt. Stir into banana mixture, mixing just until combined. Stir in nuts, chocolate chips or raisins. Pour batter into prepared loaf pan. Bake for 45 minutes or until loaf tests done. Run knife around edge of pan to loosen. Cool 10 minutes in pan, then turn out onto rack to finish cooling. Freezes well.

Cranberry Walnut Bread

2 cups	all purpose flour	500 mL
1/4 teaspoon	cinnamon	1 mL
1 teaspoon	salt	5 mL
1 1/4 teaspoons	baking soda	6 mL
3/4 cup	granulated sugar	175 mL
1/2 teaspoon	grated orange rind	3 mL
1 cup	whole cranberry sauce	250 mL
1 1/4 cups	walnuts, coarsely chopped	300 mL
1	egg, beaten slightly	1
2/3 cup	milk	150 mL
1/4 cup	butter, melted and cooled	50 mL

Preheat oven to 375°F (190°C). Grease well one 9" x 5" x 3" (2 L) loaf pan. Sift together flour, cinnamon, salt, baking soda and sugar. Mix together orange rind, cranberry sauce and nuts. In another bowl, combine egg with milk and butter. Mix and add to cranberry-nut mixture. Blend into flour mixture lightly. Do not beat. Stir until just blended. Pour into prepared pan. Bake 50 – 60 minutes. Let stand 5 minutes before turning out onto rack to cool. Leave uncovered at least 4 hours, or overnight. Bread cuts more easily if firm and cold.

Parve Cranberry Bread

GRETA COOPERSMITH LISS

1 cup	whole wheat flour	250 mL
1 cup	all purpose flour	250 mL
1/2 – 2/3 cup	granulated sugar, to taste	125 – 175 mL
1 1/2 teaspoons	baking powder	7 mL
1/2 teaspoon	baking soda	2 mL
3 tablespoons	vegetable oil	45 mL
4 teaspoons	grated orange rind	20 mL
3/4 cup	orange juice	175 mL
1	egg	1
1 1/3 cups	fresh cranberries, halved	325 mL
1/2 cup	chopped pecans or walnuts	125 mL

Preheat oven to 350°F (180°C). In a large bowl, stir together whole wheat flour, all purpose flour, sugar, baking powder and baking soda. In a small bowl, whisk together the oil, orange rind, orange juice and egg. Add this mixture to the flour mixture, stirring just to moisten the dry ingredients. Fold in the cranberries and nuts, and pour the batter into a greased 9" x 5" x 3" (2 L) loaf pan or two mini-loaf pans. Bake for 1 hour or 50 minutes for a mini-loaf pan, or until loaf tests done. Cool on a rack for 10 minutes before turning out of pan. Cool. Wrap the bread well, and let it stand overnight before slicing. This can be doubled, and freezes very well.

Date and Nut Loaf

2 cups	chopped dates	500 mL
1 teaspoon	salt	5 mL
1 cup	brown sugar	250 mL
3/4 cup	boiling water	175 mL
2	eggs	2
1 teaspoon	vanilla	5 mL
1 cup	dry red wine	250 mL
	grated rind of 1 orange	
2 tablespoons	lemon juice	30 mL
3 cups	all purpose flour	750 mL
2 teaspoons	baking powder	10 mL
2 teaspoons	baking soda	10 mL
1 cup	walnuts or pecans, chopped	250 mL
1/2 cup	melted butter or margarine	125 mL

Preheat oven to 325°F (160°C). Grease and line with waxed paper, a 9" x 5" x 3" (2 L) loaf pan. Mix dates, salt, and brown sugar in a bowl. Add boiling water. Stir well and cool. Add eggs, vanilla, wine, rind and lemon juice. Sift together flour, baking powder and soda, and add to egg mixture. Add nuts and butter or margarine. Mix well, and pour into prepared loaf pan. Bake 1 1/2 hours. Let stand 24 hours before cutting.

Whole Wheat Quickbread

VERA SANDERS

1 cup	boiling water	250 mL
1 cup	raisins or cut up dried apricots	250 mL
1 teaspoon	baking soda	5 mL
3/4 cup	natural bran	175 mL
1 cup	whole wheat flour	250 mL
1 cup	rolled oats	250 mL
1/3 cup	granulated sugar	75 mL
1 teaspoon	baking powder	5 mL
1/4 teaspoon	salt	1 mL
1 cup	milk	250 mL

Preheat oven to 350°F (180°C). Grease and flour a 9" x 5" x 3" (2 L) loaf pan. In a large bowl, pour boiling water over raisins or apricots. Add soda and let stand for 5 minutes. Add remaining ingredients and mix until well combined. Pour batter into prepared pan. Bake 70 to 80 minutes or until loaf tests done.

Purple Plum Loaf

BARBARA PERLO

2 cups	fresh prune plums, pitted	500 mL
1 cup	butter	250 mL
2 cups	granulated sugar	500 mL
4	eggs	4
1 teaspoon	vanilla	5 mL
3 cups	all purpose flour	750 mL
1 teaspoon	cream of tartar	5 mL
1 teaspoon	salt	5 mL
1/2 teaspoon	baking soda	2 mL
1/2 teaspoon	baking powder	2 mL
3/4 cup	plain yogurt	175 mL
1 teaspoon	grated lemon rind	5 mL
1 cup	chopped nuts	250 mL

Preheat oven to 350°F (180°C). Grease two 9" x 5" x 3" (2 L) loaf pans. Cut plums into small pieces. Cream butter with sugar until fluffy. Add eggs one at a time, beating well after each addition. Add vanilla. Sift together flour, cream of tartar, salt, baking soda and baking powder. Combine yogurt and lemon rind, and add alternately with dry ingredients to butter mixture. Fold in plums and nuts. Pour batter into prepared pans. Bake one hour or until loaves test done.

Fruit Cake

FAYE BIGMAN

1 pound	pitted dates	500 g
1 cup	raisins	250 mL
1 teaspoon	baking soda	5 mL
2 cups	boiling water	500 mL
1/2 cup	butter or margarine	125 mL
1 cup	brown sugar, packed	250 mL
2	eggs	2
12 ounce jar	red maraschino cherries, including juice	342 mL
6 ounce jar	green maraschino cherries, including juice	170 mL
4 cups	all purpose flour	1 L
1 teaspoon	salt	5 mL
3 teaspoons	baking powder	15 mL
1 cup	whole Brazil nuts	250 mL
1 cup	pecan or walnut halves	250 mL
1/2 cup	rum	125 mL

Preheat oven to 300°F (150°C). Combine dates and raisins. Sprinkle with baking soda. Pour boiling water over. Mix and cool. Cream butter. Add sugar gradually, and continue creaming. Add eggs, one at a time, and continue creaming until very well mixed. Using a mixing spoon, gradually add all remaining ingredients. Combine well. Pour batter into two greased and waxed paper lined 12" x 5" x 3" (3 L) loaf pans. Bake for 3 1/2 to 4 hours.

Lemon Loaf

FLORENCE GORDON

1/2 cup	butter or margarine	125 mL
1 cup	granulated sugar	250 mL
2	eggs, well beaten	2
	grated rind of 1 lemon	
1 1/2 cups	all purpose flour	375 mL
1/8 teaspoon	salt	0.5 mL
1 teaspoon	baking powder	5 mL
2/3 cup	milk	150 mL
1/2 cup	chopped walnuts	125 mL

Glaze:

1/3 cup	granulated sugar combined with juice of 1 lemon	75 mL

Preheat oven to 350°F (180°C). Grease a 9" x 5" x 3" (2 L) loaf pan. Cream butter well. Add sugar gradually and continue creaming. Add eggs, and lemon rind. Sift together flour, salt and baking powder. Add dry ingredients alternately with milk to butter mixture, beating well after each addition. Blend in walnuts. Pour into prepared loaf pan, and bake one hour. Mix lemon juice with 1/3 cup (75 mL) sugar. Pierce baked loaf thoroughly, and pour glaze over. Cool and decorate with lemon slices.

Variation: 1/4 cup (50 mL) poppy seeds may be used instead of nuts.

Pumpkin Bread

JUDY SISKIND

1 cup	all purpose flour	250 mL
1 1/2 cups	granulated sugar	375 mL
1/4 teaspoon	baking powder	1 mL
1 teaspoon	baking soda	5 mL
1 teaspoon	salt	5 mL
1/2 teaspoon	ground cloves	2 mL
1/2 teaspoon	cinnamon	2 mL
2	eggs	2
1/2 cup	oil	125 mL
1/4 cup	water	60 mL
1 cup	canned pumpkin	250 mL
1/2 cup	chopped nuts	125 mL

Preheat oven to 350°F (180°C). Grease a 9" x 5" x 3" (2 L) loaf pan. Into a large bowl, sift together the flour, sugar, baking powder, baking soda, salt and spices. Stir lightly with a fork until well mixed. Beat eggs, then add oil and water and beat until frothy. Stir in pumpkin. Add egg mixture to dry ingredients and beat just until mixed. Fold in nuts. Pour into prepared pan and bake for 65 minutes or until loaf tests done.

Rhubarb Loaf

BARBARA PERLO

1 1/2 cups	brown sugar, firmly packed	375 mL
2/3 cup	oil	150 mL
1 cup	buttermilk	250 mL
1	egg	1
1 teaspoon	vanilla	5 mL
1 teaspoon	baking soda	5 mL
1 teaspoon	salt	5 mL
2 1/2 cups	all purpose flour	625 mL
1 1/2 cups	chopped uncooked rhubarb, fresh or frozen	375 mL
1/2 cup	chopped nuts, pecans or walnuts	125 mL
Topping:		
1/2 cup	granulated sugar	125 mL
1 teaspoon	soft butter	5 mL
1 1/2 tablespoons	grated orange rind	20 mL

Preheat oven to 350°F (180°C). Grease two 9" x 5" x 3" (2 L) loaf pans. Combine brown sugar and oil in a large mixing bowl and mix well with a wooden spoon. Whisk buttermilk, egg, vanilla, soda and salt together in a smaller bowl. Add to brown sugar mixture and blend gently. Fold in flour, rhubarb and nuts. Divide batter into prepared loaf pans and sprinkle topping over batter. Bake in oven for 1 hour or until loaves test done. Let sit 10 minutes before removing from pans. Freezes well.

Apricot Bran Muffins

SHEILA LOFTUS

2 cups	cut up apricots and/or apples	500 mL
3 teaspoons	baking soda	15 mL
3 cups	sour cream or yogurt	750 mL
3 cups	all purpose flour	750 mL
3 cups	brown sugar	750 mL
3 cups	All Bran cereal	750 mL
3	eggs	3
1 1/2 cups	oil	375 mL
3 teaspoons	vanilla	15 mL

Soak apricots for a few minutes in hot water. Drain well. Preheat oven to 350°F (180°C). Combine soda with sour cream or yogurt. Sift flour. Mix dry ingredients. Make a well, and stir in eggs, oil, vanilla, and sour cream - soda mixture. Stir cut-up fruit into mixture carefully. Bake in greased muffin tins filled 2/3 full. Bake for 25 minutes. Makes 3 dozen muffins.

Zucchini Loaf

3	eggs, well beaten	3
1 cup	oil	250 mL
1 1/2 cups	granulated sugar	375 mL
2 teaspoons	vanilla	10 mL
2 cups	zucchini, grated (about 1 1/2 pounds)	500 mL
2 cups	all purpose flour	500 mL
1/4 teaspoon	baking powder	1 mL
2 teaspoons	baking soda	10 mL
1 teaspoon	salt	5 mL
1 cup	raisins	250 mL
1 cup	chopped nuts (optional)	250 mL

Preheat oven to 375°F (190°C). Grease two 9" x 5" x 3" (2 L) loaf pans. To well beaten eggs, add oil, sugar, vanilla and zucchini. Sift together flour, baking powder, baking soda and salt. Stir dry mixture into egg mixture. Stir in raisins and chopped nuts. Pour batter into prepared baking pans. Bake 1 hour or until loaves test done.

Variations:

1. Use 1 cup (250 mL) whole wheat flour and 1 cup (250 mL) all purpose flour instead of 2 cups (500 mL) all purpose flour.

2. Use a combination of grated carrots and grated zucchini to make up 2 cups instead of all zucchini.

3. Use half brown and half granulated sugar instead of all granulated.

Blueberry Muffins

BARBARA PERLO

2 1/2 cups	blueberries	625 mL
1/2 cup	butter	125 mL
1 1/4 cups	granulated sugar	300 mL
2	eggs	2
2 cups	all purpose flour	500 mL
2 teaspoons	baking powder	10 mL
1/2 teaspoon	salt	2 mL
1/2 cup	milk	125 mL
2 teaspoons	granulated sugar	10 mL

Preheat oven to 350°F (180°C). Mash 1/2 cup (125 mL) of the blueberries and set aside. Cream butter and sugar in bowl of electric mixer until blended. Add eggs one at a time, mixing well after each addition. Add sifted dry ingredients alternately with milk. Fold in mashed blueberries quickly, and then add rest of berries. Grease muffin pans, including the top of the pan. Pile high, using all of the batter to make 12 large muffins. Sprinkle 2 teaspoons (10 mL) sugar on top. Bake 30 minutes or until muffins test done. Cool in pan one half hour before removing muffins. Place muffins on a rack for complete cooling.

Banana Date Muffins

BARBARA ALEXANDER

2 – 3	very ripe bananas	2 – 3
6 tablespoons	melted shortening or oil	100 mL
1/2 cup	granulated sugar	125 mL
1 teaspoon	salt	5 mL
1	egg, well beaten	1
1 teaspoon	vanilla	5 mL
1 1/2 cups	all purpose flour	375 mL
1 teaspoon	baking soda	5 mL
1 teaspoon	baking powder	5 mL
1/2 cup	chopped dates	125 mL

Preheat oven to 350°F (180°C). Mash bananas. Add shortening, sugar and salt. Beat well. Add egg and vanilla, and continue beating. Sift flour, baking soda and baking powder over banana mixture. Add dates and mix by hand just until blended. Fill 12 greased muffin tins 2/3 full. Bake 15 – 20 minutes or until done.

Variation: You may use raisins and/or chopped nuts instead of dates. Grated orange rind also makes an interesting and delicious flavour.

Bran Muffins #1

JOYCE SPIEGEL

5 1/2 cups	all purpose flour	1375 mL
2 1/2 cups	granulated sugar	625 mL
3 cups	All Bran cereal	750 mL
2 cups	Bran Flakes cereal	500 mL
3 teaspoons	baking soda	15 mL
5 cups	buttermilk	1250 mL
1 1/2 cups	oil	375 mL
4	eggs	4
1/2 cup	molasses	125 mL
5 teaspoons	cinnamon	25 mL
1 teaspoon	nutmeg (optional)	5 mL
2 cups	raisins	500 mL

Combine all dry ingredients, except soda. In another bowl, combine soda and buttermilk. Add oil, eggs and molasses and mix. Make a well in the centre of the dry ingredients, and pour in wet mixture. Stir gently until moistened. Stir in raisins. Refrigerate at least 6 to 8 hours before baking. Bake as you need them in greased muffin tins at 375°F (190°C) for 25 – 30 minutes. This mixture lasts for 3 weeks in the refrigerator.

Bran Muffins #2

1 teaspoon	baking soda	5 mL
1 cup	sour cream	250 mL
1/4 cup	butter or margarine	60 mL
2/3 cup	brown sugar	150 mL
1	egg	1
1 cup	all purpose flour	250 mL
1 1/2 cups	bran flakes	375 mL
1 cup	raisins, dusted with flour	250 mL

Preheat oven to 350°F (180°C). Lightly grease 12 muffin tins. Dissolve baking soda in sour cream. Cream butter and sugar. Add egg and sour cream mixture. Fold in flour, bran flakes, and raisins. Fill muffin tins 2/3 full. Bake 25 minutes.

Buttermilk Bran Muffins

PAULINE TOKER

4 cups	All Bran cereal	1 L
2 cups	pure natural bran	500 mL
1 teaspoon	salt	5 mL
1 cup	raisins	250 mL
2 cups	boiling water	500 mL
4 cups	buttermilk	1 L
1 cup	margarine	250 mL
3 cups	granulated sugar	750 mL
4	eggs	4
5 cups	all purpose flour	1.25 L
5 teaspoons	baking soda	25 mL

Preheat oven to 350°F (180°C). Combine brans, salt and raisins. Stir in water and buttermilk. Cream margarine and sugar. Add eggs. Stir into bran mixture. Mix flour and soda and add to bran mixture. Stir enough to dampen. This batter may be refrigerated or frozen, for use at any time. Fill greased muffin tins 2/3 full and bake 20 – 25 minutes. Blueberries are a nice alternative to raisins. This recipe halves easily.

Cornmeal Muffins

These are lovely and rich. To simplify removal from pans, line with paper baking cups.

1 cup plus 2 tablespoons	all purpose flour	275 mL
3 1/2 teaspoons	baking powder	17 mL
1/2 teaspoon	salt	2 mL
3/4 cup	yellow cornmeal	175 mL
1/2 cup	butter	125 mL
1/2 cup	granulated sugar	125 mL
1	egg	1
3/4 cup	milk	175 mL

Preheat oven to 375°F (190°C). Grease 12 medium sized muffin tins. Measure once-sifted flour and sift with baking powder and salt. Add cornmeal and mix. Beat together butter, sugar and egg, until light and fluffy. Add dry ingredients alternately with milk, mixing lightly after each addition. Fill prepared tins 2/3 full. Bake for 18 – 20 minutes. Best served warm.

Cheese Scones

LILY KATZ

1	egg	1
	milk, as needed	
1 1/2 cups	grated old cheddar cheese	375 mL
1 cup	all purpose flour	250 mL
1 tablespoon	baking powder	15 mL
1/2 teaspoon	dry mustard	2 mL

Preheat oven to 425°F (210°C). Beat egg slightly in a measuring cup. Add milk to measure 1 cup (250 mL). Mix all ingredients together with a wooden spoon to form a thick batter. Fill greased muffin tins 3/4 full. Bake 10 minutes. Serve hot. Yield: 12 large or 18 small scones.

Date Orange Muffins

MARY SHENDROFF

1	whole orange	1
1/2 cup	orange juice	125 mL
1/2 cup	chopped, pitted dates	125 mL
1	egg	1
1/2 cup	butter or margarine	125 mL
1 1/2 cups	all purpose flour	375 mL
1 teaspoon	baking soda	5 mL
1 teaspoon	baking powder	5 mL
3/4 cup	granulated sugar	175 mL
1/2 teaspoon	salt	2 mL

Preheat oven to 400°F (200°C). Grease 18 medium muffin tins. Cut orange into pieces, remove seeds, and put pieces into blender or food processor. Blend until rind is finely ground. Add orange juice, dates, egg and butter, and mix again lightly. Into a bowl, sift flour, baking soda, baking powder, sugar and salt. Pour orange mixture over dry ingredients and stir lightly. Fill greased muffin tins 2/3 full. Bake about 15 minutes until done.

Carrot Muffins

NANCY POSLUNS

1 1/2 cups	all purpose flour	375 mL
1 teaspoon	baking powder	5 mL
1 teaspoon	baking soda	5 mL
1/2 teaspoon	salt	2 mL
1/2 teaspoon	cinnamon	2 mL
1/4 teaspoon	nutmeg	1 mL
	generous pinch allspice	
3/4 cup	firmly packed brown sugar	175 mL
1	egg	1
1/2 cup	buttermilk or sour milk	125 mL
1/3 cup	oil	75 mL
1/2 teaspoon	vanilla	2 mL
1 1/2 cups	finely grated carrots	375 mL
1 1/2 cups	raisins	375 mL
1/2 cup	chopped nuts	125 mL

Preheat oven to 400°F (200°C). Measure flour, baking powder, soda, salt, cinnamon, nutmeg, allspice and brown sugar into large bowl. Stir to blend all ingredients. In a smaller bowl whisk together egg, buttermilk, oil and vanilla. Pour over dry ingredients. Sprinkle on carrots, raisins and nuts and stir just enough to blend dry and liquid ingredients together. Transfer into greased or paper lined muffin tins. Bake for 20 minutes, until well risen, fragrant and spongy firm to the touch. Freezes well. Yield: 12 muffins.

Carrot-Pineapple Muffins

MARY SHENDROFF

1 · 8 1/4 ounce can	crushed pineapple	234 g
	milk, as needed	
2 cups	all purpose flour	500 mL
1/3 cup	packed brown sugar	75 mL
1 tablespoon	baking powder	15 mL
1/2 teaspoon	salt	2 mL
1	egg, beaten	1
3/4 cup	finely shredded carrot	175 mL
1/3 cup	cooking oil	75 mL
1/2 teaspoon	vanilla	2 mL
2 tablespoons	granulated sugar	25 mL
1/2 teaspoon	ground cinnamon	2 mL

Preheat oven to 400°F (200°C). Grease 12 muffin tins. Drain pineapple, reserving syrup. Add milk to syrup to make 3/4 cup (175 mL). Stir together flour, brown sugar, baking powder and salt. Combine egg, carrot, milk-syrup mixture, drained pineapple, oil and vanilla. Add all at once to dry ingredients, stirring just until moist. Fill greased muffin tins 2/3 full. Sprinkle tops with mixture of sugar and cinnamon. Bake about 20 – 25 minutes.

Oatmeal Muffins

MARY SHENDROFF

1 cup	rolled oats or quick cooking oatmeal	250 mL
1 cup	buttermilk	250 mL
1 cup	all purpose flour	250 mL
1 teaspoon	salt	5 mL
1/2 teaspoon	baking soda	2 mL
1 teaspoon	baking powder	5 mL
1	egg, well beaten	1
1/2 cup	well packed brown sugar	125 mL
1/2 cup	melted shortening or vegetable oil	125 mL
1 cup	chopped dates (optional)	250 mL

Combine oats with buttermilk and let stand 1/2 – 1 hour. Preheat oven to 400°F (200°C). Grease 12 medium sized muffin tins. Sift together flour, salt, baking soda and baking powder. Add egg, sugar and shortening to oatmeal mixture, stirring well after each addition. Stir in dry ingredients, mixing only long enough to moisten. If desired, chopped dates may be folded into the batter. Spoon into prepared muffin tins 2/3 full. Bake 15 – 20 minutes, until golden. You will have 12 light, buttery muffins.

Wheat Germ Muffins

NANCY FLORENCE

3 teaspoons	baking soda	15 mL
3 cups	buttermilk or sour cream	750 mL
3	eggs	3
2 cups	granulated sugar	500 mL
1 cup	brown sugar	250 mL
1 cup	oil	250 mL
3 cups	wheat germ	750 mL
3 cups	all purpose flour	750 mL
3 teaspoons	baking powder	15 mL
1 teaspoon	salt	5 mL
2 teaspoons	vanilla	10 mL

Preheat oven to 400°F (200°C). Grease 3 dozen muffin tins. Add baking soda to buttermilk or sour cream. Combine eggs, sugars and oil. Add buttermilk mixture and stir. Add wheat germ and flour sifted with baking powder and salt. Add vanilla. Pour into greased muffin tins, filling 2/3 full. Bake for 20 – 25 minutes.

English Tea and Breakfast Scones

LILY KATZ

2 cups	all purpose flour	500 mL
4 teaspoons	baking powder	20 mL
	pinch of salt	
1 tablespoon	granulated sugar	15 mL
1/3 cup	butter	75 g
1	beaten egg	1
1 cup	sour cream or yogurt	250 mL
	or	
3/4 cup	milk	175 mL

Preheat oven to 400°F (200°C). Sift dry ingredients. Cut in butter with a knife, or process, using a few quick on-off turns. Add beaten egg and sour cream or yogurt or milk. Drop by spoonfuls into medium-size greased muffin tins and bake 10 – 15 minutes. Serve with your favourite jam and a little cream or butter. Yield: 12 scones.

1	French stick, cut into slices, 1 1/2" – 2" (3.75 - 5 cm) thick	1
4 cloves	garlic	4
2	large tomatoes	2
6 – 8 leaves	fresh basil	6 – 8
	extra virgin olive oil	
	coarse salt	
	freshly grated pepper	
	grated Parmesan cheese	

Preheat broiler. Finely chop garlic cloves. Peel, seed tomatoes and chop into chunks. Tear basil into small pieces. In a bowl, toss lightly together the tomatoes, garlic, basil and approximately 1 tablespoon (15 mL) olive oil. Add salt and pepper to taste. Toast both sides of the bread under the broiler. Place toast on a cookie sheet and baste top side lightly with olive oil. Spoon on tomato mixture and sprinkle generously with cheese. Place under broiler until cheese turns golden. Edges of bread will continue to darken. Do not overbroil. Serve immediately. Serves 4 – 6.

To Make Bread Crumbs

Use any sliced stale bread.

Preheat oven to 200°F (100°C). Place sliced bread on a cookie sheet. Place in oven for 15 minutes. Process in food processor until finely ground. Keep in covered container in refrigerator or freezer.

Melba Toast: Slice leftover challa or other bread as thinly as possible. Place slices on a cookie sheet and bake at 300°F (150°C) about 10 minutes on each side until golden.

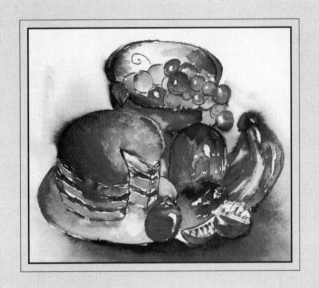

Desserts

Heavenly Angel Pie

1 1/2 cups	granulated sugar	375 mL
1/4 teaspoon	cream of tartar	1 mL
4	eggs, separated	4
3 tablespoons	shredded coconut (optional)	50 mL
3 tablespoons	lemon juice	45 mL
1 tablespoon	grated lemon rind	15 mL
1/8 teaspoon	salt	0.5 mL
2 cups	whipping cream	500 mL

Preheat oven to 275°F (140°C). Sift 1 cup (250 mL) sugar with cream of tartar. Beat egg whites until stiff but not dry. Add sugar slowly, and continue beating. When stiff glossy peaks form, spread meringue over bottom and up sides of a well greased 9" (1 L) pie plate. Sprinkle rim with part of the coconut if desired. Bake one hour. Cool. Beat 4 egg yolks slightly in top of double boiler. Stir in 1/2 cup (125 mL) sugar, lemon juice and rind, and salt. Cook over boiling water, stirring constantly, until thick, about 8 – 10 minutes. Cool. Whip 1 cup (250 mL) cream, and fold custard into it. Pour lemon-cream filling into meringue shell. Refrigerate 12 – 24 hours. Garnish with whipped cream sprinkled with **toasted coconut. Strawberries** may also be used for garnish if desired.

Easy Apple Crisp

NANCY POSLUNS

6 cups	sliced apples	1.5 L
1 teaspoon	cinnamon	5 mL
1 teaspoon	salt	5 mL
1/4 cup	water or lemon juice	60 mL

Topping:

3/4 cup	sifted all purpose flour	175 mL
1 cup	granulated and brown sugar, combined	250 mL
1/3 cup	butter	75 mL

Preheat oven to 350°F (180°C). Butter well, a 10" x 6" x 2" (1.5 L) baking dish. Place sliced apples in prepared dish. Sprinkle with cinnamon, salt and water. Rub together topping ingredients. Drop over apples. Bake 40 minutes.

Variation: A combination of flour, quick oats, and/or granola may be used instead of all flour.

Apple Dessert

2 cups	all purpose flour	500 mL
1 cup	brown sugar	250 mL
1/2 cup	butter or margarine	125 mL

Combine flour and brown sugar. Cut butter into mixture until texture of coarse meal. Press 3/4 of this mixture into an ungreased 8" x 8" (2 L) baking dish.

Filling:

4 cups	grated apples	1 L
1/2 cup	granulated sugar	125 mL
	(or more to taste)	
1 teaspoon	cinnamon	5 mL
2 tablespoons	lemon juice	25 mL

Preheat oven to 350°F (180°C). Combine apples, sugar, cinnamon and lemon juice. Put filling over base. Sprinkle remaining crumbs on top. Bake one hour. Serve warm or cold. Can be doubled for 9" x 13" (3.5 L) baking dish.

Microwave Baked Apples

VERA SANDERS

4	apples	4
1/4 cup	brown sugar	60 mL
1 teaspoon	cinnamon	5 mL
1/4 cup	raisins	60 mL

Peel apples halfway down. Combine brown sugar, cinnamon and raisins. Core apples and fill with mixture. Arrange apples in a circle in a microwavable dish. Cover with waxed paper, leaving opening for steam to escape. Cook on High (100% power) for about 8 minutes. Allow apples to stand 5 minutes before serving. If counting calories, omit sugar, and sprinkle with sugar substitute after baking.

Variation: Pears can be used instead of apples.

Family Apple Dessert

HARRIET DENNIS

	brown sugar	
	cinnamon	
8	Spy apples, peeled and cut into eighths	8
3/4 cup	granulated sugar	175 mL
1 cup	all purpose flour	250 mL
2 teaspoons	baking powder	10 mL
1/4 cup	butter or margarine	60 mL
1	egg	1
	milk or orange juice	

Preheat oven to 350°F (180°C). Grease a 2 quart (2.5 L) rectangular ovenproof baking dish with butter or margarine. Sprinkle with brown sugar. Layer apples in dish and sprinkle them with cinnamon. In a mixing bowl, sift together the sugar, flour and baking powder. Cut in butter or margarine. Break an egg into a glass measure. Add enough milk or orange juice to make 1/2 cup (125 mL) liquid. Add to flour mixture and beat with a wooden spoon until blended. Spoon over apples. Bake 3/4 hour. Best served warm.

Apple Torte

LYNDA RAPP

1 cup	butter	250 mL
2/3 cup	granulated sugar	150 mL
1/2 teaspoon	vanilla	2 mL
2 cups	sifted pastry flour	500 mL
16 ounces	cream cheese	454 g
1/2 cup	granulated sugar	125 mL
2	eggs	2
1/2 teaspoon	vanilla	2 mL
4 cups	apples, peeled and sliced	1 L
1/3 cup	granulated sugar	75 mL
1/2 teaspoon	cinnamon	2 mL
1/8 teaspoon	nutmeg	0.5 mL
1/2 cup	slivered almonds	125 mL

Preheat oven to 450°F (230°C). Cream butter and sugar. Add vanilla and flour, and blend well. Spread this dough on bottom and sides of a 9" (22.5 cm) springform pan. Combine cream cheese and sugar. Mix well. Add eggs and vanilla, and mix well. Pour into pastry. Toss apples with sugar, cinnamon and nutmeg. Arrange apples over cream cheese layer. Top with slivered almonds. Bake for 10 minutes. Reduce heat to 400°F (200°C) and bake an additional 25 minutes. Cool 3/4 hour. Best served warm.

Applesauce

PAULINE TOKER

4 quarts	apples, cut up	4 L
1/4 cup	water	60 mL
1/4 teaspoon	salt	1 mL
1 1/2 cups	granulated sugar	375 mL
	juice and rind of 1/2 lemon	
1/4 teaspoon	cinnamon	1 mL
1/8 teaspoon	nutmeg	0.5 mL

Place cut apples (including skin and core) in saucepan with water and salt. Cook until tender. Put through food mill. Return to stove. Add sugar, and cook until sugar is dissolved. Stir in lemon juice and flavouring.

Baked Apples

4 – 6	Spy apples	4 – 6
	juice of 1 lemon	
3/4 – 1 cup	brown sugar	175 – 250 mL
1 cup	water	250 mL

Preheat oven to 350°F (180°C). Wash and core apples and slice one thin slice of skin off the tops. Pour lemon juice into a baking dish and place apples in, cut side down. Let stand. Meanwhile, boil sugar and water for about 5 minutes. Turn apples right side up and pour syrup over apples. Sprinkle with **cinnamon**. Stuff **pecans** into center of each apple. Dot with **butter** and bake about 35 minutes, or until tender, basting occasionally.

Caramelized Apple Torte   M Y R T L E   C O O P E R S M I T H

1 cup plus	all purpose flour	280 mL
2 tablespoons		
1 1/2 teaspoons	baking powder	7 mL
1 3/4 cups	granulated sugar	425 mL
1/4 cup	water	60 mL
1 teaspoon	vanilla	5 mL
6	eggs	6
2 1/2 pounds	golden delicious apples, peeled, cored and roughly chopped	1 kg

Preheat oven to 350°F (180°C). Generously butter a 9" (22.5 cm) springform pan. In a large bowl, sift together the flour and the baking powder. Stir in 1 cup (250 mL) of the sugar, the vanilla and the eggs. Set aside. In a small saucepan, over medium heat, dissolve the remaining 3/4 cup (175 mL) sugar in the water, and cook without stirring until mixture is a golden caramel. Pour the hot caramel into the pan. Cover the caramel with the chopped apples, then pour the batter on top. Bake for 45 minutes or until a tester inserted into the center comes out clean. While still warm, invert springform pan onto plate and carefully release pan. Serve at room temperature. Serves 8.

French Apple Torte

VICKI CAMPBELL

This is an elegant dessert type cake. It has rum in it, as well as a custard, giving it unusual flavour and texture. Allow plenty of time for baking.

8 – 10	large apples, peeled, and quartered	8 – 10
2 tablespoons	EACH: rum, lemon juice, and sugar	30 mL
1 cup	granulated sugar	250 mL
1/2 cup	butter, melted	125 mL
2	eggs	2
1 1/2 cups	all purpose flour	375 mL
2 teaspoons	baking powder	10 mL
2 tablespoons	rum	30 mL

Preheat oven to 350°F (180°C). Grease and lightly flour a 9" (22.5 cm) springform pan. Mix together the sliced apples, the rum, lemon juice and sugar. Add 1 cup (250 mL) sugar gradually to melted butter and beat well. Add eggs, one at a time and continue beating until light and fluffy. Fold in flour which has been sifted with baking powder, and lastly add rum. Spread dough on bottom of pan and place apples around - point side down, round side up. Bake for 75 minutes.

Custard:

1/2 cup	butter, melted	125 mL
1 cup	granulated sugar	250 mL
2 teaspoons	vanilla	10 mL
2	eggs	2
2 tablespoons	rum	30 mL

Blend well, following the order of ingredients as above, at low speed. Do not overbeat. Pour custard on top of cake and continue to bake 20 – 40 minutes, until custard sets. Serve warm and sprinkle with **powdered sugar.**

Baked Apricot Custard

MYRTLE COOPERSMITH

3 1/4 pounds	ripe apricots or peaches	1.5 kg
3 tablespoons	butter	45 mL
2 tablespoons	granulated sugar	30 mL
3	eggs	3
1 1/2 cups plus 2 tablespoons	icing sugar	400 mL
1 1/2 cups plus 1 tablespoon	all purpose flour	390 mL
3 1/4 cups	milk	800 mL
1 teaspoon	vanilla	5 mL

Preheat oven to 425°F (225°C). Wash and dry apricots and cut into halves. Grease a large oval baking dish with 1 tablespoon (15 mL) of the butter. Sprinkle pan with granulated sugar. Arrange fruit in overlapping circles in the pan. Whisk together, the eggs, 1 1/2 cups (375 mL) of the icing sugar, and the flour. Gradually add milk, whisking constantly, so lumps do not form. Add vanilla. Pour mixture over apricots and dot with remaining butter. Place pan on large baking sheet to catch the drips. Bake 20 minutes. Sprinkle top with remaining icing sugar and continue to bake until a knife comes out clean - about 20 minutes more.

Baked Bananas

JOYCE LAMPERT, SAN FRANCISCO

6 medium	bananas, sliced	6
1 cup	blueberries	250 mL
1/2 cup	brown sugar	125 mL
1 cup	orange juice	250 mL

Preheat oven to 325°F (160°C). Place bananas in buttered baking dish. Add blueberries, sugar and orange juice. Dot with **butter**. Bake 20 minutes.

Blueberry Crisp

JUDY ASCH

4 cups	fresh blueberries	1 L
2 teaspoons	lemon juice	10 mL
1/3 cup	granulated sugar	75 mL
4 tablespoons	butter or margarine	60 mL
1/3 cup	brown sugar	75 mL
1/3 cup	all purpose flour	75 mL
3/4 cup	rolled oats	175 mL

Preheat oven to 350°F (180°C). Put berries in greased 1 1/2 quart (1.5 L) ovenproof dish. Sprinkle with lemon juice and granulated sugar. Cream butter and brown sugar. Add flour and oats. Mix well. Crumble over top of berries. Bake 40 minutes.

Black Forest Trifle

BERNICE GOREN, STRATFORD

3 · 14 ounce cans	pitted red cherries	398 mL each
	cherry liqueur	
1	square chocolate cake	1
1 large plus	chocolate instant pudding	1 + 1
1 small package		
1 pint	whipping cream	500 mL
	chocolate shavings	

Drain cherries and marinate in any cherry liqueur for a day or two. Make or buy a chocolate cake. Make pudding according to package directions. Whip cream. Cut cake into small pieces and sprinkle with cherry liqueur. Using a large glass bowl, layer all of the ingredients, starting with cake and ending with whipped cream. Garnish with chocolate shavings.

Blitz Torte

1/2 cup	butter or shortening	125 mL
1/2 cup	granulated sugar	125 mL
4	eggs, separated	4
1 1/3 cups	cake flour	325 mL
1 1/3 teaspoons	baking powder	7 mL
5 tablespoons	milk or lemon juice	75 mL
1 cup	granulated sugar	250 mL
	slivered almonds or	
	coconut	

Preheat oven to 325°F (160°C). Cream butter and 1/2 cup (125 mL) sugar together until fluffy. Add egg yolks, one at a time, and continue to beat. Sift flour, measure, add baking powder, and sift together three times. Add alternately with milk or lemon juice to the creamed mixture. Beat well. Spread the mixture in 2 round shallow baking pans. Beat the whites very stiff. Add the 1 cup (250 mL) sugar gradually and continue beating. Spread on the unbaked mixture in both pans. Sprinkle with almonds or coconut. Bake for 40 minutes. When cool, spread filling between layers.

Filling:

1 cup	whipping cream, whipped	250 mL
1 · 14 ounce can	apricot halves, drained and	398 mL
	arranged over whipped cream	
	or	
	your favourite lemon filling	

Filbert Torte

ESTHER GUTH

4 ounces	filberts, roasted, then ground	125 g
2 tablespoons	all purpose flour	30 mL
2 teaspoons	baking powder	10 mL
4	eggs	4
3/4 cup	granulated sugar	175 mL

Preheat oven to 350°F (180°C). Combine ingredients in large mixer bowl and mix at high speed. Pour into 2 greased and floured 8" (2 L) round pans. Bake for 30 – 35 minutes. Cool and frost.

Frosting:

1/2 pint	whipping cream	250 mL
2 tablespoons	cocoa	30 mL
2 tablespoons	granulated sugar	30 mL
1 teaspoon	vanilla	5 mL

Combine and beat until mixture forms peaks. Frost between and on top of both layers.

Blueberry Torte

1/2 cup	butter	125 mL
1/2 cup	shortening	125 mL
1 cup	granulated sugar	250 mL
1	egg	1
3 cups	all purpose flour	750 mL
1 teaspoon	baking powder	5 mL
1/8 teaspoon	salt	0.5 mL
Filling:		
3 pints	blueberries	1.5 L
1 cup	granulated sugar	250 mL
4 tablespoons	all purpose flour	60 mL
	juice and rind of 1/2 lemon	

Preheat oven to 350°F (180°C). Cream butter and shortening. Add sugar gradually and cream well. Add beaten egg. Sift dry ingredients and add to creamed mixture. Reserve 1 cup (250 mL) and pat remainder of dough into a 12" (30 cm) springform, bringing the dough up the sides to within an inch (2.5 cm) of the top. Mix blueberries, sugar, flour and lemon rind and put into prepared pan. Sprinkle with lemon juice. To remaining dough add a little flour and crumble with fingers to make a streusel. Sprinkle on top of berries. Bake for 1 1/4 – 1 1/2 hours. Before serving, dust with **icing sugar.**

Variation: A combination of cut up rhubarb and sliced strawberries can be used instead of blueberries.

Brownie Baked Alaska

DOLORES WEINER

	your favourite brownie recipe	
2 pints	vanilla ice cream	1 L
5	egg whites	5
1/8 teaspoon	salt	0.5 mL
1/2 cup plus 2 tablespoons	granulated sugar	150 mL
1/2 teaspoon	vanilla	2 mL

A few days before: Bake your favourite brownie recipe. Cool, then invert. Do not cut. Cover with 1" (2.5 cm) thick slices of ice cream, placed side by side. Wrap and freeze. Shortly before serving, preheat oven to 500°F (250°C). Beat egg whites with salt until moist peaks form. Slowly add sugar and vanilla. Beat until stiff and glossy. Spread over brownie ice cream cake, swirling into peaks on top. Bake 4 – 5 minutes. Serve immediately. Serves 8.

Crème Caramel

ETHEL KLEIN

1/2 cup	granulated sugar	125 mL
5 cups	milk	1.25 L
1/2 cup	granulated sugar	125 mL
1/4 teaspoon	salt	2 mL
4	eggs	4
1 teaspoon	vanilla	5 mL

In a small frying pan, melt 1/2 cup (125 mL) sugar and cook until caramel coloured. Pour into soufflé dish or a 6 cup (1.5 L) ring mold. Preheat oven to 350°F (180°C). In a large pot heat milk until steaming, but not boiling. Add sugar and salt. In a large bowl, beat eggs slightly. Add milk and vanilla, beating constantly. Pour into prepared dish. Place dish into a pan, larger than the dish, containing warm water. Bake for 1 hour. To test for doneness, knife inserted in the middle should come out clean. To serve, run knife around edges of ring mold. Invert onto a plate with a raised edge.

Caramel Apricot Rice Pudding

ELEANOR STEINBERG & ROZ HALBERT

2 cups (1/2 pound)	dried apricots	225 g
1/4 cup	butter or margarine, melted	60 mL
1 cup	light brown sugar	250 mL
3 cups	hot fluffy white rice	750 mL
4	eggs	4
1 cup	granulated sugar	250 mL
1 teaspoon	salt	5 mL
2 1/2 teaspoons	vanilla	12 mL
4 cups	milk, scalded	1 L
1/4 teaspoon	nutmeg	1 mL
1/2 teaspoon	cinnamon	2 mL
1 1/2 cups	heavy cream, whipped	375 mL
	unsweetened chocolate, shaved	
	slivered almonds	

Cover apricots with water. Bring to a boil, reduce heat and simmer about 5 minutes until tender. Drain. Heat oven to 350°F (180°C). Pour melted butter into 3 quart (3 L) casserole. Sprinkle brown sugar over butter. Arrange apricots, rounded side down, in a single layer over brown sugar-butter mixture. Spoon on rice. Beat eggs until light and foamy. Stir in granulated sugar, salt and vanilla. Then slowly stir in scalded milk. Pour milk mixture over rice and apricots. Sprinkle with nutmeg and cinnamon. Set casserole in pan of hot water. Bake for 1 hour or until silver knife comes out clean when inserted in center. Cool. At serving time, place spoonfuls of whipped cream on top of pudding. Sprinkle with shaved chocolate and slivered almonds. Serves 12 or more. May be halved for 5 – 6. Bake in 2 quart (2 L) baking dish for 50 minutes. Delicious!

Rice Pudding

ROSEMARY GREISMAN

1 cup	water	250 mL
1/2 cup	short grain rice	125 mL
5 cups	milk	1.25 L
2 teaspoons	corn starch	10 mL
1/2 cup	granulated sugar	125 mL
1 teaspoon	vanilla	5 mL
1/2 cup	raisins	125 mL
1 tablespoon	cinnamon	15 mL

Bring water to a boil in a saucepan. Add rice and cover. Reduce heat and simmer for 15 minutes or until water is absorbed. Place rice in 4 1/2 cups (1.125 L) of the milk in a large heavy saucepan. Cook until milk just comes to a boil. Meanwhile combine cornstarch with sugar and very gradually whisk in remaining 1/2 cup (125 mL) milk until mixture is smooth. Whisk this mixture into hot rice/milk mixture. Reduce heat to low. Cover and cook gently for 40 – 55 minutes, or until rice is very thick and creamy. Add vanilla and raisins. Pour into individual serving dishes or one large serving bowl. Sprinkle with cinnamon. Serve warm or cold. Serves 6 – 8.

Food Processor Chocolate Mousse

EVELYN BERGER

1 cup	semi-sweet chocolate pieces	250 mL
5 tablespoons	boiling water	75 mL
4	eggs, separated	4
2 tablespoons	dark rum	30 mL

Beat egg whites in electric mixer until stiff. Put chocolate pieces into food processor with steel blade and process for 5 seconds. Add water and process for 10 seconds more. Add egg yolks and rum and blend 3 seconds, or until smooth. Fold chocolate mixture into stiffly beaten egg whites. Pour into serving dish. Refrigerate for at least 6 hours before serving. Serves 6.

Chocolate Pot de Crème (parve)

ADÈLE FREEMAN

4 squares	semi-sweet chocolate	4
	or	
2/3 cup	semi-sweet chocolate chips	150 mL
4	eggs, separated	4
1/8 teaspoon	salt	0.5 mL
1 teaspoon	vanilla	5 mL
1/3 cup	finely chopped walnuts	75 mL
	whipped topping	
	walnut halves	

Melt chocolate over hot (not boiling) water. Cool slightly. Beat egg yolks and blend with cooled chocolate. Add salt, vanilla and nuts. Beat egg whites until stiff. Gently fold into chocolate mixture. Turn into custard cups or large bowl. Chill at least one hour before serving. Garnish with whipped topping and walnut halves.

Cinnamon Torte

HELAINE ROBINS

1 1/2 cups	butter	375 mL
2 cups	granulated sugar	500 mL
2	eggs	2
2 3/4 cups	all purpose flour	675 mL
2 tablespoons	cinnamon	30 mL
1 pint	whipping cream	500 mL
	chocolate shavings	

Heat oven to 375°F (190°C). Cream butter and sugar. Add eggs one at a time and continue beating. Add flour mixed with cinnamon. Grease round 8" or 9" (20 – 22 cm) pans. Divide dough into 8 – 10 pieces and pat one piece at a time into pan very thinly, pressing out bubbles. This should make 8 – 10 layers. Bake 8 – 10 minutes. Make a few days in advance and refrigerate. Before serving, whip cream and spread between layers. Decorate with chocolate shavings.

Chocolate Truffle Cake

CAROL GROSMAN

Cake:

6 squares	semi-sweet chocolate	6
3/4 cup	butter	175 mL
2/3 cup	granulated sugar	150 mL
4	eggs, separated	4
1/3 cup	all purpose flour	75 mL
2 tablespoons	granulated sugar	30 mL

Preheat oven to 375°F (190°C). Melt chocolate with butter. Cool. Beat 2/3 cup (150 mL) sugar with egg yolks until thick and lemon coloured. Add chocolate mixture and flour, blending well. Beat egg whites until soft peaks form. Add remaining 2 tablespoons (30 mL) sugar and continue beating until shiny peaks form. Fold chocolate mixture into egg whites and blend well. Pour into greased and floured 9" (22.5 cm) springform pan. Bake 35 - 40 minutes. Cool. Cake will be moist in center and will fall as it cools.

Glaze:

4 squares	semi-sweet chocolate	4
2 tablespoons	butter	30 mL
2 tablespoons	water	30 mL

Melt together and blend. Spread over cake.

Garnish:

3 ounces	white chocolate	90 g
1 teaspoon	vegetable shortening	5 mL

Melt chocolate with shortening. Make a cone out of waxed paper and and fill. Make 6 to 8 circles on top of cake. Draw a dull knife through circles toward center to make a webbed pattern.

Ice Cream Molds

FLORENCE WINBERG

Chocolate Coffee Mold:

2 quarts	coffee ice cream	2 L
1 quart	chocolate ice cream	1 L
1 can	Hershey's chocolate syrup	1

Pour 1/3 can of syrup into empty 12 cup (3 L) mold. Allow ice cream to soften slightly so that it can be handled. Consistency should still be solid. Using a large spoon, pack into mold 1 quart (1 L) of coffee ice cream. Pour 1/3 can of syrup evenly over ice cream. Pack in 1 quart (1 L) of chocolate ice cream. Pour over evenly, the last third of the chocolate syrup. Pack second quart (1 L) of coffee ice cream into mold. Pat it all in smoothly. Work quickly so flavours don't run into each other. Cover filled mold with plastic wrap and freeze.

Peanut Brittle Mold:

3 quarts	vanilla ice cream	3 L
1 pound	peanut brittle	450 g

Crush the peanut brittle between layers of waxed paper into small pieces. Soften the ice cream slightly, and mix the broken peanut brittle through the ice cream. Pack it all into your mold firmly, wrap well and freeze. This may be served with butterscotch or caramel sauce poured over the top. You may have many variations. using any flavour ice cream, sauces, candied or brandied fruits, fruit sauces. etc. Use your imagination!

To unmold: Run a sharp knife around edge to release ice cream from side. Invert on serving platter. Hold a cloth wrung out of warm water over inverted bottom for a few seconds. Remove mold. Serve at once or place in freezer until ready to serve.

Variation: If desired, line a 9" – 10" (22 – 25 cm) springform pan with ladyfingers. Pack in your favourite combination of ice creams as suggested. Freeze until firm. Make a meringue as follows:

3	egg whites	3
4 tablespoons	granulated sugar	60 mL
1/8 teaspoon	cream of tartar	0.5 mL

Preheat broiler. Beat egg whites until frothy. Add dash of cream of tartar. Add sugar gradually, beating until stiff peaks form. Pile on top of ice cream in attractive peaks. Place under broiler until meringue browns lightly. It only takes a minute. Return to freezer until ready to serve. Ice cream mold with meringue can be in the freezer for a few days. Remove sides of springform pan before serving.

Crunchy Ice Cream Pie

ANN BODLEY

1/2 cup	butter	125 mL
1 cup	brown sugar, loosely packed	250 mL
3 cups	cornflakes	750 mL
1/3 cup	toasted chopped almonds	75 mL
1 cup	flaked coconut	250 mL
1 quart	vanilla ice cream, softened	1 L
1/2 square	semi-sweet chocolate	1/2

Cream butter. Blend in sugar and continue to cream until light and fluffy. Mix in cornflakes, nuts, and coconut. Press 2/3 of this mixture over bottom and sides of 9" (1 L) pie plate. Spoon in ice cream, filling the shell evenly. Cover with other 1/3 of the nut mixture, pressing it lightly into the ice cream. Sprinkle with shaved chocolate. Freeze overnight. Remove from freezer 1/2 hour before serving. Very good and very rich. Can be made several days ahead.

Easy Chocolate Trifle

RUTH GREENSPAN

1	angel food cake or sponge cake	1
4 packages	instant chocolate pudding (4 serving size)	4
6 1/2 cups	milk	1625 mL
1 pint	whipping cream	500 mL
1 teaspoon	vanilla	5 mL
4 tablespoons	icing sugar	60 mL
1 teaspoon	liquid coffee	5 mL
	chocolate shavings	

Beat pudding with milk in large bowl of electric mixer. Set aside. Whip cream. Sweeten with vanilla, and gradually add icing sugar while beating. Into whipped cream, fold 1 cup (250 mL) of the pudding mixture blended with the coffee. Split cake in half. Using an attractive glass bowl, place one layer of cake, half the pudding, and a layer of the whipped cream. Repeat layers and top with shaved chocolate. Refrigerate.

Double Decker Mousse Pie

EDIE WINBERG

4 tablespoons	chopped pecans	60 mL
8	eggs, separated	8
1/8 teaspoon	salt	0.5 mL
1 – 2 tablespoons	brandy	15 – 30 mL
1 cup	granulated sugar	250 mL
4 squares	unsweetened chocolate, melted and cooled	4
1 cup	heavy cream	250 mL

Preheat oven to 350°F (180°C). Grease a 9" (1 L) pie plate. Sprinkle pie plate with 3 tablespoons (45 mL) of the chopped pecans. Beat egg whites until stiff, but not dry. Set aside. In a small mixing bowl, mix egg yolks, salt and brandy. Add sugar gradually and beat until thick. Add chocolate and beat well. Stir 1/4 of the egg white mixture into the yolk mixture. Then fold yolk mixture into remainder of egg whites. Pour half of the mixture into pie plate. Spread over bottom and up sides. Bake 18 – 20 minutes. Cool on rack. Center will be slightly moist. Whip cream and fold half into remaining chocolate mixture and chill. Spoon into cooled baked shell and chill overnight. Decorate with remaining whipped cream and 1 tablespoon (15 mL) chopped pecans.

Grand Marnier Soufflé

4	egg whites	4
1 cup	granulated sugar	250 mL
1 cup	whipping cream, whipped or whipped topping	250 mL
	rind of 1 orange, grated	
2 tablespoons	Grand Marnier	30 mL
	semi-sweet chocolate	

Beat egg whites until frothy. Gradually add sugar and beat until stiff. Fold in whipped cream, orange rind and liqueur. Pour into 1 large or individual serving dishes. Garnish with grated semi-sweet chocolate. Freeze for at least 5 hours. Can be made well ahead of time and frozen until ready to serve. Doubles well.

Lemon Mousse

JUDY ASCH

1 1/4 cups	graham cracker crumbs	300 mL
1/4 cup	melted butter	60 mL
7	eggs, separated	7
	juice and grated rind	
	of 3 lemons	
1 cup	granulated sugar	250 mL
1 package	unflavoured gelatin	1
1/4 cup	water	60 mL

Mix graham crumbs with butter. Pat into bottom of greased 9" (22.5 cm) springform pan. Save some for topping. Beat egg yolks with lemon juice and rind, and 1/2 cup (125 mL) of the sugar. Cook over low heat in top of double boiler until thickened, stirring constantly. Dissolve gelatin in water. Add to yolk mixture. Cook until slightly thickened. Beat egg whites until stiff, gradually adding remaining 1/2 cup (125 mL) sugar while beating. Fold whites into lemon mixture. Pour over crust, and sprinkle reserved graham crumbs on top. Chill several hours before serving.

Note: Parve whipped topping may be substituted for whipping cream.

Lemon Gelatin Dessert

DOLORES WEINER

1 · 16 ounce can	evaporated milk	425 mL
1 1/2 cups	graham wafer crumbs	375 mL
1/2 cup	brown sugar	125 mL
1/2 teaspoon	cinnamon	2 mL
2 tablespoons	melted butter	30 mL
1 package	lemon gelatin (4 serving size)	1
1 1/4 cups	boiling water	300 mL
1/3 cup	granulated sugar	75 mL
	juice and rind of 1 lemon	

Place can of milk in freezer overnight.
Prepare crust: Combine graham wafers, brown sugar, cinnamon and melted butter. Mix well, and press on bottom of 9" x 13" (3.5 L) baking dish. Save some crumbs to sprinkle on top.

Prepare gelatin: Dissolve gelatin in boiling water. Stir in sugar, lemon rind and juice. Put aside until partially set, then whip. In separate large mixer bowl, whip cold evaporated milk. Add whipped gelatin to milk and blend. Pour into prepared baking dish. Sprinkle reserved crumbs over top. Refrigerate until serving time. Serves 10 – 12.

Frozen Lemon Dessert (parve) RAYLENE GODEL

1/4 cup	margarine	60 mL
1/2 cup	brown sugar	125 mL
3 cups	corn flakes, crushed	750 mL
1 cup	pecans, chopped	250 mL
6	eggs, separated	6
1 cup	granulated sugar	250 mL
3	lemons, juice and rind	3
1 carton	parve whipped topping	500 g

Melt margarine with brown sugar. Add corn flake crumbs and pecans. Line bottom of 9" – 10" (22.5 – 25 cm) springform pan with half of this mixture. Beat 6 egg whites with sugar until stiff. Beat yolks until lemon coloured and fold into beaten whites. Alternately add lemon juice and rind with whipped topping to egg mixture. Blend and pour into springform pan. Sprinkle with remaining crumb mixture. Freeze, uncovered, until set. Then cover with foil and put into plastic bag. Can be frozen up to 2 months.

Chocolate Variation: Substitute chocolate graham cracker crumbs for corn flakes. Instead of lemon, use 10 ounces (280 g) melted unsweetened chocolate and 1 – 2 tablespoons (15 – 30 mL) Sabra liqueur.

Frozen Lemon Torte

2 – 3 packages	lady fingers (24 – 36)	2 – 3
5	eggs	5
3/4 cup	lemon juice	175 mL
	grated rind of 1 lemon	
1 1/4 cups	granulated sugar	300 mL
1 pint	whipping cream	500 mL
4 tablespoons	granulated sugar	60 mL

Line bottom and sides of buttered 9" (22.5 cm) springform pan with lady fingers. Separate 3 of the eggs. Place 2 whole eggs plus 3 yolks in top of double boiler. Beat together until smooth. Add lemon juice, rind and sugar, and beat lightly. Place over hot water and cook until thick, stirring constantly. Cool. Fold in cream, which has been whipped. Pour into prepared pan. Freeze at least 5 hours. Beat remaining 3 whites with 4 tablespoons (60 mL) sugar until stiff. Spread on cake. Place under broiler briefly until lightly browned. Return to freezer. Remove one hour before serving.

Note: Parve whipped topping may be substituted for whipping cream.

Lemon Blueberry Bread Pudding

PHYLLIS FLATT

1/2	challa, sliced,	1/2
	crusts removed	
1/4 cup	unsalted butter,	60 mL
	softened to spread	
2 cups	blueberries	500 mL
3	large eggs, lightly beaten	3
3/4 cup	granulated sugar	175 mL
2 1/2 cups	2% milk	625 mL
1/3 cup	fresh lemon juice	75 mL
1 tablespoon	grated lemon rind	15 mL
2 tablespoons	orange liqueur	30 mL
1/2 cup	orange marmalade	125 mL

Butter a 9" x 13" (3.5 L) baking dish. Spread bread with butter and arrange half in dish, buttered side down, in one layer. Sprinkle half the blueberries on top. Arrange another layer of bread on top and sprinkle with remaining blueberries. In a bowl, beat the eggs. Add the sugar, milk, lemon juice, lemon rind and 1 tablespoon (15 mL) of the orange liqueur. Pour slowly over bread mixture allowing to settle and soak in. Cover and refrigerate overnight. Preheat oven to 350°F (180°C). In a saucepan melt marmalade with remaining liqueur. Brush over pudding. Place pan in a larger pan and half fill larger pan with water. Bake 30 – 40 minutes. Serve warm.

Graham Cracker Pudding — Quick Napoleon

Line a 9" x 13" (3.5 L) baking dish with whole graham wafers. Cook 2 small packages vanilla pudding according to box instructions. Cool. Pour over graham wafers, and refrigerate.

1/2 pint	whipping cream	250 mL
1 teaspoon	vanilla	5 mL
1 teaspoon	icing sugar	5 mL

Beat together until thick. Spread over vanilla pudding. Top with whole graham wafers.

Vanilla Icing:

1	egg white	1
1 cup	icing sugar	250 mL
1 teaspoon	lemon juice	5 mL
	chocolate syrup	

Beat egg white until stiff. Gradually add icing sugar and lemon juice. Spread over crackers. Dribble chocolate syrup over as a garnish. Can be made 2 days before serving. Rich, but delicious!

Meringue Shell

5	egg whites	5
1/2 teaspoon	baking powder	2 mL
1 teaspoon	vanilla	5 mL
1 teaspoon	vinegar	5 mL
1/4 teaspoon	cream of tartar	1 mL
1 cup	granulated sugar	250 mL

Heat oven to 250°F (120°C). Beat egg whites until frothy. Add baking powder, vanilla, vinegar and cream of tartar. Gradually add sugar and continue beating until meringue is firm and shiny. Turn onto cookie sheet covered with waxed or brown paper. Form into a shell. (Hollow out center and bring up sides). Make smaller than desired size because it will spread while baking. Bake 2 1/2 hours. Cool before removing paper. Makes a delicious dessert filled with assorted ice cream balls, or filled with a lemon filling.

Peach Clafouti

3 1/2 cups	sliced fresh peaches, peeled	875 mL
2 tablespoons	peach brandy	30 mL
1/3 cup	granulated sugar	75 mL
2 cups	light cream	500 mL
3	eggs	3
1/4 cup	all purpose flour	60 mL
1 teaspoon	vanilla	5 mL
	icing sugar	

Preheat oven to 375°F (190°C). Sprinkle peach brandy over peaches. Grease a shallow 2 quart (2 L) baking dish. Sprinkle with 2 tablespoons (30 mL) of the sugar. In processor combine cream, eggs and flour and process for one minute. Add remaining sugar and vanilla and process for a few seconds more. Place peaches and juice in prepared dish. Pour mixture on top. Bake for 45 – 50 minutes or until golden and puffed. Serve warm. Sprinkle with icing sugar just before serving. (Clafouti will fall as it cools).

Peach Melba

SALLY KERR

1 · 15 ounce package	frozen raspberries	426 g
1/2 cup	red currant jelly	125 mL
1 1/2 teaspoons	cornstarch	7 mL
1 tablespoon	cold water	15 mL
	peach halves	
	vanilla ice cream	

Place the raspberries in a saucepan and allow to thaw. Mash the berries with a spoon. Add the jelly and bring to a boil over low heat. Add the cornstarch mixed with the cold water, and cook, stirring constantly, until clear. Strain and cool. Place a peach half, cut side up, in individual dessert dishes. Top each with a scoop of ice cream, and pour the cooled sauce over the top. Sauce can stay for weeks in the refrigerator.

Note: 2 – 4 tablespoons (30 – 60 mL) of Cointreau or Triple Sec adds a delightful zip to the melba sauce.

Summer Fruit Crisp

SHANEA RAKOWSKI

1/2 cup	unsalted butter	125 mL
1 cup	granulated sugar	250 mL
1 cup	all purpose flour	250 mL
1/2 teaspoon	cinnamon	2 mL
1 cup	blueberries	250 mL
1 cup	strawberries, halved	250 mL
1 cup	peaches, sliced	250 mL
1/2 cup	apricots, sliced	125 mL
1/2 cup	pitted cherries	125 mL
1/2 cup	raspberries	125 mL
2 tablespoons	cornstarch	30 mL
1/4 teaspoon	cinnamon	1 mL

Preheat oven to 400°F (200°C). Blend the first 4 ingredients until crumbly. Place the fruit in a pie plate or dish. Sprinkle with cornstarch and cinnamon. Cover with crumble. Bake for 45 minutes or until brown. Cool before serving. Serves 6 – 8.

Pears in Wine Sauce

6	uniform-size pears	6
1 teaspoon	grated lemon rind	5 mL
	Concord grape wine	
	water	
2 teaspoons	lemon juice	10 mL
4	cloves	4
1 · 2" stick	cinnamon, broken	5 cm
1 cup	granulated sugar	250 mL

Peel pears. Leave whole. Place in saucepan and cover with equal amounts of wine and water. Add remaining ingredients, cover and simmer until tender. Chill. Serve in sauce.

Poached Peaches

8	firm peaches	8
2 cups	water	500 mL
1 cup	granulated sugar	250 mL
	slice of lemon	
	slice of orange	

To remove skins pour boiling water over fruit. Immediately plunge into cold water and slip off skins. Combine water, sugar, lemon and orange slices and bring to a boil. Reduce heat to simmer and put fruit into syrup. Cover and simmer until fruit is tender, about 12 minutes.

Note: Additional orange and lemon slices may be used if desired.

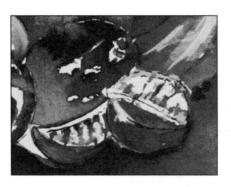

Poached Pears

Use same method as in poached peaches, except that it is not necessary to blanch fruit to peel. This fruit may take a little longer to cook.

Brandied Pears or Peaches: Substitute 1 cup (250 mL) water and 1 cup (250 mL) cognac for 2 cups (500 mL) water.

Dessert Pears with Chocolate Sauce

DOROTHY STONE

6	pears	6
1 cup	granulated sugar	250 mL
2 1/2 cups	water	625 mL
1 pint	vanilla ice cream	500 mL
	hot chocolate sauce	
	toasted almonds	

Peel and halve pears. Remove core. Dissolve sugar in boiling water. Add pears and poach until tender. Remove and drain. Surround ice cream with pears on a serving plate. Cover with chocolate sauce and sprinkle with almonds. Serve additional chocolate sauce on the side.

Chocolate Sauce

6 ounces	semi-sweet chocolate	170 g
1/2 cup	granulated sugar	125 mL
	dissolved in	
1 1/4 cups	water	300 mL

If desired, 1 1/2 cups (375 mL) of the poaching liquid may be used instead of sugar-water as above. Place syrup and chocolate in top of double boiler. Simmer over hot water for 15 minutes. Cool slightly before serving.

Strawberries Romanoff

SALLY KERR

1/2 pint	heavy cream	250 mL
1 pint	softened vanilla ice cream	500 mL
6 tablespoons	Cointreau	100 mL
2 quarts	strawberries, lightly sugared	2 L

Whip cream, and mix with softened ice cream. Blend in Cointreau and sugared strawberries. Place in stem glasses and garnish with more berries. Refrigerate until ready to serve.

Strawberry Meringue Torte

JEAN RACHLIN

Meringues:

6	egg whites	6
1/8 teaspoon	salt	0.5 mL
1/2 teaspoon	cream of tartar	2 mL
1 1/2 cups	granulated sugar	375 mL

Bake the meringue the night before putting the torte together as follows: Heat oven to 400°F (200°C). Line baking sheets with waxed or parchment paper. Trace 3 circles - 9" (22.5 cm) on the paper. Beat the egg whites with salt and cream of tartar until stiff. Gradually beat in the sugar and continue to beat until stiff and glossy. Spread the meringue evenly over the circles and place pans in the oven. Close the oven door, turn oven off, and leave the meringues in the oven overnight. (No peeking!)

The next day assemble the cake as follows:

Filling:

9 squares	semi-sweet chocolate, melted	9
4 1/2 tablespoons	water	65 mL
4 cups	heavy cream	1 L
1/2 cup	granulated sugar (scant)	115 mL
1 quart	strawberries, sliced	1 L
	whole strawberries for garnish	

Melt chocolate. Add water and blend. Whip the cream, adding the sugar gradually, beating until very stiff. Place a meringue layer on a serving plate. Spread with a thin layer of chocolate, then a 1/2" (1.75 cm) layer of whipped cream and a layer of sliced strawberries. Put a second meringue layer on top, spread with the remaining chocolate, a layer of whipped cream, and a layer of strawberries. Place third meringue layer on top. Frost sides smoothly with whipped cream and garnish with whole strawberries. Wonderful party dessert!

Strawberry Mousse

HONEY ROSENTHAL

4 cups	strawberries	1 L
3	egg whites	3
2 cups	whipping cream	500 mL
1/8 teaspoon	salt	0.5 mL
1 cup	granulated sugar	250 mL
2 tablespoons	lemon juice	30 mL

Mash strawberries. Beat egg whites until stiff. Fold into strawberries. Whip cream, adding salt, sugar and lemon juice. Fold into berry mixture. Pour into a 2 quart (2 L) mold. Freeze 12 hours. Unmold. Garnish with **whole berries**. Serves 8.

Mandarin Orange Mold

SALLY KERR

2 · 6 ounce packages	orange gelatin	340 g
3 cups	hot water	750 mL
1 pint	orange sherbet	500 mL
2 · 10 ounce cans	mandarin oranges, drained	568 mL

Dissolve gelatin in hot water. Cool. Mix orange sherbet into gelatin. Refrigerate until partially set, approximately 45 minutes. Fold in well-drained orange slices. Pour into 1 1/2 quart (1.5 L) mold. Refrigerate until firm.

Profiterole

4 tablespoons	butter	60 mL
2/3 cup	water	150 mL
1 tablespoon	granulated sugar	15 mL
1/4 teaspoon	salt	1 mL
1 cup	all purpose flour	250 mL
4	eggs	4

Preheat oven to 450°F (230°C). Place first four ingredients in a saucepan and bring to a boil. Remove from heat and add flour all at once. Stir until mixture forms a ball. Return to heat and stir vigorously until mixture appears dry and leaves a slight film on bottom of pan. Place mixture in mixer bowl and let stand until slightly cooled, about 5 minutes. Add eggs, one at a time, beating well after each addition.

Drop rounded teaspoons of dough onto a greased cookie sheet. Bake for 5 minutes. Reduce heat to 350°F (180°C) and bake another 15 minutes or until puffs are firm and golden. Cool on cake rack.

To serve: Cut tops off puffs and place a scoop of **vanilla ice cream** in each. Replace tops and spoon **hot fudge** sauce, page 146 over each. Garnish with **whipped cream** if desired.

Tiramisu

SHANEA RAKOWSKI

3	large eggs, separated (whites at room temperature)	3
2/3 cup	icing sugar	150 mL
10 ounces (about 1 1/4 cups)	marscapone cheese	300 mL
1/4 cup	dark rum	60 mL
	pinch of salt	
1 . 7 ounce	package of Biscotti di Savoiardi (Italian lady fingers)	200 g
1/3 cup	strong brewed coffee	75 mL
1/2 cup	sliced strawberries	125 mL
6 tablespoons	grated bitter chocolate	90 mL

In a large bowl, beat together the yolks and the sugar until the mixture is thick and pale. Add the marscapone and rum, and beat the mixture until smooth. In another bowl, beat the egg whites with a pinch of salt, until they hold stiff peaks, then fold this into the marscapone mixture gently. Arrange the biscotti in a shallow dish, sprinkle coffee over them, then spread sliced strawberries on top. Spread the marscapone mixture over this smoothing out the top. Sprinkle the tiramisu with chocolate, and chill covered for at least 6 hours or overnight. Serves 6 – 8.

Viennese Almond Roll

JEAN RACHLIN

6	egg yolks	6
3/4 cup	granulated sugar	175 mL
3/4 cup	chopped blanched almonds	175 mL
8	egg whites	8
	icing sugar	

Preheat oven to 350°F (180°C). Cream yolks with sugar until light and lemon coloured. Fold in almonds. Beat whites until stiff. Fold into yolk mixture. Butter a jelly roll pan 11" x 15" (27.5 x 37.5 cm). Line pan with buttered waxed paper. Spread batter evenly over pan. Bake 15 – 20 minutes until cake tests done. Cool in pan. When cool, cover for a few minutes with a towel wrung out in cold water. Remove towel and dust with icing sugar. Turn out onto waxed paper.

Fill with following:

1 1/2 cups	whipped cream	375 mL
	grated rind of 1 orange	
	and 1 lemon	
1 tablespoon	orange juice	15 mL
2 tablespoons	light rum or Cointreau	30 mL
	icing sugar	

Combine first four ingredients. Whip and spread filling over cake. Roll up with widest side facing you. Sprinkle generously with icing sugar. Cake may also be filled with flavoured whipped cream mixed with **fresh raspberries** or **fruit**.

A few easy tips: German sweet, semi-sweet and bitter chocolate are all excellent for dipping. Strawberries, cherries, orange segments and grapes are recommended for dipping. Orange segments should be placed in a sieve in a warm, turned off oven for 2 – 3 minutes to dry out the moisture.

Don't attempt chocolate dipping on a hot, humid day, because the fruits may not harden. Do not store chocolate-coated fruits in the refrigerator. This causes the chocolate to 'sweat' and turn gray.

Chocolate Coating:

4 squares	semi-sweet chocolate	4
1 tablespoon	vegetable oil	5 mL

In the top of a double boiler over hot, not boiling water, melt and stir chocolate with vegetable oil until satiny and smooth. Remove from heat and dip fruits (leave stem on) draining excess back into the pot. Place fruits on aluminum foil or waxed paper to harden. Prepare no more than 4 – 5 hours ahead. This amount will dip 26 – 30 large strawberries two-thirds of the way up.

Frosted Fruits:

1	egg white	1
2 tablespoons	water	30 mL
1 cup	granulated sugar	250 mL
2 pounds	grapes, in small bunches	1 kg

Lightly beat egg white with water in a bowl. Pour sugar into a shallow bowl. Wash and dry the clusters of grapes. Dip each cluster into egg white, covering all surfaces and letting excess drain into bowl. Set aside on waxed paper until all grapes are dipped. Surfaces will be tacky to the touch. At this point, coat clusters with granulated sugar, shaking off excess. Place on waxed paper to dry.

Note: Follow the same procedure with strawberries, cherries and other small whole fresh fruits.

Cakes and Frostings

Tips for Successful Baking

1. First, read the recipe through, and make sure that you have all the ingredients required.

2. Have ingredients at room temperature. Baking powder, baking soda and cream of tartar must be fresh. Use within six months.

3. Use the correct size of pan. Prepare the pans before you begin to make the cake. Grease and flour the bottom of the pans. Shake out any excess flour.

4. Butter is best for flavour, but margarine may also be used.

5. Always use standardized measuring utensils. All measurements should be accurate and leveled off.

6. Use all purpose flour, unless otherwise specified. Cake flour must be measured after sifting.

7. Measure dry ingredients by spooning them lightly into a measuring cup until overflowing. Do not press down or shake. Level off with a straight-edged spatula.

8. Measure liquid ingredients by pouring to the correct measuring point, looking at eye level.

9. 'Creaming' properly is extremely important. The butter should be beaten until it is light and fluffy. The sugar should be added gradually, a few tablespoons at a time, while continuing to beat until the sugar grains cannot be felt with the fingertips, and the mixture has the texture of whipped cream. Eggs should be added one at a time, and beaten well after each addition. When alternating dry ingredients with liquid, begin and end with dry ingredients. Mix just to blend. Overbeating will reduce volume.

10. When making sponge or chiffon cakes, do NOT grease the baking pan. It is best to save a pan that has never been greased for making these cakes.

11. After pouring batter into the pan, the pan should be tapped lightly on the counter top to release air. But don't do this if beaten egg whites have been folded into the batter.

12. When using raisins in a recipe, it is a good idea to soak them in very hot water for a minute or two. Drain them well, pat dry with paper toweling, and sprinkle them with a tablespoon or so of flour. This will keep them from sinking to the bottom of the cake.

13. The oven should be preheated to the proper temperature before putting in the cake. Place the cake pan on the center rack of the oven.

14. The cake is usually done when the edges have pulled away slightly from the sides of the pan, when a toothpick inserted comes out dry, or when the top springs back when lightly touched.

15. Cool cakes on racks before and after unmolding. If you are having difficulty removing cake from pan, wrap a towel which has been dipped in hot water and wrung out, around the pan, and in a few minutes you will be able to remove the cake to a rack without leaving half of it behind!

16. A crack on the top of the cake may indicate too much flour, not enough liquid, overbeating, and/or too high a temperature. If your cake has burned from too hot an oven, remove the burned crust by running the coarse side of your grater over the burned spots. It's easier than trying to cut away the burned crust. Better still - get a good oven thermometer!

17. Most cakes freeze well, although cakes that have been frosted should not be frozen.

Apple Pecan Cake

TOBY TANENBAUM

1/2 cup	oil	125 mL
3	eggs	3
2 cups	granulated sugar	500 mL
1 tablespoon	cinnamon	15 mL
2 teaspoons	vanilla	10 mL
3 cups	sifted cake flour	750 mL
1 teaspoon	baking soda	5 mL
1/2 teaspoon	salt	2 mL
1 cup	chopped pecans	250 mL
3	large Spy apples, peeled and diced	3

Preheat oven to 350°F (180°C). On slow to medium speed combine oil, eggs and sugar. Add cinnamon, vanilla, flour, soda and salt. Beat for 10 minutes. Batter will be stiff. Fold in pecans and apples. Bake in a greased 9" (2.5 L) springform pan for 1 hour and 15 minutes. Cake freezes beautifully.

Easy Apple Cake

GRETA GREISMAN

4 cups	sliced apples, preferably Spy	1 L
3 tablespoons	cinnamon, or to taste	45 mL
5 tablespoons	granulated sugar	75 mL
3 cups	all purpose flour	750 mL
2 cups	granulated sugar	500 mL
3 teaspoons	baking powder	15 mL
1 teaspoon	salt	5 mL
1 cup	oil	250 mL
4	eggs	4
1/4 cup	orange juice	60 mL
1 tablespoon	vanilla	15 mL

Preheat oven to 375°F (190°C). Grease a 10" (25 cm) tube pan. Mix together first three ingredients and set aside. Sift flour, sugar, baking powder and salt into a bowl. Make a well. Drop in oil and eggs, orange juice and vanilla. Beat with spatula or wooden spoon until smooth and shiny. Pour 1/3 of batter into greased tube pan. Add half of the apples, drained of excess moisture, and repeat, ending with last third of batter. Bake for 60 – 75 minutes or until done. If cake starts to get too brown, cover top lightly with a piece of foil.

Alternate fillings:

3 cups	blueberries, fresh or frozen	750 mL
	or	
	sliced fresh peaches	
5 tablespoons	granulated sugar	75 mL
2 teaspoons	lemon juice	10 mL

Applesauce Spice Cake

PAULINE TOKER

1/2 cup	soft butter or margarine	125 mL
1 1/2 cups	granulated sugar	375 mL
2	eggs	2
2 cups	sifted all purpose flour	500 mL
1 1/2 teaspoons	baking soda	7 mL
3/4 teaspoon	salt	3 mL
2 tablespoons	cocoa	30 mL
1/2 teaspoon each	cinnamon, ginger, nutmeg, cloves, allspice	3 mL each
1 1/2 cups	applesauce	375 mL
3/4 cup	cut up dates and/or raisins	175 mL

Preheat oven to 350°F (180°C). Grease a 12 cup (3 L) bundt pan. Cream butter and sugar until fluffy. Add eggs one at a time, beating well after each addition. Sift together flour, soda, salt, cocoa and spices, reserving 2 tablespoons (30 mL) of the flour to coat raisins. Fold in applesauce and flour mixture alternately to creamed mixture. Fold in floured raisins. Bake in well greased bundt pan for 55 to 60 minutes.

Apple Nut Coffee Cake

SHEILA MASTERS

1/2 cup	shortening	125 mL
1 cup	granulated sugar	250 mL
2	eggs	2
1 teaspoon	vanilla	5 mL
2 cups	sifted all purpose flour	500 mL
1 teaspoon	baking powder	5 mL
1 teaspoon	baking soda	5 mL
1/4 teaspoon	salt	1 mL
1 cup	sour cream	250 mL
2 cups	finely chopped apples	500 mL

Topping: Combine

1/2 cup	chopped nuts	125 mL
1/2 cup	brown sugar	125 mL
1 teaspoon	cinnamon	5 mL
2 tablespoons	melted butter	30 mL

Preheat oven to 350°F (180°C). Grease a 9" (2.5 L) springform pan. In mixing bowl, cream together shortening and sugar. Add eggs and vanilla and beat well. Sift together flour, baking powder, baking soda and salt. Add to creamed mixture alternately with sour cream. Fold in apples. Pour into prepared pan. Sprinkle topping over batter. Bake 35 – 40 minutes.

Banana Cake

Try this if you like a really rich banana flavour.

1 1/2 cups	granulated sugar	375 mL
1/2 cup	butter	125 mL
2	eggs	2
2 1/4 cups	sifted cake flour	550 mL
1/2 teaspoon	baking powder	2 mL
3/4 teaspoon	baking soda	4 mL
1/4 cup	yogurt or sour cream	60 mL
1 teaspoon	vanilla	5 mL
1 cup	lightly mashed ripe bananas	250 mL

Preheat oven to 350°F (180°C). Add the sugar to the soft butter gradually and cream until very light. Beat in the eggs one at a time. Sift together the dry ingredients. Add vanilla and yogurt to the mashed bananas. Add the dry ingredients and banana mixture alternately to the creamed butter and sugar. Stir the batter mixture after each addition until smooth. Grease and flour a 9" (2.5 L) springform pan. Add batter and bake for 1 hour.

Blueberry Dessert Cake

1/4 cup	butter	60 mL
3/4 cup	granulated sugar	175 mL
1	egg	1
2 cups	cake flour	500 mL
2 teaspoons	baking powder	10 mL
1/2 teaspoon	salt	2 mL
1/2 cup	milk	125 mL
1 1/2 cups	fresh or frozen blueberries	375 mL

Topping:
1/2 cup	granulated sugar	125 mL
1/4 cup	all purpose flour	60 mL
2 teaspoons	cinnamon	10 mL
1/4 cup	butter	60 mL

Preheat oven to 350°F (180°C). Grease an 8" (2 L) springform pan. Cream together butter and sugar. Add egg and mix well. Sift together dry ingredients and add alternately with milk to creamed mixture. Fold in blueberries. Pour into prepared pan. Mix crumb topping ingredients together by hand until crumbly. Spread evenly over top of cake. Bake for 40 – 45 minutes.

Sour Cream Blueberry Coffee Cake

1 cup	butter	250 mL
2 cups	granulated sugar	500 mL
2	eggs	2
1 cup	sour cream	250 mL
1 teaspoon	vanilla	5 mL
2 cups	sifted cake flour	500 mL
1 teaspoon	baking powder	5 mL
1/2 teaspoon	salt	2 mL
1 cup	blueberries	250 mL
2 tablespoons	all purpose flour	30 mL

Topping:

1 cup	chopped pecans	250 mL
2 tablespoons	granulated sugar	30 mL
1 teaspoon	cinnamon	5 mL
1/2 teaspoon	nutmeg (optional)	2 mL

Preheat oven to 325°F (160°C). Cream the butter and add sugar gradually, beating until light. Add the eggs, one at a time, beating until fluffy. Add sour cream and vanilla. Sift together flour, baking powder and salt. Add to creamed mixture. Lightly toss blueberries in 2 tablespoons (30 mL) flour, and fold into batter. In another bowl, combine topping ingredients. Pour half of batter into greased 10" (25 cm) bundt pan. Top with half of topping mixture. Add the remaining batter and top with second half of nut mixture. Bake for 1 hour or until cake tester comes out clean from center of cake. Cool in pan 10 minutes. Turn out onto rack and cool. Drizzle with the following glaze:

Glaze:

1 1/2 cups	confectioners sugar	375 mL
2 tablespoons	butter	30 mL
1 teaspoon	vanilla	5 mL
1 – 2 tablespoons	hot water	15 – 30 mL

Combine glaze ingredients, stirring until smooth. Drizzle over cake.

Carrot Cake

LYNN MENDELSON

1 1/2 cups	oil	375 mL
2 cups	granulated sugar	500 mL
4	eggs	4
2 cups	all purpose flour	500 mL
2 teaspoons	baking powder	10 mL
1 1/2 teaspoons	baking soda	7 mL
1 teaspoon	salt	5 mL
5 teaspoons	cinnamon	25 mL
2 cups	grated carrots	500 mL
1 cup	crushed pineapple, drained	250 mL
1 1/2 cups	chopped walnuts	375 mL
1 teaspoon	vanilla	5 mL

Preheat oven to 350°F (180°C). Grease and flour pans. Combine oil and sugar and mix with electric beater. Add eggs, one at a time, beating well after each addition. Sift together flour, baking powder, baking soda, salt and cinnamon. Add to oil mixture, beating thoroughly. Mix in carrots, pineapple, walnuts and vanilla. Pour into two 8" or 9" (20 – 22.5 cm) springform pans or a 12 cup (3 L) bundt pan. Bake 45 – 60 minutes or until cake tests done.

Icing:

8 ounces	cream cheese	225 g
1 cup	icing sugar	250 mL
1 tablespoon	orange juice	15 mL

Mix together until smooth and creamy.

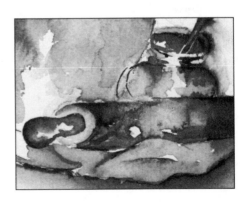

Chocolate Cake

SARA WINBERG

1/2 cup	butter or margarine	125 mL
2 cups	brown sugar	500 mL
2	eggs	2
2 cups	sifted cake flour	500 mL
1 teaspoon	baking soda	5 mL
1 1/4 cups	milk	300 mL
2 squares	unsweetened chocolate, melted and cooled	2

Preheat oven to 350°F (180°C). Cream butter or margarine. Add sugar and cream well. Add eggs, one at a time, beating well after each addition. Sift flour and soda and add to batter alternately with milk. Blend well. Add cooled chocolate. Bake in two greased 8" (1.2 L) layer pans for 35 minutes or until cake tests done.

Chocolate Cake

NANCY POSLUNS

1 3/4 cups	sifted cake flour	425 mL
1 teaspoon	baking powder	5 mL
1 teaspoon	baking soda	5 mL
1/2 teaspoon	salt	2 mL
1/2 cup	butter	125 mL
1 1/2 cups	granulated sugar	375 mL
2	eggs	2
2 tablespoons	vinegar	30 mL
1 cup	milk	250 mL
2 squares	unsweetened chocolate, melted over hot water	2

Preheat oven to 350°F (180°C). Grease two 9" (1.5 L) layer cake pans. Sift flour, baking powder, soda and salt. Cream butter. Add sugar gradually, and continue creaming. Add eggs one at a time and continue to cream until mixture is light and fluffy. Add vinegar. Add dry ingredients alternately with milk, beginning and ending with dry ingredients. Stir in melted chocolate. Pour batter into greased pans. Bake for 35 – 40 minutes. Frost with **whipped chocolate frosting**, page 320, or your favourite frosting. This cake freezes well (unfrosted).

Chocolate Cake

1/2 cup	cocoa	125 mL
3/4 cup	hot coffee	175 mL
1/2 cup	butter	125 mL
2 cups	granulated sugar	500 mL
3	eggs, separated	3
2 cups	sifted cake flour	500 mL
3 teaspoons	baking powder	15 mL
1 teaspoon	vanilla	5 mL
1/2 cup	sour cream	125 mL

Preheat oven to 325°F (160°C). Dissolve cocoa in coffee. Cream butter and sugar. Add egg yolks and blend. Add cocoa mixture and sifted dry ingredients alternately with sour cream. Add vanilla and fold in stiffly beaten egg whites. Bake in greased 9" x 13" (3.5 L) pan for 35 minutes. Frost with **jiffy frosting**, page 319.

Chocolate Banana Bundt Cake

RUTH GREENSPAN

1 cup	vegetable shortening	250 mL
2 cups	granulated sugar	500 mL
2	eggs	2
2	ripe bananas, mashed	2
1/3 cup	sour cream	75 mL
1 teaspoon	vanilla	5 mL
2 1/2 cups	all purpose flour	625 mL
2 teaspoons	baking soda	10 mL
1/3 cup	cocoa	75 mL
1/4 teaspoon	salt	1 mL
1 cup	boiling water	250 mL

Preheat oven to 350°F (180°C). Grease a 12 cup (3 L) bundt pan. Cream shortening and sugar. Add eggs one at a time and continue creaming. Add mashed bananas, sour cream and vanilla. Blend well. Add sifted dry ingredients, and stir until mixed. Add boiling water over complete mixture and blend. Batter will be loose. Pour into greased bundt pan and bake for one hour or until cake tests done.

CAKES AND FROSTINGS / 295

Chocolate Pound Cake

SHIRLEY LAZARUS

1 cup	butter, room temperature	250 mL
1/2 cup	shortening	125 mL
2 cups	granulated sugar	500 mL
5	eggs	5
3 cups	sifted all purpose flour	750 mL
1 teaspoon	baking powder	5 mL
1/4 teaspoon	salt	1 mL
1/2 cup	cocoa	125 mL
1 cup	milk	250 mL
2 teaspoons	vanilla	10 mL

Preheat oven to 325°F (160°C). Cream butter and shortening. Gradually beat in sugar. Add eggs one at a time, beating well. Sift flour with baking powder, salt and cocoa. Add dry ingredients alternately with milk and vanilla. Pour batter into a well greased and floured 10" (25 cm) tube pan. Bake 1 hour and 25 minutes. Turn out onto a rack. One day of aging improves flavour. This recipe can be halved, using 2 extra large eggs, and baked in a 9" x 5" x 3" (2 L) loaf pan.

Fudge Cake

PAULINE TOKER

2/3 cup	granulated sugar	150 mL
1/2 cup	milk	125 mL
1	egg, slightly beaten	1
3 squares	unsweetened chocolate	3

In a saucepan, combine the above four ingredients. Cook over medium heat, stirring constantly, until chocolate melts, and mixture comes to a boil. Remove from heat.

1/2 cup	butter	125 mL
1 cup	granulated sugar	250 mL
2	eggs	2
1 teaspoon	vanilla	5 mL
2 cups	sifted cake flour	500 mL
1 teaspoon	baking soda	5 mL
1/2 teaspoon	salt	2 mL
1 cup	milk	250 mL

Preheat oven to 350°F (180°C). Grease two 8" (1.2 L) layer pans and line with waxed paper. Cream butter. Add sugar gradually, beating until mixture is nice and creamy. Add eggs, one at a time, and beat well until light and fluffy. Add vanilla. Add sifted dry ingredients alternately with milk. Add cooled chocolate mixture and blend well. Bake 25 – 30 minutes. Cool and frost with **chocolate frosting**.

Fairhaven Date – Chocolate Cake

ADELE LASKIN

1 cup	dates, cut fine	250 mL
1 teaspoon	baking soda	5 mL
1 cup	boiling water	250 mL
1 cup	butter	250 mL
1 cup	granulated sugar	250 mL
2	eggs	2
1 3/4 cups	all purpose flour	425 mL
2 tablespoons	cocoa	30 mL
6 ounces	chocolate chips	170 g

Preheat oven to 350°F (180°C). Grease a 9" (3 L) square baking pan. Sprinkle dates with soda, and pour boiling water over dates. Cool. Blend date mixture in blender for 10 seconds. Cream butter and sugar well. Add eggs. Add flour sifted with cocoa, alternately with date mixture into creamed mixture. Pour into prepared pan. Sprinkle chocolate chips on top. Bake 45 – 55 minutes or until cake tests done.

Chocolate Roll

4 tablespoons	sifted cake flour	60 mL
4 tablespoons	cocoa	60 mL
1 teaspoon	baking powder	5 mL
5	eggs, separated	5
1 cup	granulated sugar	250 mL
1 1/2 tablespoons	cold water	25 mL
1 teaspoon	vanilla	5 mL

Preheat oven to 375°F (190°C). Grease and line a jelly roll pan with waxed paper. Sift dry ingredients together. Beat egg whites until stiff but not dry. Add half of the sugar while beating. Beat egg yolks. Add remaining half of sugar, water and vanilla, beating well. Fold 1/3 of egg whites into yolks, then 1/3 of flour mixture. Repeat twice. Pour batter into prepared pan and bake for 20 minutes. Turn out onto a tea towel that has been dusted with icing sugar. Remove paper. Roll towel and cake together. Cool. Unroll cake carefully, and fill with **ice cream** or your favourite **filling**.

Coffee Cake (parve)

MYRTLE COOPERSMITH

3	eggs	3
1 1/2 cups	granulated sugar	375 mL
3/4 cup	vegetable oil	175 mL
1 teaspoon	vanilla	5 mL
2 1/4 cups	all purpose flour	550 mL
1 1/2 tablespoons	baking powder	22 mL
1/2 teaspoon	salt	2 mL
3/4 cup	orange juice	175 mL

Topping:

1 cup	brown sugar	250 mL
3 teaspoons	cinnamon	15 mL
2 tablespoons	all purpose flour	30 mL
5 tablespoons	oil	75 mL
2 tablespoons	chopped nuts (optional)	30 mL

Preheat oven to 350°F (180°C). Grease and flour a 9" (2.5 L) pan. Prepare topping by combining all ingredients in a small bowl until crumbly. Set aside.

To prepare cake: Whisk together the eggs, sugar, oil and vanilla. Sift flour, baking powder and salt together, and stir into egg mixture. Stir in orange juice. Spread half of the batter in the bottom of the baking pan. Cover with half of the topping. Repeat with remaining batter and topping. Bake for 50 minutes or until cake tests done.

Coffee Cake

DOROTHY ZEIFMAN

This recipe makes a large cake.

1 cup	butter or margarine	250 mL
1 cup	granulated sugar	250 mL
4	eggs	4
1 teaspoon	vanilla	5 mL
1 teaspoon	baking soda	5 mL
1 cup	sour cream	250 mL
3 cups	all purpose flour	750 mL
4 teaspoons	baking powder	20 mL
1/2 teaspoon	salt	2 mL

Topping:

1/2 cup	brown sugar	125 mL
1/2 cup	granulated sugar	125 mL
1/2 teaspoon	cinnamon	2 mL
1 cup	chopped walnuts	250 mL

Preheat oven to 350°F (180°C). Combine topping ingredients and set aside. Cream butter and sugar until light and fluffy. Add eggs one at a time and continue to cream until well blended. Stir in vanilla. Add soda to sour cream and stir. Sift dry ingredients. Add flour mixture alternately with sour cream to egg mixture. Stir only to blend. Do not overbeat. Pour half of batter into greased 10" (25 cm) tube pan. Add 3/4 of the topping mixture. Add rest of batter and top with rest of topping. Bake for 55 minutes or until cake tests done.

Honey Cake

4	eggs	4
1 1/2 cups	granulated sugar	375 mL
1 cup	Planter's oil	250 mL
1 cup	pure natural buckwheat honey	250 mL
2 1/2 cups	all purpose flour	625 mL
2 teaspoons	baking powder	10 mL
1/2 teaspoon	cinnamon	2 mL
1/2 teaspoon	allspice	2 mL
1/4 teaspoon	ground cloves	1 mL
1/4 teaspoon	ground ginger	1 mL
1 teaspoon	baking soda	5 mL
	dissolved in	
1 cup	strong cold tea	250 mL
	juice of 1/2 lemon	

Preheat oven to 325°F (160°C). Grease and line a tube pan. Beat eggs, sugar, oil and honey. Sift together the flour, baking powder, cinnamon, allspice and cloves and add alternately with the wet ingredients to the egg mixture, beginning and ending with dry. Pour into prepared pan. Bake 1 hour and 15 minutes until cake tests done.

Mrs. Sussman's Honey Cake

3	eggs	3
2 cups	brown sugar	500 mL
3/4 cup	oil	175 mL
1 pound	honey	454 g
1	orange, juice and rind	1
1 teaspoon	baking soda	5 mL
	dissolved in	
1 cup	coffee	250 mL
4 teaspoons	baking powder	20 mL
4 cups	all purpose flour	1 L
1 teaspoon	cloves	5 mL
1 tablespoon	cocoa	15 mL
1/8 teaspoon	salt	0.5 mL

Preheat oven to 350°F (180°C). Grease and line a 9" x 13" (3.5 L) pan. Combine eggs, sugar and oil, and mix well. Add rest of ingredients and beat well. Pour batter into prepared pan. Sprinkle with **slivered almonds**. Bake 1 hour or more until cake tests done.

Light Honey Cake

PAULINE TOKER

The success of this cake depends on the thorough blending of the liquid ingredients.

6	eggs	6
1 cup	granulated sugar	250 mL
1 cup	liquid honey	250 mL
3/4 cup	vegetable oil	175 mL
1 cup	cake flour, sifted and then measured	250 mL
1 3/4 cups	all purpose flour	425 mL
1/2 teaspoon	baking soda	2 mL
1 teaspoon	baking powder	5 mL
1 teaspoon	salt	5 mL
1 teaspoon	cinnamon	5 mL
1 teaspoon	allspice	5 mL
1 teaspoon	ginger	5 mL
1/4 – 1/2 cup	dark rum, brandy or orange juice	60 – 125 mL

Preheat oven to 350°F (180°C). In large mixer bowl, beat eggs 15 minutes. Add sugar gradually and beat 10 minutes. Add honey and beat 10 minutes. Add oil and beat another 10 minutes. Sift the flours with baking soda, baking powder, salt and all the spices. Add these dry ingredients to the egg mixture on low speed, and mix only until blended. Add rum, orange juice or brandy. Pour into lightly greased 12" (30 cm) springform pan and bake for 15 minutes. Reduce oven temperature to 325°F (160°C) and bake another 55 minutes or until cake tests done. This cake freezes well.

Fruit Cake

SANDY GRANATSTEIN, OTTAWA

1 pound	pitted dates	450 g
1 cup	mixed red and green cherries	250 mL
3/4 pound	Brazil nuts	350 g
3/4 cup	granulated sugar	175 mL
3/4 cup	all purpose flour	175 mL
1/4 teaspoon	salt	1 mL
1/2 teaspoon	baking powder	2 mL
3	eggs	3
1 teaspoon	vanilla	5 mL
	rum	

Preheat oven to 300°F (150°C). Grease a 9" x 5" (2 L) loaf pan. Line pan with greased waxed paper. Put drained fruit and whole nuts into a large bowl. Measure and sift dry ingredients. Pour over fruit and nuts. Stir well. Beat eggs until light. Pour over mixture. Add vanilla and blend well. Pour mixture into pan. Bake 1 1/2 – 2 hours or until a tester comes out clean. After baking, and while still warm, pour a little rum over cake while still in pan. Remove from pan and cut into slices.

Spicy Gingerbread

2 1/2 cups	sifted all purpose flour	625 mL
1 1/2 teaspoons	baking soda	7 mL
1/2 teaspoon	ground cloves	2 mL
1 teaspoon	ground cinnamon	5 mL
1 teaspoon	ground ginger	5 mL
3/4 teaspoon	salt	4 mL
1/2 cup	soft shortening	125 mL
1/2 cup	granulated sugar	125 mL
1	egg	1
1 cup	molasses	250 mL
1 cup	hot water	250 mL

Preheat oven to 350°F (180°C). Grease and line with waxed paper, a 9" (2.5 L) square pan. Sift together flour, soda, cloves, cinnamon, ginger and salt. Cream shortening with sugar and egg until very light and fluffy. Beat in molasses. Blend in alternately, flour mixture and hot water, beginning and ending with dry ingredients. Blend just until smooth. Turn into prepared pan. Bake 50 – 55 minutes or until done. Cool on rack 10 minutes before removing from pan. Peel off paper. Cool on rack.

Coffee Sponge Cake

MYRTLE COOPERSMITH

1 tablespoon	instant coffee granules	15 mL
1 cup	boiling water	250 mL
2 cups	sifted pastry flour	500 mL
3 teaspoons	baking powder	15 mL
1/2 teaspoon	salt	2 mL
6	eggs, separated	6
1/2 teaspoon	cream of tartar	2 mL
2 cups	granulated sugar, divided	500 mL
1 teaspoon	vanilla	5 mL
1 cup	finely ground pecans or walnuts	250 mL

Preheat oven to 350°F (180°C). Dissolve instant coffee in boiling water. Cool. Sift flour with baking powder and salt. Beat egg whites with cream of tartar in a large bowl at high speed. Gradually add 1/2 cup (125 mL) of the sugar, 2 tablespoons (25 mL) at a time until very stiff. Do not underbeat. In another bowl beat egg yolks until blended. Add remaining 1 1/2 cups (375 mL) of the sugar and vanilla. Beat at high speed until thick and lemon coloured, about 4 – 5 minutes. Add the dry ingredients alternately with the cooled coffee to egg yolk mixture, beginning and ending with dry ingredients. Blend after each addition at low speed. Fold in nuts thoroughly. Fold egg yolk mixture, one quarter at a time, into egg whites. Fold 15 strokes after each addition. Pour into ungreased tube pan. Bake 60 – 75 minutes. Invert and cool.

Orange Sponge Cake

6	eggs, separated	6
1 1/4 cups	granulated sugar	300 mL
	rind of 1 orange	
1/4 cup	orange juice	60 mL
1 1/4 cups	sifted cake flour	300 mL
	sifted with	
1/4 teaspoon	salt	1 mL
1/2 teaspoon	cream of tartar	2 mL

Preheat oven to 350°F (180°C). Beat egg yolks until light. Gradually beat in sugar until mixture is fluffy. Stir in orange rind. Add juice alternately with flour/salt mixture, beating well after each addition. Beat egg whites until frothy. Sprinkle in cream of tartar, and beat until egg whites hold soft peaks. Gently fold yolks into whites. Pour into ungreased 10" (25 cm) tube pan. Bake 1 hour. Remove from oven, and invert. Let cake cool thoroughly before removing from pan. Ice with **orange frosting** on page 318.

Marble Cake

MIMI HOLLENBERG

4	eggs	4
1 cup	butter	250 mL
1 1/2 cups	granulated sugar	375 mL
2 cups	self rising flour (Brodies)	500 mL
1/2 cup	milk	125 mL
1 teaspoon	vanilla	5 mL
5 tablespoons	chocolate syrup	75 mL

Preheat oven to 350°F (180°C). Grease a 9" (22.5 cm) springform pan. Separate eggs. Cream butter with sugar until light and fluffy. Add yolks, one at a time and continue beating. Add flour and milk alternately to butter mixture. Add vanilla. Beat egg whites until stiff and fold into mixture. Remove 1/2 cup (125 mL) of the batter and combine with chocolate syrup. Pour half of plain mixture into pan, then all of the chocolate mixture, and rest of plain mixture. Cut through with a knife to marbleize. Bake 1 hour or until cake tests done.

1 cup	granulated sugar	250 mL
1	egg	1
1 cup	butter, melted	250 mL
2 1/2 cups	sifted pastry flour	625 mL
1/4 teaspoon	baking soda	1 mL

Preheat oven to 350°F (180°C). Cream sugar with slightly beaten egg. Add melted butter, flour and baking soda. Blend into a dough. Divide into 4 parts. Pat down into four 8" or 9" (1.5 L) layer cake pans. Bake about 20 minutes, or until golden brown. Turn out onto towel to cool.

Filling:

2	egg yolks	2
3/4 cup	granulated sugar	175 mL
3 tablespoons	cocoa	45 mL
4 tablespoons	cornstarch	60 mL
	dissolved in	
1/2 cup	milk	125 mL
1/2 cup	strong coffee	125 mL
1 1/2 cups	milk	375 mL
1 tablespoon	butter	15 mL
1 teaspoon	vanilla	5 mL
	sliced almonds or	
	Brazil nuts	

Mix yolks, sugar, cocoa and dissolved cornstarch. In top of double boiler combine coffee with remaining 1 1/2 cups (375 mL) milk and heat. Stir in cornstarch mixture. Cook, stirring constantly, until thick and smooth. Stir in butter and vanilla. Cool. Spread between layers and over top. Sprinkle with sliced nuts. Prepare the day before serving so that cake will soften. Refrigerate.

Spirited Marble Cake
SANDRA HABERMAN, ST. LAURENT

1 cup	margarine	250 mL
2 cups	granulated sugar	500 mL
4	eggs, separated	4
2 teaspoons	vanilla	10 mL
3 cups	all purpose flour	750 mL
3 teaspoons	baking powder	15 mL
1/4 teaspoon	salt	1 mL
1 cup	milk or juice	250 mL
1/2 cup	canned chocolate syrup	125 mL
1/4 cup	Crème de Cacao liqueur	60 mL

Preheat oven to 350°F (180°C). Grease and flour a 10" (25 cm) tube pan. Cream margarine and sugar until light and fluffy. Add egg yolks, one at a time, beating well after each addition. Stir in vanilla. Add sifted dry ingredients alternately with liquid, beginning and ending with dry. Beat whites stiff, and fold into batter. Pour 1/2 the batter into a second bowl. Add syrup and liqueur. Spoon both batters into prepared tube pan, alternating layers of white and dark. Draw a knife through batter several times to marbleize. Bake 1 hour or until cake tests done.

Marble Pound Cake
SALLY KERR

1 1/2 cups	granulated sugar	375 mL
1 cup	oil	250 mL
1 teaspoon	almond extract	5 mL
5	eggs	5
1 cup	milk	250 mL
3 squares	unsweetened chocolate, melted	3
3 cups	all purpose flour	750 mL
2 teaspoons	baking powder	10 mL
1/2 teaspoon	salt	2 mL

Preheat oven to 350°F (180°C). Beat sugar and oil in large mixing bowl. Add almond extract. Add eggs one at a time, beating after each addition. Sift flour, baking powder and salt, and add alternately with milk. Divide batter in half. To one half of batter add melted chocolate. Mix until well combined. Pour white and dark batters alternately into a greased 10" (25 cm) tube pan. Take a knife and swirl gently a couple of times to marbleize. Bake for 55 to 60 minutes.

Sponge Cake

MYRTLE COOPERSMITH

1 cup less 1 tablespoon	sifted cake flour	235 mL
1 teaspoon	baking powder	5 mL
1 tablespoon	cornstarch	15 mL
7	eggs, separated	7
1 cup	granulated sugar	250 mL
1/4 teaspoon	salt	1 mL
	juice and rind of 1/2 lemon	
	juice and rind of 1/2 orange	

Preheat oven to 350°F (180°C). Sift flour, baking powder and cornstarch together. Beat egg whites, 1/2 cup (125 mL) of the sugar and the salt, and continue beating until stiff but not dry. In another bowl, beat egg yolks and add remaining 1/2 cup (125 mL) of sugar and the rinds and juices. (Do not beat too much). Fold 1/3 of whites into yolks, then 1/3 of flour mixture. Repeat twice. Pour into ungreased tube pan and bake for 1 hour. Invert onto rack and let cool thoroughly before removing from pan.

Sponge Cake Roll

PAULINE TOKER

3	eggs	3
1 cup	granulated sugar	250 mL
1/4 cup	water	60 mL
1 cup	sifted cake flour	250 mL
2 teaspoons	baking powder	10 mL
1/2 teaspoon	salt	2 mL
1/2 teaspoon	lemon juice	2 mL
1 teaspoon	vanilla	5 mL

Preheat oven to 350°F (180°C). Line a jelly roll pan with waxed paper, overlapping edges. Beat eggs, gradually add sugar and beat until thick and lemon coloured. Add water. Sift together cake flour, baking powder and salt, and gently stir into mixture. Add flavourings. Pour batter into prepared pan smoothing out as much as possible. Bake about 12 – 14 minutes until golden. Do not overbake. Turn upside down onto tea towel covered generously with **icing sugar**. Peel off waxed paper and roll up lengthwise with towel. Let cool. Unroll cake carefully. Fill with **ice cream**. Garnish with **whipped cream** or sprinkle with **powdered sugar**. Serve with **fruit sauces** or **chocolate sauce**.

Pineapple Upside Down Cake

1/4 cup	butter	60 mL
1 cup	brown sugar	250 mL
1 · 14 ounce can	sliced pineapple	398 mL
	maraschino cherries	
	pecan or walnut halves	
1/3 cup	butter, room temperature	75 mL
1	egg	1
1 cup	granulated sugar	250 mL
1 1/3 cups	sifted all purpose flour	325 mL
2 teaspoons	baking powder	10 mL
1/2 teaspoon	salt	2 mL
2/3 cup	milk	150 mL
1 teaspoon	vanilla	5 mL

Preheat oven to 350°F (180°C). Melt butter in 9" (2.5 L) square baking pan. Sprinkle sugar evenly over butter. Place thoroughly drained pineapple rings in pan. Put a cherry in each pineapple ring, and place pecan halves between slices. Combine butter, egg and sugar in small mixer bowl. Beat at high speed until fluffy. Sift flour, baking powder and salt together. Combine milk and vanilla. Add sifted dry ingredients alternately with milk to creamed mixture. Stir after each addition until smooth. Pour batter over prepared pan. Bake about 45 minutes. Invert pan carefully onto serving plate, and let pan stand over cake for a few minutes so that all the fruit and nuts drop out. Remove pan. Serve warm or cold.

Cherry Pecan Upside Down Cake

3/4 pound	fresh sour cherries, pitted	350 g
1/2 cup	butter	125 mL
1 cup	brown sugar	250 mL
1 cup	pecan halves	250 mL
2	eggs	2
2/3 cup	granulated sugar	150 mL
1 teaspoon	vanilla	5 mL
1/2 teaspoon	almond extract	2 mL
1/3 cup plus 1 tablespoon	milk	90 mL
1 cup	all purpose flour	250 mL
1 teaspoon	baking powder	5 mL

Preheat oven to 350°F (180°C). Melt butter in a 9" (2.5 L) square baking dish. Sprinkle sugar evenly over butter and arrange pecan halves and cherries on top. In an electric mixer, beat eggs until frothy, then gradually add sugar and continue to beat until light in colour. Add vanilla, almond extract and milk and beat until smooth. Mix flour and baking powder and stir into egg mixture until just blended. Do not overbeat. Pour into prepared pan. Bake for 30 minutes or until cake tests done. Run knife around sides of pan. Let stand about 10 minutes before carefully inverting cake onto a serving plate.

Perfect Pumpkin Pound Cake

SALLY KERR

4	eggs	4
2 cups	granulated sugar	500 mL
1 cup	oil	250 mL
3 cups	all purpose flour	750 mL
2 teaspoons	baking powder	10 mL
2 teaspoons	baking soda	10 mL
1/2 teaspoon	salt	2 mL
1/2 teaspoon	cinnamon	2 mL
2 cups	canned pumpkin pie filling	500 mL
1 cup	nuts, raisins or chocolate chips (optional)	250 mL
1 teaspoon	all purpose flour	5 mL

Preheat oven to 350°F (180°C). Grease bundt or tube pan. Cream eggs and sugar. Add oil and beat to blend. Sift together flour, baking powder, baking soda, salt and cinnamon. Add dry ingredients to egg-sugar-oil mixture, alternately with pumpkin. Mix lightly, just to blend. Fold in nuts or raisins or chocolate chips which have been tossed with 1 teaspoon (5 mL) flour. Pour into prepared pan, and bake for 1 hour or more, until cake tests done.

Plain Poppy Seed Ring

1/2 cup	poppy seeds	125 mL
1 cup	milk	250 mL
1/3 cup	butter or shortening	75 mL
1 cup	granulated sugar	250 mL
4	eggs, separated	4
1 1/2 teaspoons	vanilla	7 mL
2 cups	all purpose flour	500 mL
2 teaspoons	baking powder	10 mL
1/4 teaspoon	salt	1 mL

Preheat oven to 350°F (180°C). Grease a 9" (22.5 cm) tube pan. Combine poppy seeds and milk. Cream butter or shortening and sugar until light and fluffy. Beat in egg yolks. Add poppy seed-milk mixture and vanilla. Sift flour with baking powder and salt and blend in. Beat egg whites until soft peaks form, and fold in gently. Bake in prepared tube pan for about 1 hour.

Poppy Seed Bundt Cake

RUTH GREENSPAN

1/4 cup	poppy seeds	60 mL
1 cup	buttermilk	250 mL
1/2 cup	butter or margarine	125 mL
1/2 cup	vegetable shortening	125 mL
1 1/2 cups	granulated sugar	375 mL
4	eggs, separated	4
1 teaspoon	vanilla	5 mL
2 1/2 cups	all purpose flour	625 mL
2 teaspoons	baking powder	10 mL
1 teaspoon	baking soda	5 mL
1 cup	chocolate chips	250 mL
1/2 cup	cinnamon, sugar and chocolate sprinkles, combined	125 mL

Soak poppy seeds in buttermilk 1/2 – 1 hour. Grease a bundt pan well. Preheat oven to 350°F (180°C). Cream butter or margarine, shortening and sugar until fluffy. Add yolks one at a time, beating well. Add vanilla. Mix together flour, baking powder and soda. Add alternately with poppy seed mixture to creamed mixture. Fold in stiffly beaten egg whites. On lowest speed of electric mixer fold in chocolate chips and cinnamon-sugar-chocolate sprinkle mixture. Pour into prepared pan. Bake 1 hour or until cake tests done. Leave in pan 5 minutes, then turn out onto rack to cool.

Spice Cake

2 1/4 cups	sifted cake flour	550 mL
1 teaspoon	baking powder	5 mL
3/4 teaspoon	baking soda	4 mL
1 teaspoon	salt	5 mL
3/4 teaspoon	cloves	4 mL
3/4 teaspoon	cinnamon	4 mL
3/4 cup	butter or shortening	175 mL
3/4 cup	firmly packed brown sugar	175 mL
1 cup	granulated sugar	250 mL
1 teaspoon	vanilla	5 mL
3	eggs	3
1 cup	buttermilk or sour milk	250 mL

Preheat oven to 350°F (180°C). Grease three 8" (20 cm) layer cake pans. Sift flour with baking powder, soda, salt, cloves and cinnamon. Cream butter or shortening. Add brown sugar gradually, then granulated sugar, creaming well. Add vanilla. Add eggs one at a time, beating well after each addition. Sift about 1/3 of flour mixture into batter and stir in, then half of the milk. Repeat, ending with flour. Divide batter evenly in greased pans. Bake 30 – 35 minutes.

Sour Cream Coffee Cake

Everybody's favourite

1 teaspoon	baking soda	5 mL
1 cup	sour cream	250 mL
1/2 cup	butter	125 mL
1 cup	granulated sugar	250 mL
2	eggs	2
1 teaspoon	vanilla	5 mL
2 cups	sifted cake flour	500 mL
1 teaspoon	baking powder	5 mL
1/2 teaspoon	salt	2 mL

Topping:

1/4 cup	chopped nuts	60 mL
1/2 cup	granulated or brown sugar	125 mL
1 teaspoon	cinnamon (optional)	5 mL

Preheat oven to 350°F (180°C). Grease an 8" (20 cm) springform pan. Add soda to sour cream and let stand. Cream butter and add sugar gradually, beating until creamy. Add eggs one at a time, and beat until light and fluffy. Add vanilla. Sift together flour, baking powder and salt. Fold sifted dry ingredients into butter mixture alternately with sour cream-soda mixture. Pour half of batter into greased springform pan. Sprinkle with topping. Add rest of batter and sprinkle with rest of topping. Bake for 45 – 50 minutes, or until cake tests done. Freezes well. For a nice variation, 1/4 cup (60 mL) each of **chocolate chips** and **coconut** can be added to topping mixture.

Cheesecake Squares

STELLA FREEDMAN

1 1/3 cups	graham cracker crumbs	325 mL
1/3 cup	melted butter	75 mL
1 pound	creamed cottage cheese, bulk pack	500 g
1 tablespoon	milk	15 mL
2	eggs	2
1 teaspoon	vanilla	5 mL
1/2 cup	granulated sugar	125 mL

Topping:

1 cup	sour cream	250 mL
2 tablespoons	granulated sugar	30 mL
1 teaspoon	vanilla	5 mL

Preheat oven to 350°F (180°C). Mix crumbs and butter together and pack into 8" (20 cm) square pan. Cream the cheese with the milk. Add eggs, vanilla and sugar. Whip until smooth. (Work quickly). Pour over base. Bake for 15 minutes. Cool. Preheat oven to 425°F (220°C). Mix sour cream, sugar and vanilla. Spread on top and bake for 5 minutes. Cut into squares with a wet knife.

Cheesecake #1

SANDY GRANATSTEIN, OTTAWA

2 pounds	cream cheese	1 kg
6	eggs	6
1 1/2 cups	table cream	375 mL
1 1/2 cups	granulated sugar	375 mL
2 tablespoons	all purpose flour	30 mL
	juice of 2 lemons	
1 1/2 tablespoons	vanilla	20 mL

Preheat oven to 250°F (120°C). Cream the cheese. Add rest of ingredients, one at a time, blending well. Pour into a 10" (25 cm) springform pan which has been prepared with your favourite **graham wafer crumb base**. Bake for 2 hours. Turn oven off and cool in oven overnight.

Cheesecake #2

1 1/2 cups	zweiback crumbs	375 mL
2 tablespoons	butter, melted	30 mL
2 tablespoons	granulated sugar	30 mL
1 pound	creamed cottage cheese, bulk pack	500 g
1 cup	granulated sugar	250 mL
5	eggs, separated	5
2 cups	sour cream	500 mL
1 teaspoon	vanilla	5 mL
1 teaspoon	lemon juice	5 mL
3 tablespoons	cornstarch	45 mL

Preheat oven to 300°F (150°C). Combine first three ingredients and press onto bottom of greased 9" (22.5 cm) springform pan. Cream cottage cheese and sugar. Add yolks, one at a time. Stir just enough to blend. Stir in sour cream, vanilla and lemon juice. Beat egg whites stiff, adding cornstarch while beating. Fold into cheese mixture. Pour into prepared pan. Bake 1 hour. Turn oven off and leave cake in oven for another hour. Open door for an additional half hour. Keep in refrigerator overnight.

Raspberry Swirl Cheesecake

LIBBY NAIMAN

1 cup	graham cracker crumbs	250 mL
1/2 cup	melted butter	125 mL
1 · 10 ounce package	frozen raspberries	280 g
2 tablespoons	granulated sugar	30 mL
2 tablespoons	cornstarch	30 mL
2 teaspoons	lemon juice	10 mL
16 ounces	cream cheese	454 g
3	eggs	3
2/3 cup	granulated sugar	150 mL
1/2 teaspoon	almond extract	2 mL
1 cup	sour cream	250 mL
1/2 teaspoon	vanilla	2 mL
1 tablespoon	granulated sugar	15 mL

Preheat oven to 350°F (180°C). Mix graham cracker crumbs with melted butter and press into 10" (25 cm) springform pan. Thaw berries and heat in a small saucepan. Mix cornstarch with a small amount of juice, stirring until smooth. Pour cornstarch mixture into saucepan. Add sugar and cook over medium heat, stirring constantly until thickened. Remove from heat. Stir in lemon juice and set aside.

Beat cream cheese until smooth. Add eggs one at a time and continue beating. Add sugar and almond extract. Beat until thick and lemon coloured. Pour into prepared springform pan. Spoon berry mixture on top of cheese and gently swirl into cake with a knife. Be careful not to cut through bottom crust. Bake for 25 minutes. Remove from oven and cool for 5 minutes.

Combine sour cream, vanilla and sugar. Mix until smooth. Pour over cooled cake and return to oven for about 5 minutes. Cool completely and refrigerate several hours before serving.

Mother's Cheesecake

LILLIAN VALIN

Crust:

2 cups	all purpose flour	500 mL
3 teaspoons	baking powder	15 mL
1/4 cup	granulated sugar	60 mL
1/2 cup	butter or margarine	125 mL
1/4 cup	milk	60 mL
1	egg	1

Mix all ingredients. Roll 3/4 of the dough and fit into 8" (20 cm) square baking pan. Roll remaining 1/4 of dough and set aside for top.

Filling:

1/2 pound	dry cottage cheese	250 g
1/2 cup	granulated sugar	125 mL
4	eggs	4
2 teaspoons	lemon juice	10 mL
1 teaspoon	vanilla	5 mL
1/2 cup	raisins	125 mL

Preheat oven to 350°F (180°C). Combine ingredients in a bowl and mix with a wooden spoon. Pour into unbaked crust. Place crust over filling and sprinkle with **sugar** and **cinnamon**. Bake for 50 minutes.

Chocolate Cheesecake

SUSAN MENDELSON

Preheat oven to 350°F (180°C).

Crust:

2/3 · 7 ounce package	chocolate wafers, crushed	130 g
1/3 cup	butter, melted	75 mL
1/4 cup	granulated sugar	50 mL

Combine and press into 9" or 10" (22.5 – 25 cm) springform pan. Bake for 5 minutes.

Filling:

1 pound	cream cheese, whipped style	500 g
1/2 cup	sour cream	125 mL
1 cup	granulated sugar	250 mL
2	eggs	2
6 ounces	chocolate chips, melted	170 g
1 square	unsweetened chocolate, melted	1
1 teaspoon	vanilla	5 mL

Topping: **whipped cream and shaved chocolate**

Combine all ingredients and beat in electric mixer for 15 minutes. Pour into baked shell. Bake for 30 minutes. Cool. Top with whipped cream and shaved chocolate. If desired, 1 teaspoon (5 mL) **cherry brandy** can be added to whipped cream. Refrigerate 2 – 4 hours before serving.

Pecan Cheesecake   RHODA GRANATSTEIN, WESTMOUNT

1 cup	graham crumbs	250 mL
3 tablespoons	granulated sugar	45 mL
3 tablespoons	melted butter	45 mL
3 · 8 ounce packages	cream cheese	675 g
1 1/4 cups	dark brown sugar	300 mL
2 tablespoons	all purpose flour	30 mL
3	eggs	3
1 1/2 teaspoons	vanilla	7 mL
1 cup	finely chopped pecans	250 mL

Preheat oven to 350°F (180°C). Mix graham crumbs, sugar and butter. Press into 9" (22.5 cm) springform pan. Bake 10 minutes. Combine softened cheese, brown sugar and flour. Mix in food processor or mixer until well blended. Add eggs, one at a time, mixing well after each addition. Blend in vanilla and nuts. Pour mixture into pre-baked crust. Bake 50 – 55 minutes. When done, loosen cake from rim of pan and cool. CHILL. Brush with **maple syrup** and garnish with **pecans.** Cake may be made ahead. Garnish on day you will serve it.

Chocolate Marble Cheesecake

ANNE ALLEN

Base:

1 3/4 cups	crushed graham wafer crumbs	425 mL
1/4 cup	finely ground walnuts	60 mL
1/4 cup	granulated sugar	60 mL
1/2 cup	melted butter	125 mL

Combine ingredients and blend. Grease sides of 9" – 10" (22.5 - 25 cm) springform pan. Press crumbs on bottom and up sides of pan to top. Reserve about 3 tablespoons (45 mL) of crumbs for topping.

Filling:

2 pounds	cream cheese	900 g
2 teaspoons	vanilla	10 mL
1 1/2 cups	granulated sugar	375 mL
6	eggs	6
2 cups	light cream (half and half)	500 mL
2 squares	unsweetened chocolate, melted and cooled	2

Preheat oven to 450°F (230°C). Beat cream cheese and vanilla together until fluffy. Gradually beat in sugar. Add eggs one at a time stirring until just blended. Stir in half and half. Gradually stir 3 cups (750 mL) of batter into cooled melted chocolate and blend. Pour plain batter into prepared pan. Gradually add chocolate mixture using zigzag motion. Batter will be very loose. Top with reserved crumbs. Bake 15 minutes to set batter. Reduce heat to 300°F (150°C) and bake 70 minutes longer. Remove from oven. Cool on rack one hour. Chill. Can be frozen. Serves 16.

Orange or Lemon Frosting

1/2 cup	butter or shortening	125 mL
3 cups	icing sugar	750 mL
1 tablespoon	grated orange or lemon rind	15 mL
2 – 3 tablespoons	orange or lemon juice	30 – 45 mL

Combine all ingredients and blend well, adding juice as necessary to make a spreading consistency.

Jiffy Frosting

NANCY POSLUNS

3 tablespoons	melted butter	45 mL
5 tablespoons	brown sugar	75 mL
2 tablespoons	cream or milk	30 mL
1/2 cup	shredded coconut and/or	125 mL
1/2 cup	chopped nuts	125 mL

Mix together above ingredients and spread on cake while it is still warm. Place on lowest shelf under broiler. Broil until surface bubbles and becomes brown. Do not allow to burn.

Chocolate Frosting

1 square	unsweetened chocolate	1
1/4 cup	milk	60 mL
1/2 cup	butter	125 mL
2 1/2 cups	icing sugar	625 mL
1 teaspoon	vanilla	5 mL

Combine chocolate, milk and butter in saucepan. Heat to boiling point. Remove from heat. Add sugar and vanilla. Beat until smooth and creamy. If too thin, let cool slightly. If too thick, add a few drops of milk.

Easy Milk Chocolate Frosting

Frosts a 9" x 13" (3.5 L) pan of brownies.

3 tablespoons	butter or margarine	45 mL
2 tablespoons	cocoa powder	30 mL
1 1/2 cups	icing sugar	375 mL
2 tablespoons	milk	30 mL
1 teaspoon	vanilla	5 mL

Melt butter or margarine in a medium saucepan. Stir in cocoa until dissolved. Add sugar, milk and vanilla. Stir until smooth. Add more milk if necessary, beating until of spreading consistency.

Whipped Chocolate Frosting

3 squares	unsweetened chocolate	3
1/3 cup	butter	75 mL
3 cups	icing sugar	750 mL
1/2 cup	milk	125 mL
1 teaspoon	vanilla	5 mL
1/4 teaspoon	salt	1 mL

Melt butter and chocolate together over low heat. Cool slightly. Combine sugar, milk, vanilla and salt in small mixer bowl. Place bowl in large mixer bowl half filled with **ice cubes**. Beat while adding chocolate mixture. Continue beating until of spreading consistency.

Seven Minute Frosting

2	unbeaten egg whites	2
1 1/2 cups	granulated sugar	375 mL
2 teaspoons	light corn syrup	10 mL
1/3 cup	cold water	75 mL
1/8 teaspoon	salt	0.5 mL
1 – 1 1/2 teaspoons	vanilla	5 – 7 mL

Place all ingredients except vanilla in top of double boiler, not on heat. Beat 1 minute to blend. Place over boiling water and cook, beating constantly, until frosting forms stiff peaks, about 7 minutes. Do not over-cook. Remove from boiling water. Add vanilla. Beat until of spreading consistency, about 2 minutes. Frosts two 8" or 9" (20 – 22.5 cm) layers.

Rich Butter Frosting

1/2 cup	butter	125 mL
1	egg yolk	1
2 tablespoons	buttermilk or milk	30 mL
1/2 teaspoon	vanilla	2 mL
3 cups	sifted icing sugar	750 mL

Place ingredients in small mixer bowl. Blend. Beat at medium speed 3 minutes. If soft, add a little more sugar to reach a spreading consistency. This frosts two 8" or 9" (20 – 22.5 cm) layers.

Caramel Frosting

3 cups	light brown sugar	750 mL
1 cup	light cream	250 mL
1/8 teaspoon	salt	0.5 mL
1/3 cup	butter	75 mL
1 teaspoon	vanilla	5 mL

Combine sugar, cream and salt in saucepan. Cook, stirring until sugar is dissolved, to soft ball stage, 234°F (115°C). Remove from heat. Add butter and cool without stirring until bottom of saucepan feels lukewarm. Add vanilla and beat until frosting is creamy and barely holds its shape. Spread quickly on cake before frosting hardens. Frosts tops and sides of two 9" (22.5 cm) layers.

Butter Icing

PAULINE TOKER

1/4 cup	soft butter	60 mL
2 cups	sifted icing sugar	500 mL
1/8 teaspoon	salt	0.5 mL
1 teaspoon	vanilla	5 mL
3 – 4 tablespoons	warm milk	45 – 60 mL

Beat butter until creamy. Stop mixer, and with spatula, work in sugar and salt. Mixture will be crumbly. Add 1 tablespoon (15 mL) of the warm milk and start mixer. Beat at high speed, slowly adding as much milk as needed, until mixture is fluffy and of good spreading consistency. Add vanilla. (Warm milk produces a nice shiny icing.)

Chocolate Shiny Icing

PAULINE TOKER

This recipe is sufficient for an 8" or 9" (20 – 22.5 cm) layer cake. The milk must be heated to below boiling point. This creates the shine.

3 squares	unsweetened chocolate	3
1/4 cup	butter	60 mL
3 scant cups	sifted icing sugar	725 mL
1/8 teaspoon	salt	0.5 mL
3 – 4 tablespoons (or more)	hot milk	45 – 60 mL
1 teaspoon	vanilla	5 mL

Melt chocolate and butter over hot water. Pour into small mixer bowl and with spatula, work in icing sugar which has been sifted with salt. Add 1 tablespoon (15 mL) hot milk and start mixer at high speed. Continue to add milk until mixture is of spreading consistency and shiny. Blend in vanilla.

Streusel Topping

3/4 cup	all purpose flour	175 mL
3/4 cup	granulated sugar (white or brown or in combination)	175 mL
1 teaspoon	cinnamon, optional	5 mL
3/4 cup	butter	175 mL
3/4 cup	chopped pecans	175 mL

Combine flour, sugar and cinnamon. Cut in butter until crumbly. Add pecans. Sprinkle on batter before baking. This is an easy topping for coffee cakes or muffins. Can be doubled and frozen for use as desired.

Pies and Pastries

2 cups	all purpose flour	500 mL
1 teaspoon	salt	5 mL
1/3 cup	vegetable shortening	75 mL
1/3 cup	butter or margarine	75 mL
5 tablespoons	orange juice	75 mL

Mix flour and salt in bowl. Cut in shortening to texture of coarse meal. Cut in butter to texture of small peas. Add juice gradually, stirring with a fork. Using fingers, work mixture into a ball. Divide in half. Roll each half between floured pieces of waxed paper, into a thin circle. Remove paper and lift dough carefully into pie plate. Yield: one 9" or 10" pie (1.5 L). Double recipe will yield enough for two 9" pies, plus one 9" shell.

To freeze: Wrap pie well. It is not necessary to defrost before baking. If desired, all vegetable shortening may be used instead of butter or margarine/vegetable combination.

For processor: Place flour and salt in bowl fitted with steel blade. Process briefly to sift. Cut cold butter or margarine into pieces and add to bowl. Add shortening. Process with on/off turns until crumbly. Pour juice through the feed tube while motor is running. Process until a ball is formed.

Baked Pastry Shell

Follow previous recipe. Moisten rim of pie plate before crimping edges. Prick bottom and sides of pastry with a fork to prevent puffing up during cooking. Bake at 450°F (230°C) 8 – 10 minutes until golden brown. Finish pie according to recipe.

Hint: A large square of aluminum foil may be fitted into shell before baking. Fill with about 1 cup (250 mL) of raw rice to weight down shell. Bake as directed, removing rice with foil last 3 or 4 minutes to allow bottom to brown evenly.

One Crust Pie

1 cup	all purpose flour	250 mL
1/2 teaspoon	salt	2 mL
1/3 cup	shortening	75 mL
2 – 3 tablespoons	cold water or orange juice	30 – 45 mL

Mix together flour and salt. Cut in shortening with pastry blender to the texture of coarse meal. Sprinkle with water or juice. Work with a fork and/or with fingers to form a ball of dough. Roll out into a circle 1" (2.5 cm) larger than pie plate. Fit pastry into pan. Trim edges, leaving 1/2" (1.5 cm) all around. Fold overhang under, building up edge. Crimp with fingers. Pour in filling. Bake according to recipe instructions.

Three Pie Pastry

JOYCE SPIEGEL

5 cups	all purpose flour	1.25 mL
1 cup	Crisco, room temperature	250 mL
1 cup	butter, room temperature	250 mL
1	egg	1
1 tablespoon	white vinegar	15 mL
	tap water	
	salt	

In a large bowl, cut butter and shortening into flour. In an 8 ounce (250 mL) measuring cup, beat egg lightly. Add vinegar and enough tap water to make 3/4 cup (175 mL). Add a dash of salt. Pour liquid into flour, and blend with a fork. Divide into 6 balls, wrap individually, and freeze. Defrost and roll as desired. Unused bits may be refrozen. Yield: pastry for 3 double crust 9" (22.5 cm) pies.

Baked Crumb Crusts

Kind and Amount	Butter	Granulated Sugar
Graham Crackers: 1 1/3 cups (325 mL)	1/4 cup (60 mL)	1/4 cup (60 mL)
Chocolate Wafers: 1 1/3 cups (325 mL)	3 tbsp. (45 mL)	None
Vanilla Wafers: 1 1/3 cups (325 mL)	1/4 cup (60 mL)	None
Gingersnaps: 1 1/3 cups (325 mL)	6 tbsp. (90 mL)	None
Corn Flakes: 1 1/3 cups (325 mL)	1/4 cup (60 mL)	2 tbsp. (30 mL)

The measurement above represents CRUMBS.

Roll crackers, wafers or corn flakes between layers of waxed paper to get crumbs. Roll gently with a rolling pin. Measure. Combine crumbs, sugar and melted butter in a bowl, stirring with a fork until crumbly. Set aside 3 tablespoons (45 mL) for topping. Press rest of crumb mixture onto bottom and sides of 9" (22.5 cm) pie plate, forming a small rim. Bake at 375°F (190°C) for 8 minutes. Cool, fill, and top with reserved crumbs.

Unbaked Crumb Crust

1 1/3 cups	graham cracker crumbs	325 mL
1/3 cup	brown sugar	75 mL
1/2 teaspoon	cinnamon	2 mL
1/3 cup	melted butter	75 mL

Mix all ingredients together until crumbly. Set aside 3 tablespoons for topping. Press remaining crumbs onto bottom and sides of greased 9" (22.5 cm) pie plate. Do not spread up on rim. Chill well. Fill.

1/2 cup plus 4 tablespoons	butter	175 g
1/2 cup	granulated sugar	125 mL
1	egg	1
1 tablespoon	oil	15 mL
2 1/2 cups	all purpose flour	625 mL
1 teaspoon	baking powder	5 mL
	pinch of salt	

Cream butter and sugar. Add egg and oil and beat until well blended. Add sifted dry ingredients and form into ball. (This may be done in a food processor). Press dough into an oiled jelly roll pan, 10" x 15" (25 cm x 37.5 cm). Press dough up the sides of the pan as well, to form a ridge. Prick dough with a fork, and refrigerate for about an hour. Preheat oven to 375°F (190°C). Bake dough 10 – 15 minutes, until golden. Remove from oven.

Filling:

1 · 8 ounce jar	apricot jam	250 mL
1/2 cup plus 2 tablespoons	butter	155 mL
3/4 cup	granulated sugar	175 mL
3 tablespoons	milk	45 mL
1 cup	slivered almonds, toasted	250 mL
1/2 teaspoon	almond flavouring	2 mL

While base is baking, warm jam in a saucepan to enable it to be spread easily. Place butter, sugar, milk and toasted almonds in a saucepan. Bring to a boil, and simmer for 2 – 3 minutes. Add almond flavouring. Remove from heat. Reduce oven temperature to 350°F (180°C). Spread jam lightly over base, to cover. Pour filling over, spreading mixture evenly with a knife. Bake 10 – 15 minutes. Remove pan to cooling rack. Carefully run a knife along edges of pan to loosen, but do not attempt to remove tart from pan until it is completely cooled. When cool, invert tart carefully onto a cooling rack. Use another rack or serving plate to correct position. This tart may be cut into squares, which store very well in a covered container.

Apple Pie

NANCY POSLUNS

	pastry for 9" (1.5 L) pie	
7 – 8	Spy apples, peeled and sliced	7 – 8
1/4 cup	brown sugar	60 mL
1/3 cup	granulated sugar	75 mL
1 tablespoon	lemon juice	15 mL
1 teaspoon	cinnamon	5 mL

Preheat oven to 425°F (220°C). Mix all ingredients. Place in pastry shell. Dot with butter if desired. Cover with top pastry and crimp edges. Sprinkle top of crust lightly with white sugar. Bake 20 minutes at 425°F (220°C). Reduce heat to 350°F (180°C) and make slits in top crust. Bake an additional 40 minutes.

To freeze: Freeze before baking. Wrap well. Do not defrost. Bake as above. Pie will likely require an additional 20 minutes at 350°F (180°C).

Blueberry or Raspberry Pie

NANCY POSLUNS

	pastry for 9" (1.5 L) pie	
4 cups	fresh blueberries or raspberries or a combination of both	1 L
1 cup	granulated sugar	250 mL
5 tablespoons	all purpose flour	75 mL
1 teaspoon	cinnamon	5 mL
1 tablespoon	lemon juice	15 mL
1 1/2 tablespoons	butter	20 mL

Preheat oven to 425°F (180°C). Combine sugar, flour and cinnamon. Sprinkle blueberries or raspberries with lemon juice. Lightly mix flour mixture through berries. Place berry mixture in pie plate lined with pastry. Dot with butter. Top with crust. Seal and crimp edges. Bake 20 minutes. Reduce heat to 350°F (180°C). Make slits in top crust. Bake an additional 25 minutes or more until juices are bubbling.

Option: The bottom pastry may be sprinkled with fine bread crumbs before adding berry mixture.

Cherry Pie

Follow directions for blueberry or raspberry pie, except use sour pitted cherries instead of blueberries. Omit lemon juice. Add 1 teaspoon (5 mL) almond extract. Use 1 1/4 cups (300 mL) sugar, instead of 1 cup (250 mL).

Sour Cream Apple Pie   PEARL LITWIN

1	9" (22.5 cm) unbaked pie shell	1
4 – 5 cups	peeled, sliced apples	1.25 mL
1 tablespoon	lemon juice	15 mL
2 tablespoons	all purpose flour	30 mL
3/4 cup	granulated sugar	175 mL
2	eggs, slightly beaten	2
1 cup	sour cream	250 mL
1/2 teaspoon	vanilla	2 mL
1/4 teaspoon	salt	1 mL

Topping:

1/3 cup	granulated sugar	75 mL
1/3 cup	finely chopped almonds	75 mL
1/4 cup	butter	60 mL

Preheat oven to 350°F (180°C). Toss the sliced apples with lemon juice and set aside. In a bowl, mix flour and sugar. Add eggs, sour cream, vanilla and salt, and stir until smooth. Stir in apples and pour into pie shell. Bake for 30 minutes. Meanwhile, mix sugar and almonds together and cut in butter until mixture resembles coarse crumbs. Spoon topping over pie, and bake 15 – 18 minutes more until lightly golden on top. May be served hot or cold. Other fruits may be substituted.

Chocolate Cream Pie

1	baked pie shell 9" (22.5 cm)	1
1 · 6 ounce package	chocolate bits	170 g
2 tablespoons	granulated sugar	30 mL
3 tablespoons	milk	45 mL
4	eggs, separated	4
1 teaspoon	vanilla	5 mL

Melt chocolate bits in top of double boiler. Add sugar and milk and stir to blend well. Cool. Beat in yolks, one at a time. Add vanilla. Fold in stiffly beaten egg whites. Pour into cooled baked pie shell. Garnish when cold with **whipped cream** and **chocolate shavings**, if desired. Chill until serving time.

Jean's Coconut Pie

1	baked 9" (22.5 cm) pie shell	1
1/2 cup	granulated sugar	125 mL
2 tablespoons	cornstarch (heaping)	2
2	eggs, separated	2
2 cups	milk	500 mL
1 tablespoon	butter	15 mL
1 teaspoon	vanilla	5 mL
3 tablespoons	granulated sugar	45 mL
1/4 teaspoon	cream of tartar	1 mL
	coconut	

Combine 1/2 cup (125 mL) sugar and cornstarch in a saucepan. Add egg yolks mixed with milk. Cook over medium heat, stirring until thick. Add butter and vanilla. Pour into pie shell.

Meringue: Preheat oven to 400°F (200°C). Beat egg whites until frothy. Add a pinch of cream of tartar, and gradually add 3 tablespoons (45 mL) sugar while beating until stiff peaks form. Pile on filling. Sprinkle with coconut. Brown meringue in oven until golden brown, about 5 minutes.

Lemon Meringue Pie

VIOLET BROWN, KITCHENER

1	baked 9" (22.5 cm) pie shell	1
5 tablespoons	cornstarch	75 mL
1/4 teaspoon	salt	1 mL
1 cup	granulated sugar	250 mL
2 cups	water	500 mL
1 tablespoon	grated lemon rind	15 mL
3	eggs, separated	3
1 tablespoon	butter (optional)	15 mL
6 tablespoons	lemon juice	90 mL
6 tablespoons	granulated sugar	90 mL

Preheat oven to 400°F (200°C). Combine cornstarch, salt and sugar in saucepan. Gradually stir in water and add lemon rind. Cook over medium heat stirring constantly until mixture thickens and comes to a boil. Boil gently for 1 minute. Beat the egg yolks lightly, and add a little of the hot mixture to the yolks, stirring well. Return to mixture in saucepan and blend. Cook and stir for 1 minute. Remove from heat. Add butter and lemon juice. Beat one egg white stiff, and fold lemon mixture into it, blending well. Pour into pie shell. Beat remaining two egg whites until stiff, gradually adding sugar while beating. Spread over lemon filling, making sure the meringue touches the crust all the way around. Bake 5 – 10 minutes, or until lightly browned.

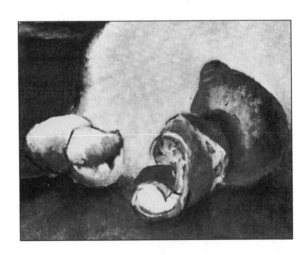

Key Lime Pie

ELEANOR LAMBERT, ST. CATHARINES

1	baked 9" (22.5 cm) pie shell	1
1 · 14 ounce can	sweetened condensed milk	395 g
1/2 cup	lime juice	125 mL
3	eggs, separated	3
	green food colouring	
1/8 teaspoon	salt	0.5 mL
	grated lime rind (optional)	

Chill condensed milk several hours or overnight. Put milk in large mixer bowl, and beat at high speed for 3 minutes. Add lime juice slowly, scraping as you do. (Mixture looks like soft marshmallows). Add egg yolks, one at a time, beating well after each addition. Add enough food colouring to tint a delicate green. Beat egg whites and salt until stiff peaks form. Fold into condensed milk mixture. Pour into cooled, baked pie shell. Sprinkle with grated lime rind. Chill several hours.

Peaches 'n Cream Pie

HOLLY GOREN LASKIN

	pastry for 2 crust pie	
1 · 28 ounce can	peach halves	796 mL
	or	
6 – 8	fresh peaches,	6 – 8
	peeled and halved	
2 tablespoons	all purpose flour	30 mL
1/2 cup	granulated sugar	125 mL
1/2 cup	sour cream	125 mL
1 tablespoon	grated lemon rind	15 mL
1/2 cup	brown sugar	125 mL

Preheat oven to 425°F (220°C). Roll out half of dough to fit 9" (22.5 cm) pie plate. Drain peach halves. Arrange, cut side down, in pie shell. Reserve remaining dough in refrigerator. Combine flour, granulated sugar, sour cream and lemon rind. Beat until smooth, and pour over peach halves. Crumble together the remaining dough and the brown sugar. Sprinkle over filling. Bake 15 minutes. Reduce heat to 350°F (180°C) and bake an additional 20 – 25 minutes.

Fresh Peachy Praline Pie

LILLIAN MANDEL

Pecans and brown sugar give this summer pie superb flavour.

1	unbaked 9" (22.5 cm) pie shell	1
3/4 cup	granulated sugar	175 mL
3 tablespoons	all purpose flour	45 mL
4 cups	sliced peeled peaches, or more, if desired	1 L
1 1/2 teaspoons	lemon juice	7 mL
1/3 cup	brown sugar, firmly packed	75 mL
1/4 cup	all purpose flour	60 mL
1/2 cup	chopped pecans	125 mL
3 tablespoons	butter or margarine	45 mL

Preheat oven to 400°F (200°C). Combine sugar and flour in a large bowl. Add peaches and lemon juice. Combine brown sugar, flour and pecans in a small bowl. Mix in butter until mixture is crumbly. Sprinkle 1/3 of the pecan mixture over bottom of pie shell. Cover with the peach mixture and sprinkle with remaining pecan mixture. Bake until peaches are tender, about 40 minutes.

Pecan Pie

SANDY GRANATSTEIN, OTTAWA

1	unbaked 9" (22.5 cm) pie shell	1
1 cup	corn syrup	250 mL
1 cup	dark brown sugar	250 mL
1/4 teaspoon	salt	1 mL
1/3 cup	melted butter or margarine	75 mL
1 teaspoon	vanilla	5 mL
3	eggs, lightly beaten	3
1 cup	shelled pecan halves, heaping whipped cream or ice cream (optional)	300 mL

Preheat oven to 350°F (180°C). Combine syrup, sugar, salt, butter and vanilla and mix well. Add eggs. Pour into pie shell. Sprinkle pecans over all. Bake about 45 minutes. When cool, may be topped with whipped cream or ice cream.

Pecan Pie (parve)

ROZ HALBERT

1	unbaked 9" (22.5 cm) pastry shell	1
3	eggs	3
1/2 cup	brown sugar	125 mL
1/2 cup	granulated sugar	125 mL
1 cup	corn syrup	250 mL
1 cup	pecan halves	250 mL
1 teaspoon	vanilla	5 mL

Preheat oven to 300°F (150°C). Break about 3/4 of the pecans. Save the rest for the top of the pie. Beat eggs and both sugars very well, until thick. Beat in corn syrup and vanilla. Fold in broken nuts. Pour into unbaked pie shell. Dot with reserved pecan halves. More nuts may be sprinkled on top if desired. Bake 1 – 1 1/2 hours until set. Top will crack. Serve warm with **French vanilla ice cream**, or **coffee flavoured whipped cream**. For parve pie, use whipped topping flavoured with instant coffee, instead of whipped cream or ice cream. For 10" (25 cm) pie, use 1 1/3 recipe.

Raisin Pie

ELEANOR LAMBERT, ST.CATHARINES

	pastry for 2 crust pie	
2 cups	raisins	500 mL
1 cup	boiling water	250 mL
3/4 cup	brown sugar	175 mL
2 tablespoons	corn starch	30 mL
1/4 cup	cold water	60 mL
1/4 teaspoon	salt	1 mL
1 tablespoon	vinegar	15 mL
1 teaspoon	vanilla	5 mL
1 – 2 tablespoons	butter	15 – 30 mL

Preheat oven to 425°F (220°C). Combine raisins and boiling water and simmer for 5 minutes. Stir in brown sugar and cornstarch which has been blended with cold water. Cook, stirring, until clear. Add rest of ingredients. Pour into prepared pie plate. Cover with top crust, sealing edges well. Cut slits in top crust. Bake for 15 minutes. Reduce heat to 350°F (180°C) and bake for an additional 20 minutes.

Quickie Pie

1	baked 9" (22.5 cm) pastry shell	1
1 package	raspberry gelatin	1
	(4 serving size)	
1 2/3 cups	hot water	400 mL
1 tablespoon	lemon juice	15 mL
1 pint	vanilla ice cream	500 mL
1 cup	crushed raspberries	250 mL

Dissolve gelatin in hot water. Add lemon juice. Chill until partially set. Beat ice cream into gelatin. Fold in crushed raspberries. Pour chilled filling into cool pie shell. Chill pie 1 or 2 hours until firm.

Old-Fashioned Rhubarb Pie

MYRTLE COOPERSMITH

	pastry for 2 crust pie	
4 cups	diced tender red rhubarb	1 L
1 1/4 cups	granulated sugar,	325 mL
	or more to taste	
5 tablespoons	all purpose flour	75 mL
1 1/2 tablespoons	butter or margarine	20 mL

Preheat oven to 400°F (200°C). Line pan with rolled out pastry. Wash but do not peel rhubarb, discarding leaves and stem ends. Cut into 1/4" (0.6 cm) pieces, and measure 4 cups (1 L). Mix sugar and flour, and sprinkle enough over pastry just to cover. Add half the rhubarb, half the sugar/flour mixture, then remaining rhubarb, and remaining sugar mixture. Dot with butter. Dampen rim of lower crust and cover with rolled out pastry. Seal, trim and crimp edges. Slit top. Bake about 40 – 50 minutes, or until pastry is golden brown and juice bubbles through crust.

Strawberry Pie

ADÈLE FREEMAN

1	baked 9" (22.5 cm) pastry shell	1
2 quarts	strawberries	2 L
1/2 cup	icing sugar	125 mL
1 cup	water	250 mL
2 tablespoons	corn starch	30 mL
3/4 cup	granulated sugar	175 mL

Add icing sugar to strawberries, and let stand in refrigerator one hour. Crush 1 cup (250 mL) of the smallest berries with a fork. Save the largest and nicest to fill the shell. Cook crushed berries with water over medium heat. Bring to a boil, and boil gently for 2 minutes. Press mixture through a sieve. Mix the cornstarch with the sugar. Add a little of the crushed strawberry mixture to the cornstarch-sugar mixture to make a paste. Then stir cornstarch mixture into the crushed strawberry mixture. Cook over medium heat, stirring constantly, until clear and slightly thickened. Add a drop or two of **red food colouring**, if desired. Arrange reserved whole strawberries in pie shell, and pour glaze over all.

Butterless Butter Tarts

FLORENCE BEGG

1	recipe pie pastry	1
1	egg	1
	beaten with	
2 tablespoons	cream	30 mL
1 teaspoon	vanilla	5 mL
1 cup	brown sugar	250 mL
1/2 cup	currants	125 mL
1/4 cup	chopped walnuts	60 mL

Line tart pans with pastry dough. Preheat oven to 375°F (190°C). Mix and fill shells 2/3 full. Bake until bubbling and golden, about 10 – 15 minutes. Yield: 12 – 14 tarts.

Butter Tarts

FLORENCE BEGG

1	recipe pie pastry	1
1 cup	raisins or currants	250 mL
1/2 cup	butter	125 mL
1 cup	brown sugar	250 mL
1 cup	corn syrup	250 mL
1/2 teaspoon	salt	2 mL
1 teaspoon	vanilla	5 mL
2	eggs, slightly beaten	2
1 tablespoon	vinegar	15 mL

Line tart pans with pastry dough. Preheat oven to 425°F (220°C). Combine raisins, butter, sugar, corn syrup and salt in a heavy saucepan. Cook over low heat until butter is melted and mixture is warm. Remove from heat and add vanilla, beaten eggs, vinegar and **2 dashes of nutmeg**. Fill pastry shells 2/3 full. Bake 10 minutes. Reduce heat to 350°F (180°C) and bake an additional 5 minutes, or until pastry is golden. Yield: 18 medium or 24 small tarts.

Butterhorns

JUDY SWARTZ

2 cups	all purpose flour	500 mL
1 cup	butter or margarine	250 mL
1	egg yolk	1
3/4 cup	sour cream	175 mL
3/4 cup	granulated sugar	175 mL
1 teaspoon	cinnamon	5 mL
3/4 cup	chopped nuts	175 mL

Measure flour into a bowl. Cut in butter or margarine and mix with fingers until crumbly. Add 1 egg yolk and sour cream. Mix well. When blended, shape into a ball. Sprinkle waxed paper with flour. Wrap and chill dough several hours or overnight. Grease a cookie sheet lightly. Preheat oven to 375°F (190°C). Combine sugar, cinnamon and chopped nuts. Divide dough into five pieces. Roll each piece separately on floured board into a circle. Sprinkle with cinnamon mixture, leaving center of dough free of filling. Cut into wedges (16ths) and roll each wedge up from wide end toward center. Place on cookie sheet. Bake 25 – 30 minutes until browned.

Cinnamon Rolls

SANDRA HABERMAN, ST. LAURENT

3 tablespoons	butter	45 mL
3 tablespoons	granulated sugar	45 mL
1	egg	1
1 1/2 cups	all purpose flour	375 mL
3 teaspoons	baking powder	15 mL
1/2 cup	sour cream	125 mL
	melted butter, cinnamon and brown sugar	

Cream butter and sugar. Add egg and mix well. Add sifted dry ingredients alternately with sour cream, and mix until dough is formed. Chill dough, if desired. Divide dough in two. Roll dough out into rectangular shape. Spread melted butter generously over dough. Sprinkle with cinnamon and brown sugar. Roll dough as for jelly roll, and slice. Place in greased muffin tins. Bake at 375°F (190°C) for 18 minutes. This freezes very well.

Cheese Knishes

PEARL MEKLER

Pastry:

2 cups	all purpose flour	500 mL
1 cup	margarine	250 mL
1 cup	sour cream	250 mL

Process ingredients to form a ball and refrigerate overnight.

Filling:

1 pound	pressed cottage cheese	454 g
1	egg	1
2 tablespoons	granulated sugar	30 mL
1/2 teaspoon	vanilla	5 mL

Combine all ingredients. Preheat oven to 350°F (180°C). Divide dough in half. Roll out each half, separately, into a rectangular shape. Place cheese mixture along the long edge. Roll as for jelly roll. Using the edge of your hand, cut into 1" (2.5 cm) slices. Place on ungreased cookie sheet and bake 45 minutes until golden.

Hot Cheese Pie

SHIRLEY LAZARUS

Dough:

1/2 cup	butter	125 mL
1/2 cup	granulated sugar	125 mL
1	egg	1
2 tablespoons	sour cream	30 mL
1 1/2 cups	all purpose flour	375 mL
1 1/2 teaspoons	baking powder	7 mL
1/2 teaspoon	salt	2 mL
1 teaspoon	vanilla	5 mL

Preheat oven to 350°F (180°C). Grease a 10" (25 cm) pie plate. Cream butter and sugar. Add egg, sour cream and beat. Sift together flour, baking powder and salt and add to butter mixture. Add vanilla. Divide dough in half. Flour hands, and pat one half into prepared pie plate, on bottom and half way up sides.

Filling:

1 pound	cottage cheese	450 g
2	eggs	2
1/4 cup	granulated sugar	60 mL
2 tablespoons	sour cream	30 mL
1/2 teaspoon	salt	2 mL
1/2 teaspoon	lemon juice	2 mL

Beat cheese with eggs. Add sugar, and continue beating. Blend in sour cream, salt and lemon juice. Beat until creamy. Pour over dough. Flour hands well, and with other half of dough, make 6 rolls for a lattice top. Bake until golden, about 1 hour. Let stand out of oven for 10 – 15 minutes before serving.

Cheese Pie

JUDY ASCH

1 pound	cottage cheese	450 g
1 cup	granulated sugar	250 mL
1 cup	sour cream	250 mL
4	eggs	4
1/4 teaspoon	salt	1 mL
1/2 teaspoon	baking powder	2 mL
1 · 14 ounce can	crushed pineapple, drained	398 mL
1 cup	cream, whipped	250 mL

Crust:

3 cups	crushed crumbs; corn flakes, frosted flakes or ginger snaps	750 mL
1/4 cup	melted butter	60 mL
2 tablespoons	icing sugar	30 mL

Preheat oven to 400°F (200°C). Combine ingredients for crust. Pat into greased 10" (25 cm) pie plate. Beat cheese with sugar, sour cream, eggs, salt and baking powder. Fold in one half of the crushed pineapple. Pour into prepared pie plate. Bake 15 minutes. When cool, frost with whipped cream mixed with other half of the crushed pineapple.

Cream Cheese Pastry

SARAH SLOBINSKY

1 cup	butter	250 mL
1 cup	cream cheese	250 mL
2 cups	all purpose flour	500 mL
1/8 teaspoon	salt	0.5 mL

Mix above ingredients. Knead well. Shape into a ball. Wrap in waxed paper and chill well.

Preheat oven to 350°F (180°C). Roll 1/4 of dough at a time into circular shape, as thin as possible* and cut into wedges. On outer edge place a **date**, or mixture of any **fruit and nuts**. Sprinkle **ground nuts** and **brown sugar** over top. Roll each edge toward center. Bake until golden.

Caraway, Sesame and Poppy Seed Pastries

Follow previous recipe to *. Cut dough into 3" (7.5 cm) rounds. Brush each round lightly with a mixture of:

1	egg white beaten with	1
2 tablespoons	cold water	30 mL

Sprinkle some rounds with **caraway seeds**, some with **sesame seeds**, and some with **poppy seeds**. Bake at 425°F (220°C) for 5 minutes. Reduce heat to 350°F (180°C) and bake until golden and crisp. These can be made ahead and stored in an airtight container. Reheat in 300°F (150°C) oven to crisp.

Flan Pastry

MYRTLE COOPERSMITH

2 cups	all purpose flour	500 mL
1 cup	butter, room temperature	250 mL
1/2 cup	granulated sugar	125 mL
2 tablespoons	vinegar	30 mL

Preheat oven to 350°F (180°C). Combine ingredients. Press into 10" (25 cm) flan pan. Bake until golden.

Note: Sugar may be omitted for quiche pastry.

Variation: Pastry may be pressed into tart pans for individual tartlets.

Blueberry Flan

1	baked 10" (25 cm) flan shell	1
2 quarts	blueberries	2 L
1/2 cup	granulated sugar	125 mL
1/4 cup	Grand Marnier	60 mL

Combine sugar with 1 quart (1 L) berries and Grand Marnier in saucepan and heat until sugar is dissolved. Add remaining berries and pour into baked flan shell. Serve with **ice cream** or **whipped cream.**

Apple Flan Filling

S U E   D E V O R

1/2 cup	granulated sugar	125 mL
1/4 cup	all purpose flour	60 mL
2	eggs	2
1/2 cup	unsalted butter or margarine, melted and slightly browned	125 mL
1/4 teaspoon	vanilla	2 mL
2 tablespoons	finely grated lemon peel	30 mL
3 large, or 6 small	MacIntosh or Spy apples, peeled, cored and thinly sliced icing sugar	3 – 6

Preheat oven to 375°F (190°C). Prepare your favourite 10" (25 cm) flan pastry.

Filling: Combine sugar, flour and eggs, and whisk until smooth. Stir in melted butter or margarine, vanilla and lemon peel. Arrange apple slices, cartwheel fashion, on pastry in flan pan. Pour the filling over the apples and bake for 30 – 40 minutes until golden brown. Cool. Sift icing sugar over flan. Serves 10 – 12.

Strawberry Flan

| 1 | baked 10" (25 cm) flan shell | 1 |
| 1 – 2 quarts | strawberries, washed and hulled | 1 – 2 L |

Arrange whole berries in baked flan shell.

Glaze:

1/4 cup	apricot jam	60 mL
1/2 cup	crabapple jelly	125 mL
2 tablespoons	orange juice or Cointreau	30 mL

Combine and dissolve over low heat. Brush over berries with a pastry brush. Refrigerate until serving.

Raspberry Roll-ups

SANDRA HABERMAN, ST. LAURENT

2 cups	all purpose flour	500 mL
1 teaspoon	baking powder	5 mL
1 cup	butter	250 mL
1/2 cup	sour cream	125 mL
1	egg, separated	1
	raspberry jam	
	granulated sugar	

Sift flour with baking powder. Cut in butter with pastry blender. Mix yolk into sour cream, and add to flour mixture, mixing well with a fork, only until blended. Divide dough into quarters, and form each piece into a ball. Wrap in waxed paper, and refrigerate for several hours. On floured board, roll each ball into a 10" (25 cm) circle. Spread with raspberry jam. Cut into 12 pie shaped wedges. Roll from the outside in. Brush tops with beaten egg white, and sprinkle with sugar. Bake on ungreased cookie sheet at 350°F (180°C) for 20 – 25 minutes, until golden. A mixture of **brown sugar**, **cinnamon** and **ground nuts** may be substituted for jam. These freeze very well.

Pear Tart

PAULINE MENKES

Use Flan Pastry recipe on page 341.

Filling:

6	large, ripe pears, peeled, cored and sliced	6
1 tablespoon	lemon juice	15 mL
1/2 cup	granulated sugar	125 mL
3 tablespoons	all purpose flour	45 mL
1 tablespoon	grated ginger	15 mL

Preheat oven to 425°F (220°C). Place pears in pastry lined 12" (30 cm) flan pan. Sprinkle with lemon juice. Combine sugar, flour and ginger, and pour over top of pears.

Topping:

1/3 cup	brown sugar	75 mL
1/4 cup	all purpose flour	60 mL
1/8 teaspoon	ground ginger	0.5 mL
1/4 cup	butter	60 mL
1/4 cup	chopped pecans	60 mL

Combine ingredients in processor bowl fitted with steel blade. Process with quick on/off turns until crumbly. Spread mixture over top of pear mixture. Bake 10 minutes. Reduce heat to 350°F (180°C) and bake an additional 30 minutes or until bubbly.

Caramelized Pear Tart

PAULINE MENKES

1 cup less 2 tbsp.	butter	220 mL
1/2 cup	granulated sugar	125 mL
3	egg yolks	3
	zest of 1 lemon, grated	
3/4 cup	ground almonds	175 mL
1 3/4 cups	all purpose flour	425 mL

Process all ingredients to form a ball. Divide dough into 4 pieces. Place the pieces on top of one another. Press together and repeat the dividing, stacking and pressing 3 more times. Wrap dough in plastic wrap and chill for 1 hour.

Filling:

2 1/2 pounds	ripe, firm pears	1.25 kg
1/2 cup	butter	125 mL
3/4 cup	granulated sugar	175 mL
1/3 cup	sliced almonds	75 mL

Preheat oven to 400°F (200°C). Butter a 10" (25 cm) tart pan with a removable bottom. On a lightly floured surface, roll out the dough to a thickness of 1/8" (0.3 cm). Line pan with dough. Place foil over dough and fill with dried beans or pie weights. Bake 20 minutes. Remove beans and foil and bake an additional 3 minutes or until crust is golden.

While crust is baking, peel and core pears. Cut into large cubes. Melt butter in a large pan. Sauté pears over medium heat until tender. Sprinkle with sugar, and cook until fruit is caramelized. Place filling in crust. Brown almonds under broiler 1 minute and sprinkle on top.

Apple Strudel

3 cups	all purpose flour	750 mL
1 cup	shortening	250 mL
1/2 teaspoon	salt	3 mL
2	eggs, slightly beaten	2
1/2 cup	ginger ale or water	125 mL

Cut shortening into flour and salt. Add eggs and liquid. Mix well. Wrap in waxed paper and chill overnight. Preheat oven to 400°F (200°C). Divide dough into 6 pieces. Roll each out as thin as possible into a rectangle. On the edge of each piece, put filling and bake as below.

6 – 8	apples, peeled and chopped	6 – 8
3/4 cup	granulated sugar	175 mL
	grated rind of 1 lemon	
3 tablespoons	melted butter	45 mL
1/2 cup	bread crumbs	125 mL

Add sugar, lemon rind, butter and bread crumbs to apples. Roll dough as thin as possible. Sprinkle top of dough with **oil**, **sugar** and **cinnamon** to taste. Place apple mixture at edge of dough. Fold over a little dough to seal ends. Roll as a log. Bake in slightly oiled pan for 20 – 30 minutes.

Dough:

1 3/4 cups	**all purpose flour**	425 mL
1 cup	**butter**	250 mL
1/2 cup	**granulated sugar**	125 mL
1	**egg yolk**	1
3 tablespoons	**sour cream or yogurt**	45 mL

Combine ingredients in processor fitted with steel knife. Process until dough gathers into a ball. Divide in half, cover with waxed paper and let it rest for at least an hour.

Preheat oven to 375°F (190°C). Roll each half of dough separately, between two sheets of waxed paper. Measure to fit a 9" x 13" (3.5 L) baking pan. Place one dough on bottom of pan.

Filling:

7	**eggs, separated**	7
1 cup	**granulated sugar**	250 mL
4 ounces	**semi-sweet chocolate, melted**	125 g
10 – 12 ounces	**walnuts, chopped**	275 – 325 g
2	**green apples, grated**	2

In large bowl of electric mixer, beat egg whites, gradually adding one half cup (125 mL) of the sugar, and continue to beat until stiff but not dry. In a separate bowl, beat egg yolks, gradually adding the other half cup (125 mL) of the sugar. Add melted chocolate, walnuts and apples. Combine mixture with beaten egg whites folding carefully. Pour into prepared pan. Place the second half of dough on to the mixture, carefully anchoring the dough on top of the filling. Prick with a fork. Bake 45 – 60 minutes. Cut into squares when cold, and sprinkle with **icing sugar.**

# Chocolate Tart

Pastry:

1 cup	all purpose flour	250 mL
1/8 teaspoon	salt	0.5 mL
1/3 cup	granulated sugar	75 mL
6 tablespoons	unsalted butter, chilled and cut into pieces	90 mL
1	small egg, slightly beaten	1

Process flour, salt, sugar and butter for 10 seconds. Add egg and process until dough forms a ball. Press dough into a 9" (22.5 cm) flan pan with a removable bottom. Prick dough and chill, uncovered, for 1 hour.

Preheat oven to 375°F (190°C). Bake pastry for 20 minutes. (Rice or pie weights placed on foil in pan can be used to prevent bubbling.) Remove foil and weights, and bake another 10 minutes until golden brown. Cool at least 10 minutes before filling.

Filling:

5 ounces	bittersweet chocolate	150 g
1	whole egg	1
2	egg yolks	2
2 tablespoons	granulated sugar	30 mL
1 teaspoon	icing sugar	5 mL

Reduce oven temperature to 350°F (180°C). Melt chocolate in top of double boiler. Set aside. In large bowl of electric mixer, combine egg, egg yolks, and granulated sugar. Beat until thick and lemon coloured. Add cooled chocolate and whisk until well combined. Pour mixture into cooled shell. Bake only about 10 minutes, until chocolate is set. Cool. Sift icing sugar over the top.

3 cups	self-rising flour	750 mL
1 cup	margarine	250 mL
3/4 cup	yogurt	175 mL

Cut margarine into flour as for pastry. Lightly stir in yogurt. (One or two extra tablespoons of yogurt may be necessary if dough seems too dry). Form dough into a ball. Divide into four parts. Roll each part out thinly into a rectangular shape. Spread with your favourite filling. (See below). Roll up as for jelly roll. Place on cookie sheet, seam side down, two rolls per sheet. Oil top lightly and sprinkle with **sesame seeds** or **chopped nuts**. Bake at 350°F (180°C) about 30 minutes, or until lightly browned.

Filling:

1. Purim Combination:

1/2 pound	chopped pitted dates	225 g
1 cup	raisins	250 mL
	grated rind of 1 orange	
2 tablespoons	lemon juice	30 mL
1/2 – 1 cup	apricot jam	125 – 250 mL

Barely cover dates and raisins with water and simmer until soft and thick, about 10 minutes. Add rest of ingredients and stir until combined. Mixture should be thick and tart.

2. Combine: Quantities according to your taste.

strawberry jam
orange marmalade
raisins
chopped nuts

3. Cheese treats - Combine:

1/2 pound	dry cottage cheese	225 g
1	egg	1
	raisins and cinnamon	
	grated lemon or orange rind	

This makes a lovely cheese pastry.

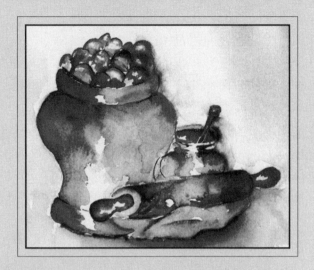

Cookies

Almond Cookies

ANN BODLEY

1 cup	butter	250 mL
1 cup	granulated sugar	250 mL
1	egg	1
1	egg yolk	1
	grated rind of 1 lemon	
2 cups	all purpose flour	500 mL
1 cup	finely chopped or ground almonds	250 mL

Topping:

1	egg white	1
2 tablespoons	granulated sugar	30 mL
1/3 cup	finely chopped or ground almonds	75 mL
1 teaspoon	cinnamon	5 mL

Cream butter. Gradually beat in sugar. Add eggs, one at a time and blend. Stir in rind, flour and chopped almonds. Form dough into a ball and chill a few hours or overnight. Preheat oven to 400°F (200°C). Roll out dough on floured board and cut into desired shapes with a cookie cutter. Place on a greased cookie sheet. Brush top with unbeaten egg white, and sprinkle with mixture of remaining sugar, almonds and cinnamon. Bake about 8 minutes or until golden.

Almond Lace Cookies

PAULINE MENKES

1/2 cup	unsalted butter	125 mL
3/4 cup	ground almonds	175 mL
1 tablespoon	all purpose flour	15 mL
1/2 cup	granulated sugar	125 mL
1 tablespoon	cream	15 mL
1 tablespoon	milk	15 mL
1 cup	chocolate chips	250 mL

Preheat oven to 350°F (180°C). Place all ingredients except for chocolate chips in a saucepan. Heat gently until butter melts, stirring constantly. Let cool. Drop by teaspoonfuls on ungreased heavy duty foil lined cookie sheet about 2" (5 cm) apart, to allow for spreading. Do only 5 or 6 at a time. Bake about 5 minutes until golden. Let cool a few seconds before trying to lift from pan. Lift with a spatula, and cool on paper towels. Melt chocolate chips and spread between cookies to make a sandwich.

Melba Toasted Almond Slices   PEARL MEKLER

A very low-fat, low calorie cookie.

4	egg whites	4
1/2 cup	granulated sugar	125 mL
1/2 teaspoon	vanilla	2 mL
	grated rind and juice	
	of 1/2 lemon or orange	
	(i.e. 1 tablespoon – 15 mL)	
2 tablespoons	oil	30 mL
3/4 cup plus 1 tablespoon	all purpose flour	200 mL
1/4 teaspoon	salt	1 mL
3/4 cup	toasted almonds	175 mL

Preheat oven to 350°F (180°C). Beat egg whites, adding sugar gradually and beat until stiff. Combine vanilla, rind, juice and oil. Fold into whites. Sift flour and salt and fold into white mixture. Carefully fold almonds into mixture. Spoon batter into an ice cube tray, or a 10" x 3.5" x 2.5" (25 x 8.75 x 6.25 cm) loaf pan which has been greased and waxed paper lined. Bake for 30 minutes. Turn out and remove waxed paper immediately. Wrap in a tea towel. Cool and refrigerate or freeze overnight. With a very sharp knife or slicer, slice thinly and bake at 350°F (180°C) until golden.

No-Bake Arrowroot Squares

ROSE MALLIN

30	Arrowroot cookies, broken into pieces	30
1 cup	chopped walnuts	250 mL
2	eggs	2
1/2 cup	granulated sugar	125 mL
1/8 teaspoon	salt	0.5 mL
4 tablespoons	cocoa	60 mL
1/2 cup	butter or margarine	125 mL
1 teaspoon	vanilla	5 mL

Combine cookie pieces and walnuts. Crumble with fingers. Combine eggs, sugar, salt, cocoa, butter and vanilla in top of double boiler. Cook until thickened. Pour egg mixture over the cookie nut mixture and blend well. Place mixture into greased 8" (2 L) square baking pan. Frost with Butter Icing when cool.

Butter Icing:

1 cup	icing sugar	250 mL
2 tablespoons	butter	30 mL
1 teaspoon	vanilla	5 mL
3-4 teaspoons	milk	15-20 mL
1 square	unsweetened chocolate, melted	1

Blend together all ingredients except chocolate. Frost. Dribble melted chocolate over frosting. Refrigerate overnight. No baking required.

Brown Eyed Susans

BERNICE GOREN

1 cup	butter	250 mL
1 teaspoon	almond extract	5 mL
1/2 teaspoon	salt	2 mL
3 tablespoons	granulated sugar	45 mL
2 cups	all purpose flour	500 mL

Preheat oven to 400°F (200°C). Cream butter. Add remaining ingredients and mix until smooth. Roll into walnut-size balls. Place on greased cookie sheet and flatten slightly. Bake 10 – 12 minutes.

Frosting:

1 cup	icing sugar	250 mL
2 tablespoons	cocoa	30 mL
1 1/2 tablespoons	water	20 mL
1/2 teaspoon	vanilla	3 mL
1/2 teaspoon	almond extract	3 mL
	blanched almonds	

Combine sugar and cocoa. Add water, vanilla and almond extract. Mix well. Place 1/2 teaspoonful (2 mL) on each cookie. Top with 1 blanched almond.

Brown Yummies

VICKI CAMPBELL

4 squares	unsweetened chocolate	4
1 cup	butter	250 mL
4	eggs	4
1 1/2 cups	granulated sugar	375 mL
1 1/3 cups	sifted cake flour	325 mL
1 teaspoon	baking powder	5 mL
1/2 teaspoon	salt	3 mL
2 teaspoons	vanilla	10 mL
6 ounces	semi-sweet chocolate bits	170 g
1/2 cup	chopped walnuts	125 mL

Preheat oven to 350°F (180°C). Combine chocolate and butter in top of double boiler and melt over boiling water. Cool. Beat the eggs until frothy and gradually add sugar, mixing just until blended. Add flour which has been sifted with baking powder and salt. Add vanilla. Add chocolate mixture and blend just until mixed through. Do not overbeat. Fold in chocolate bits. Pour into greased 9" x 13" (3.5 L) pan. Sprinkle top with chopped walnuts. Bake 30 minutes. Cool. Put in refrigerator to chill. Cut into squares.

Iced Brownies

1/2 cup	butter	125 mL
2 squares	unsweetened chocolate	2
1/2 cup	all purpose flour	125 mL
1/2 teaspoon	baking powder	2 mL
1 cup	granulated sugar	250 mL
2	eggs	2
1 teaspoon	vanilla	5 mL
1/2 cup	chopped nuts (optional)	125 mL

Preheat oven to 350°F (180°C). Grease an 8" – 9" (2 – 3 L) square baking pan. Melt butter and chocolate over hot water. Cool. Sift together flour, baking powder and sugar. Add eggs, vanilla and chocolate-butter mixture. Beat for 1 minute. Add nuts if desired. Pour into prepared pan. Bake for 20 – 25 minutes. Cool. Ice with the following icing:

Icing:

1 cup	sifted icing sugar	250 mL
2 tablespoons	butter, softened	25 mL
1 tablespoon	milk or cream	15 mL
1/8 teaspoon	peppermint extract	0.5 mL
1 square	unsweetened chocolate	1
1 tablespoon	butter	15 mL

Beat first four ingredients in small bowl of mixer until of spreading consistency. Spread over brownies. Let set 5 – 10 minutes. Melt chocolate with butter over hot water. Pour over icing. Tip pan until white icing is completely covered with chocolate. Refrigerate until ready to serve. **To freeze:** Wrap well. Defrost before serving.

Butter Cookies

PAULINE TOKER

1 cup	butter	250 mL
1 cup	brown sugar	250 mL
1	egg yolk	1
1 teaspoon	vanilla	5 mL
2 cups	all purpose flour	500 mL
1	egg white	1
1/4 cup	ground nuts	50 mL
1 tablespoon	granulated sugar	15 mL
1/4 teaspoon	cinnamon	1 mL
1 cup	chocolate chips	250 mL
1/2 cup	sliced almonds or chopped nuts	125 mL

Preheat oven to 350°F (180°C). Cream butter, sugar and egg yolk. Add vanilla. Add flour and blend. Press thinly on 2 greased jelly roll pans. Using fingers brush top of one with lightly beaten egg white. Sprinkle with ground nuts mixed with cinnamon and sugar. Melt chocolate chips. Spread over second pan, and sprinkle with sliced almonds, or chopped nuts. Bake both pans for 12 – 15 minutes. Cut while hot into squares, or diamond shapes. Remove from pan. Can be frozen. This makes two different varieties with one recipe. Lovely for a tea table.

Cheese Squares

BARBARA GOLDBERG, HALIFAX

1/2 cup	brown sugar	125 mL
1 cup	all purpose flour	250 mL
1 teaspoon	salt	5 mL
1 · 8 ounce	package processed yellow cheese	225 g
1/4 pound	butter	125 mL

Preheat oven to 325°F (160°C). Place sugar, flour and salt in a bowl and mix. Cut in cheese and butter until blended. Pat half the dough down into lightly greased 8" (2 L) square pan. Spread generously with your favourite **tart jam** or **jelly**. Crumble remaining dough on top. Sprinkle top with a little **grated Parmesan cheese**. Bake about 25 – 35 minutes until lightly browned. Cut into squares.

Cherry Pecan Bars

JUDY ASCH

1/3 cup	butter or margarine	75 mL
2/3 cup	brown sugar, packed	150 mL
1 1/3 cups	all purpose flour	325 mL
1/2 teaspoon	baking powder	2 mL
2	eggs	2
3/4 cup	corn syrup	175 mL
1/3 cup	brown sugar	75 mL
3 tablespoons	all purpose flour	45 mL
1/2 teaspoon	salt	2 mL
3/4 cup	chopped maraschino cherries	175 mL
3/4 cup	pecans	175 mL

Preheat oven to 350°F (180°C). Grease a 9" x 13" (3.5 L) baking pan. Cream together butter and sugar until light and fluffy. Stir in flour mixed with baking powder, until crumbly. Press into prepared baking pan. Bake 10 minutes. Beat eggs until foamy. Mix in corn syrup, brown sugar, flour, salt and cherries. Spread over base. Dot with pecans. Return to oven and bake an additional 25 – 30 minutes. Cut into bars. Yield: 48.

Chocolate Chip Cookies

FERN COOPERSMITH

1/2 cup	soft butter	125 mL
3/4 cup	brown sugar	175 mL
1	egg	1
1 teaspoon	vanilla	5 mL
1 cup	cake flour	250 mL
1/2 teaspoon	baking soda	2 mL
1/2 teaspoon	salt	2 mL
1 · 6 ounce package	chocolate chips	170 g

Preheat oven to 350°F (180°C). Cream butter and sugar. Add egg and vanilla. Combine flour, soda and salt and add to creamed mixture. Fold in chocolate chips. Drop by spoonfuls onto greased cookie sheet, allowing room for spreading. Bake 10 – 12 minutes.

Chocolate Cookies

SHIRLEY LAZARUS

2 cups	granulated sugar	500 mL
1/2 cup	oil	125 mL
4 squares	unsweetened chocolate, melted	4
4	eggs	4
2 cups	all purpose flour	500 mL
2 teaspoons	baking powder	10 mL
1/2 teaspoon	salt	2 mL
2 teaspoons	vanilla	10 mL

Blend sugar with oil and chocolate. Add eggs, one at a time, beating after each addition. Sift together flour, baking powder and salt, and blend into sugar mixture. Add vanilla. Refrigerate overnight. Preheat oven to 350°F (180°C). Make balls the size of walnuts. Roll in **powdered sugar**. Place far apart on ungreased cookie sheet (they spread). Bake 12 minutes. Cool on rack. Keep in covered tins. Can be frozen.

Chocolate Chip or Raisin Drop Cookies

RUTH SADOWSKI

1 cup	butter	250 mL
1 cup	granulated sugar	250 mL
1/2 cup	brown sugar	125 mL
2	eggs	2
2 teaspoons	vanilla	10 mL
2 cups	all purpose flour	500 mL
1 teaspoon	baking soda	5 mL
1 teaspoon	salt	5 mL
1 · 12 ounce package	chocolate chips or raisin drops	340 g

Preheat oven to 375°F (190°C). Cream butter. Add sugars and continue creaming. Add eggs, and mix well. Add vanilla. Combine flour, soda and salt, and blend into butter mixture, a little at a time. Stir in chocolate chips or raisin drops (chocolate covered raisins). Drop by teaspoonfuls on greased cookie sheet. Bake 8 – 10 minutes. Yield: 72 cookies.

Chocolate Chunk Cookies

LILLIAN MANDEL

2 cups	all purpose flour	500 mL
1 cup	granulated sugar	250 mL
1/4 teaspoon	salt	1 mL
1/4 teaspoon	baking soda	1 mL
1 cup	unsalted butter	250 mL
1 cup	light brown sugar	250 mL
2	large eggs	2
1 1/2 cups	semi-sweet or bittersweet chocolate, chopped into chunks	375 mL

Sift together flour, sugar, salt and baking soda. Cream butter and brown sugar until light and fluffy. Add eggs. Stir in flour mixture. Add chocolate chunks. Cover dough and refrigerate overnight. Preheat oven to 350°F (180°C). Lightly grease a cookie sheet. With an ice cream scoop, place scoops of dough onto prepared pan. Bake for 15 minutes or until golden. Yield: 18 super large cookies.

Chocolate Chip Granola Cookies

SANDY GRANATSTEIN, OTTAWA

1 cup	soft butter	250 mL
3/4 cup	granulated sugar	175 mL
3/4 cup	brown sugar, packed	175 mL
1	egg	1
1 teaspoon	vanilla	5 mL
1 1/2 cups	all purpose flour	375 mL
1 teaspoon	baking soda	5 mL
1/2 teaspoon	salt	2 mL
1 3/4 cups	granola cereal	425 mL
1 cup	chocolate chips or raisins	250 mL

Preheat oven to 350°F (180°C). Cream butter and sugars well. Add egg and continue creaming, until light and fluffy. Add vanilla. Add flour mixed with soda and salt and blend well. Stir in granola and chips. Drop by teaspoonfuls on lightly greased cookie sheet. Bake about 15 minutes until golden. Yield: 72 cookies.

Coconut Crisp Cookies

GLADYS FOGLER

1 cup	butter	250 mL
1 cup	granulated sugar	250 mL
1 cup	brown sugar	250 mL
1	egg, beaten	1
1 1/2 cups	all purpose flour	375 mL
1 1/4 cups	rolled oats	300 mL
1/2 teaspoon	salt	2 mL
1/2 teaspoon	baking soda	2 mL
1 teaspoon	baking powder	5 mL
3/4 cup	shredded coconut	175 mL

Preheat oven to 375°F (190°C). Grease a cookie sheet. Cream butter. Add sugars and beaten egg, and beat until fluffy. Combine dry ingredients and add to creamed mixture. Drop by teaspoonfuls onto prepared cookie sheet and press lightly with a fork. Bake about 8 – 10 minutes until golden. Let cool a few minutes before removing from pan. Yield: 60 cookies.

Crisp Cornflake Cookies

SHEILA LOFTUS

1 cup	butter	250 mL
1 cup	granulated sugar	250 mL
1	egg	1
1 1/2 cups	all purpose flour	375 ml
3 1/2 teaspoons	baking powder	17 mL
1/2 teaspoon	salt	2 mL
1 teaspoon	vanilla	5 mL
5 cups	cornflakes, uncrushed	1250 mL

Preheat oven to 350°F (180°C). Cream butter, and gradually blend in sugar. Beat in egg. Combine and sift in flour, baking powder and salt. Add vanilla. Measure cornflakes before crushing. Crush and add to butter mixture. Drop by teaspoons about 1 1/2" (4 cm) apart on greased cookie sheet. Press as flat as possible with fork dipped in cold water. Bake about 10 minutes. Yield: 6 – 8 dozen cookies.

Cream Cheese Refrigerator Cookies

MYRNA WEBBER

1/2 cup	butter	125 mL
1 cup	granulated sugar	250 mL
1	egg, well beaten	1
1 1/2 ounces	cream cheese	50 mL
2 tablespoons	sour milk	30 mL
1/2 teaspoon	vanilla	3 mL
2 1/2 cups	all purpose flour	625 mL
1/8 teaspoon	baking soda	0.5 mL
1/2 teaspoon	baking powder	2 mL
1/2 teaspoon	salt	2 mL
2 tablespoons	chopped nuts	30 mL

Blend butter with sugar and egg until creamy. Soften cream cheese slightly. Beat it into the butter mixture with sour milk and vanilla. Beat in flour mixed with soda, baking powder and salt. Form dough into long roll. Cover with waxed paper and chill. Preheat oven to 350°F (180°C). Cut dough into slices. Sprinkle each slice with chopped nuts and cinnamon and sugar mixture. Bake 12 – 15 minutes.

Currant Crisps

MYRTLE COOPERSMITH

1 1/2 cups	all purpose flour	375 mL
1 cup	corn starch	250 mL
1 teaspoon	baking powder	5 mL
1/2 teaspoon	salt	2 mL
1 cup	unsalted butter, softened	250 mL
1 cup	granulated sugar	250 mL
1	egg, lightly beaten	1
2 teaspoons	vanilla	10 mL
1 cup	dried currants	250 mL

Sift together the flour, cornstarch, baking powder and salt into a bowl. In large bowl of electric mixer, cream butter. Add sugar a little at a time, beating after each addition. Continue beating for two minutes. Add the egg, and vanilla and beat for one minute longer. Add the flour mixture in two batches at low speed until it is just combined. Stir in currants. Chill dough covered for 3 hours or overnight. Preheat oven to 375°F (190°C). Roll level teaspoons of the dough into balls and arrange them 2" (5 cm) apart on baking sheets. Flatten with a fork dipped in water, and bake in centre of oven for 8 – 9 minutes or until golden around the edges. Cool on rack. Yield about 10 dozen cookies.

Ginger Snaps

GRETA COOPERSMITH LISS

3/4 cup	vegetable shortening	175 mL
1 1/3 cups	granulated sugar	325 mL
1/4 cup	molasses	60 mL
1	egg, slightly beaten	1
1 1/2 cups	all purpose flour	375 mL
1 teaspoon	baking soda	5 mL
1 teaspoon	ground ginger	5 mL
1/2 teaspoon	cinnamon	2 mL
1/2 teaspoon	ground cloves	2 mL
1/2 teaspoon	salt	2 mL

In large bowl of electric mixer, cream the shortening, and add 1 cup (250 mL) of the sugar a little at a time, beating until light and fluffy. Stir in the molasses, and add the egg. Combine flour, baking soda, ginger, cinnamon, cloves and salt. Add to mixture a little at a time. Chill the dough, covered, until firm, about 2 hours. Preheat oven to 325°F (160°C). Form the dough into 3/4" (2 cm) balls and roll the balls in the remaining 1/3 cup (75 mL) sugar. Arrange on a cookie sheet 2" (5 cm) apart and bake for 10 – 12 minutes or until set. Cookies will be soft in the center and they will flatten a bit. Cool on rack. Yield: 48 cookies.

Date Nut Squares

IRENE FINK

1/3 cup	butter	75 mL
1 cup	brown sugar	250 mL
1	egg	1
1 teaspoon	vanilla	5 mL
1 cup	all purpose flour	250 mL
1/4 teaspoon	baking soda	1 mL
1/2 teaspoon	baking powder	2 mL
1/2 teaspoon	salt	2 mL
1 cup	chopped pecans	250 mL
1 cup	chocolate chips	250 mL
1/2 cup	chopped dates	125 mL

Preheat oven to 350°F (180°C). Grease a 9" x 9" (2 L) pan. In large bowl of electric mixer cream together butter and sugar until light and fluffy. Beat in egg and vanilla. Sift together flour, baking soda, baking powder and salt and add to egg mixture. Beat until well combined. Add nuts, chocolate chips and dates. Dough will be stiff. Spread in pan and bake for 30 minutes. Cut into squares while still warm. Delicious!

Date Squares

PAULINE TOKER

Base:

1 cup	butter	250 mL
1 1/3 cups	rolled oats	325 mL
1 1/2 cups	all purpose flour	375 mL
1 teaspoon	salt	5 mL
1/2 teaspoon	baking soda	3 mL
1 cup	brown sugar	250 mL

Cut butter into dry ingredients. Crumble with fingers until well combined. Pat half of mixture on bottom of greased 9" x 13" (3.5 L) baking pan.

Filling:

1 1/4 pounds	dates, cut up	600 g
1 cup	granulated sugar	250 mL
1 cup	water	250 mL
	juice of 1 lemon	
1/8 teaspoon	salt	0.5 mL

Preheat oven to 350°F (180°C). Combine all of the ingredients in a saucepan and boil gently until thickened. Spread over base and sprinkle remaining crumbs on top. Bake 20 – 25 minutes or until light brown.

Hermits

1/2 cup	butter or shortening	125 mL
1 cup	brown sugar, lightly packed	250 mL
2	eggs	2
1/2 teaspoon	vanilla	2 mL
1 3/4 cups	all purpose flour	425 mL
1 teaspoon	baking soda	5 mL
1/2 teaspoon	salt	2 mL
1/2 teaspoon	cinnamon	2 mL
1/8 teaspoon	allspice	0.5 mL
1/8 teaspoon	nutmeg, grated	0.5 mL
1 cup	raisins	250 mL
1 cup	chopped dates	250 mL
1 cup	chopped walnuts	250 mL

Preheat oven to 350°F (180°C). Cream butter or shortening and sugar. Beat in eggs and vanilla. Sift dry ingredients and add to creamed mixture. Mix in fruit and nuts. Drop by teaspoonfuls onto a greased baking sheet. Bake 10 – 12 minutes until golden. Yield: 36 cookies.

Lacey Cookies

DOLORES WEINER

1/4 cup	butter	60 mL
1/2 cup	corn syrup	125 mL
1/3 cup	sifted all purpose flour	75 mL
1/2 cup	quick oats	125 mL

Preheat oven to 350°F (180°C). Melt butter in small saucepan over low heat. Remove from heat. Stir in corn syrup, and then flour. Stir until smooth. Stir in oats. Drop batter in rounded 1/4 teaspoonfuls (2 mL) onto greased cookie sheet 2" (5 cm) apart. Do only five or six at a time. Bake 5 – 6 minutes, or until golden brown. Remove pan from oven and let sit for a few seconds before trying to lift from cookie sheet. Working quickly, lift cookie from sheet with spatula, place around rolling pin, and gently slide off onto rack to cool.

Easy Lemon Squares

EVELYN LIEFF, OTTAWA

Base:

1/2 cup	butter	125 mL
1 cup	all purpose flour	250 mL
1/4 cup	icing sugar	50 mL

Topping:

2	eggs, beaten	2
1 cup	granulated sugar	250 mL
4 tablespoons	lemon juice	60 mL
1 teaspoon	lemon rind	5 mL
2 tablespoons	all purpose flour	30 mL
1/2 teaspoon	baking powder	2 mL

Preheat oven to 350°F (180°C). Mix all base ingredients together until well blended. Press into bottom of 9" (3 L) square baking pan. Bake 20 minutes. Process topping ingredients briefly until blended. Pour over baked base. Bake 25 minutes. Cool on rack. Cut into squares and sprinkle with icing sugar.

Marble Bars

JUDY ASCH

1 cup	soft butter	250 mL
2 cups	granulated sugar	500 mL
4	eggs	4
1 3/4 cups	all purpose flour	425 mL
1/2 teaspoon	salt	3 mL
2 teaspoons	vanilla	10 mL
1 cup	chopped nuts	250 mL
2 squares	unsweetened chocolate, melted	2

Preheat oven to 350°F (180°C). Grease a 9" x 13" (3.5 L) baking pan. Cream butter. Beat in sugar. Add eggs, one at a time, beating well after each addition. Mix flour and salt, and gradually add to butter mixture. Stir in vanilla and nuts. Divide batter in half. Stir melted chocolate into one part. Drop batter alternately by spoonfuls into greased pan, running a knife through to marbleize. Bake for 40 – 45 minutes. Cool completely. Frost with Chocolate Buttercream Icing.

Icing:

2 squares	unsweetened chocolate, melted	2
1/4 cup	butter	50 mL
1	egg	1
2 cups	sifted icing sugar	500 mL
1/2 teaspoon	vanilla	2 mL

Melt chocolate over hot water. Cool. Cream butter. Beat in chocolate and egg. Gradually beat in sifted icing sugar and vanilla.

Mandel Bread

2	eggs	2
1 cup	granulated sugar	250 mL
1/2 cup	vegetable shortening	125 mL
3 cups	all purpose flour	725 mL
1 teaspoon	salt	5 mL
2 teaspoons	baking powder	10 mL
1/2 cup	orange juice	125 mL
1/2 cup	melted butter	125 mL
1 teaspoon	vanilla	5 mL
1 cup	ground or finely chopped almonds	250 mL

Mix eggs and sugar in large mixer bowl. Add shortening and cream lightly. Sift together flour, salt and baking powder. Add dry ingredients to egg-sugar-shortening mixture alternately with orange juice and melted butter. Add vanilla. Stir in almonds. Chill about 1 hour. Preheat oven to 350°F (180°C). Divide and roll on floured board into rolls about 1" (2.5 cm) thick. Place on greased cookie sheet. Bake 20 minutes until lightly golden. Remove from oven. Slice diagonally. Turn each piece on its side and return to oven for 5 minutes. Remove from oven - turn each piece over and return to oven for another 5 minutes or so, until golden brown.

Meringue Cookies

2	egg whites	2
1/8 teaspoon	salt	0.5 mL
1/8 teaspoon	cream of tartar	0.5 mL
1 teaspoon	vanilla	5 mL
3/4 cup	granulated sugar	175 mL
1 · 12 ounce package	chocolate chips	340 g
1/4 cup	chopped walnuts	50 mL

Preheat oven to 300°F (150°C). Beat egg whites, salt and cream of tartar until soft peaks form. Add vanilla. Gradually add sugar, beating until stiff. Fold in chips and nuts. Place a paper towel on a cookie sheet. Drop by spoonfuls onto lined cookie sheet. Bake 25 minutes. Yield: 24 cookies.

Mandelbrot

E D I E   W I N B E R G

3	eggs	3
1 cup	granulated sugar	250 mL
1 cup	oil	250 mL
1 teaspoon	vanilla	5 mL
2 cups	all purpose flour	500 mL
1/2 teaspoon	salt	2 mL
2 teaspoons	baking powder	10 mL
2 cups	Special K or Grape Nuts	500 mL
1/2 pound	chopped almonds	225 g
	cinnamon	

Preheat oven to 350°F (180°C). Beat eggs and sugar well. Add oil and vanilla. Sift flour, salt, baking powder and add to egg mixture. Add almonds and cereal. Batter will be loose. Form into rolls 2" (5 cm) in diameter on greased cookie sheets. Bake 15 minutes. Remove from oven. Lower temperature to 325°F (160°C). Slice, turn each piece on its side, sprinkle with cinnamon, and bake, turning occasionally until brown on all sides.

Oatmeal Cookies

E L L E N   C O L E

1 cup	butter	250 mL
1 1/4 cups	lightly packed brown sugar	300 mL
1 1/2 cups	sifted all purpose flour	375 mL
1/2 teaspoon	salt	2 mL
1 teaspoon	baking soda	5 mL
1/4 cup	boiling water	60 mL
3/4 cup	yellow raisins or chocolate chips	175 mL
1 3/4 cups	rolled oats	425 mL
1/4 – 1/2 cup	toasted wheat germ	75 – 125 mL

Preheat oven to 350°F (180°C). Cream butter. Add sugar and continue creaming. Add flour mixed with salt. Stir in soda dissolved in water, raisins or chips, oats and wheat germ. Place by spoonfuls on ungreased cookie sheet. Flatten with fork. Bake 8 – 10 minutes.

Oatmeal Coconut Bars

ELLEN COLE

2 cups	all purpose flour	500 mL
1/4 teaspoon	salt	1 mL
1 cup	rolled oats	250 mL
1 cup	shredded coconut	250 mL
1 cup	butter	250 mL
1 cup	brown sugar	250 mL
2 teaspoons	vanilla	10 mL
1 teaspoon	baking soda dissolved in	5 mL
1/4 cup	hot water	60 mL

Preheat oven to 350°F (180°C). Grease a 10" x 15" (25 x 37.5 cm) jelly roll pan. Mix together flour, salt, oats, and coconut. Cream butter and brown sugar, and add vanilla. Add baking soda, which has been dissolved in hot water. Add dry ingredients, and mix well. Press into prepared jelly roll pan. Bake 20 – 25 minutes, or until light brown. Cut into squares while warm.

Oatmeal Chippers

JUDY SAPERA

1 1/2 cups	packed brown sugar	375 mL
1 1/2 cups	vegetable oil	375 mL
2	eggs, beaten	2
2 1/2 cups	quick cooking rolled oats (not instant)	625 mL
1 1/2 cups	whole wheat flour	375 mL
1 cup	wheat germ	250 mL
1 teaspoon	baking soda	5 mL
1 cup	semi sweet chocolate chips	250 mL
1 cup	chopped almonds	250 mL

Preheat oven to 350°F (180°C). In large bowl stir together brown sugar, oil and eggs until well combined. Stir in oats, flour, wheat germ and baking soda until well blended. Stir in chocolate chips and almonds. Drop by teaspoonfuls onto ungreased cookie sheet. Flatten slightly with fork. Bake 8 – 10 minutes or until set and golden brown. Let cool completely.

Citrus Oatmeal Cookies

MYRTLE COOPERSMITH

2 cups	sifted all purpose flour	500 mL
2 cups	granulated sugar	500 mL
4 teaspoons	baking powder	20 mL
1 teaspoon	salt	5 mL
1 teaspoon	nutmeg	5 mL
1 teaspoon	cinnamon	5 mL
1 cup	unsalted butter, room temperature	250 mL
2	eggs	2
1 tablespoon	fresh lemon juice	15 mL
1 tablespoon	fresh orange juice	15 mL
1 tablespoon	lemon rind	15 mL
2 teaspoons	orange rind	10 mL
2 cups	quick rolled oats	500 mL

Preheat oven to 350°F (180°C). Sift flour, sugar, baking powder, salt, nutmeg and cinnamon into a large mixing bowl. Add the butter, eggs, lemon juice, orange juice and beat until smooth. Mix in orange and lemon rinds, and the rolled oats. Drop from a teaspoon onto an ungreased cookie sheet. Bake 12 – 15 minutes. Cool cookies on rack. Yield: 5 – 6 dozen.

Pecan Drop Cookies

1/2 cup	butter	125 mL
1 cup	brown sugar	250 mL
1	egg	1
1 cup	pastry flour	250 mL
1/2 cup	broken pecans	125 mL
1/2 teaspoon	vanilla	2 mL

Preheat oven to 350°F (180°C). Cream butter and sugar. Add egg, flour, pecans and vanilla. Drop from teaspoon onto buttered cookie sheet 1 1/2" (4 cm) apart. Place half pecan in centre of each cookie and bake 10 minutes.

Orange Poppy Seed Cookies MYRTLE COOPERSMITH

2 cups	all purpose flour	500 mL
2 teaspoons	baking powder	10 mL
1/2 teaspoon	salt	2 mL
1/2 teaspoon	nutmeg	2 mL
2/3 cup	vegetable oil	150 mL
1 cup	granulated sugar	250 mL
2	eggs, lightly beaten	2
1/3 cup	poppy seeds	75 mL
1 tablespoon	grated orange rind	15 mL
1 teaspoon	orange extract	5 mL

Sift together flour, baking powder, salt and nutmeg. In large bowl of electric mixer, combine oil and sugar and beat for 2 minutes. Add the eggs. Beat mixture for 1 minute and stir in the poppy seeds, orange rind and extract. Add the flour mixture in two batches, beating at low speed until just blended. Chill dough covered for at least 3 hours. Preheat oven to 400°F (200°C). Roll level teaspoons of the dough into balls and arrange 2" (5 cm) apart on baking sheets. Flatten each ball with the palm of the hand, then press with a fork dipped in warm water. Bake in middle of the oven for 6 – 7 minutes or until puffed and lightly golden around the edges. Cool on rack. Yield: 84 cookies.

Cookies with Poppy Seeds RHODA GRANATSTEIN

1 cup plus 1 tablespoon	butter or margarine	265 mL
3/4 cup	granulated sugar	175 mL
2 1/2 cups	all purpose flour	625 mL
	poppy seeds	

Preheat oven to 325°F (160°C). Mix butter, sugar and flour together with fingers. Pat down in a buttered jelly roll pan. Sprinkle with poppy seeds. Bake 18 – 20 minutes until lightly brown. Cut into squares while warm.

Palm Leaves

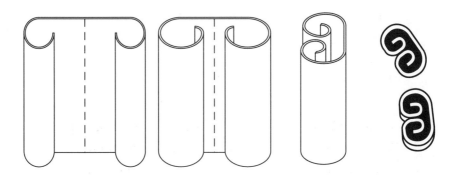

RAY ZUCKERMAN

1 1/2 cups	unsifted flour	375 mL
1 cup	butter	250 mL
1/2 cup	sour cream	125 mL
	granulated sugar	

Place the flour in a bowl. Coarsely cut the butter over the flour. With a pastry blender cut the butter into the flour until the mixture has the texture of coarse crumbs. Stir in the sour cream. Knead briefly until mixture holds together. Form into a ball. Wrap in waxed paper, and refrigerate for 2 hours. Place half the dough on a smooth working surface, sprinkled generously with granulated sugar. Keeping the dough well sugared on both sides, roll into a square about 1/8" (0.3 cm) thick and 10" (25 cm) square. Trim the edges. Sprinkle top of dough with additional sugar. Mark the center of the dough. Fold each side in towards the center. Then fold along the marked center, vertically, like a book, making a compact roll about 2" (5 cm) wide, 3/4" (2 cm) thick and 10" (25 cm) long. Wrap in waxed paper and refrigerate for 1 hour, or place in freezer for 1/2 hour.

Preheat oven to 400°F (200°C). Line a cookie sheet with aluminum foil. With a sharp knife, slice the roll into 1/2" (1.5 cm) pieces. Dip both cut sides in sugar, and place on cookie sheet cut side down, 2 1/2" (7 cm) apart as they will spread. Bake 12 minutes or until sugar is well caramelized. Remove from oven and turn palm leaves over and bake another 3 minutes until lightly browned. Remove palm leaves from foil and cool on rack. Yield: 3 1/2 dozen.

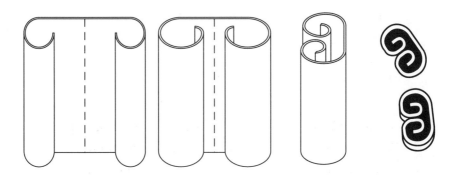

Peanut Butter Pillows

PHYLLIS FLATT

1 1/2 cups	sifted all purpose flour	375 mL
1/2 teaspoon	baking soda	2 mL
1/4 teaspoon	salt	1 mL
1/2 cup	butter	125 mL
1/2 cup	creamy peanut butter	125 mL
1/2 cup	granulated sugar	125 mL
1/4 cup	light corn syrup	60 mL
1 tablespoon	milk	15 mL
	chunky peanut butter	
	for filling	

Sift together flour, baking soda and salt. In electric mixer, cream butter, add peanut butter and sugar and beat until smooth. Beat in corn syrup and milk. Reduce speed and add sifted dry ingredients. Beat until well combined. Turn dough out onto a board and knead briefly. Form into 2 rolls 2" (5 cm) in diameter, and refrigerate for several hours or overnight.

Preheat oven to 350°F (180°C). With sharp knife, slice rolls in 1/8" (0.3 cm) slices. Arrange slices on ungreased cookie sheet 2" (5 cm) apart. Place a teaspoon of chunky peanut butter in the center. Spread to flatten leaving 1/2" (1.3 cm) border. Cover with cookie to make a sandwich and allow the cookies to stand for 2 – 3 minutes enabling them to soften slightly. Seal the edges by pressing them lightly with a flour dipped fork. Bake 12 – 15 minutes or until lightly coloured.

Optional: To decorate, a peanut may be pressed into the center.

Pecan Bars

NANCY POSLUNS

1/3 cup	butter or margarine	75 mL
1/2 cup	brown sugar, firmly packed	125 mL
1 1/3 cups	all purpose flour, sifted	325 mL
1/2 teaspoon	baking powder	2 mL
1/4 cup	pecans, chopped fine	60 mL

Topping:

2	eggs	2
3/4 cup	dark corn syrup	175 mL
1/4 cup	brown sugar, firmly packed	50 mL
3 tablespoons	all purpose flour	45 mL
1/2 teaspoon	salt	2 mL
1 teaspoon	vanilla	5 mL
3/4 cup	pecans, coarsely chopped	175 mL

Preheat oven to 350°F (180°C). Cream together butter and sugar. Sift flour with baking powder, and add to butter mixture. Mix until mixture resembles coarse meal. Stir in finely chopped pecans. Pat firmly into bottom of greased baking pan 9" x 13" (3.5 L). Bake for 10 minutes. Beat eggs until foamy. Add corn syrup, brown sugar, flour, salt and vanilla. Mix well. Pour over base. Sprinkle with coarsely chopped pecans. Bake for 25 to 30 minutes. Cool in pan before cutting into bars. Yield: about 30 bars.

Pecan Buttercrunch Squares   J U D Y   A S C H

1/2 cup	sweet butter	125 mL
1 1/4 cups	graham cracker crumbs	300 mL
1 cup	semi-sweet chocolate chips	250 mL
3/4 cup	butterscotch chips	175 mL
1 · 14 ounce can	sweetened condensed milk	395 mL
2 cups	pecan halves	500 mL

Line sides and bottom of 9" x 13" (3.5 L) pan with foil. Preheat oven to 350°F (180°C). Melt butter and pour into lined pan. Sprinkle crumbs over butter. Sprinkle chocolate and butterscotch chips over base. Pour condensed milk over top. Cover with pecan halves. Bake 5 minutes, then carefully press nuts down so they won't fall off later. Bake another 20 – 25 minutes, until milk has turned golden brown in colour. Cool to room temperature, then refrigerate 1 – 2 hours before cutting.

Pecan Crescents

BERNICE GOREN, STRATFORD

1 cup	butter	250 mL
1/2 cup	icing sugar	125 mL
2 teaspoons	vanilla	10 mL
2 cups	all purpose flour	500 mL
1/2 teaspoon	salt	2 mL
2 cups	chopped pecans	500 mL

Preheat oven to 325°F (160°C). Cream butter and sugar until light and fluffy. Add vanilla. Add flour and salt. Add pecans. Roll one tablespoonful of dough at a time between the palms of hands and shape into a crescent. Bake on an ungreased cookie sheet for 20 minutes. Dust with icing sugar before serving. Delicious! Yield: about 60 cookies.

Pumpkin Seed Orange Cookies

PHYLLIS FLATT

1/3 cup	soft butter or margarine	75 mL
1/2 cup	granulated sugar	125 mL
1	egg	1
1/2 teaspoon	vanilla	2 mL
2 tablespoons	orange juice	30 mL
2 tablespoons	grated orange rind	30 mL
1 cup	sifted whole wheat flour	250 mL
1/2 teaspoon	baking soda	2 mL
1/2 teaspoon	salt	2 mL
1 1/2 cups	quick cooking rolled oats	325 mL
1 cup	seedless raisins	250 mL
1/2 cup	pumpkin seeds, shelled, toasted and chopped	125 mL

Beat together butter, sugar, egg and vanilla in large bowl of electric mixer until fluffy. Stir in orange juice and orange rind. Combine flour, baking soda and salt and blend into butter mixture. Add oats, raisins and pumpkin seeds and mix until well blended. Chill for about 2 hours. Preheat oven to 350°F (180°C). Shape dough into 1" (2.5 cm) balls and arrange on lightly greased cookie sheets. Flatten with a fork that has been dipped in warm water. Bake 12 – 15 minutes or until brown around the edges. Yield: 36 cookies.

Prune Bars

SANDRA HABERMAN

Base:

1/2 cup	margarine	125 mL
1/2 cup	brown sugar	125 mL
1 cup	all purpose flour	250 mL

Filling:

1 1/4 cups	prunes, about 20	300 mL
1/3 cup	brown sugar	75 mL
2 tablespoons	cornstarch	30 mL
1/8 teaspoon	salt	0.5 mL
1 tablespoon	orange rind, grated	15 mL
1/4 cup	orange juice	60 mL
1 cup	chopped walnuts	250 mL
2	egg whites	2

Preheat oven to 350°F (180°C). Grease an 8" square (2 L) pan. Blend together margarine, brown sugar and flour. Pat into prepared pan. Bake 5 – 10 minutes. Cook prunes in enough water to cover, approximately 20 minutes. Drain, reserving 2 tablespoons (30 mL) liquid. Remove pits, and cut into quarters. Mix liquid from prunes with next five ingredients. Simmer 2 – 3 minutes. Stir in walnuts. Spread over base. Beat whites until stiff, and spread over filling. Bake 25 minutes. Cool and cut into squares.

Shortbread Cookies

PAULINE MENKES

1 cup	unsalted butter	250 mL
3/4 teaspoon	salt	3 mL
3/4 cup	firmly packed brown sugar	175 mL
2 cups	sifted all purpose flour	500 mL

Preheat oven to 300°F (150°C). In mixer, cream butter, salt and brown sugar. When creamed, add flour in batches of 1/3 cup (75 mL), creaming well after each addition. When blended, divide dough into 4 parts. Place mounds in balls on two greased cookie sheets. Pat with your hand to spread out into 8" (20 cm) circles. Perforate with a fork into wedges. Bake for 25 – 30 minutes. Cool about 5 minutes. Cut perforations into wedges.

Shortbread Crescents

SALLY KERR, CALGARY

1 cup	butter or margarine	250 mL
1/3 cup	granulated sugar	75 mL
1 teaspoon	vanilla	5 mL
1/2 teaspoon	almond extract	2 mL
1 2/3 cups	all purpose flour	400 mL
1/8 teaspoon	salt	0.5 mL
1/2 cup	finely ground almonds	125 mL
1/4 cup	granulated sugar	60 mL
2 teaspoons	cinnamon	10 mL

Preheat oven to 325°F (160°C). Cream butter. Add sugar gradually, and continue creaming. Add vanilla and almond extract. Blend in flour mixed with salt, and stir in ground almonds. Roll walnut-sized pieces one at a time between palms of hands, and shape into crescents. Place on ungreased cookie sheet 1" (2.5 cm) apart. Sprinkle with sugar-cinnamon mixture. Bake 15 to 20 minutes, until very lightly golden.

Shortbread Cookies with Apricot Jam

VERA SANDERS

1/4 cup	granulated sugar	60 mL
1 cup	soft sweet butter	250 mL
	powdered sugar	

Preheat oven to 350°F (180°C). Measure flour and sugar into a bowl. Cut in butter and knead until soft and pliable and of workable consistency. Roll out on floured surface 1/8" (0.3 cm) thick. Cut into rounds with cookie cutter or brandy glass. As you use up dough, reroll remaining bits, and cut again into rounds. Count cookies, and cut centers from half the number made. A thimble makes a nice sized hole. Place cookies on an ungreased cookie sheet and bake about 10 minutes. They should be light in colour. Cool, remove from cookie sheet, and spread a thin layer of apricot jam on whole cookies. Place cookie with hole on top, sandwich style. Sprinkle with powdered sugar before serving. Freezes well. Yield: about 40 cookies.

Lemon Shortbread Cookies

MYRTLE COOPERSMITH

1 1/2 cups	all purpose flour	375 mL
1 teaspoon	baking powder	5 mL
1/2 teaspoon	salt	2 mL
1/2 cup	butter	125 mL
1 cup	granulated sugar	250 mL
1	whole egg	1
1	egg yolk	1
1/4 cup	lemon juice	50 mL

Preheat oven to 350°F (180°C). Sift together flour, baking powder and salt. Cream butter and sugar thoroughly. Add egg and egg yolk separately and continue beating. Add sifted dry ingredients alternately with lemon juice. Add **grated rind of 1 lemon**. Drop on greased cookie sheet. Bake 12 – 15 minutes. Remove and cool on racks. Sprinkle with icing sugar.

Nicko's Shortbread

MRS. ELIE SPIVAK

1 cup	butter, room temperature	250 mL
1/2 cup	icing sugar	125 mL
2 1/4 cups	all purpose flour	550 mL

Preheat oven to 300°F (150°C). Cream butter and icing sugar until fluffy. Gradually add flour and knead to mix into a smooth dough. Roll out on floured board. Cut into desired shapes. Bake on an ungreased cookie sheet about 20 minutes.

Mrs. Levine's Spritz Cookies

1 cup	butter, room temperature	250 mL
1/2 cup	icing sugar (scant)	115 mL
1 3/4 cups	all purpose flour	425 mL

Preheat oven to 275°F (130°C). Cream butter. Add sugar and continue creaming. Blend in flour. Put dough in cookie press, and press onto ungreased cookie sheet. Bake 30 minutes.

Raisin Honey Drops

NANCY POSLUNS

3/4 cup	honey	175 mL
3/4 cup	granulated sugar	175 mL
3/4 cup	butter or margarine	175 mL
1	egg	1
2 cups	all purpose flour	500 mL
1 teaspoon	salt	5 mL
1 teaspoon	cinnamon	5 mL
1/2 teaspoon	baking soda	2 mL
2 cups	rolled oats	500 mL
1 cup	raisins	250 mL

Preheat oven to 375°F (190°C). Cream honey, sugar, butter and egg. Sift together flour, salt, cinnamon and soda. Stir dry ingredients into creamed mixture. Add oats and raisins. Drop by spoonfuls onto greased cookie sheet. Bake 12 – 14 minutes until lightly browned. Yield: about 48 cookies.

Sesame Cookies #1

ESTELLE ZALDIN

1/2 cup	butter (not margarine)	125 mL
1/2 cup	granulated sugar	125 mL
2 teaspoons	instant coffee granules	10 mL
1 tablespoon	all purpose flour	15 mL
2 tablespoons	milk	30 mL
2 cups	sesame seeds	500 mL

Preheat oven to 375°F (190°C). Melt butter in saucepan. Add rest of ingredients. Combine and stir over low heat until blended. Drop onto foil-lined cookie sheet by spoonfuls, about 2" (5 cm) apart. Bake 6 minutes until golden. Cool just 3 minutes on cookie sheet before lifting off with spatula. This cooling time is important - too little or too much time on the cookie sheet makes the cookies difficult to remove without breaking. Make on a cool day. Store in a covered tin.

Sesame Cookies #2

1 cup	butter, room temperature	250 mL
2/3 cup	granulated sugar	150 mL
2 cups	all purpose flour	500 mL
1	egg, beaten with	1
1 tablespoon	water	15 mL
	sesame seeds	

Preheat oven to 350°F (180°C). Cream butter. Add sugar, and continue creaming until fluffy. Stir in flour. Chill for 10 – 15 minutes. Break off pieces the size of a walnut or smaller. Roll each piece into a smooth ball and press lightly between palms of hands. Place on ungreased cookie sheet. Press flat, and very thin. Brush top with beaten egg and water mixture, and sprinkle with sesame seeds. Bake 15 – 20 minutes until lightly golden.

Strudel

GINA BROWN

1 cup	butter, room temperature	250 mL
2 cups	all purpose flour	500 mL
1	egg yolk	1
8 tablespoons	sour cream	125 mL
1 cup	icing sugar	250 mL
1 cup	finely ground walnuts	250 mL
	for rolling	
1/2 – 1 pound	Turkish Delight	225 – 450 g
	jam, walnuts and coconut	

Preheat oven to 350°F (180°C). Cut butter into flour with pastry blender until consistency of coarse meal. Add egg yolk and sour cream. Work in with pastry blender and fingers until dough forms a ball. Wrap in waxed paper and refrigerate overnight. Divide into 6 pieces. Roll each piece out onto mixture of icing sugar and ground walnuts. Spread jam, walnuts and coconut over dough. Sprinkle sparingly with cut up pieces of Turkish Delight. Roll up as for jelly roll and bake 3 rolls at a time on Teflon pan. Bake 20 – 25 minutes until golden. Run spatula under rolls to release from pan after 2 – 3 minutes to prevent from sticking. Cut before cooled into 1" (2 cm) slices.

Sugar Cookies

SHIRLEY LAZARUS

1 3/4 – 2 cups	all purpose flour	400 – 500 mL
2 teaspoons	baking powder	10 mL
1/4 teaspoon	salt	2 mL
2	eggs	2
1/2 cup	granulated sugar	125 mL
1/2 cup	oil	125 mL
1/2 teaspoon	vanilla	3 mL
1/2 teaspoon	almond extract	3 mL
	finely chopped nuts	
	additional granulated sugar	

Preheat oven to 350°F (180°C). Mix 1 3/4 cups (400 mL) flour with baking powder and salt. Add rest of ingredients. Mix dough and knead on board, using more flour as needed. Divide dough in four. Roll out thin. Cover dough with a mixture of sugar and finely chopped nuts. Go over dough with rolling pin. Cut into shapes. Place on a greased cookie sheet. Bake until golden and toasty.

Thimble Cookies

BERNICE GOREN, STRATFORD

1/2 cup	butter	125 mL
1/4 cup	granulated sugar	60 mL
1	egg, separated	1
1 cup	all purpose flour	250 mL
1 teaspoon	vanilla	5 mL
1 cup	walnuts, very finely chopped	250 mL
	jam	

Preheat oven to 350°F (180°C). Cream butter and add sugar gradually. Add egg yolk, flour and vanilla. Shape into balls. Dip into unbeaten egg white, and then into chopped nuts. Make a dent in center. Bake for 5 minutes, and dent again. Bake another 10 – 12 minutes. When cool, fill with your favourite jam.

Toffee Bars

ELLEN COLE

1 cup	butter	250 mL
1 cup	brown sugar	250 mL
1 teaspoon	vanilla	5 mL
2 cups	all purpose flour	500 mL
3/4 cup	chocolate chips	170 g
1 cup	chopped pecans	250 mL

Preheat oven to 350°F (180°C). Cream together thoroughly, butter, sugar and vanilla. Add flour and mix well. Add chocolate chips and pecans. Press into ungreased jelly roll pan. Bake 25 minutes, or until brown. Cut into squares while warm.

Viennese Squares

VERA SANDERS

1/2 cup	sweet butter	125 mL
1 cup	all purpose flour	250 mL
1/2 teaspoon	salt	2 mL
1/2 cup	apricot or raspberry jam	125 mL
3 tablespoons	butter	45 mL
1 1/4 cups	granulated sugar	300 mL
6	eggs, separated	6
1/2 pound	walnuts, grated	225 g

Preheat oven to 350°F (180°C). Butter a 9" x 13" (3.5 L) baking dish. Cut butter into flour and salt and mix until crumbly. Press mixture into baking dish, and bake for 15 minutes. Spread jam on base. Cream 3 tablespoons butter and sugar well. Beat egg yolks until light. Add to butter mixture and stir until blended and foamy. Add grated nuts gradually, stirring well after each addition. Beat egg whites until stiff. Gently fold whites into nut mixture. Pour filling onto base. Lower oven temperature to 325°F (170°C) and bake for 40 minutes or until toothpick inserted in center comes out clean.

Toffee Fingers

EDIE WINBERG

27	graham wafers	27
1 cup	butter	250 mL
1 cup	brown sugar	250 mL
1 · 4 ounce package	slivered almonds	113 g
	or	
2 tablespoons	sesame seeds	30 mL

Preheat oven to 350°F (180°C). Cover jelly roll pan with foil. Cover with wafers, touching. Melt butter, stir in brown sugar, and bring to a boil. Add almonds or sesame seeds and spread immediately over wafers. Bake 9 minutes or until very bubbly. Cut while warm. Store in refrigerator. May be frozen. Quick, easy, and delicious!

Whole Wheat Sugar Cookies

JEAN RACHLIN

1/2 cup	brown sugar	125 mL
1/2 cup	granulated sugar	125 mL
1 teaspoon	baking powder	5 mL
1/2 teaspoon	salt	2 mL
1/2 teaspoon	baking soda	2 mL
1/2 teaspoon	nutmeg	2 mL
1/2 cup	butter, softened	125 mL
2 tablespoons	milk	30 mL
1 tablespoon	grated lemon or orange rind	15 mL
1 teaspoon	vanilla	5 mL
1	egg	1
2 cups	whole wheat flour	500 mL

Preheat oven to 375°F (190°C). Mix first 11 ingredients well in large mixer bowl. Gradually add flour and blend. Roll small pieces of dough into approximately 1" (2.5 cm) balls and place on ungreased cookie sheet about 2" (5 cm) apart. Flatten with fork dipped in flour. Sprinkle with **cinnamon** mixed with **sugar**. Bake until lightly browned, about 8 – 10 minutes. Centers will be slightly soft. Cool on racks.

Snacks and Treats

Almond Bark

1 cup	toasted almonds*	250 mL
1/2 pound	semi-sweet chocolate, white or dark	225 g
1 teaspoon	butter or shortening	5 mL

Grease a 9" (22.5 cm) square pan with a little oil. Melt chocolate with butter or margarine. Add almonds and mix well. Pour mixture into prepared pan. Refrigerate until hardened. Break into irregular pieces to serve.

*To toast almonds, place on a pie tin and bake in a 300°F (150°C) oven for 20 minutes.

Almond Brittle

1 1/2 cups	slivered, toasted almonds	375 mL
1 cup	butter	250 mL
1 cup	granulated sugar	250 mL
1/3 cup	brown sugar	75 mL
2 tablespoons	water	30 mL
1/2 teaspoon	baking soda	2 mL
3 squares	semi-sweet chocolate, grated	3

Sprinkle 1 cup (250 mL) nuts in buttered 9" x 13" (3.5 L) pan. Melt butter in a saucepan, add sugars and water and mix well. Bring to a boil, stirring constantly. Continue to cook without stirring until mixture reaches 300°F (150°C). Remove from heat and stir in soda. Carefully pour mixture over nuts. Cool about 5 minutes, and then sprinkle chocolate over top. Press remaining nuts over all. Cool. Break into pieces.

Sugared Almonds

1 pound	unblanched almonds	500 g
1/2 cup	water	125 mL
1 cup	granulated sugar	250 mL
1 teaspoon	cinnamon	5 mL

Preheat broiler to 250°F (125°C). Mix water, sugar and cinnamon in a heavy saucepan. Bring mixture to a boil, stirring constantly. Stir in almonds and cook until all liquid is evaporated. Pour almonds onto a jelly roll pan, spreading evenly over pan. Broil on center rack for 40 minutes, stirring frequently. If temperature cannot be controlled, bake at 350°F (180°C) for 15 minutes, stirring frequently. Watch carefully to avoid scorching.

Penuche

1/4 cup	butter or margarine	60 mL
2 cups	light brown sugar	500 mL
3/4 cup	milk	175 mL
1 teaspoon	vanilla	5 mL
1 cup	chopped nuts	250 mL

Melt 2 tablespoons (30 mL) butter in heavy saucepan. Add sugar and milk and stir. Cook over low heat stirring occasionally to 240°F (120°C). Remove from heat. Add remaining butter or margarine. Do not stir. Cool, without stirring, until outside of pan feels lukewarm. Add vanilla and nuts and beat until mixture loses its gloss and a small amount dropped from spoon will hold its shape. Pour into 8" (2 L) square greased pan. Cool and cut into squares.

Chocolate Fruit Clusters

DOROTHY ZEIFMAN

4 squares	semi-sweet chocolate	4
1 1/2 cups	chopped candied citrus peel	375 mL
1/2 cup	finely chopped nuts and/or	125 mL
1/2 cup	flaked coconut	125 mL

Melt chocolate in a pan over hot water. Stir in chopped candied peel, and mix well. Stir in nuts and/or coconut. Drop by half-teaspoons onto waxed paper on a baking sheet. Chill 30 minutes. Store between layers of waxed paper in a covered container in a cool place.

Spicy Nuts

VERA SANDERS

1 tablespoon	vegetable oil	15 mL
1 1/3 cups	whole almonds	325 mL
1 1/4 cups	pecan halves	300 mL
1 cup	walnut halves	250 mL
1 teaspoon	cumin	5 mL
1 teaspoon	curry powder	5 mL
1/4 teaspoon	cayenne	1 mL
1/8 teaspoon	white pepper	0.5 mL
1/4 teaspoon	salt (optional)	1 mL

Preheat oven to 350°F (180°C). Toss the oil with nuts in bowl. Combine spices (except salt). Add to nuts, mixing well. Spread nuts on baking tray in a single layer. Bake 10 minutes. Sprinkle with salt, if desired.

Chocolate Noodles

JUNE FILLER

12 ounces	chocolate chips	340 g
1 cup	Chinese noodles	250 mL
1/2 cup	shredded coconut	125 mL
1/2 cup	dark raisins	125 mL

Melt chocolate chips in top of double boiler. Add rest of ingredients. Mix well. Drop by teaspoonfuls onto waxed paper. Refrigerate or freeze until hardened.

Magic Chocolate French Fudge

GRETA COOPERSMITH LISS

18 ounces	semi-sweet chocolate chips	500 g
1 1/3 cups	sweetened condensed milk	325 mL
1 1/2 teaspoons	vanilla	7 mL
1/2 cup	chopped nuts, optional	125 mL

In top of double boiler, melt chocolate over hot water, stirring occasionally. Remove from heat. Add sweetened condensed milk, vanilla and nuts. Stir only until smooth. Turn into waxed paper lined 8" (2 L) square pan. Spread mixture evenly and smooth surface. Refrigerate about 2 hours or until firm. Turn candy out onto cutting board. Peel off paper. With a sharp knife, cut fudge into serving sized pieces. Store in an airtight container.

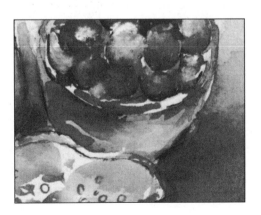

Taffy Apples

2 cups	granulated sugar	500 mL
2/3 cup	corn syrup	150 mL
1 cup	water	250 mL
1	cinnamon stick, broken	1
4	cloves	4
	dash of salt	
	red food colouring	
6	red apples	6
6	wooden skewers	6

Combine sugar, corn syrup and water in a saucepan. Stir over medium heat until sugar is dissolved. Add cinnamon, cloves and salt and bring to a boil. Cover and boil gently 3 minutes. Uncover and boil, stirring occasionally, to 350°F (150°C). Remove from heat. Add a few drops of red food colouring. Stir well. Insert skewer in each washed and dried apple. Dip in hot syrup, swirling quickly, and spooning syrup over to coat. Place on waxed paper to set. If syrup becomes too thick while you are working, place over boiling water.

No Bake Peanut Butter Squares

PHYLLIS FLATT

3/4 cup	brown sugar	175 mL
3/4 cup	corn syrup	175 mL
2/3 cup	crunchy peanut butter	150 mL
1 teaspoon	vanilla	5 mL
1 cup	Rice Krispies, crushed	250 mL
2 cups	corn flakes, crushed	500 mL
1 1/2 cups	chocolate chips	375 mL

Grease a 9" x 13" (3.5 L) pan. In a double boiler heat sugar and syrup until dissolved. Remove from heat and stir in peanut butter and vanilla. Cool. Mix in cereals. Press into prepared pan. Melt chocolate chips and drizzle over top. Cut into squares. Yield: 24 squares.

Heavenly Hash

ETHEL KLEIN

4 squares	unsweetened chocolate	4
2 tablespoons	margarine	30 mL
2	eggs	2
1 cup	icing sugar	250 mL
40	marshmallows	40
1 cup	blanched almonds, whole, toasted	250 mL
	coconut	
	crushed nuts	

Melt chocolate and margarine. Mix eggs and icing sugar. Add to chocolate mixture. Add marshmallows and almonds. Mix well, and cook until slightly thickened. Divide into 4 rolls on sheets of waxed paper which have been sprinkled with coconut or crushed nuts. Put rolls in freezer. Remove from freezer a few hours before serving. Slice to serve.

Chocolate Nut Clusters

SALLY KERR

1/2 cup	granulated sugar	125 mL
1/2 cup	evaporated milk	125 mL
1 tablespoon	corn syrup	15 mL
1 teaspoon	vanilla	5 mL
1 cup	chocolate chips	250 mL
1 cup	pecan halves or toasted almonds	250 mL

Combine sugar, evaporated milk, and corn syrup in a saucepan. Cook and stir until bubbles form on top. Boil another minute or two, stirring constantly. Remove from heat. Stir in vanilla and chocolate chips until melted. Add nuts. Drop by spoonfuls onto waxed paper or baking parchment. Chill until firm.

No Bake Macaroons

SALLY KERR

2/3 cup	evaporated milk	150 mL
3/4 cup	granulated sugar	175 mL
1 tablespoon	butter or margarine	15 mL
1 teaspoon	vanilla	5 mL
1 cup	chocolate chips	250 mL
2 cups	corn flakes	500 mL
1 1/4 cups	coconut	300 mL
1/2 cup	chopped nuts	125 mL

Combine milk, sugar and butter or margarine in a saucepan. Cook and stir until bubbles break the top of the mixture, approximately 2 minutes. Remove from heat. Add vanilla and chocolate chips, stirring until melted. Add corn flakes, coconut and nuts. Drop from a tablespoon onto waxed paper or baking parchment. Chill until firm.

Pralines

1 3/4 cups	granulated sugar	425 mL
1 cup	boiling water	250 mL
	pinch of salt	
1 tablespoon	butter	15 mL
1/2 teaspoon	vanilla	3 mL
1 cup	pecan halves	250 mL

Melt 1/2 cup of the sugar in a saucepan over medium heat until syrupy. Remove from heat and carefully add the boiling water. Return pan to heat and stir until smooth. Stir in salt, butter and remaining sugar and boil, stirring constantly until soft ball stage, 285°F (114°C). Remove from heat, let stand 5 minutes and stir in vanilla and pecans. Stir until creamy, about 4 minutes, then drop by spoonfuls onto waxed paper. Let stand until set.

Microwave Peanut Brittle

1 cup	granulated sugar	250 mL
1/2 cup	corn syrup	125 mL
1 1/2 cups	unsalted peanuts, dry roasted	375 mL
1 teaspoon	butter	5 mL
1 teaspoon	vanilla	5 mL
1 teaspoon	baking soda	5 mL

Combine sugar and corn syrup in a 2 quart (2 L) mixing bowl. Cook on High for 4 minutes. Stir in peanuts using a wooden spoon. Cook on High for 3 minutes. Stir in butter and vanilla and cook on High an additional 3 minutes or until candy thermometer registers 300°F (140°C). Blend in baking soda and stir until mixture is light and foamy. Pour onto a greased baking sheet. Spread as quickly as possible, using the back of a wooden spoon or roll with the side of a glass. The mixture hardens very quickly. Don't worry if it doesn't reach the ends of the pan, just spread it as thinly as possible. When cool, break into pieces. Store in an airtight container.

Frosted Pecans

1 pound	pecan halves	450 g
1	egg white	1
1 tablespoon	water	15 mL
1 cup	granulated sugar	250 mL
1/2 teaspoon	salt	3 mL
1 teaspoon	cinnamon	5 mL

Preheat oven to 200°F (100°C). Beat egg white with water until foamy. Blend in sugar, salt and cinnamon. Add pecans and stir until nuts are evenly coated. Spread in one layer on a baking sheet. Bake for 45 minutes, stirring every 15 minutes until nuts are dry. Remove from oven. When cool, store in a covered container.

Healthy Snacks

In keeping with today's growing interest in health foods, we are including a few tasty and nourishing snacks.

Carob powder is a healthy chocolate substitute available in health food stores. It is also called St John's Bread, and is mentioned in the Christian, as well as in the Jewish Bible. In Yiddish it is known as "Bokser". It is a fruit pod of the carob tree that grows throughout the Middle East. The pods are picked and roasted, and then ground into a powder which looks and tastes like chocolate.

Carob powder has no sugar, no fat, and is filled with vitamin B. It is a pure, wholesome, natural dried fruit, and is also available mixed with sugar as a drink mix, and as carob chips, which can be used like chocolate chips.

Bokser is traditionally eaten around the world by Jewish people on the holiday of Tu B'Shevat, our first spring holiday. It is the holiday of "the planting of trees" and the bokser is eaten as the symbol of the first fruits of the trees.

Carob Covered Banana Popsicles   MERLE GOULD

6	bananas, ripe but firm	6
12 ounces	carob chips	340 g
6 teaspoons	oil	30 mL

Cut peeled bananas into thirds or halves. Place each on a popsicle stick, and place on sheet of waxed paper in freezer for 1 hour. While freezing, melt chips in top of double boiler. Add oil and stir until smooth. Take bananas from freezer a few at a time. Dip into carob coating to cover. Shake off excess. If desired, banana may also be rolled in coconut. When coating congeals - this just takes a few seconds - place on individual squares of foil. Wrap and freeze. This will keep for weeks in freezer.

Carob Brownies

MERLE GOULD

1 cup	carob powder	250 mL
1 cup	oil	250 mL
2/3 cup	honey	150 mL
4	eggs	4
	dash of salt	
1 cup	peanut flour*	250 mL
4 tablespoons	rye or other flour	60 mL
1 cup	chopped nuts, optional	250 mL
1 cup	raisins, optional	250 mL
2 teaspoons	pure vanilla	10 mL

Preheat oven to 325°F (160°C). Oil a 9" (2.5 L) square pan. Combine carob powder, oil and honey in a small bowl. In a larger bowl, beat eggs and salt until light. Beat in carob mixture. Stir in peanut flour and rye flour. Mix well. Add nuts, raisins, and vanilla. Spread evenly in prepared pan. Bake 20 – 25 minutes until surface is firm to touch. If desired, unsweetened coconut may be sprinkled over top before baking, or you may frost with carob frosting.

*Peanut flour is made by putting shelled raw or roasted unsalted peanuts through blender, food processor, or nut grinder, until texture of flour. Don't process too long, or you will get peanut butter. If a very fudgy texture is desired, peanut butter may be substituted for peanut flour.

Carob Frosting

MERLE GOULD

1/3 cup	carob powder	75 mL
2/3 cup	powdered milk (not instant) available in health food stores	150 mL
2 tablespoons	oil or butter	30 mL
1/4 cup	honey	60 mL
4 – 6 tablespoons	milk or cream	60 – 90 mL
1 teaspoon	pure vanilla	5 mL

Mix all ingredients with a beater and spread on cool brownies.

Healthy Carob Fudge

MERLE GOULD

1 cup	peanut butter, freshly ground	250 mL
1 cup	honey	250 mL
1 cup	carob powder	250 mL
1/2 cup	sunflower seeds	125 mL
1/2 cup	sesame seeds	125 mL
1/2 cup	unsweetened coconut	125 mL
1/2 cup	raisins	125 mL
1/2 cup	crushed peanuts	125 mL
1 teaspoon	pure vanilla	5 mL
1/4 teaspoon	salt	1 mL
1/4 teaspoon	cinnamon	1 mL

Lightly toast the sunflower and sesame seeds in a 300°F (150°C) oven for 10 minutes. Meanwhile, melt peanut butter and honey in a heavy pot just until melted and blended. Add the carob powder and continue stirring. Scrape out into a large mixing bowl. Add all other ingredients. Use hands to knead the mixture until it is thoroughly blended. Shape into walnut-sized balls and roll in coconut if desired. Store in a plastic bag in refrigerator. Makes about 30 balls. This is a wholesome snack for lunchboxes.

Yogurt Popsicles

MERLE GOULD

1 pint	plain yogurt	500 mL
1 small can	frozen fruit juice, thawed (orange, grape, lemonade, etc.)	1
2 teaspoons	pure vanilla extract	10 mL

Stir all ingredients together. Pour into paper cups. Cover with a square of aluminum foil, and push **popsicle stick** into center. Freeze. If available, a popsicle maker may be used instead of paper cups.

Cereal Snack

PEARL MEKLER

4 cups	bite size Shreddies	1 L
4 cups	Rice Krispies	1 L
4 cups	Cheerios	1 L
1 small box	pretzel sticks	1
6 ounces	peanuts or toasted almonds	175 g
1/2 cup	butter or margarine	125 mL
2 teaspoons	celery seed	10 mL
1 - 2 teaspoons	seasoned salt	5 - 10 mL
1/2 teaspoon	curry powder (optional)	2 mL
2 tablespoons	Worcestershire sauce	30 mL

Preheat oven to 250°F (125°C). Mix first five ingredients in a large, shallow baking pan. In a small saucepan, melt butter or margarine. Add seasonings. Pour over dry mixture and stir. Toast in oven for 1/2 hour stirring often. When cool, store in covered containers.

Pumpkin Seeds

2 cups	pumpkin seeds, washed	500 mL
1 1/2 tablespoons	oil	25 mL
1 teaspoon	salt	5 mL

Preheat oven to 250°F (125°C). Remove all fibrous part from seeds. Mix seeds with oil and salt. Spread out onto a cookie sheet and bake, stirring occasionally, until crisp and brown. Add more salt to taste, if desired.

Homemade Granola

1. Combine:

2 1/2 cups	mixed rolled oats and 100% bran (total amount)	625 mL
1 cup	shredded coconut	250 mL
3/4 cup	coarsely chopped almonds	175 mL
1/2 cup	sesame seeds	125 mL
1/2 cup	sunflower seeds, shelled	125 mL
1/2 cup	wheat germ	125 mL

2. Combine:

1/2 cup	honey*	125 mL
1/2 cup	soybean oil	125 mL

Add #2 mixture to #1 mixture and stir to mix thoroughly. Spread mixture evenly on a greased, shallow baking sheet. Bake at 300°F (150°C) for 20 minutes. Remove from oven and add:

3/4 cup	dried apricots, coarsely chopped	175 mL
1/2 cup	raisins	125 mL

Mix mixture well. Continue baking for about 20 minutes more. Stir every 5 – 8 minutes to allow for even browning. Remove from oven. Cool. Stir from time to time to prevent sticking. Store in tightly sealed jars, keeping extra portion in refrigerator or freezer. Make this recipe a few days before using. Flavour improves upon standing. Yield: 7 cups (1.75 L).

* For richer flavour, use buckwheat honey.

Yeast

Baking with Yeast

Contrary to popular opinion, working with yeast is quite simple and very rewarding. Here are a few hints to help make it even easier.

Cake yeast and granular yeast can be used interchangeably. Cake yeast must be fresh, and granular keeps well in the refrigerator. The package will usually be dated. One envelope of granular yeast measures 1 scant tablespoon (about 13 mL).

Always dissolve yeast in lukewarm liquid in which a teaspoon (5 mL) of sugar has been dissolved. This helps to activate it more quickly.

Dough can be made the day before and refrigerated overnight. Bring it back to room temperature before shaping.

Yeast dough has to be placed in a warm, draft-free place to rise. An unheated oven with just the light burning is an excellent place.

To rise in a microwave: Put yeast dough into a greased 2 quart (2 L) bowl that is microsafe. Cover bowl with plastic wrap, leaving one corner open for venting. Place this into a larger microsafe bowl. Pour 3 cups (750 mL) of lukewarm water into the larger bowl. Microwave on low for 20 minutes. Let stand in microwave without power for 10 – 15 minutes longer. Dough will have doubled in bulk. Punch down and shape as desired.

Holiday Challa

DOROTHY GELLMAN

1/2 cup	unsalted margarine	125 mL
1/2 cup	granulated sugar	125 mL
1 teaspoon	salt	5 mL
1 cup	very hot water	250 mL
2	eggs	2
2 ounces	moist (cake) yeast	56 g
3 1/2 – 4 1/2 cups	all purpose flour	875 – 1125 mL

Into a large bowl put margarine, sugar and salt. Pour hot water over and stir to help margarine melt. Beat in eggs. Crumble the yeast and add it to the mixture. Beat until everything is blended. Add flour slowly until beaters can take no more. Then beat in the rest of the flour by hand with a wooden spoon. Remove dough from the bowl and knead for 10 minutes on a board adding just enough flour to make sure the dough does not stick to your hands. Put dough into a greased bowl, cover with greased waxed paper and transparent wrap. Refrigerate for at least 8 hours to a few days.

Before shaping the dough, let it stand at room temperature for 45 – 60 minutes. Divide dough into 2 parts. Cut each part into 3 and roll snake fashion. Join the three rolls at the top and braid. This recipe makes 2 nice size breads.

Put loaves on a greased cookie sheet or in greased loaf pans. Brush with beaten **egg yolk** and sprinkle with **sesame** or **poppy seeds** and allow it to rise until double in bulk (1 – 1 1/2 hours). Bake at 375°F (190°C) for about 40 minutes or until brown. If it browns too quickly, cover loosely with foil until the bread is baked. A nice variation is to use half white and half whole wheat flour.

Shaping Loaves

ESTHER SCHWARTZ

Challa buns: Divide dough into small pieces. Knead each piece a little, then roll into a rope. Knot, tuck ends under, and place on a greased foil lined pan, (shiny side up).

Mock 6 Braid Challa: Divide dough into two pieces, one slightly larger than the other. Divide the larger part into three pieces. Roll each piece into a rope, thicker in the middle than at the ends. Attach the three ropes at the top, and braid, tucking ends under. Place on a greased foil lined cookie sheet (shiny side up). Divide smaller portion of dough into 3 sections. Roll into ropes as above, and braid. Place on top of previously braided dough.

Round Challa: Make a rope, 18" (45 cm) long, thicker at one end. Starting with the thicker end, roll into a circle, tucking thinner end underneath at the end.

Six Braid Challa: Divide dough into six equal pieces. Knead each piece a little before rolling into a rope, slightly thicker in the center than at the ends. Arrange ropes as below:

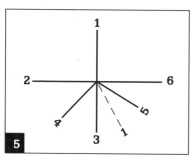

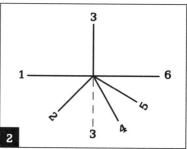

Take 3 up to top.

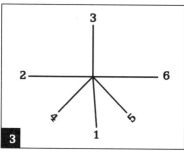

Bring 1 under 2 and 4, bringing 2 into 1 position.

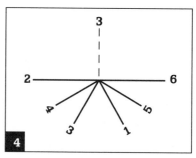

Bring 3 down between 4 and 1.

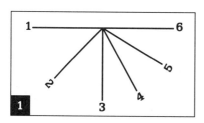

Lift 1 to top.

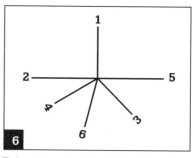

Bring 6 under 5 and 3, taking 5 to 6 position.

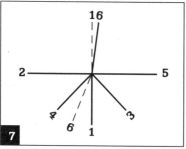

Bring 1 down over top between 3 and 6. Then lift 6 up to top.

Starting now with step No.3, repeat process, alternating left and right. Practice a few times with pipe cleaners or pieces of rope. It's easier than it looks, and makes a beautiful challa!

Food Processor Challa

ESTHER SCHWARTZ

1 envelope	granular yeast	13 mL
1 teaspoon	granulated sugar	5 mL
1 cup	warm water (a little hotter than lukewarm)	250 mL
1	vitamin C tablet (500 mg), crushed (optional)	1

Combine above ingredients and mix well.

3 cups plus 2 tablespoons	all purpose flour	780 mL
1/4 – 1/2 cup	granulated sugar	75 – 125 mL
1 teaspoon	coarse salt	5 mL
1	egg	1
1/4 cup	oil	60 mL

Using the metal blade, add flour, sugar and salt to the bowl. Turn on/off. With machine running, add through the feed tube, the egg, oil and yeast mixture. Process until ball forms, and sides of bowl are clean, about 40 seconds. Turn dough out onto a lightly floured board and knead until smooth and satiny, about 1 minute. Place in a greased bowl, turning to coat all sides. Cover with greased waxed paper and a damp towel. Let rise in a warm place 1 1/2 – 2 hours until doubled. When poked with 2 fingers, the indentations should remain. Punch down.

Or

Place in refrigerator overnight. (It doubles in bulk, then stops rising.) In the morning, punch down. Let stand at room temperature to take the chill off. Knead for 1 minute. Shape loaves. Place loaves on a greased pan. Cover with a damp towel. Let rise again in warm place until doubled, about 1 hour. Brush with beaten egg. Sprinkle with poppy seeds or sesame seeds. Bake in a preheated oven 375°F (190°C) 35 – 40 minutes or until nicely crusted and golden. Bottom should sound hollow when tapped. Makes 1 large loaf or 2 small ones. Bake miniature rolls in preheated oven 375°F (190°C) 20 – 25 minutes or until golden.

Bagels

1 cup plus 2 tablespoons	warm water	280 mL
1 teaspoon	granulated sugar	5 mL
1 envelope	granular yeast	13 mL
3 cups	all purpose flour	750 mL
1 tablespoon	granulated sugar	15 mL
1 1/2 teaspoons	salt	7 mL
1 tablespoon	corn syrup	15 mL
1/3 cup	oil	75 mL
1 tablespoon	honey	15 mL
	sesame seeds	
	poppy seeds	

Dissolve 1 teaspoon (5 mL) sugar in water. Add yeast and let stand 10 minutes.

Food processor method: In processor bowl, place flour, sugar and salt. Process with several on/off motions to blend. Add corn syrup and oil to yeast mixture. With motor running, add yeast mixture through feed tube and process until dough forms a ball, adding more flour, if necessary. Turn onto floured board and knead by hand 1 or 2 minutes.

Electric mixer with dough hook method: In a large bowl, place 2 cups (500 mL) of the flour, salt and sugar and make a well. Add yeast mixture, oil and corn syrup. Beat until dough forms. Turn out onto floured board and knead, adding flour until dough is smooth and elastic.

Place dough in a greased bowl, cover, put in a warm place and let rise until doubled in bulk.

Divide dough into 12 pieces. Roll each piece into a rope 8" (20 cm) long. Wrap around hand and roll to join the ends. Place on floured board. Let rise 1/2 hour.

Preheat oven to 400°F (200°C). In a large pot, bring 10 cups (2.5 L) water to a boil. Add honey, turn heat down and let water simmer. Add bagels, 4 at a time and cook 5 minutes, turning once. Remove to rack and cool slightly. Line large cookie sheet with foil and grease well. Dip both sides of bagels in sesame or poppy seeds. Place on prepared pan, and bake 30 minutes or until golden brown. Cool on rack.

Middle Eastern Flat Bread

1/4 cup	butter	60 mL
1 teaspoon	granulated sugar	5 mL
1 cup	warm water	250 mL
1 envelope	granular yeast	13 mL
1 1/2 teaspoons	salt	7 mL
2 – 3 1/2 cups	all purpose flour	500 – 875 mL
1	egg white	1
	poppy seeds	
	sesame seeds	

Melt butter and cool to lukewarm. Dissolve sugar in water. Sprinkle yeast on top and let stand 10 minutes. Stir. Add cooled butter. Place salt and 2 cups of the flour in bowl of food processor. With motor running, add yeast mixture through the feed tube. Add more flour as necessary. Dough should come away from the sides of the bowl and should be smooth. *Knead by hand for 1 minute and place in buttered bowl, turning to coat dough with butter on both sides. Cover and let rise in a warm place until doubled in bulk.

Preheat oven to 350°F (180°C). Divide dough into 4 pieces. Roll each piece into a rectangle approximately 10" x 14" (25 cm x 35 cm). Dough should be very thin. Place on ungreased cookie sheet, paint with slightly beaten egg white, and sprinkle lightly with poppy seeds and sesame seeds. Bake for 20 minutes or until brown. Cool on rack and store in tightly covered tin or large plastic bag.

* If not using processor, place salt and 2 cups of the flour in a large bowl. Make a well in center and add yeast mixture. Stir until all flour is absorbed, adding more until dough is manageable. Turn onto floured board and knead until dough is smooth and elastic. Continue from * above.

Whole Grain Bread

2 cups	warm water	500 mL
4 teaspoons	yeast (1 1/2 envelopes)	20 mL
1/2 cup	honey	125 mL
1/4 cup	oil	60 mL
1/2 cup	rye flour	125 mL
1/2 cup	oats	125 mL
1/2 cup	dry milk	125 mL
2 teaspoons	salt	10 mL
2 1/2 cups	whole wheat flour	625 mL
2 cups	all purpose flour	500 mL

Place water, yeast, honey and oil in a large bowl and let stand 10 minutes. Mix well. Add remaining ingredients, except all purpose flour, mix and stir until dough leaves sides of bowl. Turn out onto floured board and knead in white flour until dough becomes smooth and elastic. Place in a greased bowl turning to coat. Cover and let rise 1 1/2 hours in a warm place. Separate into 2 loaves. Roll out dough and tightly roll up, squeezing out air bubbles. Place in well greased bread pans. Let rise 45 minutes. Split top of bread with knife. Brush with a small amount of **honey** and sprinkle with **sesame seeds**. Let rise 30 minutes.

Preheat oven to 350°F (180°C). Bake for 35 minutes or until golden brown. Let stand about 5 minutes. Remove from pans. Cool on rack.

Dill Bread

SHIRLEY LAZARUS

1 envelope	granular yeast	13 mL
1/4 cup	lukewarm water	60 mL
1 cup	lukewarm cottage cheese	250 mL
2 tablespoons	butter	30 mL
2 tablespoons	grated onion	30 mL
1 teaspoon	salt	5 mL
2 teaspoons	dill seed	10 mL
1/4 teaspoon	baking soda	1 mL
1	egg	1
2 – 2 1/2 cups	all purpose flour	500 – 625 mL

Sprinkle yeast in lukewarm water. Let stand for 10 minutes. Stir. In large bowl of mixer, combine cottage cheese, butter, onion, salt, dill seed, baking soda and egg. Add the yeast mixture and mix well. Gradually add flour to make a stiff dough. Knead on a floured surface for 10 minutes. Place in a greased bowl, cover with greased waxed paper and a damp cloth and let rise in a draft-free place for 50 - 60 minutes. Punch down, turn into well buttered 1 1/2 quart (1.5 L) casserole and let rise for 30 – 40 minutes. Preheat oven to 350°F (180°C). Bake for 40 – 50 minutes. When baked, brush with soft butter.

French Bread

LOIS FRIEDMAN

1 envelope	granular yeast	13 mL
1 tablespoon	granulated sugar	15 mL
1 1/2 cups	warm water	375 mL
2 teaspoons	salt	10 mL
4 cups	all purpose flour	1 L
1	egg white	1
1 tablespoon	water	15 mL

In a large bowl, dissolve sugar in 1/2 cup (125 mL) of the water, sprinkle yeast on top and let stand for 10 minutes. Stir. Add remaining water, salt and 3 cups (750 mL) of the flour. Beat with wooden spoon until dough comes away from the sides of the bowl, adding more flour if necessary. Turn out onto floured board and knead, adding flour as necessary until dough is smooth and elastic. Place in greased bowl, turning to coat both sides, cover and let rise until doubled in bulk. Punch down and let rise 45 minutes more.

Grease a large baking sheet or baguette pan and sprinkle with **cornmeal**. Divide dough in half. Shape each piece into a long, thin loaf and place on prepared pan. On top of each loaf cut 4 shallow, slanted slits with a sharp knife. Let rise 30 minutes.

Preheat oven to 400°F (200°C). Beat egg white lightly with water. Brush tops of loaves. Bake 45 minutes or until golden and loaves sound hollow when tapped. Cool on rack.

Basic Yeast Dough

LOIS FRIEDMAN

1 envelope	granular yeast	13 mL
1 1/4 cups	lukewarm milk	325 mL
1 teaspoon	granulated sugar	5 mL
1 cup	butter	250 mL
1/2 cup	granulated sugar	125 mL
3	eggs	3
1 teaspoon	salt	5 mL
4 – 5 1/2 cups	all purpose flour	1 – 1.375 L
1/2 cup	raisins, optional	125 mL

Dissolve 1 teaspoon (5 mL) sugar in 1/2 cup (125 mL) of the milk. Add yeast and let stand 10 minutes. Cream butter, add 1/2 cup (125 mL) sugar, cream well. Add eggs, one at a time, beating well after each addition. Add yeast mixture, remaining milk, salt, and 3 cups (750 mL) of the flour. Beat on low speed until well blended. Continue to add flour until dough is too stiff for mixer. Use your hand to add enough flour so that dough does not stick to hand. Add raisins and mix through. Place in greased bowl, turning to coat the dough, cover with waxed paper, then a tea towel, and let rise in warm place until double in bulk. Continue with specific recipe.

Blueberry Buns

LOIS FRIEDMAN

1 recipe	yeast dough, omitting raisins	1
2 pints	blueberries	1 L
3/4 cup	granulated sugar	175 mL
3 tablespoons	minute tapioca	45 mL

Mix berries, sugar and tapioca. Set aside. Divide dough into 4 pieces. Roll each piece to a thickness of 1/4" (0.6 cm). Cut with a large cookie cutter or large glass. Place as much filling as possible on dough, pull edges to the top and pinch seam **very well**. Place on buttered cookie sheets and let rise, covered with waxed paper and a tea towel, for 45 minutes. Preheat oven to 350°F (180°C). Brush buns with **1 egg** mixed with **1 tablespoon (15 mL) water**. Bake 25 minutes or until golden. Remove to wire rack. Buns tend to open while baking. Be sure to pinch them well.

Sticky Buns

LOIS FRIEDMAN

1 recipe	basic yeast dough	1
1/2 cup	butter	125 mL
3/4 cup	brown sugar	200 mL
1/2 cup	honey, warmed	125 mL
1/4 pound	pecan halves	115 g
1 1/2 cups	granulated sugar	375 mL
2 tablespoons	cinnamon	30 mL

Prepare muffin tins by placing 1 teaspoon (5 mL) melted butter, 1 teaspoon (5 mL) honey, 1 rounded teaspoon (about 8 mL) brown sugar, and a few pecan halves in each buttered section. Break off small pieces of dough the size of a golf ball. Roll into mixture of cinnamon and sugar, and place in prepared tins. Let rise 1/2 hour, and bake at 400°F (200°C) for 15 minutes. Reduce heat to 325°F (160°C) and bake for an additional 10 minutes. Let cool for 1 minute before removing from pan.

Cinnamon Buns

LOIS FRIEDMAN

1 recipe	basic yeast dough	1
1/2 cup	butter	125 mL
1 1/2 cups	granulated sugar	375 mL
2 tablespoons	cinnamon	30 mL

Divide dough into 4 pieces, and each piece into 10 balls. Melt butter. Combine sugar and cinnamon. Brush an 11" x 15" (27.5 x 37.5 cm) jelly roll pan with melted butter. Roll each ball into a 3" (7.5 cm) rope, dip it in melted butter, and then in cinnamon-sugar mixture. Tie in a knot, or form into a pinwheel. Place in the pan in rows, 5 across and 8 down. When finished, cover pan with waxed paper and a tea towel, and let rise 30 minutes. Preheat oven to 375°F (190°C). Bake for 25 minutes. Remove from oven, and allow to stand a few minutes before inverting onto wire rack.

To freeze: Divide into packages of 8 or 10. Wrap in foil, and place in freezer. To serve, remove from freezer and place in 350°F (180°C) oven for 20 – 25 minutes.

Quick Rise Cinnamon Buns

Fleischmann's Quick-Rise instant yeast reduces preparation time by eliminating one rising. Do not substitute other types of yeast.

4 1/2 cups	all purpose flour	1.125 L
1 envelope	Quick-Rise yeast	8 g
1 teaspoon	salt	5 mL
1/4 – 1/2 cup	granulated sugar	60 – 125 mL
1/2 cup	butter, margarine or vegetable shortening	125 mL
1/4 cup	water	60 mL
1 cup	milk	250 mL
2 – 4	eggs, well beaten	2 – 4

Set aside 1 1/2 cups (375 mL) of the flour. Mix remaining flour, yeast, salt and sugar in large bowl of electric mixer. Heat butter with water and milk until hot to touch - 125 – 130°F. Stir the hot liquid into the dry mixture and mix 3 – 5 minutes on medium speed. Slowly add the beaten eggs and blend well. Mix enough of the reserved flour for desired consistency, soft but not sticky. If mixer does not take it, mix in by hand. Knead 5 minutes with dough hook or 10 minutes by hand. Cover and let rest for 10 minutes.

To Shape: Divide dough in half. Roll 1/4" (0.6 cm) thick on a floured surface. Paint the rolled dough with **melted butter** or **margarine**. Sprinkle with **cinnamon**, **sugar** and **raisins** or **nuts** if desired.

Roll as for jelly roll, stretching to uniform thickness. Cut into 1 1/2" (3.75 cm) slices. Place, loosely touching, in buttered pan. One half recipe will fit 8" (20 cm) square pan, a whole recipe will fit a 9" x 13" (22.5 cm x 32.5 cm) pan. Cover with a tea towel and let rise for 45 – 60 minutes. Bake in preheated 375°F (190°C) oven about 20 minutes until golden.

Dough may be frozen after shaping but before rising. Return to room temperature and let rise, about 3 – 4 hours before baking. Dough may be refrigerated after shaping for up to 2 days. Return to room temperature, about 1 hour before baking.

Cousin Phyllis' Chocolate Yeast LOIS FRIEDMAN

1 cup	warm milk	250 mL
1 teaspoon	granulated sugar	5 mL
1 envelope	granular yeast	13 mL
3 cups	all purpose flour	750 mL
1/2 cup	granulated sugar	125 mL
1 teaspoon	salt	5 mL
2	eggs	2
1/2 cup	melted butter	125 mL

Dissolve 1 teaspoon (5 mL) sugar in warm milk. Sprinkle yeast on top and let stand 10 minutes. In a large bowl, place flour, sugar and salt. Make a well in center and add eggs. melted butter and yeast mixture. Beat with wooden spoon until dough forms. Turn out onto floured board and knead until smooth and elastic, adding flour if necessary. Place in greased bowl, cover, and let rise until doubled in bulk.

Glaze:

4 tablespoons	butter	60 mL
1/2 cup	brown sugar	125 mL
2 tablespoons	boiling water	30 mL
1/4 cup	toasted, slivered almonds or pecan halves	60 mL

In skillet, melt butter, add sugar and mix well. Add water and whisk until smooth. Bring to a boil and cook about 3 minutes, whisking constantly. Pour into well greased bundt pan and sprinkle nuts on top.

Filling:

3 tablespoons	melted butter	45 mL
1/2 cup	brown sugar	125 mL
2 tablespoons	cocoa	30 mL
1/4 teaspoon	cinnamon	1 mL
1/2 cup	raisins (optional)	125 mL

Roll dough into a rectangle 16" x 20" (40 x 50 cm). Paint with melted butter. Mix sugar, cocoa and cinnamon together. Sprinkle on top. Add raisins. Roll, lengthwise, from both sides and when they meet in the middle, place one on top of the other. Form a circle, sealing ends carefully, and place in prepared bundt pan. Cover and let rise until doubled in bulk.

Preheat oven to 375°F (190°C). Bake for 45 – 55 minutes. Remove from oven, let stand 10 minutes. Invert pan and let stand another 10 minutes before removing pan.

Cottage Cheese Danish

JOAN SOLWAY

2 envelopes	granular yeast	26 mL
2/3 cup	warm water	175 mL
1 teaspoon	granulated sugar	5 mL
4 1/2 cups	all purpose flour	1.125 L
1 cup	granulated sugar	250 mL
1 teaspoon	salt	5 mL
2/3 cup	butter	150 mL
1 pound	creamed cottage cheese	500 g
2	eggs	2

Dissolve 1 teaspoon (5 mL) sugar in water. Add yeast and let stand 10 minutes. Place flour, sugar and salt in a large bowl. Cut in butter with pastry blender until it is in small particles. Add cottage cheese and mix well. Make a well in flour mixture and add yeast and eggs. Mix well. Knead until smooth, adding more flour when kneading if dough is too sticky to handle. Cover and let rise in a warm place until double in bulk. Refrigerate overnight. Leave at room temperature 1 hour before shaping. Divide dough into 4 pieces. Roll each piece into a rectangle 1/4" (0.6 cm) thick.

Brush each piece with either **apricot jam**, or a mixture of **cinnamon** and **sugar**. If desired, a row of stewed prunes may be placed down one side before rolling. Roll as for jelly roll. Cut into 1" (2.5 cm) slices and place on slightly buttered cookie sheet. Let rise, covered, until double in bulk. Preheat oven to 375°F (190°C). Bake 15 minutes. Glaze with icing sugar mixture while hot.

Glaze for Yeast:

1 cup	icing sugar	250 mL
4 teaspoons	hot milk	20 mL
1/4 teaspoon	vanilla	1 mL

Combine well. Dribble over warm yeast cake.

Butter Kuchen Crescents (Rogella)

PAULINE TOKER

3 cups	all purpose flour	750 mL
1/2 cup	granulated sugar	125 mL
1/4 teaspoon	salt	1 mL
1 teaspoon	granulated sugar	5 mL
1/4 cup	warm water	60 mL
1	cake of yeast	1
2	eggs	2
1/2 cup	butter, melted	125 mL
1 cup	sour cream	250 mL
	softened butter	
	granulated sugar	
	cinnamon	
	raisins	
	chopped nuts (optional)	

Sift flour, sugar and salt into a bowl. Add 1 teaspoon (5 mL) sugar to warm water and sprinkle in yeast. Let stand for 10 minutes. Stir. Add beaten eggs, yeast mixture, melted butter and sour cream to flour mixture. Beat until flour has been absorbed and is of elastic consistency. Knead by hand or pastry hook until dough leaves sides of bowl. Place dough in greased bowl, and cover with greased waxed paper, then with a cloth. Refrigerate overnight. Remove from refrigerator and let stand for a short time at room temperature. Divide dough into 4 parts. Roll each part on floured board, into a circle. Cut each circle into 6 or 8 triangles. Spread with softened butter and a mixture of sugar, cinnamon and raisins. Chopped nuts may be added if desired. Roll up, starting at the outside edge. Place on greased pans, and let stand in a warm place covered, until double in bulk. Bake at 375°F (190°C) for 15 minutes.

European Bobke

JEAN RACHLIN

1	cake of yeast	1
1 cup	milk	250 mL
1 teaspoon	granulated sugar	5 mL
3 1/2 cups	sifted all purpose flour	875 mL
1/2 teaspoon	salt	2 mL
3/4 cup	granulated sugar	175 mL
1/2 cup	butter	125 mL
1 tablespoon	shortening	15 mL
3	large eggs	3
1 teaspoon	vanilla	5 mL
1 cup	raisins	250 mL
1/4 cup	granulated sugar	60 mL
1/2 cup	chopped walnuts or pecans	125 mL
1/4 cup	all purpose flour	60 mL

Scald milk with 1 teaspoon (5 mL) sugar. Cool to lukewarm. Crumble in yeast and let stand 10 minutes. Stir. Measure flour and sift with salt and sugar. Make a well in the flour mixture. Melt and cool butter and shortening, and pour into well. Add eggs, vanilla and yeast. Stir well, starting in center, gradually incorporating flour into liquid. Beat until very smooth and elastic, with wooden spoon, or by machine. This will take 10 – 15 minutes. Cover and let rise in warm, draft-free place until doubled in bulk, about 1 1/2 hours. Steam raisins until plump, and cool.

Beat risen mixture again, about 8 minutes on mixer, or knead well by hand. Beat or knead in raisins. Reserve 1/2 cup (125 mL) of batter. Turn into well buttered 10" (25 cm) tube pan. Mix reserved batter with nuts, sugar and flour, and sprinkle over top. Cover and let rise again until doubled in bulk, about 1 1/2 hours. Bake in preheated 375°F (190°C) oven about 40 minutes.

Traditional

Holidays and Festivals

ESTELLE ZALDIN

The observance of our Jewish holidays and festivals is part of an evolving process based on historic events and geared to seasonal festivals and fast days. During each holiday, we eat traditional foods which have symbolic and spiritual significance.

On Rosh Hashanah, the New Year, a round challah is served as a symbol of life without end. The meal begins with challah or apple dipped in honey to symbolize our hopes for a sweet year.

Succot and Simhat Torah, which occur during the fall harvest, are full of joy in the Torah. Appropriately, we eat filled foods such as stuffed cabbage and potato knishes.

Chanukah and Purim have completely different food observances, based on a particular historic event. On Chanukah we eat latkes or doughnuts fried in oil because of the miracle of the oil burning for eight days in the rededicated Temple. On Purim we eat three cornered filled pastries called Hamantashen, to remember the victory over the tyrant Haman, who was said to have worn a three cornered hat.

The major spring holiday, Passover (Pesach), requires that we have fresh greens and lamb in our menu. The Haggadah, which we read together as we sit around the holiday table, tells in detail the symbolic foods that are traditionally eaten, and the reasons for eating them.

Since Shavuot is the birthday of the Torah, and because the Torah is compared to milk and honey, we eat foods made with milk, and other dairy products such as blintzes and cheesecake.

Sabbath is something else again. The Jewish Sabbath is a day blessed and hallowed for refreshing body and spirit. It is personified in Jewish lore as a bride whose bridegroom is Israel, and for this reason we feast and drink as for a wedding celebration.

Our traditional Jewish dishes have their origins in central European cuisines. Jewish women have always used their imagination and ingenuity to adapt indigenous foods and seasonal ingredients for the Jewish festivals. In our time and place, 20th century North America, we are evolving a new and unique cuisine which is a synthesis of our traditional European foods, our health-conscious, low calorie eating habits and the contemporary food ideas, foods, and techniques available to us. The possibilities are endless.

Potato Cholent

ESTHER SCHWARTZ

2 tablespoons	chicken fat or	30 mL
	Vegarine vegetable spread	
5 pounds	baking potatoes	2.5 kg
1	large onion, grated	1
2 teaspoons	salt	10 mL
1/4 teaspoon	pepper	1 mL
3/4 cup	challa crumbs	175 mL
1 pound	flanken (short ribs),	500 g
	cut at each bone	

Melt chicken fat or Vegarine in bottom of a heavy pot. Grease sides of pot. Grate potatoes into water and strain through a fine strainer. Mix the potatoes with the grated onion, salt, pepper, and challa crumbs. Pour half the potato mixture into the pot. Place flanken pieces in the center and top with remaining potato mixture. Cover. Heat on top of the stove, and when it begins to steam, turn to a very low heat (simmer) and cook for 6 - 7 hours, mixing with a wooden spoon every two hours. Leave covered all the time it is cooking. The bottom gets crusty. Cook on Thursday for Shabbat as it is better the second day. If it is too solid the second day, reheat with a little stock or gravy. Freezes well. Delicious!

Farfel Mold

3	medium onions, chopped	3
1	green pepper,	
	seeded and chopped	1
2 tablespoons	oil	30 mL
1 · 6.5 ounce package	farfel	183 g
1/2 teaspoon	salt	2 mL

Preheat oven to 350°F (180°C). Sauté onions and green pepper in oil until onions are golden brown. Boil farfel in **salted boiling water** until soft, according to package directions. Mix sautéed vegetables with farfel. Place in greased mold and bake for 15 minutes.

Hamantashen

3 cups	all purpose flour	750 mL
3 teaspoons	baking powder	15 mL
1/2 cup	granulated sugar	125 mL
1/4 teaspoon	salt	1 mL
3/4 cup	butter or vegetable shortening	175 mL
3	eggs	3
	additional egg, beaten, for brushing dough	

Preheat oven to 400°F (200°C). Sift together flour, baking powder, sugar and salt. Cut in shortening. Add well beaten eggs and mix to a soft dough. Roll out on a floured board to 1/4" (5 mm) thickness. Cut with a large, round cookie cutter. Put a spoonful of desired filling in center, and pinch together to form a triangular pocket. Brush with beaten egg and place on a well greased pan. Bake for 12 - 15 minutes.

Suggested Fillings:

Poppy seed filling:

1/2 pound	poppy seed	225 g
1/2 cup	honey	125 mL
	juice and rind of 1/2 lemon	
	or	
1 teaspoon	vanilla	5 mL
1/2 cup	granulated sugar	125 mL

Scald poppy seed with boiling water 2 or 3 times. Put through food chopper or food processor. Add honey, flavouring, sugar and blend.

Apple filling:

4 pounds	apples, sliced	1.75 kg
1 1/2	lemons, juice and rind	1 1/2
2 cups	granulated sugar	500 mL

Cook all together, stirring frequently, until thick. Cool before using.

Date filling:

1 pound	pitted dates	450 g
1/2 cup	honey	125 mL
1 cup	chopped nuts	250 mL
1/2 cup	water	125 mL
1	lemon, juice and rind	1

Combine and cook all ingredients slowly until dates are tender. Cool before using.

Prune filling #1: Put uncooked pitted prunes through food chopper or food processor. To 1 pound (450 g) prunes, add the juice of 1 lemon and 1/2 cup (125 mL) honey. Blend well.

Prune filling #2:

1 pound	large prunes	450 g
1/2 cup	granulated sugar	125 mL
1 tablespoon	lemon juice	15 mL
	grated rind of 1 lemon	

Stew prunes. Remove pits. Process lightly with sugar and flavouring. If too wet, add 1 tablespoon (15 mL) **bread crumbs** and 2 tablespoons (30 mL) **chopped nuts**.

Apricot filling: Soak apricots overnight in water to cover. Drain well. Put through food chopper or processor. To 1 pound (450 g) apricots, add 1 cup (250 mL) honey, 1 tablespoon (15 mL) grated orange rind, and the juice of 1/2 orange.

Egg Noodles

MYRTLE COOPERSMITH

6	eggs	6
	dash nutmeg	
	dash pepper	
2 tablespoons	oil	30 mL

Beat eggs. Mix in nutmeg, pepper and oil. Oil well, a 6" (15 cm) frying pan or crepe pan. (One oiling is enough). Drop egg mixture from a ladle onto hot pan. Tilt over medium heat until even and thin. Pour off excess. Brown lightly. Turn over for 10 seconds. Remove to paper towel. When cool, roll up and slice thinly. Serve in chicken soup. Serves 4 - 6.

Honey Soufflé

4	eggs, separated	4
2 tablespoons	all purpose flour	30 mL
1/4 teaspoon	nutmeg	1 mL
3/4 cup	icing sugar	175 mL
2 tablespoons	sherry or sweet wine	30 mL
1/2 cup	honey	125 mL
1/2 cup	unsalted parve margarine, melted	125 mL
1 teaspoon	grated lemon rind	5 mL
2 tablespoons	finely ground almonds	30 mL

Preheat oven to 350°F (180°C). Beat yolks until light and creamy. Sift flour, nutmeg, and sugar together. Stir into yolks. Add wine. Mix honey and melted margarine together, and add slowly to egg mixture. Add rind and beat smooth. Beat whites until stiff but not dry, and fold into honey mixture. Pour into ungreased 1 1/2 quart (1.5 L) soufflé dish. Sprinkle with almonds. Place dish in shallow pan of hot water and bake 30 - 40 minutes. This is a lovely Rosh Hashanah dessert. Serves 4.

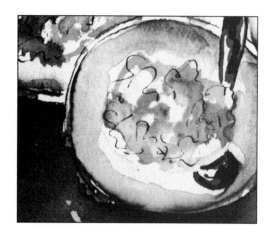

Meringues:

6	egg whites, room temperature	6
1/2 teaspoon	cream of tartar	2 mL
1/2 teaspoon	salt	2 mL
1 cup	granulated sugar	250 mL

Preheat oven to 275°F (135°C). In a large mixing bowl, beat the egg whites until foamy. Add cream of tartar, salt and sugar gradually. Beat until stiff. Lightly grease and flour 2 large cookie sheets. Drop meringues by tablespoons, 1" (2.5 cm) apart. Use a spatula to push meringues from spoon. Bake for one hour until crisp and golden. Remove and place on a rack.

Filling:

2	bananas	2
	orange juice or liqueur	
2 cups	whipping cream	500 mL
1/2 cup	icing sugar	125 mL
1/2 cup	chopped pecans	125 mL
1 · 19 ounce can	pineapple chunks, well drained	540 mL

Slice bananas and marinate in orange juice or liqueur for 10 minutes. Drain very well. Whip cream with icing sugar. Combine drained banana slices, pineapple chunks and pecans. Fold fruit-nut mixture into sweetened whipped cream. Shape into a pyramid by placing a round base of 10 meringues on a platter. Spoon some of the cream mixture on the base and make sure 1" (2.5 cm) is left uncovered around base. Make next layer smaller, adding cream, and continue building pyramid with meringues and cream mixture. Finish with a single meringue on top.

Garnish: Sprinkle **shaved chocolate** over all. If desired the platter can be decorated with small clusters of **green grapes** and/or **strawberries**.

Passover Substitutes

6 ounces (175 g) **semi-sweet chocolate** = 6 tablespoons (90 mL) unsweetened cocoa powder plus 1/4 cup (50 mL) oil and 7 tablespoons (100 mL) granulated sugar

1 tablespoon (15 mL) **flour** = 1/2 tablespoon (7 mL) potato starch

1 tablespoon (15 mL) **cornstarch** = 1 tablespoon (15 mL) potato starch

1 cup (250 mL) **bread crumbs** = 1 cup (250 mL) matzo meal

1 cup (250 mL) **milk** = 1 cup (250 mL) water plus 2 tablespoons (30 mL) margarine

Some ingredients in the following recipes are not available in all communities. For strictly Kosher use, buy products appropriately labeled for Passover. When in doubt, consult your Rabbi.

Versatile Passover Dough
ESTHER SCHWARTZ

1 cup	water	250 mL
1/2 cup	oil	125 mL
1 teaspoon	salt	5 mL
2 tablespoons	granulated sugar	30 mL
1 1/2 cups	matzo meal	375 mL
4	large eggs	4

Bring water, oil, salt and sugar to boiling point. Remove from heat, and stir in matzo meal, mixing thoroughly. Return to heat for 3 minutes, stirring constantly. Remove from heat. Let stand 10 minutes. Add eggs one at a time, beating well after each addition until dough is smooth.

Bagels: Preheat oven to 400°F (200°C). Oil hands and tablespoon lightly. Measure 2 tablespoons (30 mL) of dough and form into a ball. Roll in **cinnamon**. Place on lightly greased cookie sheet 1 1/2" (3.75 cm) apart. Dip finger in oil and make a hole in center of each bagel. Bake for 40 - 45 minutes or until nicely browned. Yield: 16 bagels.

Cream Puffs: Preheat oven to 400°F (200°C). Oil hands slightly. Measure 2 tablespoons (30 mL) of the dough and form into a ball. Place on greased cookie sheet and bake for 20 - 25 minutes or until golden brown. Cool. Cut off tops. Remove webbing, and fill with your favourite filling. Yield: 16 cream puffs.

Soup Nuts (Mandlach): Preheat oven to 400°F (200°C). Oil hands slightly. Measure 1/2 teaspoon (2 mL) of the dough at a time and shape into small balls. Place on a greased cookie sheet and bake 20 - 25 minutes, or until puffed and brown. Yield: 128 soup nuts (mandlach).

Bubbela

RUTH GOLDBERG

Use 1 1/2 tablespoons (25 mL) **matzo meal** per **egg**. Beat whites until stiff. Add beaten egg yolk to white. Then fold in matzo meal. Cook slowly in well buttered frying pan over low heat. When brown and pulling away from sides of pan, flip and cook on other side. These can be made in individual pancakes or 1 large one. Just be sure to cook slowly, adding butter if necessary, so it gets done in the middle. Serve with **sugar** and **cinnamon** or **applesauce**.

Passover Cream Puffs

1 cup	boiling water	250 mL
1/4 cup	butter or oil	60 mL
2 teaspoons	granulated sugar	10 mL
1/2 teaspoon	salt	2 mL
1 cup	cake meal	250 mL
3	eggs	3

Preheat oven to 375°F (190°C). Place first four ingredients in pot and bring to a boil. Add cake meal all at once and stir rapidly. Cool slightly. Add eggs one at a time and beat well after each addition. Drop by spoonfuls onto a greased cookie sheet. Bake for 40 minutes.

Basic Blintz Leaves:

4	eggs	4
1 3/4 cups	water	425 mL
1/2 teaspoon	salt	2 mL
1 tablespoon	oil	15 mL
3/4 cup	sifted cake meal	175 mL
	oil for skillet	

Beat the eggs, water, salt, and oil in a medium bowl. Gradually add the cake meal, beating until the mixture is the consistency of light cream. Stir the batter periodically while preparing.

Heat a 7" - 8" (20 - 25 cm) lightly greased skillet over moderately high heat. Ladle in sufficient batter to thinly coat the bottom of the pan. Quickly tilt and rotate the pan to distribute the batter evenly. Pour off excess batter. Cook until the batter sets and the edge of the pancake starts to leave the sides of the pan. Invert the skillet over a clean cloth. Repeat until all the batter is used up. Yield: 12 - 14 blintz leaves.

Suggested Fillings:

Cheese Filling:

1 pound	cottage cheese	500 g
1	egg	1
1/2 teaspoon	salt	2 mL
1/2 teaspoon	granulated sugar	2 mL
1/2 teaspoon	cinnamon	2 mL
1/4 cup	raisins (optional)	60 mL
	oil for frying	

In a small mixing bowl thoroughly combine all of the ingredients. Divide the filling evenly among the blintz leaves. Fold the sides of the leaves over filling and roll up to make an envelope. Brown in a little butter or shortening over medium heat. Sprinkle with additional **sugar** and **cinnamon** if desired.

Meat Filling:

2 cups	ground cooked meat or chicken	500 mL
2 teaspoons	chopped onion	10 mL
2 tablespoons	chopped celery	30 mL
1 tablespoon	oil	15 mL
1 teaspoon	salt	5 mL
1/2 teaspoon	pepper	2 mL

Slowly sauté the onion and celery in the oil in a small skillet over low heat for 5 minutes. Transfer to a bowl and combine with meat, salt and pepper. Continue as for cheese blintzes, using vegetable shortening to brown.

Passover Apple Pudding   MYRTLE COOPERSMITH

6	matzot	6
4	beaten eggs	4
2 cups	sour cream	500 mL
2 tablespoons	melted butter	30 mL
1 teaspoon	salt	5 mL
1 cup	granulated sugar	250 mL
1/2 cup	raisins	125 mL
1 cup	diced apples	250 mL
	cinnamon and sugar mixture	

Preheat oven to 350°F (180°C). Break matzot into small pieces and cover with boiling water. Drain. Cover with cold water. Drain. Beat in eggs, sour cream, butter, salt and sugar. Fold in the raisins and apples. Turn into a greased deep-dish casserole. Sprinkle with sugar and cinnamon. Bake 45 - 60 minutes.

Apple Pudding

JOYCE POSLUNS

6 - 8	medium apples, peeled and sliced	6 - 8
3/4 cup	granulated sugar	175 mL
6	eggs, separated	6
3/4 cup	water	175 mL
3/4 cup	matzo meal	175 mL
4 tablespoons	margarine or vegetable shortening	60 mL

Preheat oven to 350°F (180°C). Grease a 9" x 13" (3.5 L) baking dish. Mix apples with sugar. Beat egg whites until stiff. Fold in beaten yolks. Add water, matzo meal, margarine or shortening and a pinch of **salt**. Pour half of batter into prepared baking dish. Put in apples which have been sprinkled with **cinnamon**. Add rest of batter. Bake 1 hour.

Farfel Pudding

JOYCE CHARENDOFF

2 tablespoons	oil	30 mL
1 1/2 cups	boiling water	375 mL
2 cups	matzo farfel	500 mL
3/4 cup	granulated sugar (scant)	175 mL
3	apples, grated	3
3/4 cup	orange juice	175 mL
	juice and rind of 1/2 lemon	
4	eggs, beaten	4
	cinnamon to taste	
1/2 cup	raisins, soaked in hot water, then drained	125 mL

Preheat oven to 350°F (180°C). Heat oil in an 8" (2 L) baking dish in the oven. Watch so that oil does not burn. Add boiling water to farfel. Drain and add the remaining ingredients. Pour into prepared pan. Sprinkle **chopped nuts** and **cinnamon** on top. Bake one hour.

Note: Recipe may be doubled for a 9" x 13" (3.5 L) baking dish. It is not necessary to double oil or sugar.

Carrot Apple Pudding

ANNE HANDELMAN

3	eggs, separated	3
1/2 cup	butter	125 mL
3/4 cup	slivered almonds	175 mL
1	large tart apple, pared and grated	1
1 cup	grated carrots	250 mL
1/2 cup	raisins or chopped dates	125 mL
1/2 cup	matzo meal	125 mL
1/2 cup	granulated sugar	125 mL
3 tablespoons	lemon juice	45 mL
1 teaspoon	cinnamon	5 mL

Preheat oven to 350°F (180°C). Set aside egg whites. Melt butter in a large saucepan. Remove from heat. Mix in 1/2 cup (125 mL) of the almonds, egg yolks, and all remaining ingredients. Beat egg whites until stiff. Fold into pudding. Pour into greased 1 quart (1 L) soufflé or baking dish. Sprinkle with remaining almonds. Bake about 40 minutes until brown. Delicious! Serves 4 - 6.

Cottage Cheese Pudding

HELAINE ROBINS

4	matzot	4
6 tablespoons	melted butter	100 mL
1 pound	cottage cheese	500 g
3	eggs	3
1/2 teaspoon	salt	2 mL
1/2 cup	granulated sugar	125 mL
	juice of 1/2 lemon	
1/2 teaspoon	grated lemon rind	2 mL
1/2 cup	raisins	125 mL

Preheat oven to 325°F (160°C). Soak matzot briefly in water and drain well. Pour 3 tablespoons (45 mL) of the melted butter into bottom of an 8" (2 L) square pan. Make a layer with 2 broken matzot. Combine cheese with remaining ingredients. Make a layer of half the cheese mixture. Repeat layers of matzot and cheese, and top with remaining melted butter. Bake for 30 minutes. Cut into squares while hot. Serve with **sour cream**. May be reheated.

Farfel Casserole

ADÈLE FREEMAN

2 cups	matzo farfel	500 mL
1	egg, lightly beaten	1
	oil for frying	
1 tablespoon	oil	15 mL
1 1/2 cups	hot chicken soup	375 mL
1/2	Spanish onion, chopped	1/2
1 cup	finely chopped celery	250 mL
1/4 pound	mushrooms, sliced	125 g
1/2 pound	chicken livers, cut up (optional)	250 g
	salt and pepper	

Preheat oven to 350°F (180°C). Combine farfel and egg. Stir with a fork in a frying pan over medium heat with a little oil until dry. Add 1 tablespoon (15 mL) oil and hot soup. Stir*. In another pan, in a small amount of oil, sauté onion, celery, mushrooms and livers. Mix with farfel mixture. Add salt and pepper to taste. Place in casserole. Bake 1 hour. Serves 8. This recipe doubles or triples well.

Variation #1: Prepare matzo farfel as above to *. Set aside. Sauté onion, celery, mushrooms, green pepper, zucchini and/or any available fresh greens, Chinese vegetables etc., in oil until just crisp-tender. Combine with farfel. Heat and serve.

Variation #2 "Kugel": Prepare variation #1 as above. Add 4 well beaten eggs. Mix well. Pour into a 9" (2.5 L) square greased casserole. Bake 30 minutes at 350°F (180°C). Cut into squares to serve.

Passover Beef Pie

HONEY ROSENTHAL

Filling:

2 pounds	stewing beef	1 kg
2 tablespoons	oil	30 mL
2	large onions, chopped	2
1 tablespoon	granulated sugar	15 mL
	salt and pepper to taste	
	chicken stock to cover	

Cut meat into cubes. Brown in hot oil on bottom and sides. Add onions to pan and sauté until brown. Add sugar, salt, pepper and stock. Simmer until beef is quite tender.

Crust:

5	large potatoes	5
2 tablespoons	oil	30 mL
	salt and pepper	
2	eggs	2
2 teaspoons	chopped parsley	10 mL

Boil potatoes until tender. Mash over low heat, adding oil and seasonings to taste. Remove from heat. Mix in eggs and parsley.

Preheat oven to 400°F (200°C). Line the bottom and sides of a well greased casserole with 2/3 of the crust mixture. Pour hot stew into crust. Cover with remaining potato mixture. Bake 20 minutes or until golden brown. Serves 4.

Chicken Quiche

ESTHER-ROSE ANGEL

12	eggs	12
2 cups	boiled chicken, cubed	500 mL
1/2 cup	fresh dill (more if desired)	125 mL
	salt and pepper to taste	
6	matzot	6
4 cups	chicken soup	1 L
	oil	

Preheat oven to 325°F (160°C). Grease a 9" x 13" (3.5 L) baking pan. Beat eggs. Add chicken, dill, salt and pepper. Soak matzot in chicken soup. Divide into 4 parts. Line baking dish with matzot. Pour 1/3 of chicken mixture over. Repeat twice and top with matzot. Drizzle with oil. Cover and bake for 20 minutes. Uncover, and bake for an additional 20 minutes. Serves 10.

Passover Lasagna

ADÈLE FREEMAN

3 tablespoons	butter	45 mL
1	large Spanish onion, thinly sliced	1
2	eggplants	2
1/2 pound	mushrooms, thinly sliced	225 g
1 cup	celery, thinly sliced	250 mL
3	medium zucchini, well scrubbed and thinly sliced	3
1	green pepper, seeded and diced	1
3	tomatoes, peeled and diced	3
1/4 teaspoon	pepper	1 mL
1 teaspoon	salt	5 mL
2 cloves	garlic, minced	2
	dash of paprika	
1/2 cup	freshly chopped parsley	125 mL
1 · 10 ounce can	tomato mushroom sauce	284 mL
	Swiss cheese slices	
1	egg, beaten with	1
2 tablespoons	milk	30 mL
2 - 4	matzot	2 - 4

Preheat oven to 350°F (180°C). Sauté onion in butter. Peel eggplant and cut into 1/2" (1.5 cm) cubes. Combine onion with vegetables (except tomatoes), adding one at a time. Add seasonings and sauce, and cover. Simmer 15 minutes or until eggplant is tender. Stir in tomatoes and simmer a few more minutes. Grease a 2 quart (2 L) baking dish. Dip matzot in egg mixture and line bottom of pan. Arrange alternate layers of sauce, cheese slices and soaked matzot. End with sauce and cheese slices. Bake for 30 minutes. Serves 6.

Sweet Potato & Apple Casserole

Preheat oven to 350°F (180°C). Grease casserole, and arrange layers of par-boiled **sweet potatoes** and raw peeled **apples**. Dot with **butter**, sprinkle with **brown sugar*** and pour a little **orange juice** over mixture. Bake for 45 - 60 minutes. *For Passover, use **white sugar** or **honey**.

Granny Mehr's Tzimmes

GRETA GREISMAN

3 pounds	flanken	1.5 kg
2	onions, sliced	2
5 pounds	carrots, sliced	2.5 kg
5	sweet potatoes, peeled and quartered	5
1 1/2 cups	brown sugar	375 mL
	salt to taste	
8	large potatoes	8
2	eggs	2
	salt to taste	
2 tablespoons	vegetable shortening	30 mL

Place meat and onions in a large roaster. Cover with water and cook, covered, on top of stove, for one hour. Add carrots. Cook, covered, for an additional hour. Add sweet potatoes, salt and sugar. Bake in 350°F (180°C) oven for another hour. Note: This can be done in advance and refrigerated. The next day, preheat oven to moderate 350°F (180°C) and reheat tzimmes while preparing potato topping. Peel and grate potatoes on top of ice cubes. Drain. Add salt, eggs, and shortening. Spoon over tzimmes and bake for 1 1/2 hours, until well browned. Tzimmes improves with age. Simply add a little water each time before reheating.

Fried Matzo

LOIS FRIEDMAN

6	matzot	6
4	eggs	4
	salt to taste	
2 tablespoons	water	30 mL
	butter for frying	

Soak matzot in water for just a few seconds. Break into pieces. Beat eggs, add salt and the water. Pour over matzot and mix until all pieces are well coated. Heat butter in frying pan. Fry batches until brown. Add butter as needed. Salt before serving, or serve with sprinkled **sugar** or **jam**.

Passover Stuffing for Fowl

LOIS FRIEDMAN

4	large potatoes	4
2	large onions, chopped	2
2	ribs of celery, diced	2
2 tablespoons	margarine	30 mL
2 tablespoons	oil	30 mL
1	egg	1
	salt and pepper to taste	
2 tablespoons	chopped parsley	30 mL
3	matzot	3

Boil, drain and mash potatoes. Sauté onions and celery in margarine and oil until golden. Add to potatoes. Add egg and seasoning and mix well. Add chopped parsley. Soak matzot in cold water for a few seconds. Drain and break into small pieces. Fold into potato mixture. Stuff fowl loosely.

Vegetable Cutlets

ANNE HANDELMAN

3 tablespoons	butter or margarine	45 mL
1/4 cup	chopped green pepper	60 mL
1/2 cup	chopped onion	125 mL
1 1/2 cups	grated raw carrots	375 mL
1 · 10 ounce package	spinach, chopped, cooked and well drained	280 g
3	eggs, beaten	3
1 1/2 teaspoons	salt	7 mL
	pepper to taste	
3/4 cup	matzo meal	175 mL
	oil for frying	

Preheat oven to 350°F (180°C). Sauté green pepper, onion and carrots in butter until onions are lightly golden. Mix in spinach and balance of ingredients. Put in refrigerator for 15 minutes. Form into cutlets. Fry in about 2 tablespoons (30 mL) oil on both sides until golden brown. Bake on a rack for 15 minutes to crisp and drain.

Party Apple Tart

GRETA GREISMAN

2 cups	matzo meal	500 mL
1 cup	cake meal	250 mL
6 tablespoons	granulated sugar	100 mL
	pinch of salt	
1 cup	butter or margarine	250 mL
3 tablespoons	vinegar	45 mL
3 tablespoons	water	45 mL
1	egg	1
	apples (preferably Spy)	
3/4 cup	granulated sugar	175 mL
1	egg	1

Preheat oven to 350°F (180°C). Combine matzo meal, cake meal, sugar and salt. Cut in butter or margarine to the texture of coarse meal. Combine vinegar, water and egg. Add to dry mixture and form into a ball. Pat 1/2 the dough onto bottom and up sides of large 11" (27.5 cm) springform pan. Peel and slice apples to fill springform. Add sugar. Roll remaining dough on waxed paper and cover top of apples with dough. Seal and crimp edges. Make slits in top. Beat egg with a few drops of water and brush top of dough. Sprinkle with chopped **nuts**. Brush again with egg. Bake 1 hour, or until apples are soft. May be served with or without lemon sauce. Recipe on page 438.

Fruit Compote

PAULINE TOKER

**Use any assortment of dried fruits, e.g:
prunes, apricots, apple rings,
peaches, pears, etc.**

Preheat oven to 350°F (180°C). Use proportionately more prunes and apricots than the other fruits. Arrange the fruit attractively in a baking dish. Do not pile too high. A double layer of fruit is fine. Cover fruit generously with water, and cover dish loosely with foil. Bake for 40 minutes. Turn off oven and leave the baking dish in the oven overnight. Before serving, sprinkle with **cinnamon.**

Dried Fruit Pudding

HELAINE ROBINS

4	eggs	4
1 teaspoon	salt	5 mL
2 cups	water	500 mL
1/2 cup	oil	125 mL
2/3 cup	granulated sugar	150 mL
1 · 8 ounce package	dried fruit, cut into pieces	224 g
3	grated apples	3
	cinnamon	
	lemon rind	
1 1/2 cups	matzo meal	375 mL

Preheat oven to 350°F (180°C). Beat eggs and salt. Add water, oil and sugar. Add fruit, apples, cinnamon and rind. Fold in matzo meal, and let stand 15 minutes. Bake in a well greased baking dish for 1 1/2 hours.

Passover Wine Spice Cake

DOROTHY ZEIFMAN

9	eggs, separated	9
1 1/2 cups	granulated sugar, divided	375 mL
3/4 cup	potato starch	175 mL
1/4 cup	cake meal	60 mL
2 teaspoons	cinnamon	10 mL
1/2 teaspoon	ginger (optional)	2 mL
1/4 cup	grape wine	60 mL
1/4 teaspoon	salt	1 mL

Preheat oven to 325°F (160°C). Beat egg yolks until thick and creamy. Add 1 cup (250 mL) of the sugar gradually, and beat until light and fluffy. Sift potato starch and cake meal with spices. Gradually blend dry ingredients and wine alternately into yolk mixture. Add salt to whites and beat until foamy. Gradually add remaining 1/2 cup (125 mL) of the sugar, beating until stiff but not dry. Fold into yolk mixture. Pour into ungreased 10" (25 cm) tube pan. Bake for 1 hour or until cake tests done. Invert to cool.

Passover Sponge Cake

ANNE HANDELMAN

9	eggs, separated	9
2 cups	granulated sugar	500 mL
6 tablespoons	fresh orange juice	100 mL
2 1/2 teaspoons	lemon rind	12 mL
1/4 cup	fresh lemon juice	50 mL
3/4 cup	cake meal	175 mL
3/4 cup	potato starch	175 mL
1 cup	chopped pecans	250 mL

Preheat oven to 325°F (160°C). Beat yolks lightly. Add sugar and beat until fluffy. Add juices and rind. Sift cake meal and potato starch. Add to yolk mixture. With clean beaters and bowl, beat egg whites very stiff. Fold whites into yolks. Gently fold in nuts. Bake in ungreased 10" (25 cm) tube pan for 1 1/4 hours. Invert to cool.

Potato Starch Sponge Cake

FLORENCE WINBERG

8	eggs	8
1 1/2 cups	granulated sugar, sifted	375 mL
4 tablespoons	lemon juice	60 mL
2 1/2 teaspoons	grated lemon rind	12 mL
3/4 cup	potato starch, sifted	175 mL
	dash of salt	

Preheat oven to 350°F (180°C). Separate the eggs. Using electric mixer, beat the yolks for 2 minutes at high speed. Add sugar, lemon juice and rind and mix well. Gradually add the sifted potato starch and continue mixing at medium speed for an additional 2 minutes. With clean beaters and bowl, beat the egg whites until foamy. Add salt and beat until stiff. Fold them gently but thoroughly into the yolk-sugar-starch mixture. Pour into an ungreased 10" (25 cm) tube pan and bake for 1 hour and 10 minutes, or until the cake springs back when firmly touched with the fingers. Invert pan and cool thoroughly before removing cake from pan.

Decadent Chocolate Passover Cake

SUE DEVOR

8 ounces	semi-sweet chocolate, broken into pieces	250 g
3 tablespoons	water	45 mL
1/2 cup	unsalted margarine or butter	125 mL
3	eggs, separated	3
2/3 cup	granulated sugar	150 mL
2 tablespoons	cake meal	30 mL
2/3 cup	ground almonds	150 mL
1/2 teaspoon	vanilla	2 mL
	pinch of salt	
	strawberries dipped in chocolate	

Preheat oven to 350°F (180°C). Grease a 9" (22.5 cm) round cake pan or springform pan. Dust with potato starch or line bottom with parchment paper. Melt chocolate with water. Stir in margarine or butter until melted. Cool. Beat egg yolks with sugar until pale and creamy. Stir in chocolate mixture, cake meal, nuts, vanilla and salt. With clean beaters, whip egg whites until stiff. Fold egg whites into chocolate mixture and turn into pan. Spread batter evenly. Bake 35 to 40 minutes. (Cake does not rise much, but it is very rich). Cool 15 minutes. Do not worry if a crust forms on top of cake. Press it down gently but firmly. Invert cake on to serving platter so that the bottom becomes the top. If cake is uneven, press gently to even it. Decorate the middle and around the outside edge with chocolate dipped berries. Serves 8 -10.

Note: For chocolate dipped berries, see page 284.

Chocolate Chip Cake

ELINORE ASHER

10	large eggs, separated	10
1 1/2 cups	granulated sugar	375 mL
1/2 cup	cake meal, sifted	125 mL
1/4 cup	potato starch	60 mL
2-3 ounces	grated bitter-sweet chocolate	60 - 90 g
1 teaspoon	lemon juice	5 mL

Preheat oven to 325°F (160°C). Beat egg whites until they form soft peaks. Gradually add sugar and continue to beat until stiff, shiny and of a meringue consistency. In a separate bowl, beat egg yolks until foamy and thick. Carefully fold yolks into whites. Gradually fold cake meal, potato starch, grated chocolate and lemon juice into egg white mixture. Pour batter into 10" (25 cm) ungreased tube pan. Bake 40 - 50 minutes. Invert to cool. Freezes well.

Passover Chocolate Banana Cake

ADÈLE FREEMAN

3/4 cup	grated bittersweet chocolate	175 mL
3/4 cup	cake meal	175 mL
1/3 cup	potato starch	75 mL
9	eggs, separated	9
1/2 teaspoon	salt	2 mL
1 1/2 cups	granulated sugar, sifted	375 mL
1 cup	ripe mashed bananas	250 mL
	juice and rind of 1/2 orange	
1 tablespoon	lemon rind	15 mL

Preheat oven to 325°F (160°C). Grate chocolate. Sift cake meal and potato starch twice and combine with the grated chocolate. Beat whites with salt until foamy, then begin to add sugar gradually and beat until of a meringue consistency. In a separate bowl, beat yolks, add banana and flavourings and beat well. Fold yolk mixture into stiffly beaten whites. Gradually fold dry ingredients into batter. Pour into ungreased 10" (25 cm) tube pan and bake for 1 hour or until done. Invert until cool.

Variation: Omit chocolate and replace with 1/2 - 1 cup (125-250 mL) chopped nuts.

Passover Sponge Cake

ANNE HANDELMAN

9	eggs, separated	9
2 cups	granulated sugar	500 mL
6 tablespoons	fresh orange juice	100 mL
2 1/2 teaspoons	lemon rind	12 mL
1/4 cup	fresh lemon juice	60 mL
3/4 cup	cake meal	175 mL
3/4 cup	potato starch	175 mL
1 cup	chopped pecans	250 mL

Preheat oven to 325°F (160°C). Beat yolks lightly. Add sugar and beat until light and lemon coloured. Add juices and rind. Sift cake meal and potato starch. Add to yolk mixture. With clean beaters and bowl beat egg whites very stiff. Fold whites into yolks. Gently fold in nuts. Bake in ungreased 10" (25 cm) tube pan for 1 1/4 hours. Invert to cool.

Passover Nut Torte

ETHEL KLEIN

7	eggs, separated	7
1 1/4 cups	granulated sugar	300 mL
3 tablespoons	lemon and	45 mL
	orange juice, combined	
	rind of 1/2 lemon	
	rind of 1/2 orange	
1/2 pound	almonds, finely ground	225 g
3 tablespoons	cake meal	45 mL

Preheat oven to 325°F (160°C). Beat egg whites until stiff but not dry. Add 1/4 cup (60 mL) of the sugar gradually, and beat until stiff and shiny. In another bowl, beat egg yolks. Gradually add remaining 1 cup (250 mL) of the sugar and beat until light and lemon coloured. Add juice and rinds, and fold in almonds and cake meal. Lastly, fold in egg whites. Pour batter into an ungreased tube pan. Bake 1 1/4 hours. Remove from oven and invert until cake cools.

Parve Chocolate Mousse

DOROTHY ZEIFMAN

4 ounces	unsweetened chocolate	120 g
3/4 cup	granulated sugar	175 mL
1/4 cup	water	60 mL
5	eggs, separated	5
1 teaspoon	vanilla	5 mL
	or	
1 tablespoon	Avdat or Sabra brandy*	15 mL
	or	
2 tablespoons	sherry	30 mL

Combine chocolate, sugar and water in top of double boiler. Heat until chocolate has melted, stirring occasionally. Add the egg yolks, one at a time, while the double boiler is still over the heat. Beat well after each addition. Remove from heat and let cool. Beat egg whites until stiff. Fold whites into yolk mixture very gently and flavour with vanilla, brandy, or sherry. Pour the mixture into a dessert bowl or individual cups. Refrigerate for at least 12 hours before serving. Serves 8. *For Passover.

Mocha Squares

NANCY KRAFT

6 tablespoons	cocoa	90 mL
1/2 cup plus 2 tablespoons	butter or margarine	155 mL
2	eggs	2
1 cup	granulated sugar	250 mL
1/4 teaspoon	salt	1 mL
1 tablespoon	instant coffee	15 mL
1/2 cup	sifted cake meal	125 mL
1/2 cup	chopped walnuts	125 mL

Preheat oven to 325°F (160°C). Melt chocolate and butter or margarine in top of double boiler. Cool. Combine eggs, sugar and salt. Add cooled chocolate mixture. Beat well. Stir in remaining ingredients except nuts. Pour into greased 8" (2 L) baking pan. Sprinkle chopped nuts on top. Bake 30 minutes. Cool before cutting into squares.

3	egg whites	3
2 · 12 ounce cans	frozen unsweetened orange juice concentrate	340 mL each
	or	
2 quarts	fresh strawberries	2 L
1/4-1/2 cup	granulated sugar	60-125 mL
2 teaspoons	lemon juice	10 mL

Beat egg whites until stiff but not dry. Blend juice or fruit until smooth. Add sugar to fruit in blender (sugar is not necessary with orange version). Add lemon juice and blend. Fold fruit mixture into egg whites in large mixer bowl. Beat at top speed for 20 minutes. This will grow! (Orange version may be flavoured with brandy or white wine). For year round use, liqueur may be used, about 1 tablespoon (15 mL). Freeze 3/4 of mixture in serving bowl. Keep 1/4 separate in refrigerator. Pile this extra on top before serving. Garnish with **strawberries** or **grated dark chocolate**, or **chopped chocolate covered orange rind**.

Note: This recipe can be used to fill chocolate cups.

Lemon Sauce

1 cup	granulated sugar	250 mL
2 tablespoons	potato starch*	30 mL
2 cups	water	500 mL
3 tablespoons	butter	45 mL
3 tablespoons	lemon juice	45 mL
	grated rind of 1 lemon	

Combine sugar and potato starch in top of double boiler. Add water gradually, stirring. Cook and stir over hot water until thickened. Remove from heat. Stir in butter, lemon juice and rind. *For year round use, substitute cornstarch. Can be used over cake or fresh fruit.

Passover Jelly Roll

TOBY DUNKELMAN

4	eggs, separated	4
1/2 cup	granulated sugar	125 mL
	grated rind of 1/2 lemon	
	grated rind of 1/2 orange	
1/2 cup	cake meal	125 mL
1/4 teaspoon	salt	1 mL

Preheat oven to 350°F (180°C). Line a jelly roll pan with waxed paper. In large mixmaster bowl, beat yolks, sugar and rinds together until light in colour. Add cake meal. Add salt to egg whites, and beat until stiff. Fold whites into yolk mixture. Pour into prepared jelly roll pan. Bake for 12 minutes, or until cake tests done. Place a sheet of waxed paper on a damp towel for a few minutes. When jelly roll is done, remove from oven, and invert onto waxed paper which has been sprinkled with icing sugar. Peel off paper, spread with **jelly**, **jam** or **lemon filling** (see page 440) and roll up. Wrap in waxed paper first, and then put damp towel around the waxed paper for 15 minutes to help the roll keep its shape.

Passover Blueberry Muffins

PHYLLIS FLATT

1/2 cup	oil	125 mL
1 cup	granulated sugar	250 mL
3	eggs	3
1/4 cup	potato starch	60 mL
1/2 cup	cake meal	125 mL
1 1/2 cups	blueberries	375 mL
	cinnamon-sugar mixture	

Preheat oven to 325°F (160°C). Grease and/or line with paper cups, 12 muffin tins. Combine oil and sugar and beat until light. Add eggs, beating well. Sift together potato starch and cake meal and fold into egg mixture by hand. Fold in blueberries. Fill muffin tins 2/3 full. Sprinkle with cinnamon-sugar mixture. Bake for 35 - 40 minutes. Yield: 12 muffins.

Lemon Filling:

4	eggs, separated	4
1 teaspoon	grated lemon rind	5 mL
1/4 cup	lemon juice	60 mL
1/4 cup	water	60 mL
1 cup	granulated sugar	250 mL

Beat egg yolks in top of double boiler over lightly boiling water, stirring occasionally, until thick. Gradually stir in lemon rind, lemon juice, water and 1/2 cup (125 mL) of the sugar. Cook slowly, stirring frequently until thickened, about 15 minutes. Remove from heat. Beat egg whites until frothy. Gradually add remaining 1/2 cup (125 mL) of sugar, beating until lightly stiff. Fold 1/3 of this meringue mixture into warm lemon mixture. Pour into cooled almond matzo crust. (See below). Top with remaining meringue sealing well to crust. Bake in preheated 325°F (160°C) oven for 25 to 30 minutes, or until meringue is browned. Cool.

Almond Matzo Crust:

1/2 cup	ground almonds	125 mL
1/2 cup	matzo meal	125 mL
2 tablespoons	granulated sugar	25 mL
1/4 teaspoon	salt	1 mL
1/4 cup	peanut oil	50 mL
1	egg white	1

Mix the almonds, matzo meal, sugar and salt together. Combine peanut oil and egg white. Beat slightly. Stir into almond mixture. Press firmly and evenly against sides and bottom of an 8" or 9" (22 cm) pie plate. Bake in preheated 375°F (190°C) oven for 15 - 20 minutes, until golden brown. Cool thoroughly.

Lemon Dessert

7	eggs, separated	7
1 cup	granulated sugar	250 mL
3	lemons, grated rind and juice	3
3 tablespoons	potato starch	45 mL
2 cups	cold water	500 mL
1 teaspoon	lemon juice	5 mL
1/4 cup	granulated sugar	60 mL
	grated chocolate (optional)	

Beat egg yolks until light. Slowly beat in 1 cup (250 mL) of the sugar, until light and lemon coloured. Add lemon rind and juice. Transfer to top of double boiler. Cook and stir until thick. Remove from heat. Dissolve potato starch in 1/2 cup (125 mL) of the water. Add to lemon mixture with remaining 1 1/2 cups (375 mL) water. Cook, stirring constantly until thick. Cool. Beat egg whites until soft peaks form. Add lemon juice and 1/4 cup (60 mL) sugar gradually, beating until stiff peaks are formed. Fold the cooled lemon mixture into the whites gently. Pour into a serving bowl and refrigerate overnight. Decorate with grated chocolate.

Simple Pie Crust

MYRTLE COOPERSMITH

1 can	almond flavoured macaroons	1
2 tablespoons	liquid (orange or apple juice)	30 mL

Combine in processor fitted with steel blade. Process for 8 - 10 seconds. Press into a pie plate or springform pan. May be filled with Lemon Filling on page 440 or Strawberry Passover Dessert on page 438.

Macadamia Torte for Passover

5 ounces	unsalted Macadamia nuts	140 g
8 ounces	bittersweet parve chocolate bar	225 g
2 tablespoons	instant coffee, dissolved in	30 mL
1/3 cup	water	75 mL
4	eggs, separated	4
12 tablespoons	parve margarine, cut into pieces and softened	185 mL
1/3 cup	potato starch	75 mL
1/2 cup	granulated sugar, divided	125 mL
	pinch of salt	
Glaze:		
6 ounces	bittersweet chocolate	170 g
2 tablespoons	instant coffee dissolved in	30 mL
1/3 cup	water	75 mL

Preheat oven to 350ºF (180ºC). Grease a 9" (22.5 cm) round cake pan. Cover bottom with a circle of waxed paper, cut to fit, and grease the paper. Toast nuts on a baking sheet in oven for 8 - 10 minutes until golden brown. Cool. Raise oven temperature to 375ºF (190ºC).

Melt chocolate and coffee in a saucepan over low heat, stirring until smooth. Remove from heat and stir in egg yolks one at a time. Return saucepan to medium heat and stir gently until mixture is slightly thickened. Remove from heat and stir in margarine, mixing until blended. Using a processor, grind nuts until fine but not oily. Add potato starch and 1/4 cup (60 mL) of the sugar to nuts. Add to chocolate mixture.

Beat egg whites and salt until soft peaks form. Fold whites into chocolate mixture. Pour into cakepan. Bake 20 - 25 minutes until cake is puffed and knife inserted in center comes out with a slightly creamy coating. Cool on rack 45 minutes before removing from pan. (Cake may sink and surface may crack).

Melt chocolate and coffee for glaze in a small saucepan over low heat, stirring until smooth. Cool slightly. When cake is cold, invert onto serving dish. Remove paper and spread glaze over top and sides of cake. Refrigerate overnight or freeze. Remove from refrigerator 30 minutes before serving.

Passover Mandel Brot

FLORENCE ROSS

3	eggs, beaten	3
1/2 cup	granulated sugar	125 mL
3/4 cup	oil	175 mL
1/4 cup	potato starch	60 mL
1 1/4 cups	cake meal	300 mL
	juice and rind of 1/2 lemon and 1/2 orange	
3/4 cup	chopped almonds	175 mL
1/2 teaspoon	cinnamon	2 mL

Preheat oven to 350°F (180°C). Combine all ingredients in order given and mix well. Rub hands with cake meal and shape into 3 rolls. Place on a lightly greased baking sheet. Bake for 30 minutes. Slice rolls diagonally into pieces about 1" (2.5 cm) thick. Reduce oven temperature to 300°F (150°C). Return slices to oven and toast until lightly browned. Turn and toast other side.

Passover Brownies

NANCY POSLUNS

2 tablespoons	cocoa	30 mL
4 teaspoons	hot water	20 mL
1/2 cup	butter, melted	125 mL
1 cup	granulated sugar	250 mL
2	eggs, well beaten	2
6 tablespoons	cake meal	90 mL
2 tablespoons	potato starch	30 mL
1/2 cup	chopped nuts	125 mL

Preheat oven to 350°F (180°C). Mix cocoa with water to make a paste. Add melted butter and sugar. Stir well. Add the well beaten eggs, cake meal, potato starch and nuts. Mix well. Place in well buttered 9" (2.5 L) square pan. Bake 20 minutes or until set. Cool on rack. Cut into squares when cool.

Brownie Meringues

2	egg whites	2
	dash of salt	
1/2 teaspoon	vinegar	2 mL
1/2 teaspoon	vanilla	2mL
1/2 cup	granulated sugar	125 mL
6 ounces	semi-sweet chocolate, melted and cooled	170 g
3/4 cup	chopped walnuts	175 mL

Preheat oven to 350°F (180°C). Beat egg whites with salt, vinegar and vanilla until soft peaks form. Gradually add sugar, beating to stiff peaks. Fold in chocolate and nuts. Drop from teaspoon onto greased pan. Bake 10 minutes.

Candied Orange Peel

	peel of 2 large oranges or 3 large lemons	
2 cups	water	500 mL

Cut orange or lemon peel into thin shreds, about 1 1/2" (3.75 cm) long. Bring water to a simmer in a small saucepan. Add peel and cook about 5 minutes until tender. Drain, run under cold water and drain again. Dry on paper towels.

Syrup:

1 cup	granulated sugar	250 mL
6 tablespoons	water	90 mL
1/2 teaspoon	vanilla or Passover liqueur	3 mL

Combine sugar and water in a small saucepan. Stir over medium heat until sugar is dissolved. Cover and continue cooking until syrup registers 230°F (110°C) on a candy thermometer (thread stage). Remove from heat. Stir in flavouring and orange peel. Let stand at least 30 minutes. Drain before using. Undrained peel may be stored several weeks in refrigerator.

Preserves
and Condiments

Things to Keep in Mind

Make only as much as you will use before the next season. Quality deteriorates over long periods. **Never double or halve recipes**.

For top products, use top quality fruits bought at their peak. Use a heavy-based saucepan – not aluminum.

To reduce foaming, add 1/4 teaspoon (1 mL) butter to an average batch of jam. If you do not use butter make sure that you use a pot large enough to leave room for the boiling liquid to rise.

To remove scum, pat a large piece of waxed paper lightly over the slightly cooled jam. Scum will lift off with the paper.

To test for jellying point when making jam or jelly, dip a spoon into the boiling syrup and let syrup run off the spoon. The last few drops will thicken slightly and run together when ready. Jam will thicken as it cools.

To sterilize jars, place washed jars in a large kettle and cover with warm water. Cover the kettle and boil fifteen to twenty minutes. When ready to use, remove with tongs and drain. The jars should be hot when hot mixture is poured in to prevent breakage.

To sterilize rubber rings, dip three or four times into boiling water. For best results, use only new rings. Dip rubber rings in fruit juice, before putting on jar.

To seal, fill jars 1/4" (1 cm) from top, and let set. Then cover with 1/8" (3 mm) layer of hot, melted paraffin wax. When cool, cover with another layer of wax, turning jar slightly so that wax is completely sealed to edges of jar.

Screw tops: Test for leakage by putting a little water in jar; fit with rubber ring, glass and screw top. Invert. If water leaks from jar, it is not air-tight and should be refitted. Wash jars in hot, soapy water and rinse. Sterilize jars, glass and screw tops. Place in kettle, cover with cold water, heat gradually to boiling. Boil 15 minutes, lift out, drain and fill at once.

Strawberry Jam

4 cups	strawberries	1 L
3 cups	granulated sugar	750 mL
1/4 cup	lemon juice	60 mL

Wash and hull fruit. Put the strawberries into a large, heavy saucepan with the sugar and allow to come to a boil slowly so as not to burn. When the mixture comes to a bubbling mass, cook for about 15 minutes. Exact time will vary depending on the berries. Remove saucepan from heat and as the jam settles, skim off the scum that has bubbled to the top. Let the jam cool for 10 minutes, then stir in the lemon juice. With a slotted spoon, fill each jar two-thirds full with whole berries, until you have used all the strawberries. Bring the remaining jelly to a rolling boil, and top the jars to 1/4" (1 cm) from the top. Some of the berries will float to the top. Push them down with a clean knife so that the top of the jar is all jelly. Allow to cool for 30 minutes, then seal with melted paraffin. Store in a cool dark place.

Raspberry Jam

Do not wash raspberries, as they become mushy. Add sugar and lemon juice and cook as above. Cooking time will be less than for strawberries.

Apricot Spread   VERA SANDERS

| 3 ounces | dried apricots | 90 g |
| 1/2 cup | unsweetened apple juice | 125 mL |

Coarsely chop apricots. Combine fruit and juice in a saucepan, and bring to a boil, stirring. Cover, reduce heat and simmer for about 45 minutes, stirring occasionally. Cool and process in a blender or food processor until smooth. Chill, covered, before serving. Makes a delicious low calorie spread.

Fresh Apricot Jam

MRS. J. SCHIPPER

4 cups	diced fresh apricots	1 L
3 cups	granulated sugar	750 mL
1	orange, thinly sliced, with peel	1

Wash, pit, and dice fruit. Cover with sugar and allow to stand overnight to extract juice. Pour off juice and sugar from fruit and boil syrup for 15 minutes. Add the fruit and continue to cook gently for about 20 minutes. Stir frequently. Pour into sterilized jars. Seal while jam is still hot. This method provides a very clear and delicious jam.

Peach Jam

Blanch and peel peaches before proceeding as for Apricot Jam.

Tangy Apricot Jam

8 cups	quartered apricots (about 3 pounds)	2 L
4 1/2 cups	granulated sugar	1.125 L
3/4 cup	brown sugar	175 mL
1	orange	1
1 cup	canned crushed pineapple, with juice	250 mL
	pinch of salt	

Combine apricots and sugars in a heavy preserving kettle. Coarsely grate orange rind, squeeze its juice, and add both to apricots. Add pineapple and salt. Stir over medium-high heat until sugar dissolves, then bring to boiling point. Cook rapidly, stirring frequently for about 30 minutes. Skim, then seal in sterilized jars. Yield: 8 small jars.

Cantaloupe Peach Jam

MYRTLE COOPERSMITH

5 cups	diced peeled cantaloupe	1.25 L
5 cups	diced peeled peaches	1.25 L
3	medium-sized oranges	3
5 cups	granulated sugar	1.25 L

Combine cantaloupe and peaches in a preserving kettle. Grate bright outer rind from oranges and squeeze their juice. Add orange juice, sugar and rind to cantaloupe mixture. Let stand for about an hour, stirring occasionally, to dissolve sugar. Bring to boiling point, stirring occasionally. Cook for about 30 minutes or until thick, stirring frequently from the bottom to prevent sticking. Seal in sterilized jars. Yield: 8 small jars.

Peach Conserve

SHEILA LOFTUS

2	oranges	2
1	lemon	1
	diced peeled peaches	
4 cups	granulated sugar	1 L
	blanched almonds	
	maraschino cherries (optional)	

Chop oranges and lemon finely, including rind and pulp. Add diced fresh peaches to make 4 cups (1 L). Add sugar. Boil softly for 15 minutes. Skim if necessary. Add blanched almonds and cherries, if desired. Cook another 3 minutes until thickened. Pour into sterilized jars and seal.

Marmalade

SHEILA LOFTUS

2	grapefruit	2
4 – 5	oranges	4 – 5
3	lemons	3
5 pounds	granulated sugar	2.2 kg
6 cups	water	1.5 L

Squeeze fruit to extract juices. Blend with 3 cups (750 mL) of the water. Mince pulp. Combine and boil for 20 minutes. Mix sugar with remaining 3 cups (750 mL) water and cook for 20 minutes. Blend together and cook for about 2 hours. Pour into sterilized jars and seal.

Grape Jelly

1 · 6 quart basket	grapes	6.8 L
	granulated sugar	

Wash and stem grapes. Place in a preserving kettle. Mash. Boil for 30 minutes. Strain through a jelly bag into a pot overnight. Do not squeeze bag if clear jelly is desired. Measure juice. Measure an equal quantity of sugar. Place sugar in a pan in the oven to heat. In the meantime, heat the juice. When the sugar is hot, add to juice which has boiled for 5 minutes. Boil together 3 minutes longer. Bottle in sterilized jars and let stand until cold. Seal and store in a cool dark place.

Herb Butter or Cream Cheese Spread ED FIFE

1 pound	butter or cream cheese	454 g
1/4 cup	loosely packed herbs	60 mL
	e.g. basil, thyme, tarragon,	
	parsley, rosemary	

Slightly soften butter. Process herbs and butter or cream cheese in food processor with steel blade, until smooth. Package in covered containers. Can be frozen.

Apple Chutney

2 1/2 cups	apples, peeled, cored and chopped	625 mL
1 cup	tomato sauce	250 mL
3/4 cup	brown sugar, firmly packed	175 mL
1/2 cup	raisins	125 mL
1/2 cup	cider vinegar	125 mL
1	medium onion, chopped	1
1	red pepper, seeded and chopped	1
1 teaspoon	fresh ginger, finely chopped	5 mL
1/4 teaspoon	red pepper flakes	1 mL
1/2 teaspoon	salt	3 mL

Combine all ingredients in a saucepan and bring to a boil stirring frequently. Reduce heat and simmer until thickened, stirring occasionally, about 45 minutes. Remove from heat. When cool, pour into sterilized jars. Cover tightly. Keep refrigerated. Yield: 3 cups (750 mL).

Cranberry Chutney SANDRA HABERMAN, ST. LAURENT

1 pound	cranberries	450 g
1 1/2 cups	granulated sugar	375 mL
1 cup	water	250 mL
1 cup	orange juice	250 mL
1 cup	raisins	250 mL
1 cup	chopped celery	250 mL
1 cup	chopped walnuts	250 mL
1	apple, diced	1
1 tablespoon	grated orange rind	15 mL
1 teaspoon	ginger	5 mL

Boil cranberries, sugar and water until skins of berries pop. Stir in remaining ingredients. Mix well and refrigerate.

Bread and Butter Pickles

FREDA LUBIN

16 cups	thinly sliced, unpeeled cucumbers	4 L
8 cups	sliced onions	2 L
1/2 cup	coarse salt	125 mL
4 cups	white vinegar	1 L
5 cups	granulated sugar	1.25 L
2 tablespoons	mustard seeds	30 mL
1 tablespoon	celery seeds	15 mL
1 1/2 teaspoons	turmeric	7 mL
1/2 teaspoon	white pepper	2 mL

Combine cucumbers, onions and salt in a very large bowl or crock. Gently stir until the salt is evenly distributed. Cover with **ice cubes**. Let stand at room temperature for 3 hours, or until the cucumbers are cold and crisp. Add more ice if necessary. Then drain well, but do not rinse.

Meanwhile, sterilize enough jars to hold about 16 cups (4 L). Combine the remaining ingredients in a large saucepan and bring to a boil. Boil, covered, for 10 minutes. Add the well drained vegetables and bring back to the boiling point.

Keep the vinegar solution simmering while packing the vegetables into one sterilized jar. Pour a bit of the vinegar mixture into a measuring cup and fill the jar to a half inch from the top, being sure to cover the vegetables with the vinegar mixture. Seal at once. Repeat until all the jars are filled.

Variation: If a little colour is desired, you can add:

2	green peppers, thinly sliced	2
1	red pepper, thinly sliced	1

If you do not use ice cubes, let vegetables stand for 12 hours. Drain well.

Red Pepper Pickles

2 1/2 dozen	large red peppers	30
4 cups	vinegar	1 L
2 cups	granulated sugar	500 mL
1/2 teaspoon	pickling spices	2 mL

Cut peppers in quarters and remove seeds. Mix vinegar, sugar, spices and **salt** to taste, in a large pot. Bring to boil, add peppers and boil for 5 minutes. Cool. Seal in sterilized jars.

Mother's Mustard Pickles   LOIS FRIEDMAN

6 quarts	gherkins	6 L
2	heads cauliflower	2
6	green peppers	6
6	red peppers	6
2 quarts	small white onions	2 L
2	bunches celery	2

Clean and cut up vegetables. Cut cauliflower into small rosettes, peppers into strips 1 1/2" x 1/2" (3.75 cm x 1.25 cm), celery into 1" (2.5 cm) strips. Cut small gherkins in half (leave whole if very small). Cut larger gherkins into 3 or 4 pieces. Soak vegetables in salted water overnight.

Paste for mustard pickles:

3 quarts	white vinegar	3 L
6 cups	granulated sugar	1.5 L
1/2 cup	dry mustard	125 mL
1 ounce	turmeric powder	28 g
3 cups	all purpose flour	750 mL
	pinch of cayenne pepper	

Make a paste with dry ingredients and part of the vinegar. Bring balance of vinegar to a boil and add paste, stirring constantly. Boil for 30 minutes. Drain vegetables well and add to mustard sauce. Heat for a few minutes. Remove from heat and let stand several hours before placing in sterilized jars.

Ethel Brenner's Pepper Relish

2 cups	prepared peppers, about 12	500 mL
7 cups	granulated sugar	1.75 L
1 1/2 cups	cider vinegar	375 mL
1 · 6 ounce bottle	liquid pectin	170 mL
	or	
2 packets	liquid pectin	85 mL each

Prepare peppers: Cut about 12 medium sized peppers and discard seeds. For best colour, use half red, and half green. Chop finely.

Measure 2 cups (500 mL) into a very large saucepan. Add sugar and vinegar and mix well. Place over high heat, and bring to boiling point. Let boil rapidly for one minute, stirring constantly. Remove from heat and stir in pectin. Skim off any foam with a metal spoon. Stir and skim for 5 minutes to cool and prevent floating fruit. Ladle into sterilized jars. Cover with 1/2" (1 1/4 cm) melted, hot paraffin.

Kosher Dill Pickles   MRS. FRANK SILVERMAN

1 · 6 quart basket	dill cucumbers	6 L
	garlic cloves	
	fresh dill	
	mixed pickling spices	
16 cups	water	4 L
3/4 cup	salt	175 mL
1 cup	vinegar	250 mL
1 rounded teaspoon	alum	7 mL

Wash cucumbers thoroughly and pack firmly into sterilized jars. Place 1 clove garlic, sprig of dill and 2 teaspoons (10 mL) mixed pickling spices in each jar. Bring water, salt, vinegar, and alum to a boil. Pour hot solution into jars to overflowing and seal immediately. Let stand two weeks in a cool dark place before using. Then store in refrigerator.

Tomato Relish

20 large or 30 medium	tomatoes, coarsely chopped	20 – 30
6 cups	finely chopped celery	1.5 L
4 cups	finely chopped onions	1 L
1/4 cup	coarse salt	60 mL
4 cups	granulated sugar	1 L
1 cup	cider vinegar	250 mL
2	sweet peppers, red or green, seeded and chopped	2
	dash crushed hot red pepper flakes	
2 tablespoons	mustard seeds	30 mL
2 tablespoons	ground fresh ginger	30 mL

In a glass or ceramic bowl, gently mix tomatoes, celery, onion and salt. Cover with plastic wrap and let sit overnight. Drain off liquid. Transfer to a heavy pot. Add remaining ingredients. Bring to a slow boil, stirring occasionally. Boil 10 – 15 minutes. Sterilize six 1 pint (.5 L) jars. Add relish to jars, using a slotted spoon. Seal immediately and cool. Store in a cool place up to 2 years. Remaining liquid can be used for other cooking or may be discarded.

Granny Mehr's Brown Chili Sauce

8 cups	peeled tomatoes	2 L
2	large Spanish onions, coarsely grated	2
2 cups	brown sugar	500 mL
1 cup	cider vinegar	250 mL
1 teaspoon	ground cloves	5 mL
1 teaspoon	cinnamon	5 mL
1 teaspoon	allspice	5 mL

Combine all ingredients in a saucepan. Bring to a boil, and then let simmer uncovered 2 hours or until thick. Stir occasionally. Bottle and seal.

Spicy Orange Flavoured Beets

An easy way to perk up beets, to serve as an interesting relish.

1/2 cup	cider vinegar	125 mL
1/4 cup	granulated sugar	50 mL
2	bay leaves	2
1/2 cup	orange juice	125 mL
2 · 19 ounce cans	beets, sliced or whole, drained	1080 mL

Place vinegar, sugar and bay leaves in a saucepan. Bring to a boil, reduce heat and simmer uncovered for 5 minutes. Remove bay leaves. Stir in orange juice and pour over drained beets. Cover or place in a jar and refrigerate at least overnight to blend flavours.

Tangy Sweet Mustard

HELAINE ROBINS

4 ounces	dry mustard	115 g
1 cup	cider vinegar	250 mL
3	eggs	3
1 cup	brown sugar	250 mL

Combine vinegar and mustard. Let stand overnight. Next day, beat eggs and sugar together. Stir into mustard-vinegar mixture. Cook in a double boiler, stirring constantly until thick. Fill jars and let cool. Store in refrigerator.

Hot Mustard

1 cup	dry mustard	250 mL
1 cup	granulated sugar	250 mL
1/2 cup	boiling water	125 mL
1 tablespoon	oil	15 mL
1 tablespoon	vinegar	15 mL

Combine mustard and sugar in processor bowl fitted with steel blade. With motor running, pour boiling water through the feed tube. Add oil and vinegar and process briefly to blend well.

Making Flavoured Vinegars

These suggestions were given to us by Ed Fife, naturalist, and Professor of Landscape Architecture at University of Toronto.

To Make Herb Vinegar:

1. Use clear, clean wide mouth jars. Into each gallon jar place 2 – 3 large handfuls of herbs such as: tarragon, basil, mint or thyme. Use singly or in any combination - experimentation is fun! An herb to avoid using is summer savory. It is very strong and would take over the other flavours.

2. *Fill jar with good quality vinegar - either white, cider or red wine vinegar. Leave a little space at the top of the jar to allow for expansion.

3. Cover top of jar with plastic wrap and then place cover of jar on top. Plastic wrap keeps top of jar from rusting.

4. Place jar in sun - protect it from being knocked over - and allow to remain outside for 4 – 6 weeks. If left inside, leave it for 6 – 8 weeks.

Start making vinegar in August - you will not have to worry about freezing temperatures. Taste periodically - if too strong, you can add additional vinegar.

Fruit Vinegars:

To each gallon container add 1 – 1 1/2 quarts (1 – 1 1/2 L) raspberries or blueberries instead of herbs and continue from * above.

Helpful Hints

Stain Removal:

To remove candle wax, rub washable materials with ice or put into freezer to harden the wax. Scrape off excess wax. Then, if wax is white, place stain between layers of white paper towelling. Press with a warm iron. (Do not press coloured wax - you may set the stain). Use cleaning fluid to sponge off any traces of wax.

To remove wax from silver, hold under hot running water until wax is melted. Then wipe off and rub with a soft dry cloth.

To remove wax from furniture, let wax stand overnight until it has solidified. Then lay a large piece of aluminum foil over wax. Soak a terrycloth washcloth in very hot water, and wring it out thoroughly. Place the hot folded cloth on top of the foil for a few minutes. Do not let the damp cloth come in direct contact with the wood. Remove foil. If wax has formed a soft wad, it will slide off easily. If the wax is still too hard, reapply steaming hot cloth on top of the foil. After wax has been removed, rub warm wood with facial tissues with the grain of the wood. Never use a knife to remove wax from wood or silver.

To remove "hot pot" or water stains from wood furniture, rub a little mayonnaise into the spot with your fingers. Let stand an hour or so. Then wipe clean with a soft, dry cloth.

To remove lipstick from napkins, try pouring a little undiluted liquid shampoo onto the stain. Let stand about half an hour. Then wash as usual.

To remove wine stain from tablecloth, stretch stained area over a bowl. Secure with a rubber band, sprinkle with salt, and pour boiling water through stained area from about 12"(30 cm) above. Be careful not to splash yourself!

To melt paraffin for preserving, press sides of a clean soup can lightly to form a pouring spout. Put paraffin in can and place in pan of hot water over low heat to melt. When finished, cover cooled can with a plastic bag to store until ready to reuse.

To cut through meringue easily, dip your cutting knife in hot water and cut through meringue (not the pie) while the pie is still hot.

To prevent "tears" on meringue, be sure your egg whites are at room temperature, and be sure to beat sugar in gradually and thoroughly, until you can feel no grains when you rub a little of the beaten meringue between your fingertips.

To soft boil eggs properly, place in a saucepan and cover with cold water. Bring water to a boil. Turn off heat. Cover pan, and let eggs stand 2 – 4 minutes according to taste. To hard cook eggs, let stand in water 15 minutes, then cool eggs immediately by letting cold water run over them. Fast cooling will make the shells easier to remove.

To remove cooking odours, especially from fish, add a piece of cinnamon stick and one vanilla bean, or 1/2 teaspoon (5 mL) of vanilla to a pan of water. Simmer gently on the stove.

Index

For additional copies contact:

Hadassah-WIZO Organization
788 Marlee Avenue, Toronto,
Ontario, Canada M6B 3K1

Mrs. J. Posluns
23 Park Lane Circle, Don Mills,
Ontario M3B 1Z8

Mrs. H. Coopersmith
409 Glenayr Road, Toronto,
Ontario M5P 3C8

Credits:

Design: Barr Associates,
Design Consultants, Toronto
Illustrations: Vera Sanders
Photography: Eekoff and Muir
Printed in Canada by Webcom